PROFESSIONAL FASH
ILLUSTRATION RESOUR

- Garment drawing templates: men, women, children, swimwear and lingerie for women

- More than 700 hand drawn illustrations

- Step by step tutorials on drawing fashion flats: t-shirt, skirt, pants, jacket, and swimwear

- Detailed do's and don'ts of technical drawing

- Basic garment details terminology

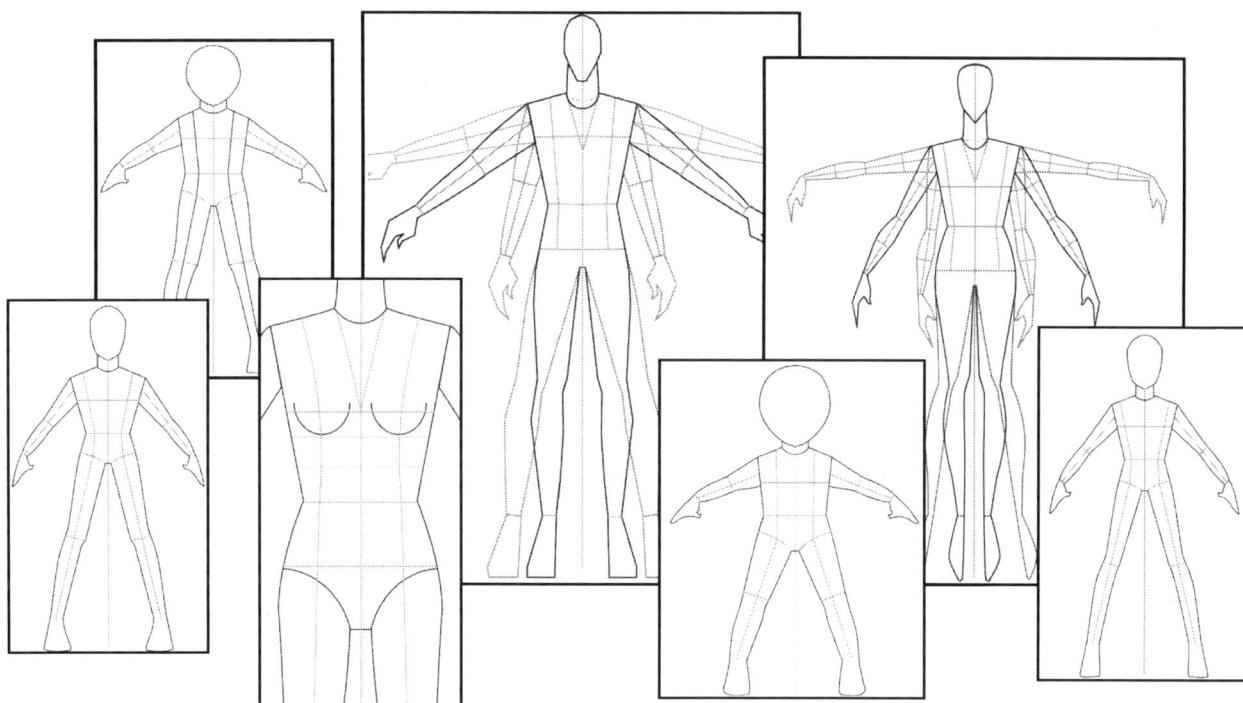

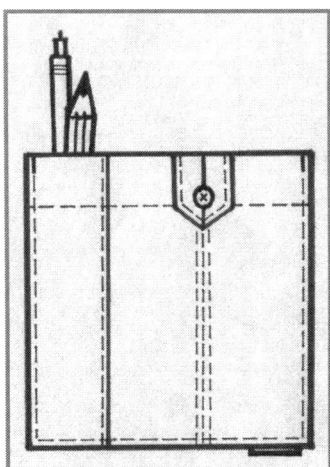

FASHION DRAWING:
STYLISH AND ACCURATE

Fashion Croquis

IRINA V. IVANOVA

With dedication to memory of Maya F. Rybalkina.

Teacher, mother and friend.

How to Draw Fashion Flats

A practical guide to fashion technical drawing
(pencil and marker techniques)

by Irina V. Ivanova

book designed by Andre L. Milman

Art Design Project, Inc

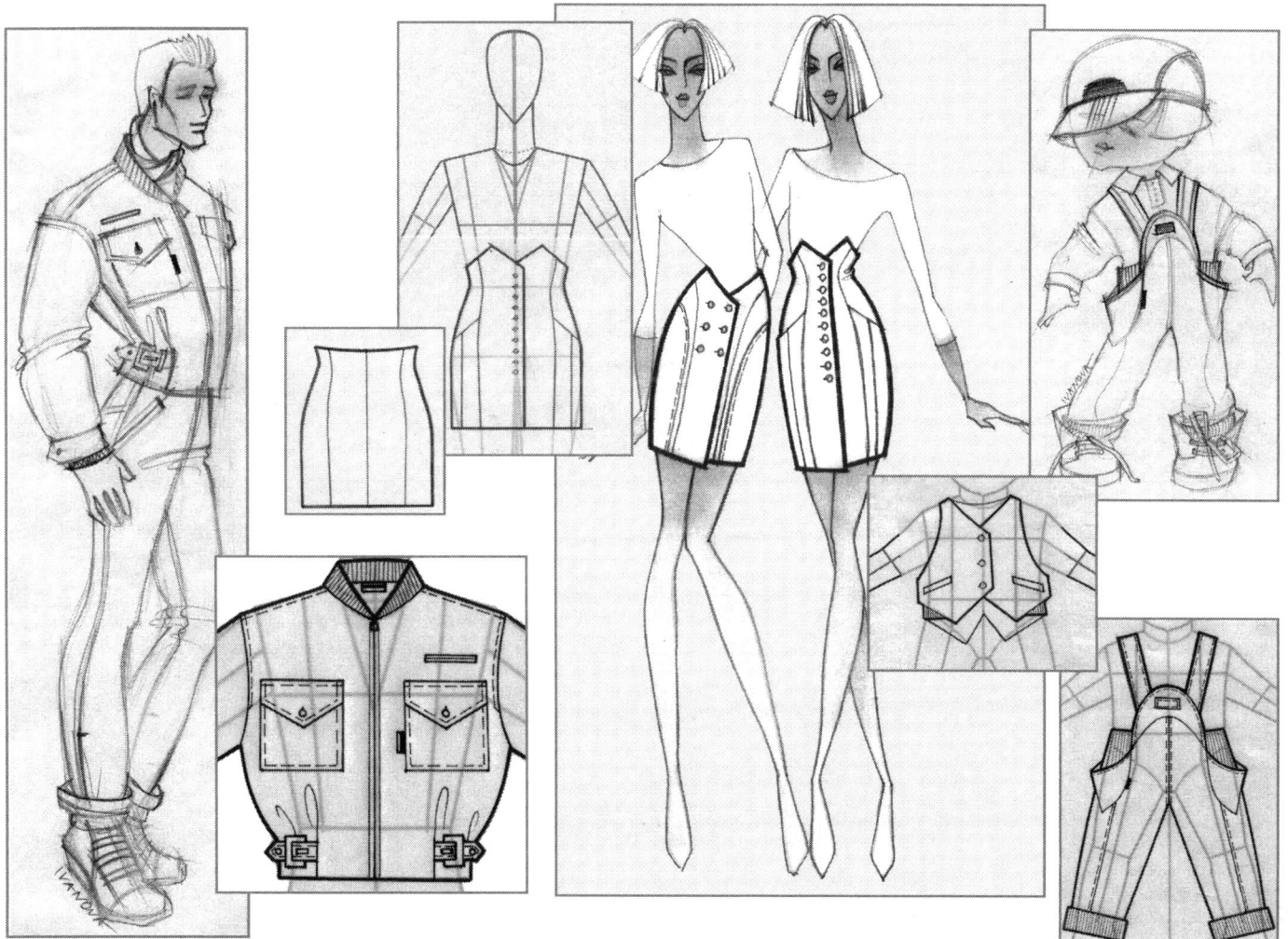

How to Draw Fashion Flats

A practical guide to fashion technical drawing (pencil and marker techniques)

by Irina V. Ivanova

ISBN-13:978-0984356027

ISBN-10:0984356029

(Art Design Project, Inc.)

Book Websites

www.fashioncroquis.com

www.fashion-flats.com

Email: contact@artdesignproject.com

Give feedback on the book at: contact@artdesignproject.com

Art Design Project, Incorporated

Printed in U.S.A.

CONTENTS

Chapter 1

Introduction/ Preparation

What are fashion flats?

Flats (technical drawing for fashion industry) are garment drawings without drawing of a body.

Technical drawing for fashion could be implemented either by hand or with an aid of a computer.
Hand drawn technical drawing is a form of manual garment drawing with rulers, set of French curves, pencils, and markers.

CAD (Computer Aided Design) is a computer generated technical drawing created most often in one of the vector graphic programs. The most common choice for computer aided technical drawings are Adobe Illustrator or Corel Draw.

In this book, we will explain how to do hand-drawn flats. Once you mastered the basic rules and requirements for hand drawn technical drawings, you can move to computer-aided flats.

Why we need flats?

1. The purpose of technical drawing for fashion or flats is to form a basis for further product development process.
2. Technical drawing for fashion is used in:
   - tech packs, specifications, cost sheets,
   - pattern cards and patternmaking documentation,
   - line sheets and production related presentations.

Tools and supplies

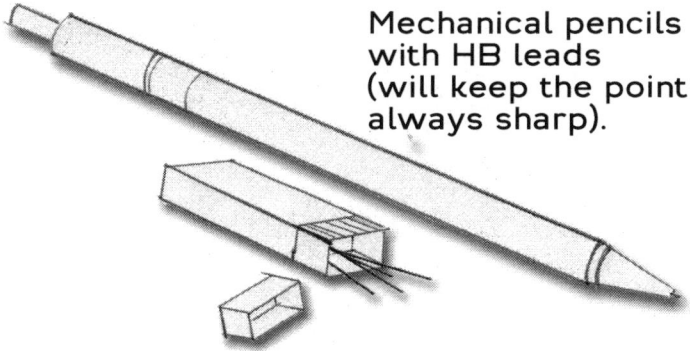

Mechanical pencils with HB leads (will keep the point always sharp).

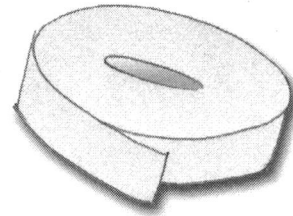

Low-tack adhesive tape (to hold your drawings in place without shifting).

Tip

Keep the open point of a marker on the paper in one dot for a few seconds. If the dot is not increasing in size, then your marker is not bleeding.

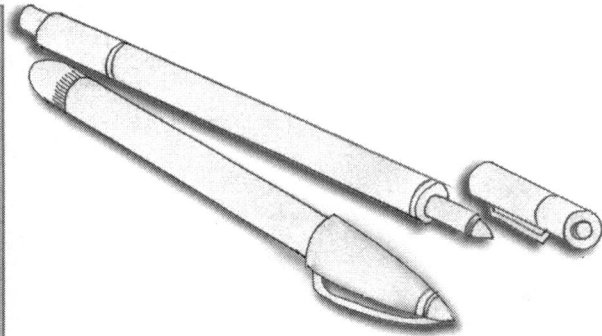

Markers or felt-tip pens with different thickness of a line (use a fine line for topstitching, and inner garment details, and broad line for garment outlining). Make sure your markers do not "bleed."

Sketch paper (use for sketching images from real life to remember your ideas for future implementation into flats and illustrations).

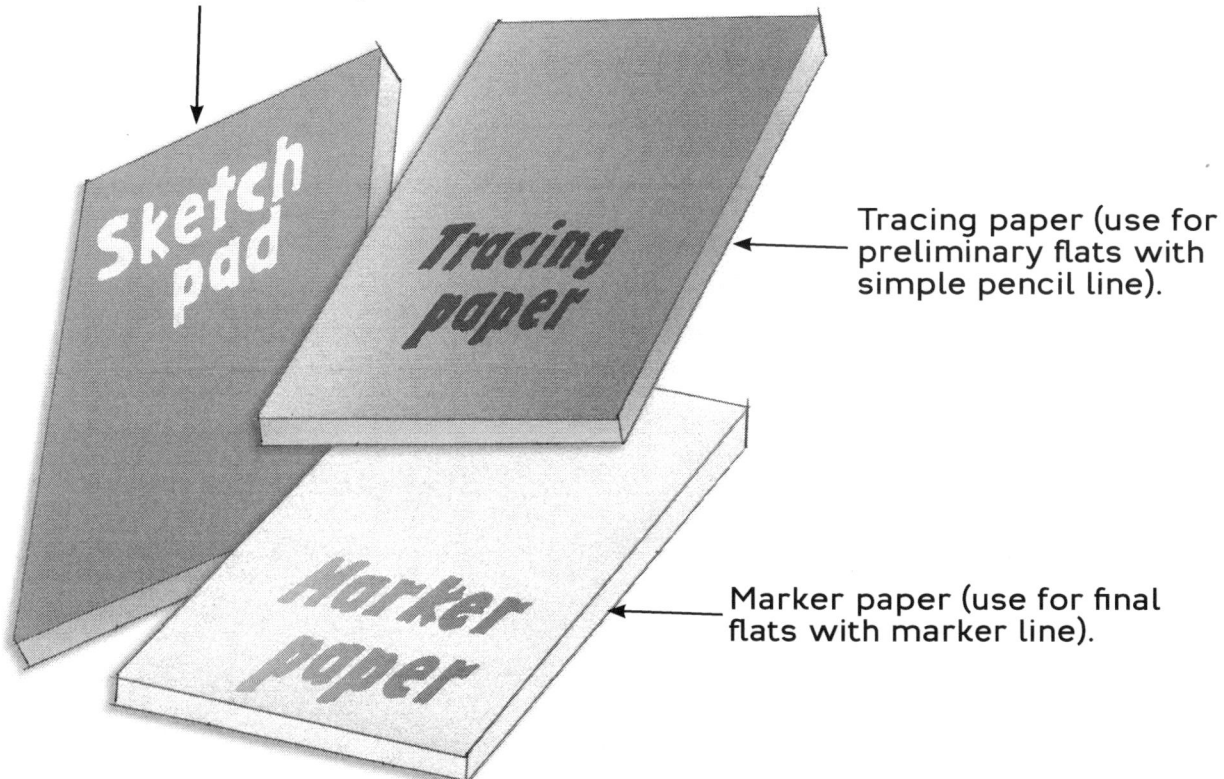

Sketch pad

Tracing paper

Marker paper

Tracing paper (use for preliminary flats with simple pencil line).

Marker paper (use for final flats with marker line).

See-through triangle ruler (will use to check all 90-degree angles and build perpendiculars).

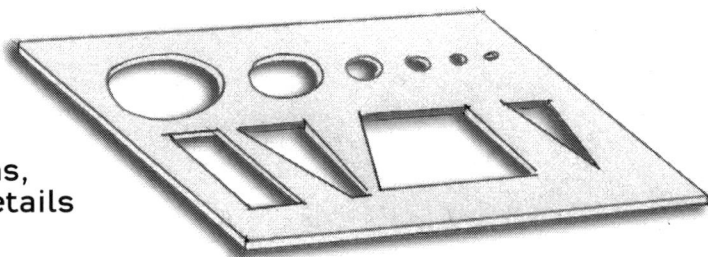

Stencil (to perfect buttons, pockets and any small details on your flats).

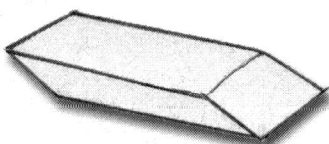

Pink, white, or kneaded eraser (to remove all your mistakes).

Plastic see-through French curve assorted sizes (to draw the perfect curve lines).

Move French curve around your drawing to find the best curve line you want to draw.

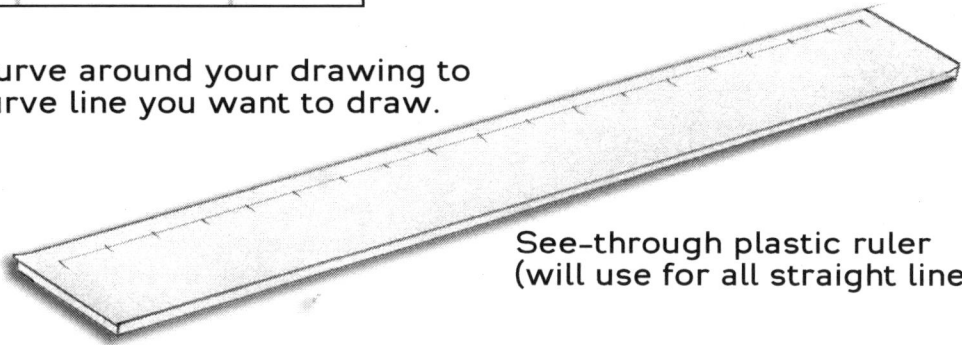

See-through plastic ruler (will use for all straight line).

Rulers and French curves may have different shape of the edge

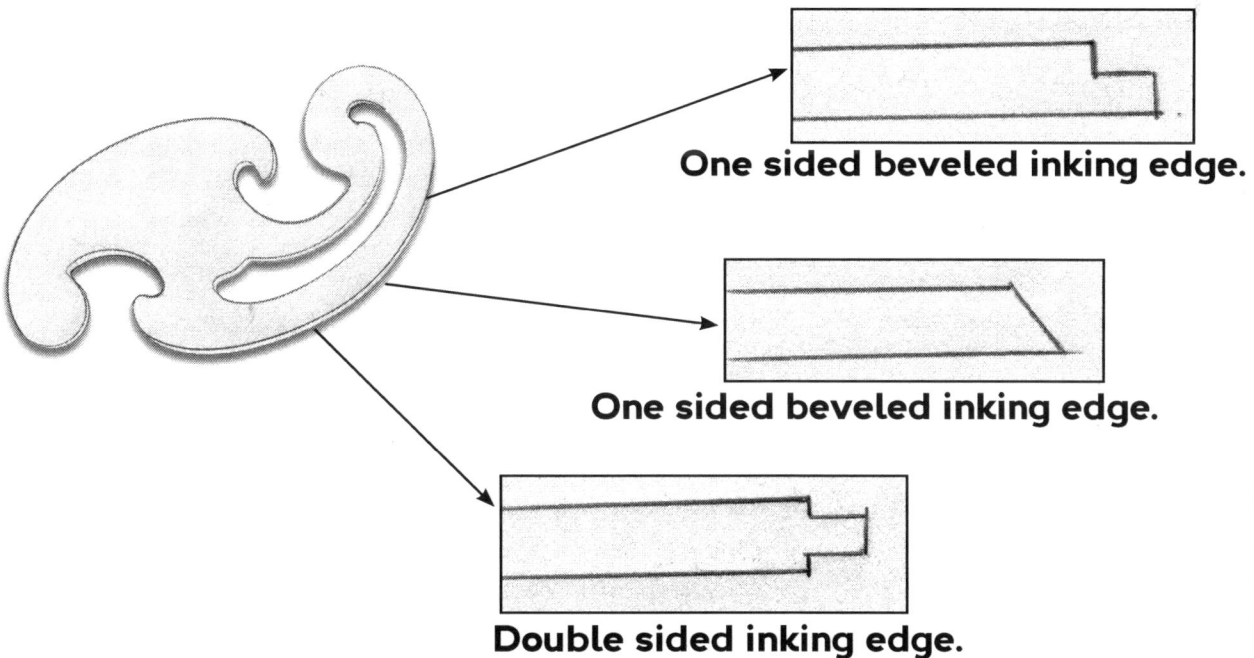

One sided beveled inking edge.

One sided beveled inking edge.

Double sided inking edge.

How to prevent smudging the marker line

Case #1. How to use one sided beveled inking edge of the French curve or the ruler to eliminate smearing.

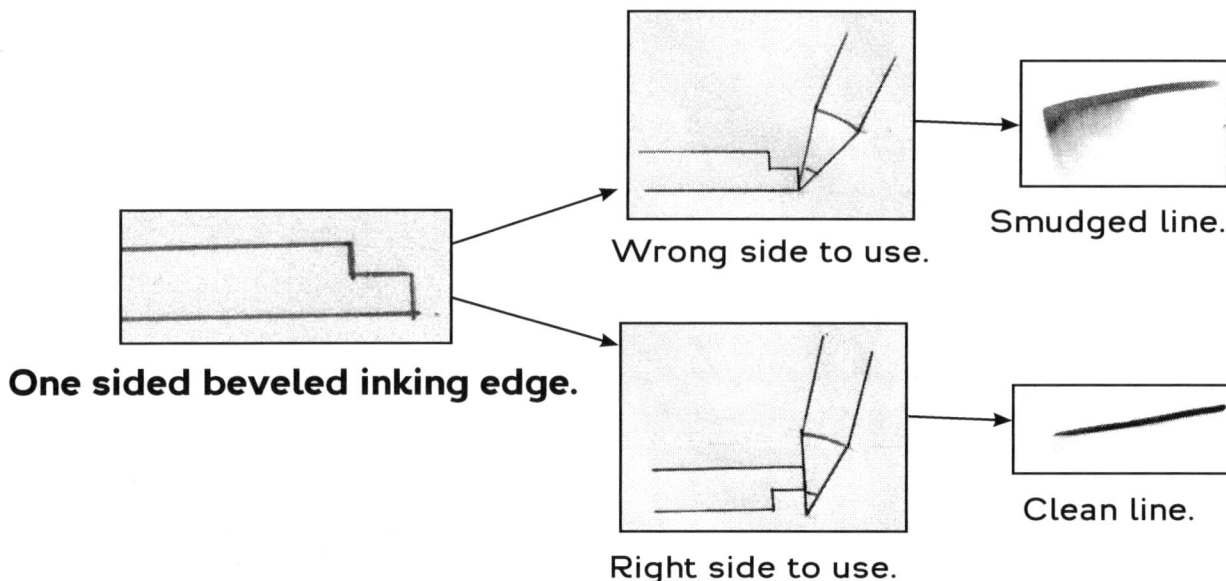

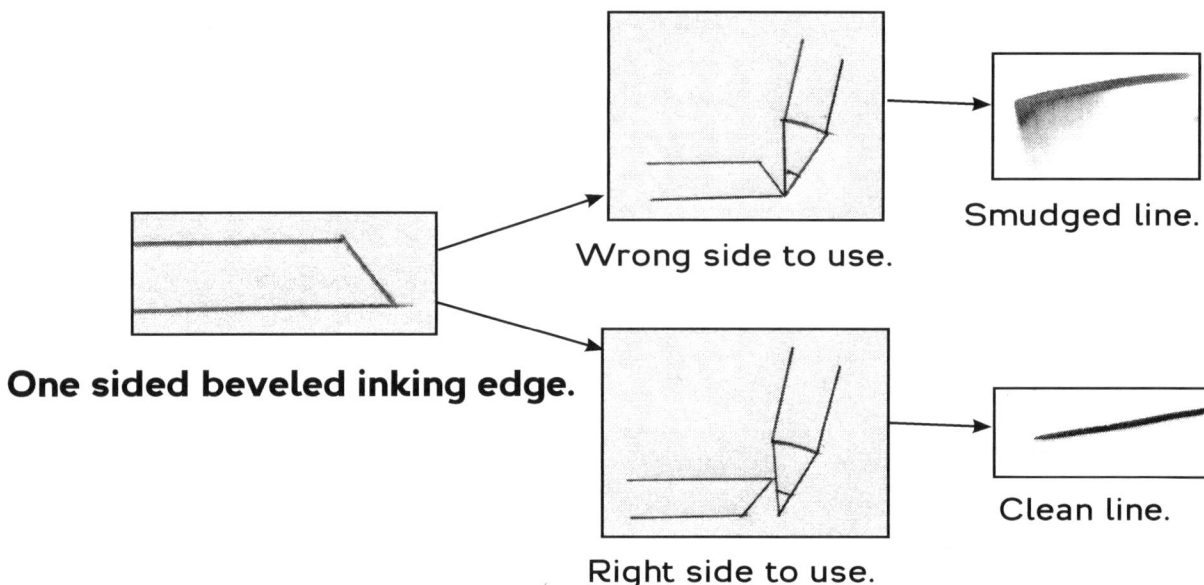

Wrong side to use.

Smudged line.

One sided beveled inking edge.

Clean line.

Right side to use.

Case #2. How to use one sided beveled inking edge of the French curve or the ruler to eliminate smearing.

Wrong side to use.

Smudged line.

One sided beveled inking edge.

Clean line.

Right side to use.

How to Draw **Fashion Flats** A practical guide to fashion technical drawing by Irina V. Ivanova

CHAPTER 1

Case #3 (the best). How to use double sided inking edge in the French curve or the ruler will permit the use of the either side up.

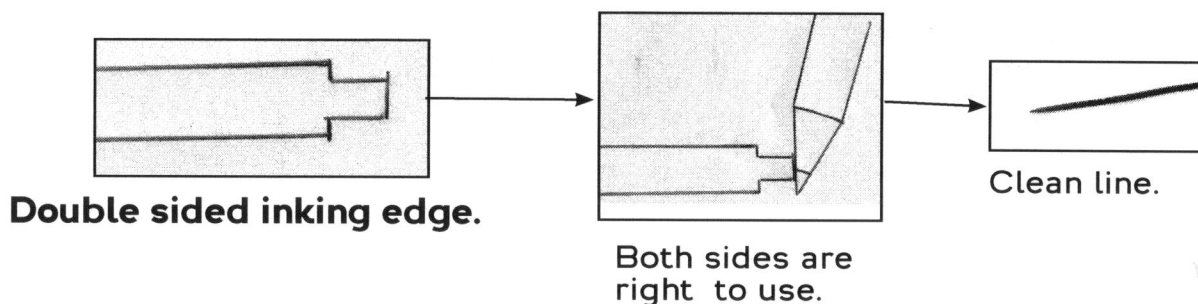

Double sided inking edge.

Both sides are right to use.

Clean line.

Rules to follow to avoid smearing of marker line:

• For the best result use double sided inking edge in the French curve or the ruler.

• Make sure your markers do not "bleed."

• Use marker paper. It is a most friendly paper for marker work.

• If you have difficulties seeing through marker paper:
  • use light box or
  • replace your marker paper with lighter (easier to see through) marker paper.

• Wash hands regularly to avoid leaving finger prints on your flats.

• Clean the edge of the ruler and French curve with napkin regularly to avoid line smudging.

• Do not rush. With practice, you will become faster. It takes time!

How to choose right figure template for flat drawing

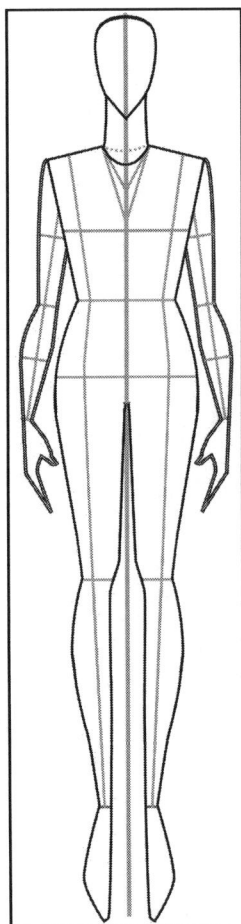

Fashion croquis (garment drawing figure template) is a basic, simplified figure intended to be used as a foundation for creating flats, fashion illustrations or floats.

Tip

Use realistic body proportions for flats and elongated figure to create fashion illustrations.

Realistic body proportions with less contrast between waist and hip lines.

Exaggerated body proportions with more contrast between waist and hip lines.

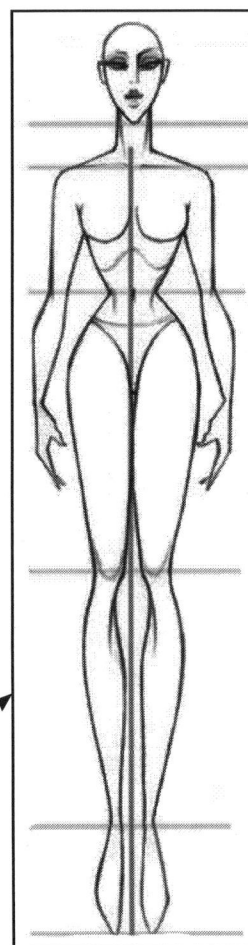

Croquis for fashion flats

Croquis for fashion illustrations

Croquis for fashion illustrations

Croquis for fashion illustrations can have slightly stylized proportions (to depict a fashion style better) and typically has a variety of poses. Fashion croquis for fashion illustrations should have all or some technical lines (for example waist, hip and balance lines).

Croquis for fashion flats

Croquis for flats is a simplified and true to actual body anatomy of the human figure with proportions of a sewing mannequin and not proportions of a runway model.
Croquis for the technical drawing must have various arms and legs positions. It is critical to have many options for a position of arms and legs which better illustrate the garment.
Croquis for flats is typically offered only in static (still) poses and must have all technical lines depicted on a fashion figure (bust, hip, waist and princess lines).

How to choose the right type of drawing

There are five main types of fashion drawing for the fashion industry.

Fashion float is a combination of a fashion illustration (drawing with a garment in movement) and flats (drawing without of body). It could be used for fashion presentation boards or apparel line sheets.

Fashion float

Fashion flat (fashion technical drawing) is a drawing of a garment without any movement and without body outlining.

Fashion flat

Fashion spec drawing (garment spec drawing) is a fashion flat with measurements for garment production purposes.

Fashion spec

Sketch is a rough or incomplete drawing. Can be a preliminary step in illustration or quick way to visualize an initial idea.

Sketch

Fashion illustration

Fashion illustration is a drawing of a garment on a figure.

How to prepare garment for flat drawing

Technical drawings are called **"flats"** for a reason, and the reason is that technical drawing depicts garment in its flattened condition, not the way it looks on a body.

There are **two different ways** to prepare garment for technical drawing.

1. Lay the garment down on the table

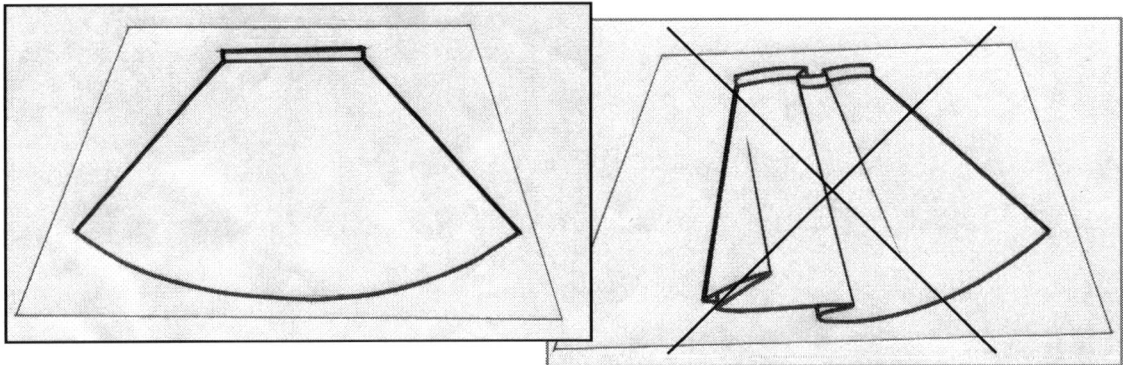

A flared hem could be illustrated as flattened as patterns (without flared line).

Make sure the garment is completely flat. Do not use any garment distortions!

2. Hang the garment on a hanger

- A flared hem could be illustrated as if hanging on a hanger (with flared lines).
- Make sure the garment hangs symmetrically!

How to draw garment from stretchy fabric

If the garment is created out of **stretchy fabric**, it must be depicted the way it is plainly flattened on a desk, not the way it fits a body.

Tip

Drawing of a garment which is created out of stretchy fabric must be more closely related to sewing garment patterns than to the actual look of a garment on a body.

The correct way to draw flat for pants from stretchy fabric.

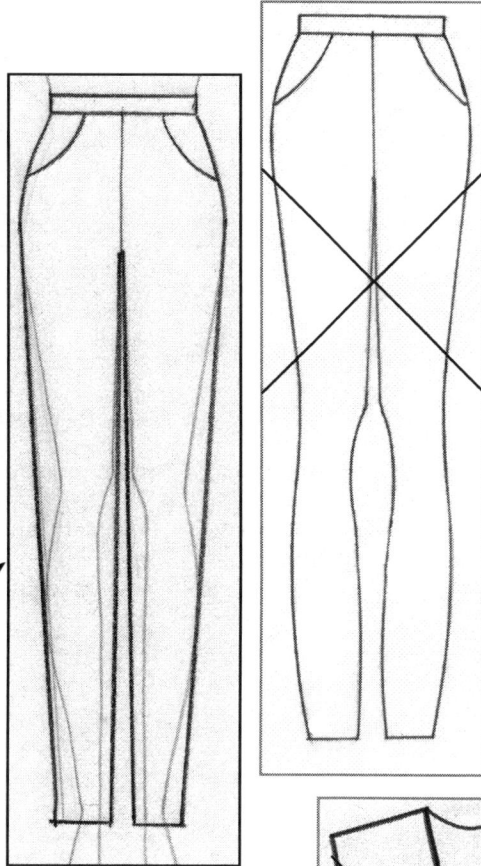

The incorrect way to draw flat for pants from stretchy fabric.

When you draw flat for pants from stretchy fabric, do not outline leg but show outlining for pants patterns.

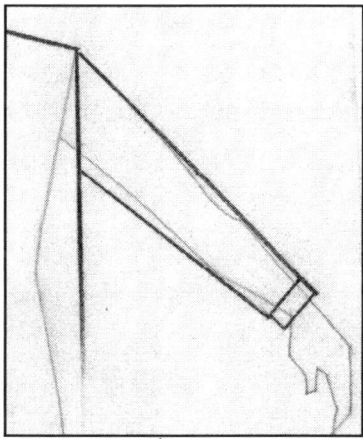

The correct way to draw flats for sleeves from stretchy fabric.

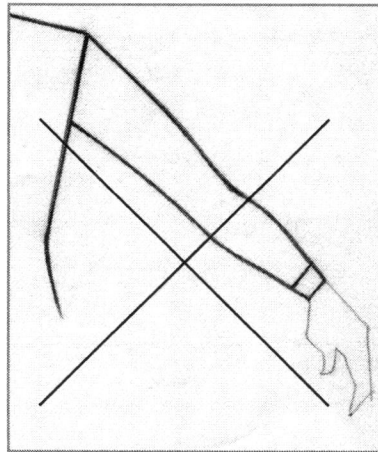

The incorrect way to draw flat for sleeves from stretchy fabric.

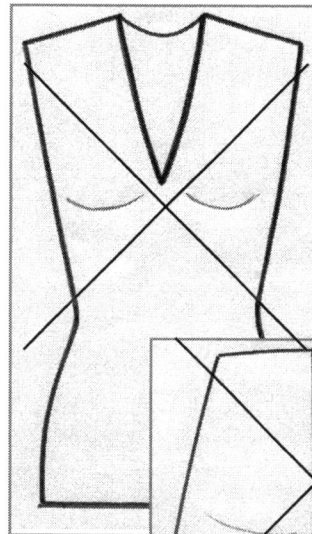

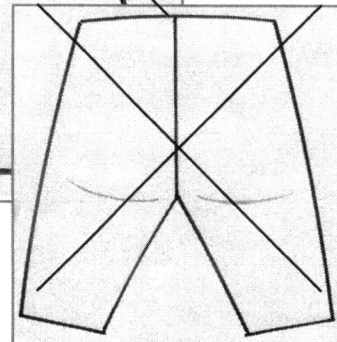

Do not show any parts of the body on the flats! Remember that flats are a garment drawing without a body.

When you draw sleeves from stretchy fabric do not outline arm but show outlining for sleeves patterns.

How to draw folded sleeves

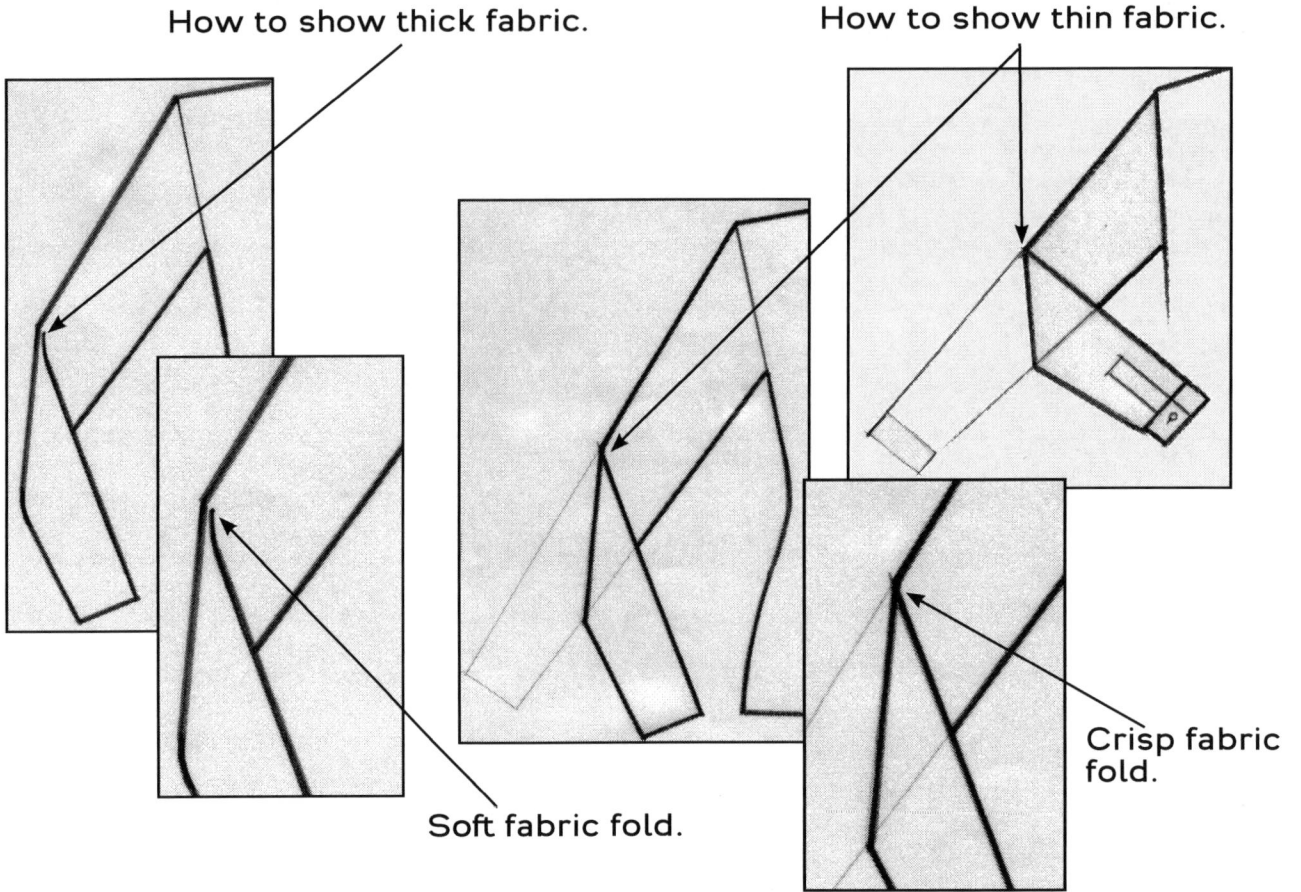

How to show thick fabric.

How to show thin fabric.

Soft fabric fold.

Crisp fabric fold.

How to draw hemlines

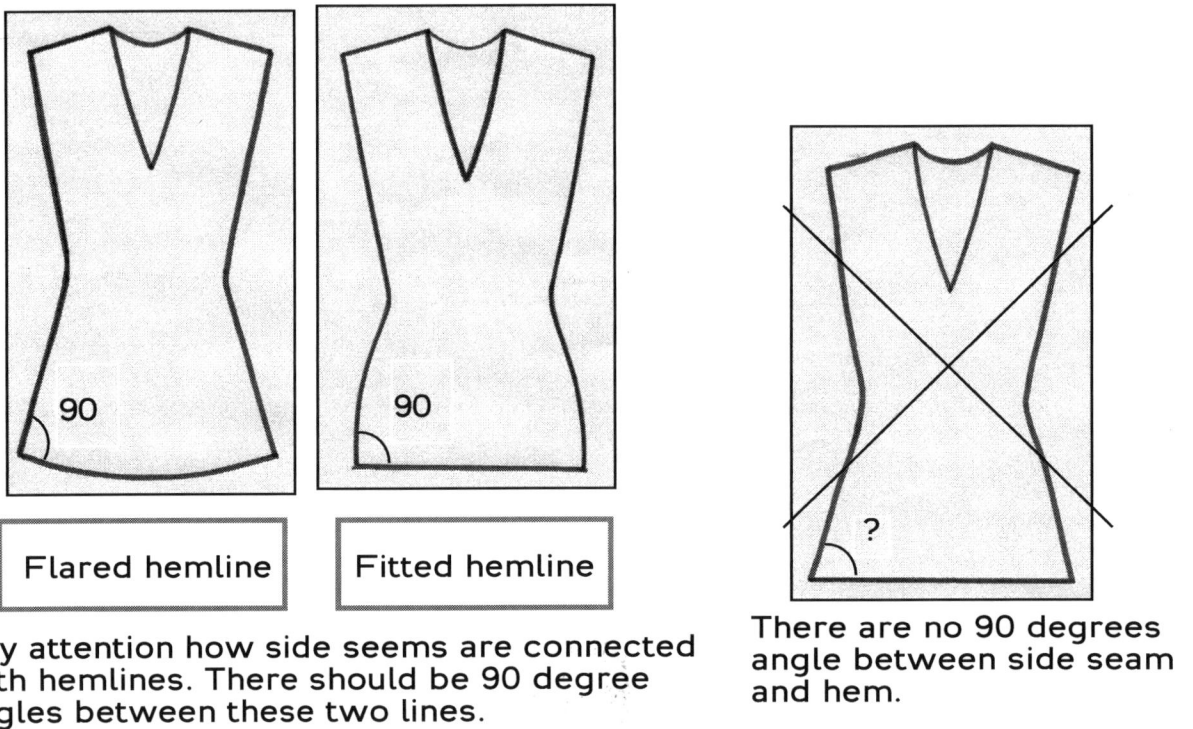

90

Flared hemline

90

Fitted hemline

?

Pay attention how side seems are connected with hemlines. There should be 90 degree angles between these two lines.

There are no 90 degrees angle between side seam and hem.

20

How to draw armholes

Armholes sometimes are impossible to flatten.

So, you can use one of the ways below to show armhole. Both ways are correct.

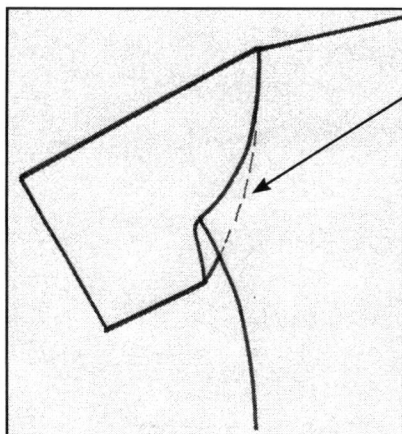

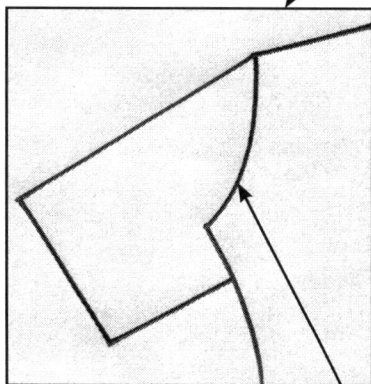

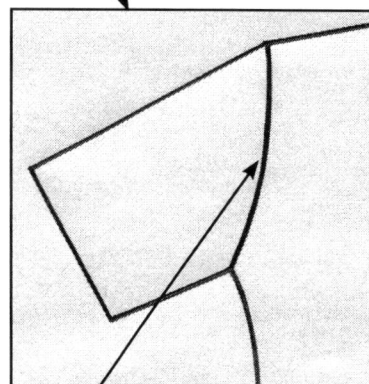

Armhole

How to draw center seam for pants

Rise

Center seam

Crotch point

Center seam for pants sometimes is impossible to flatten.

Rise is distance between waistline and crotch point.

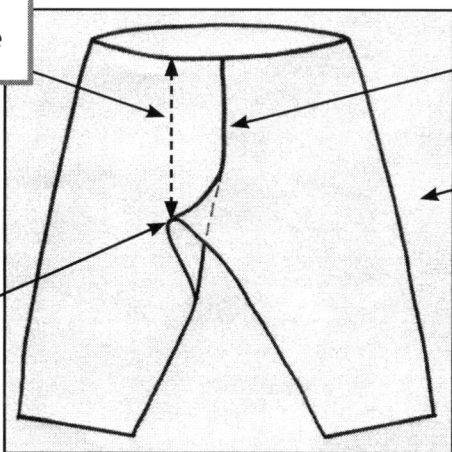

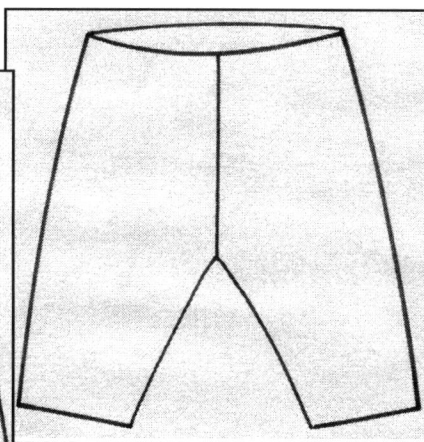

So, you can use one of the ways above to show center seam. Both ways are correct.

Chapter 2

Basic requirements for technical drawing

How to draw seams and stitches

Technical drawing for fashion design must accurately and clearly communicate how the garment is constructed.

All aspects and details of sewing have to be accurately visualized (seams, top stitching, trimming, darts, gores, buttonholes).

Difference between seam and stitch

A **stitch** is an interlacing thread between two passes of a needle through the material.
A stitch is the smallest element of a seam.
A **seam** is a line created when two or more layers of material are sewn (stitched) together.
So, a seam is a set of stitches.

Difference between industrial and handmade topstitching

In **industrial topstitching** spaces between stitches are shorter than the length of the stitches themselves.

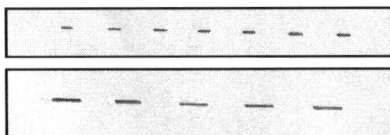

In **handmade topstitching** spaces between stitches are longer or equal to the length of the stitches themselves.

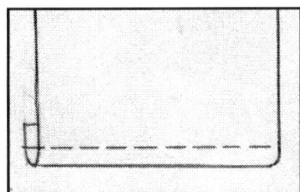

Tip

Pay attention how close or far from folded edge seam is placed.

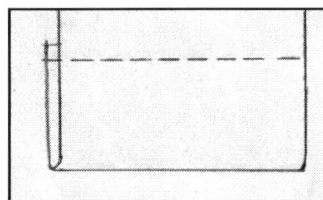

Seam with minimum distance from folded edge (**edgestitching**).

Used mostly in other then hem cases (for example, for attaching a patch pocket to a garment).

Seam with extra distance from folded edge.

Used mostly for the hem.

Basic seams and stitches

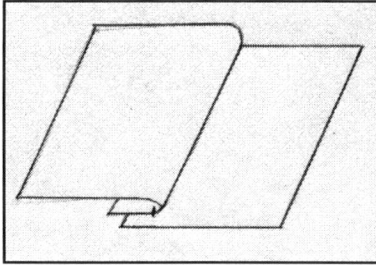

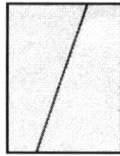

Seam (always use a solid line to show the seam).

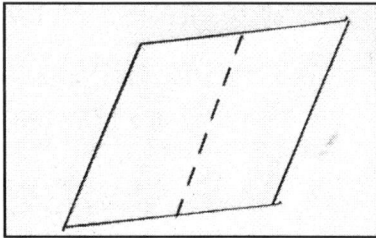

Topstitching (always use a dashed line to show topstitching).

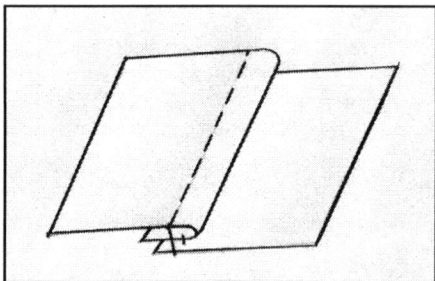

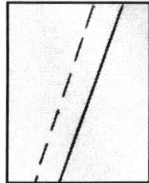

Seam and single line of topstitching. Top stitching is always parallel to the seam.

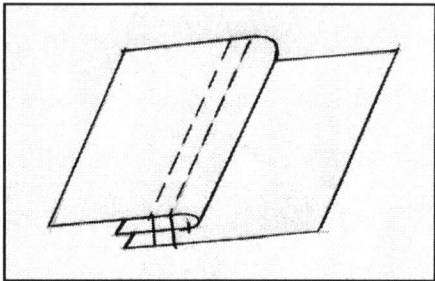

Seam and a double line of topstitching. Topstitching is always parallel to each other and the seam.
All stitches in double topstitching, as a rule, are aligned.

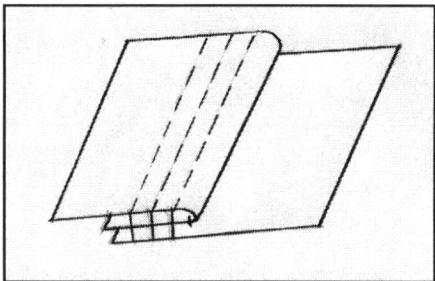

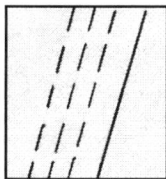

Seam and triple line of topstitching.

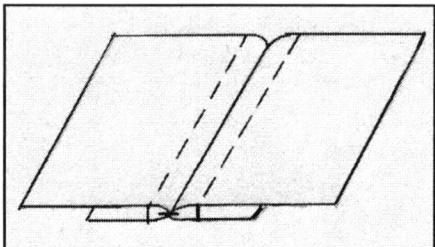

Seam and topstitching on both sides of the seam.

25

Step by step garment flats drawing at glance

Front view garment flats drawing (simple pencil line)

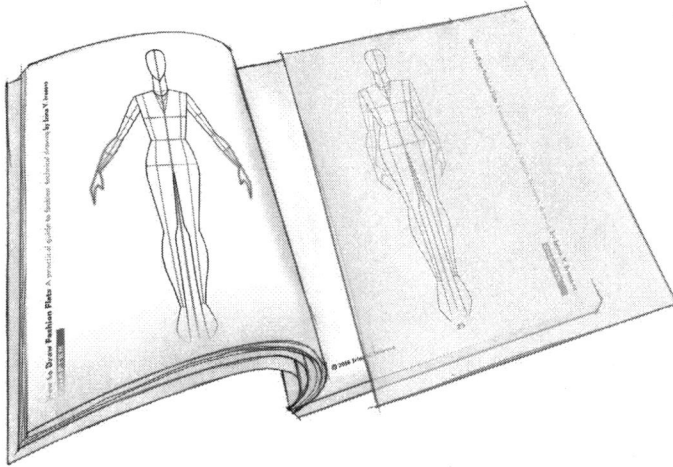

Step #1

Pick the template from the book and cover it with tracing paper.

> # Tip
>
> Do not use too strong tape for easy removal it afterward.

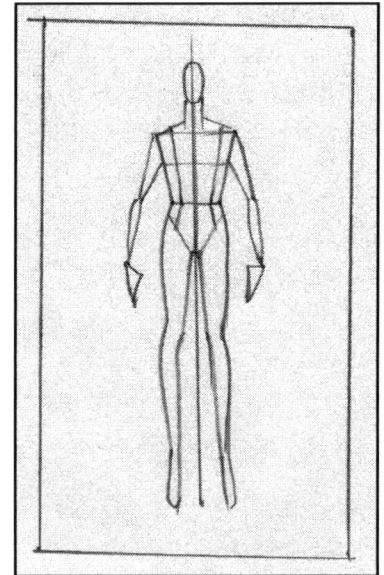

Step #2

Copy the template from the book with all inner technical lines. Now you are ready to start your flat drawing.

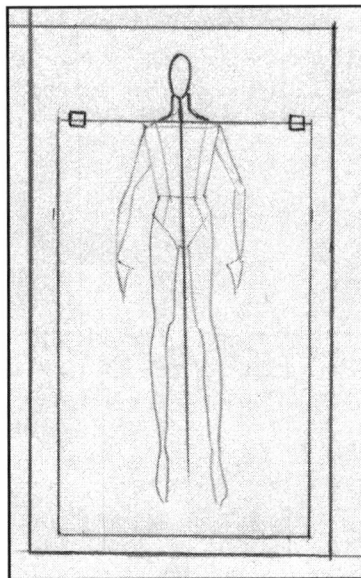

Step #3

Cover the template with a new sheet of tracing paper. Fix tracing paper to the template with tape and draw a center line.

> # Tip
>
> Always draw only one half (right or left) of flats and trace the second half to make sure the garment is symmetrical.

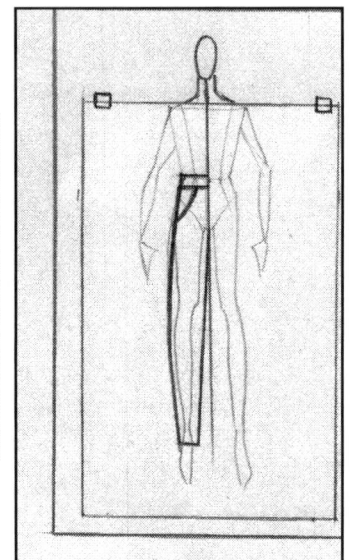

Step #4

Draw half of garment flat (right or left).

26

© 2016 Irina V. Ivanova

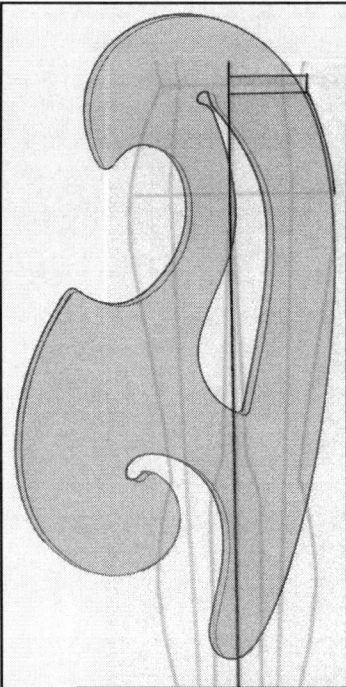

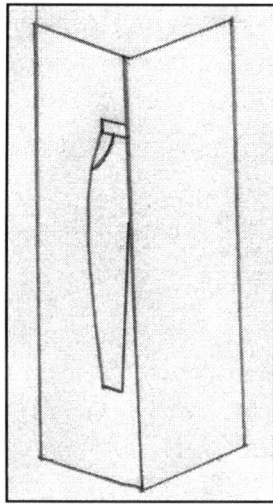

Step #5

Remove the tape and fold accurately the tracing paper along the center line.

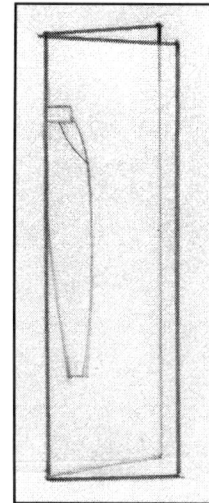

Step #6

Trace the second half of the flat.

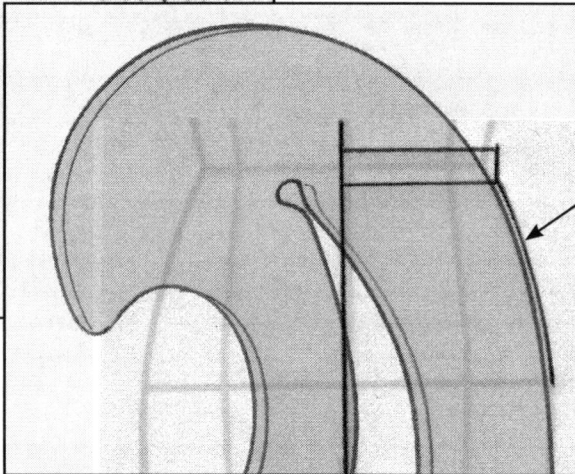

Tip

Use the French curve for all curves.

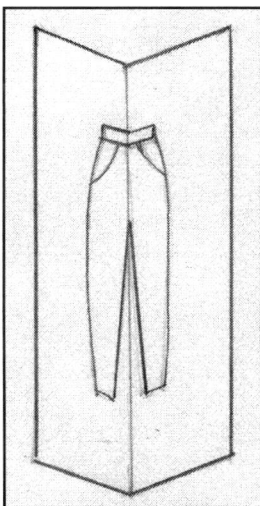

Tip

Use mechanical pencil for clean and sharp line.

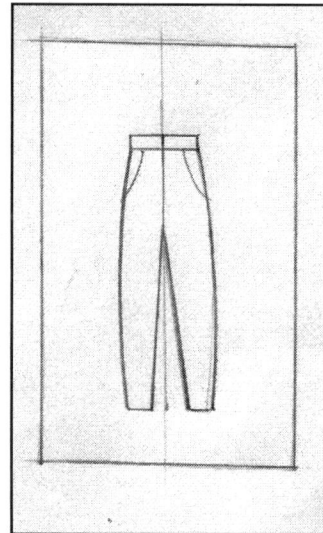

Step #7

Do corrections, add the details or openings if necessary.

Step #8

Front view flat is ready. Make sure that any lines which are crossing the center line are smoothly connected.

Back view garment flats drawing (simple pencil line)

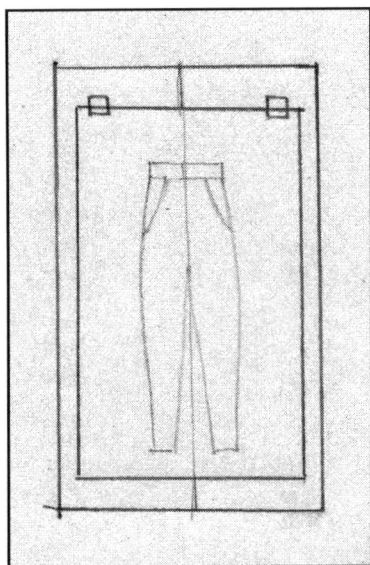

Step #9

Cover the front view flat with a sheet of marker paper and fix it with tape to avoid shifting.

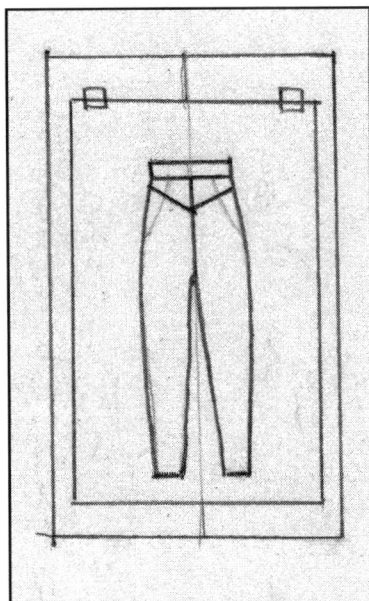

Step #10

Outline (with simple pencil line) basic shape of the front view flat.

Tip

Never use the body template for drawing back view flat but for only a front view flat. A front view flat as underdrawing will help to keep the front and back views identical in general outlining.

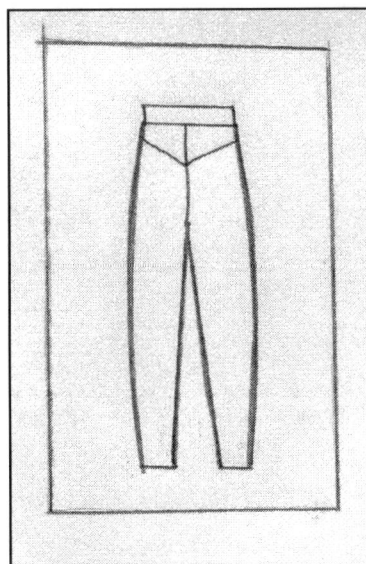

Step #11

Add all details which are necessary to show for the back view flat.

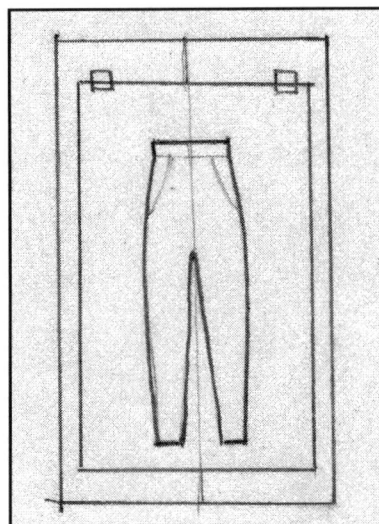

Step #12

Remove the tape and do corrections if necessary.

Garment flats drawing (marker line)

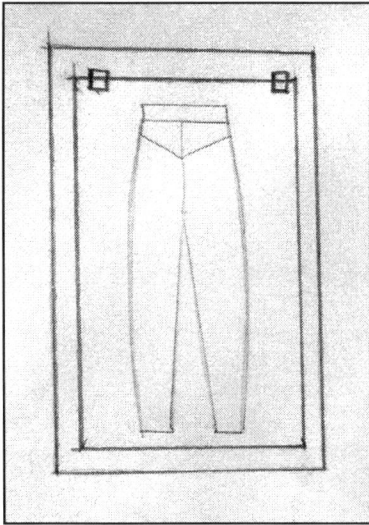

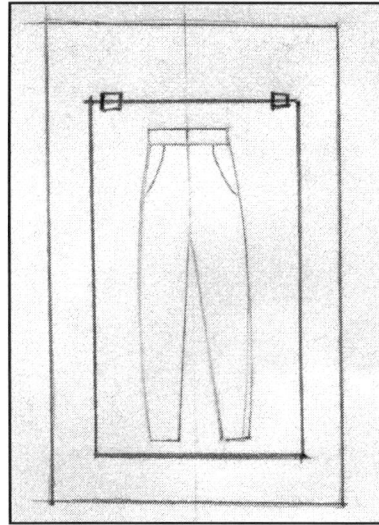

Step #13

Tip

Use double sided inking edge French curve or ruler for perfect outlining (see pages 14-15).

To draw front and back views flats with black marker line use a front and back views flats with simple pencil line as a underdrawing.

Cover your simple pencil flats with a new sheet of marker paper.

Use tape to avoid shifting. Trace flats with marker line.

Tip

Use markers which are not bleeding (see page 11).

Tip

Wash hands and clean with a napkin the edge of the ruler and French curve regularly to avoid line smudging.

Step #14

So, front and back views of the flat are completed!

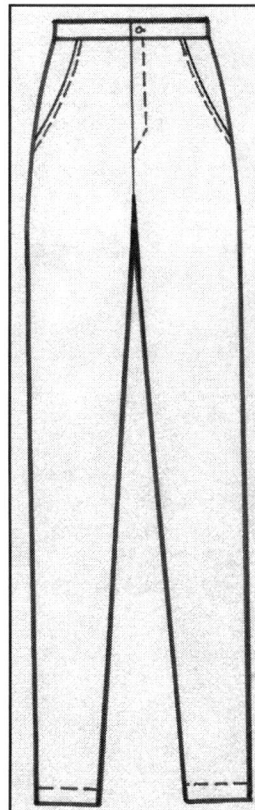

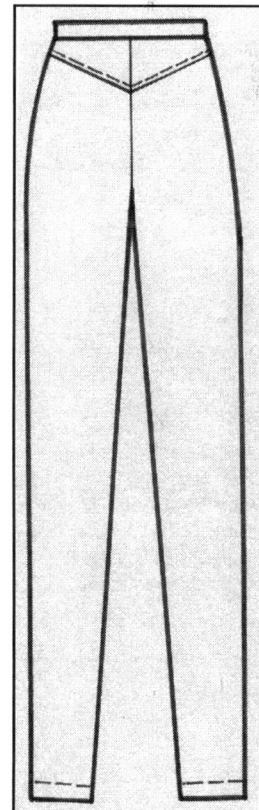

CHAPTER 2

Chapter 3

T-shirts

Terminology of crew collar

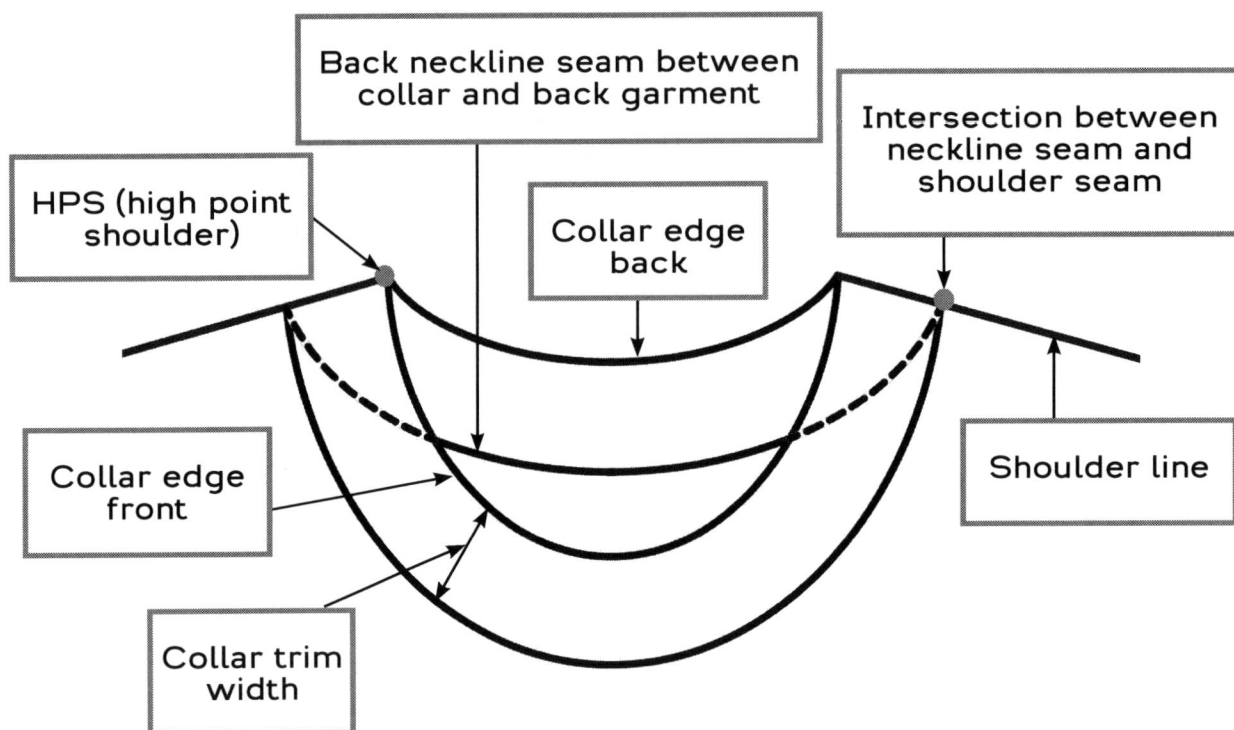

Back neckline seam between collar and back garment

Intersection between neckline seam and shoulder seam

HPS (high point shoulder)

Collar edge back

Collar edge front

Shoulder line

Collar trim width

How to draw crew and stand collars for T-shirts

Front neckline, as a rule, is deeper than back neckline (exceptions are designs with deeper neckline (décolleté) on the back).

Structural variations of T-shirt crew and stand collars

Crew (flat) collar

Crew (with "soft" stand) collar

Stand collar

Depending on the deepness of front neckline you may have more or less open view for back neckline.

How to show rib on T-shirt crew and stand collars

Tip

Add details (for example, rib drawing) only after you have the collar structure drawing done correctly.

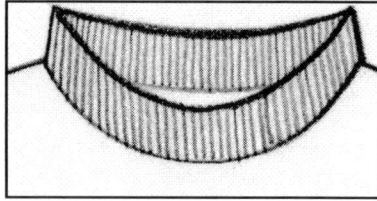

T-shirt crew ribbed collars

T-shirt stand ribbed collar

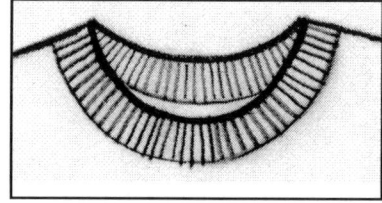

How to draw topstitching and serge finish for crew collar

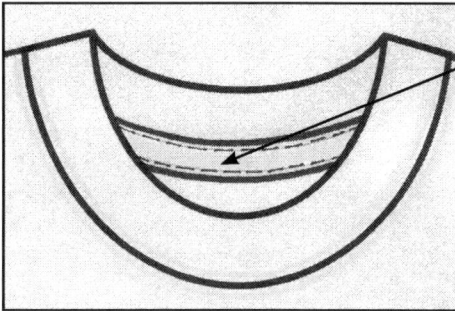

Tape to cover seams on the back neckline

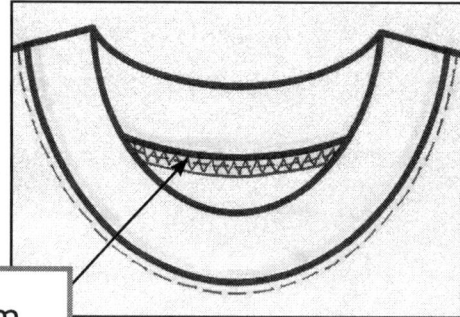

Serge seam

Serge seam is a finished edge sewn on a serge machine.

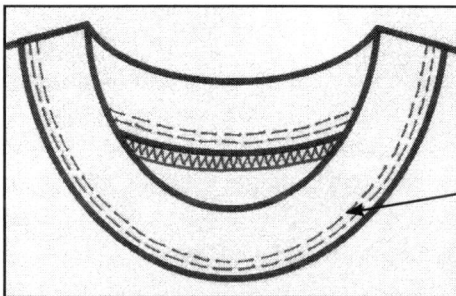

Topstitching

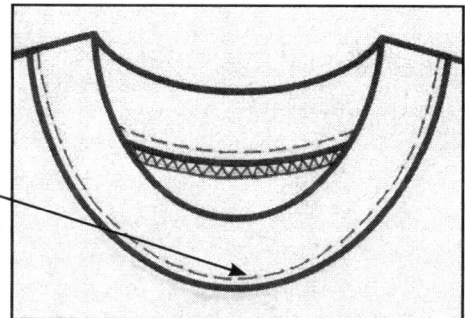

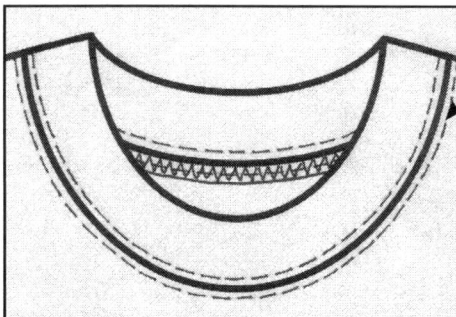

Tip

Always keep topstitching parallel to neckline seams.

Depending on the design of neckline you may have one or more lines of topstitching around neckline seam.
The topstitching for back and front necklines are not necessary the same.

How to draw V-neck for T-shirts

V-neck structure

Tip

Do not forget to show how you want to complete the V-point (overlapping or center seam).

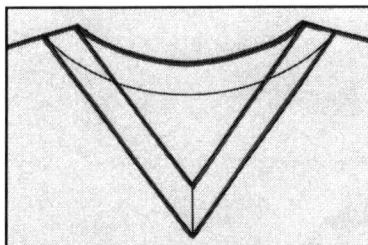

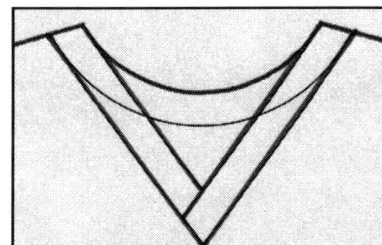

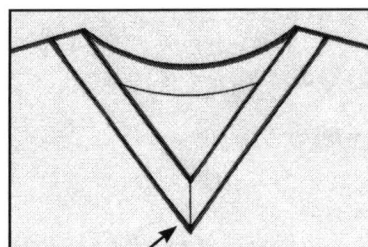

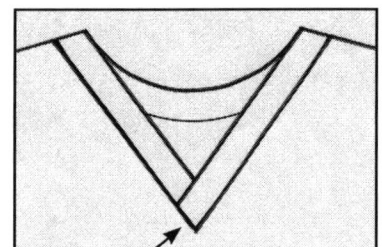

V-point with center seam

Overlapped V-point

How to draw ribbed V-neck for T-shirts

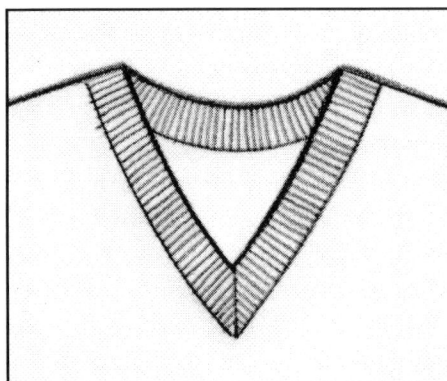

Ribbed V-point with center seam.

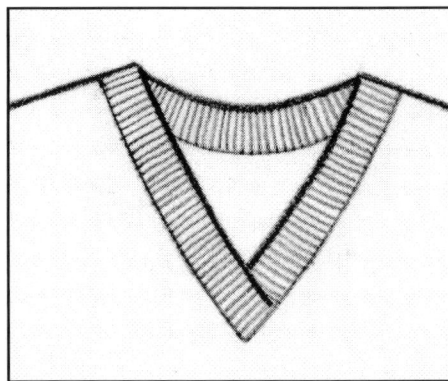

Ribbed V-neck with overlapped V-point.

Common mistakes in drawing crew collar

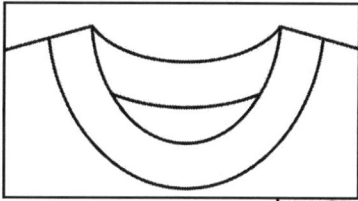

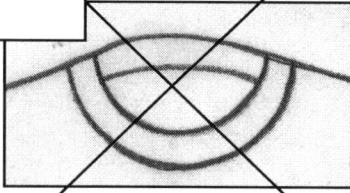

Do not curve up back neckline.

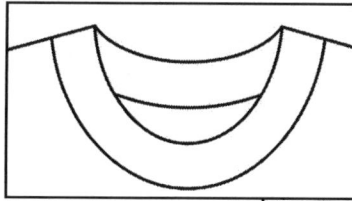

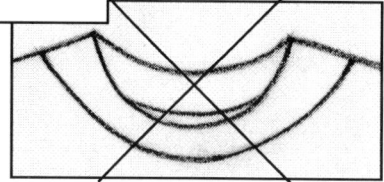

Keep the same width of the collar.

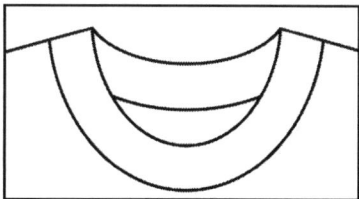

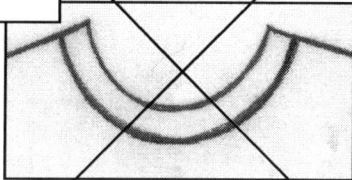

Always show back neckline on the front view of T-shirt.

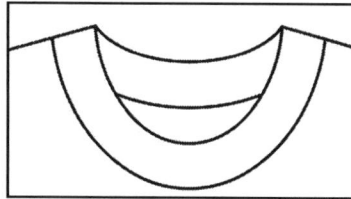

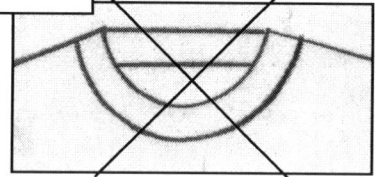

Back neckline should not be straight.

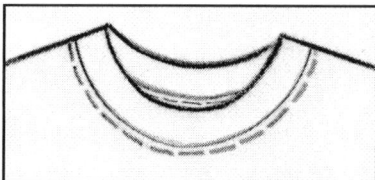

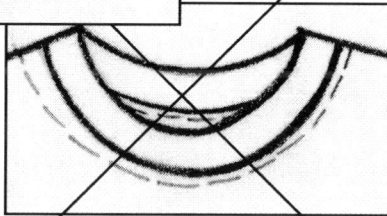

Always keep topstitching parallel to seams.

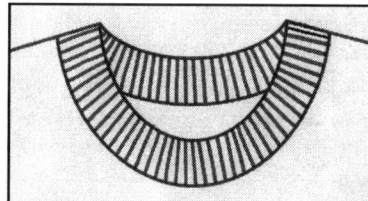

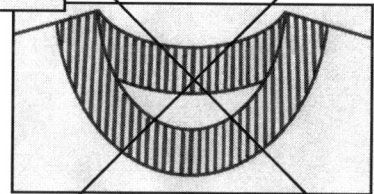

To show rib structure follow the shape of collar.

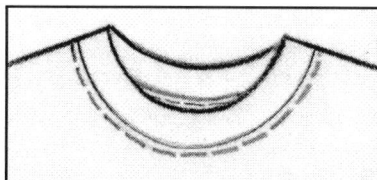

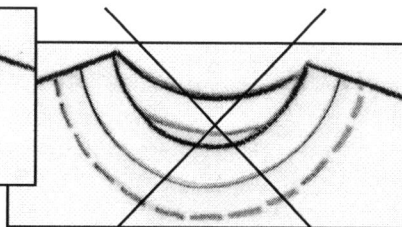

Always keep topstitching close to neckline seam.

T-shirt

How to draw front view flat for T-shirt
(simple pencil line)

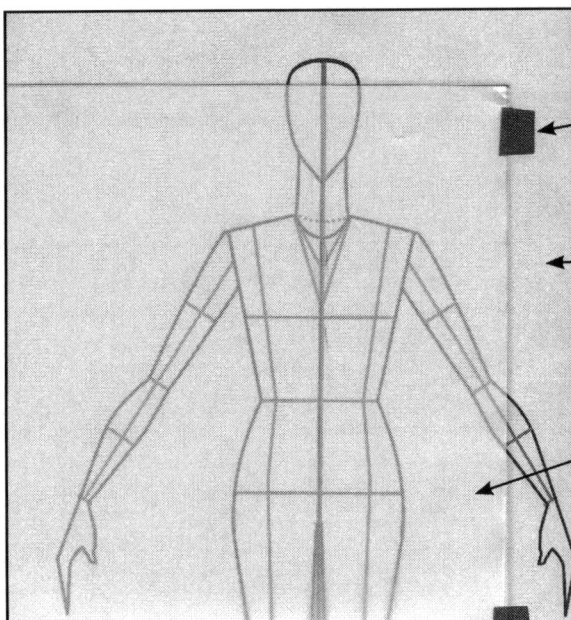

Tape to avoid shifting.

Sheet of paper with template on it.

Sheet of tracing paper.

Step #1

Cover template with tracing paper and tape it to avoid shifting.

Tip

Always draw only one side of flats and trace the second side to make sure the garment is symmetrical.

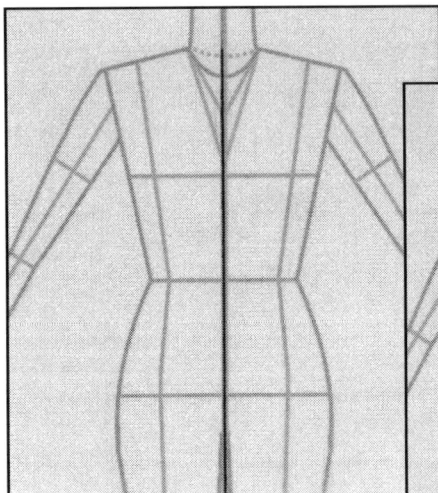

Step #2

Draw center line.

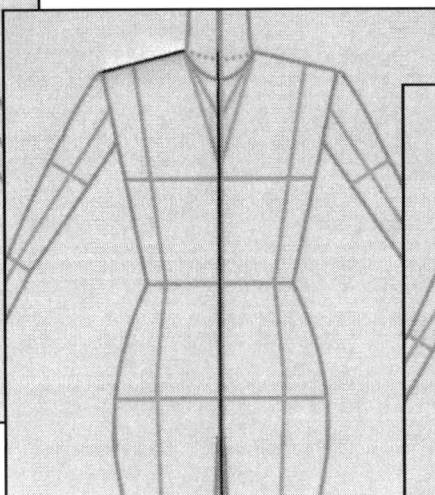

Step #3

Draw shoulder line.

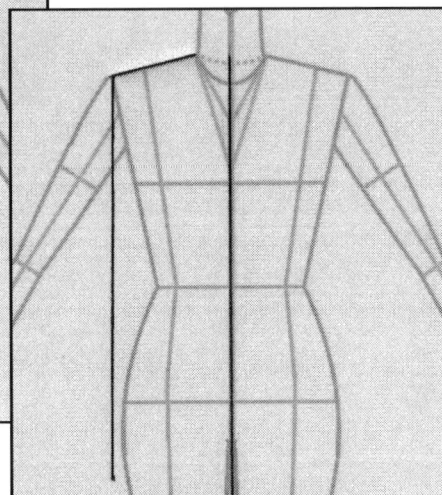

Step #4

Draw side line. Keep side line parallel to center line.

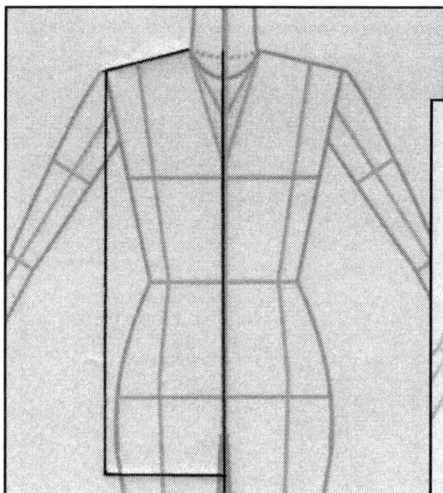

Step #5

Draw hemline. Make sure you have 90 degree angle between side and hemlines.

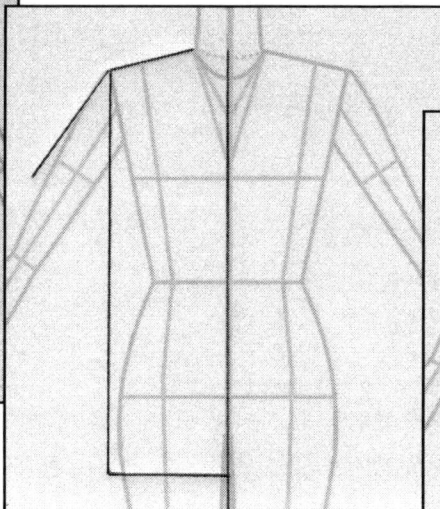

Step #6

Start sleeve outlining.

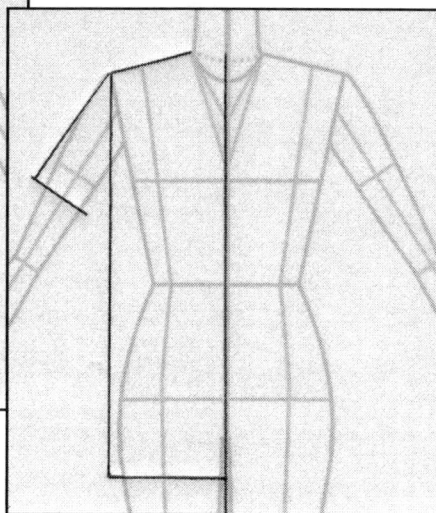

Step #7

Show hemline for sleeve.

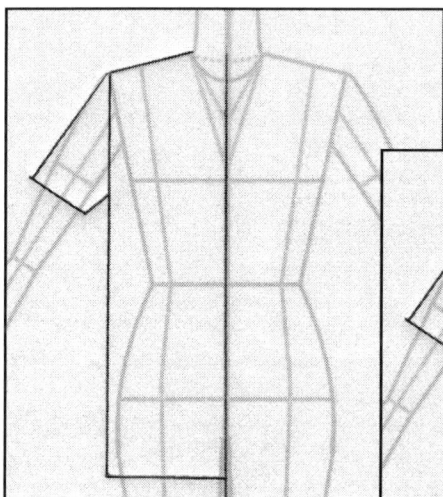

Step #8

Finish sleeve outlining.

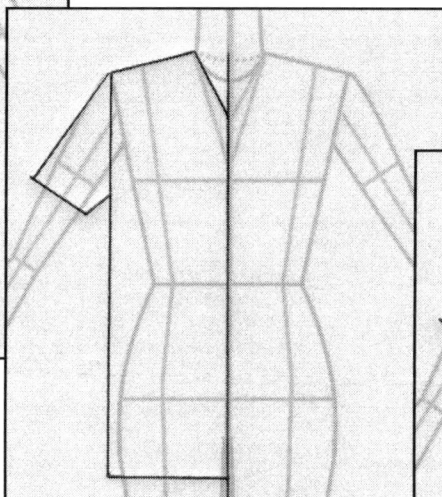

Step #9

Draw front neckline.

Step #10

Draw back neckline.

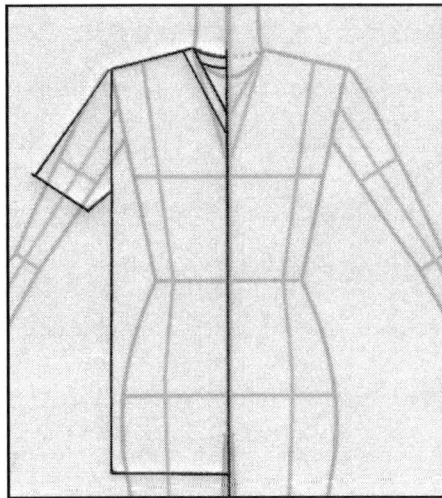

Step #11

Draw binding neckline.

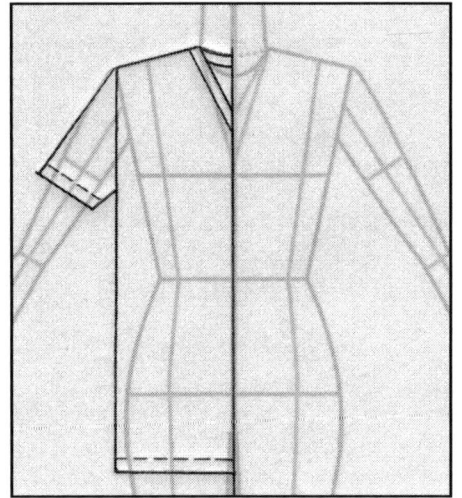

Step #12

Draw topstitching for hemlines.

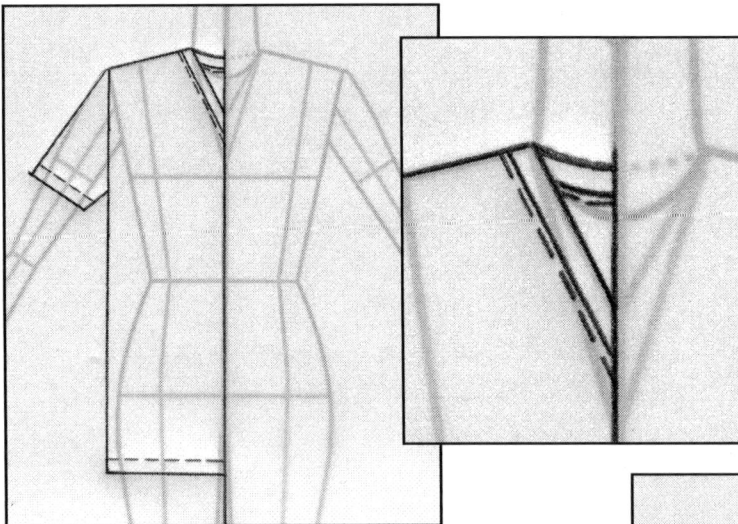

Step #13

Draw topstitching around neckline.

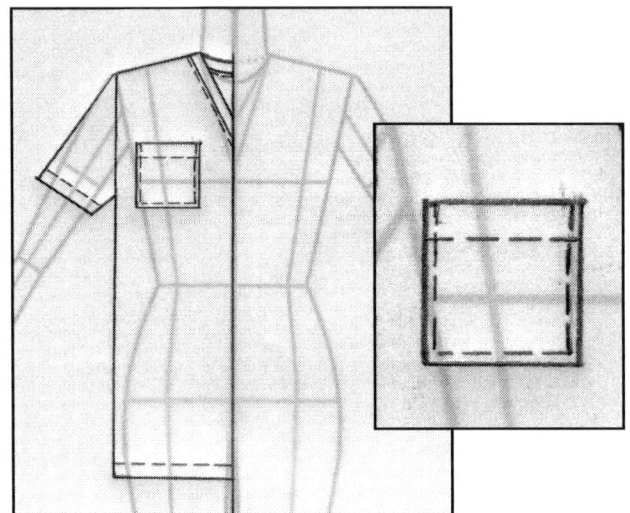

Step #14

Draw patch pocket with topstitching.

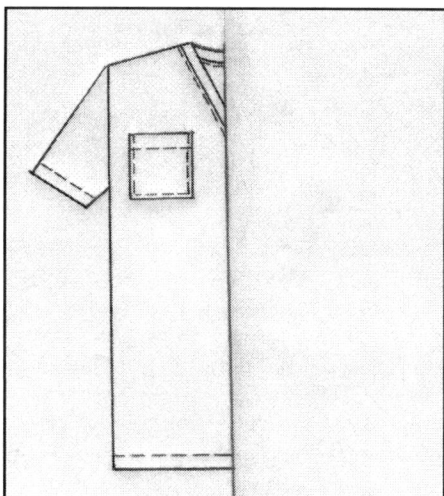

Step #15

So, the half of the flat is completed!

Now we should copy or trace second half of the flat.

Step #16

Fold your flat along the center line and trace second half.

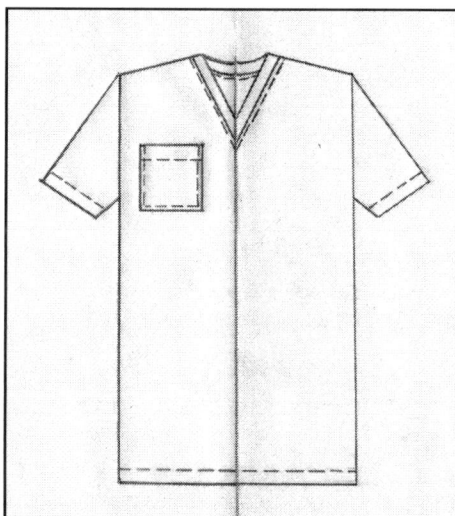

Step #17

So, front view of the flat is completed! It is time to do corrections if needed.

Now we are ready to do back view flat.

Tip

See more patch pocket designs on page 70.

How to draw back view flat for T-shirt
(simple pencil line)

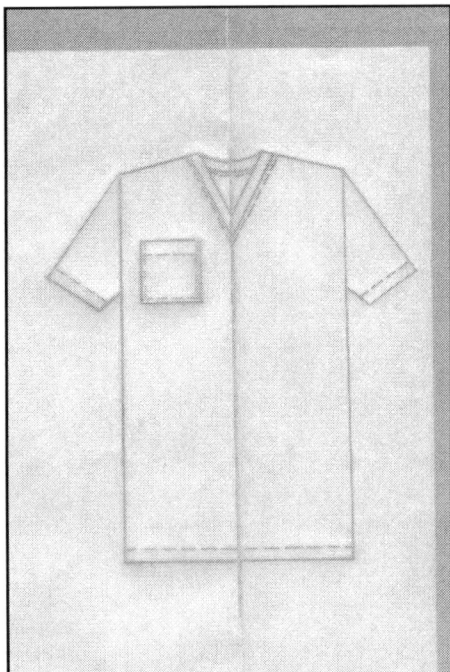

CHAPTER 3

Tip

Never use the body template for drawing back view flat but for only a front view flat. A front view flat as underdrawing will help to keep the front and back views identical in general outlining.

Step #18

Cover the front view flat with a new sheet of tracing paper.

Use tape to avoid shifting.

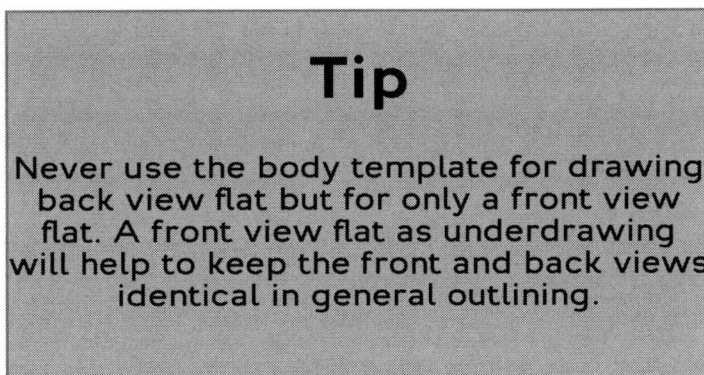

Step #19

Outline the basic shape of the T-shirt and show topstitching for hemlines.

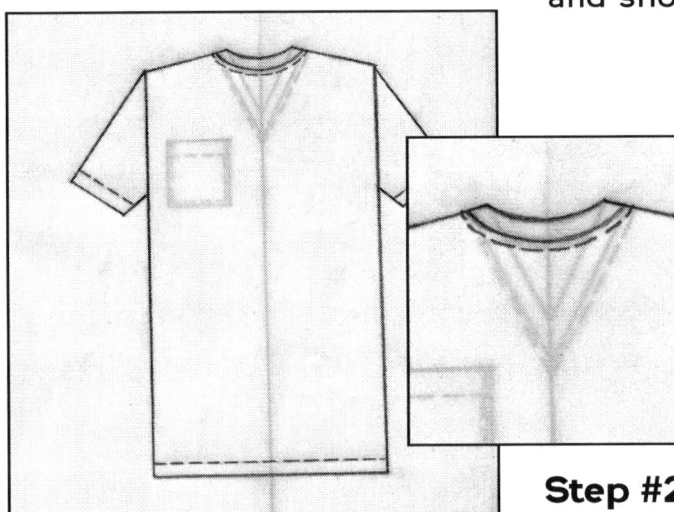

Step #20

Show back neckline, binding and topstitching. So, the back view of the flat in simple pencil line is completed!

How to draw final front view of flats for T-shirt
(marker line)

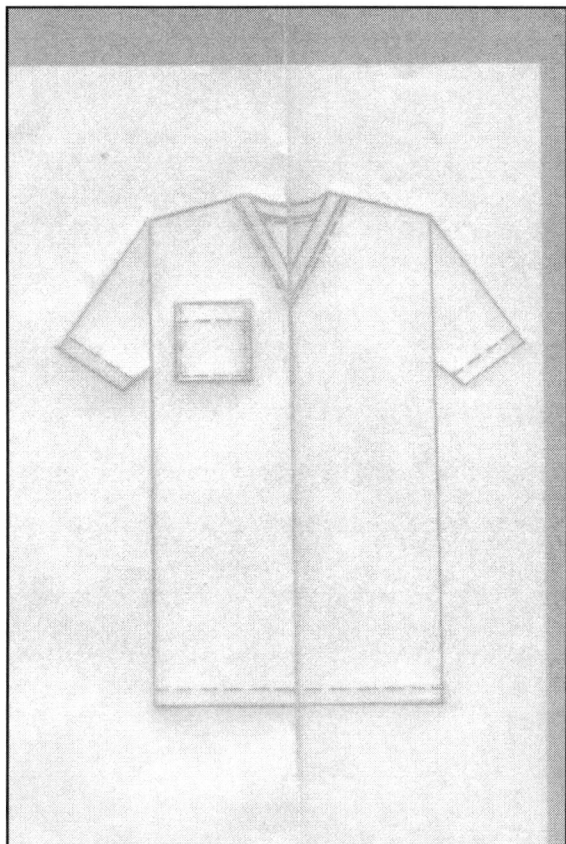

Step #21

To draw a front view flat with black marker line use a front view flat with simple pencil line.

Cover your simple pencil front view flat with a new sheet of marker paper.

Use tape to avoid shifting.

Tip

Use double sided inking edge French curve or ruler for perfect marker outlining (see pages 14–15).

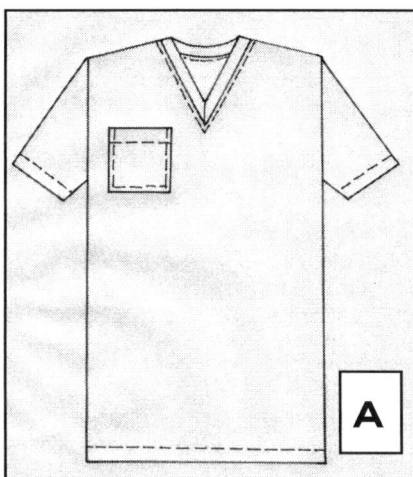

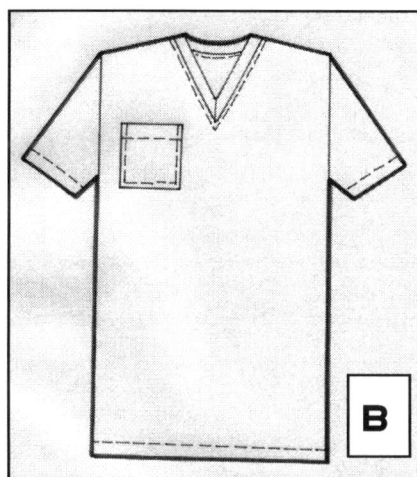

Step #22

For final outlining, you can use only one marker (A) or a few different markers (B) to show a thicker line for the basic shape and skinnier lines for details of the T-shirts and topstitching.

How to draw final back view of flats for T-shirt (marker line)

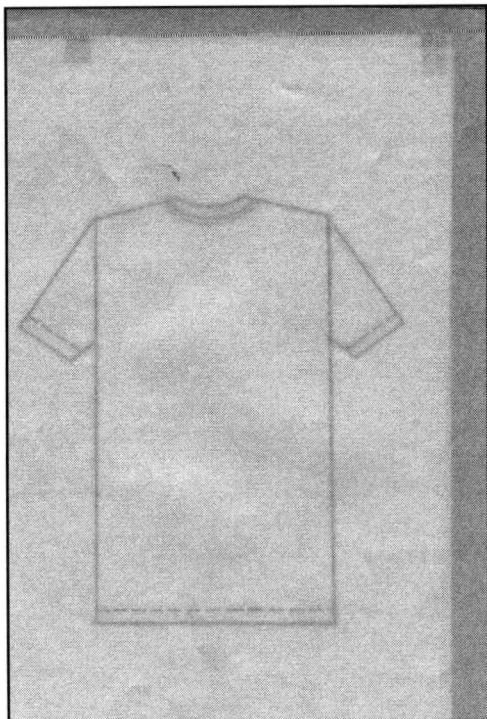

Step #23

To draw a back view flat with black marker lines use a back view flat with simple pencil line.

Cover your simple pencil back view flat with a new sheet of marker paper.

Use tape to avoid shifting.

Tip

Use markers which are not bleeding (see page 11).

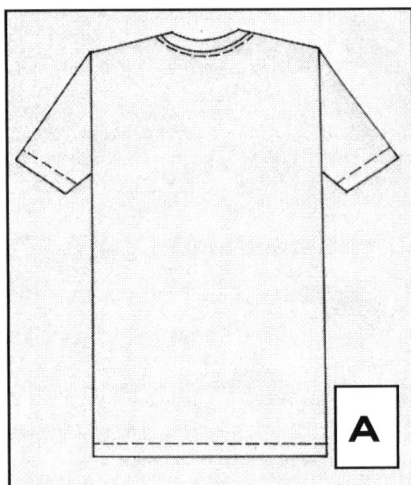

A

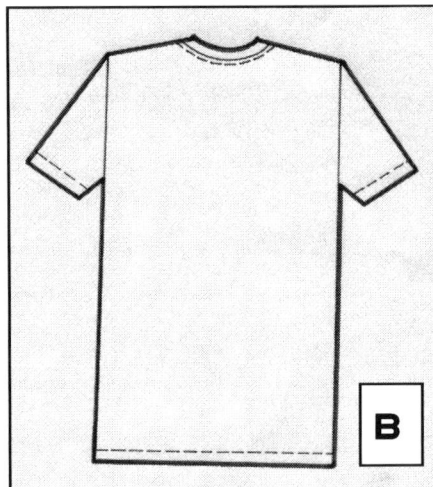

B

Step #24

For final outlining, you can use only one marker (A) or a few different markers (B) to show a thicker line for the basic shape and skinnier lines for details of the T-shirts and topstitching.

The most preferred method is the contrast technique with thick garment outlining and a thin line for inner details.

How to draw different styles of armholes for set-in sleeves in T-shirts

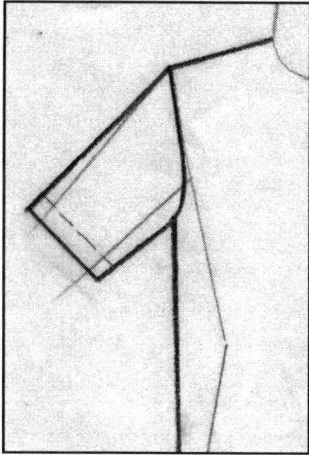

Tip

There is no "one and the only way" to draw armhole. So, chose the style you want.

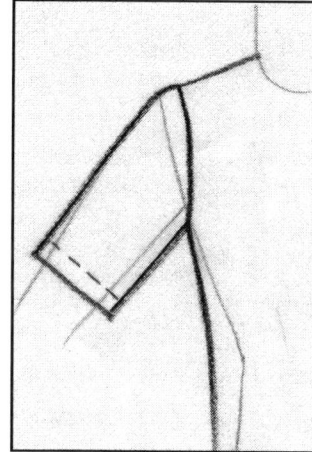

Not fitted T-shirt with standard shoulder seam and curved set-in armhole.

Not fitted T-shirt with standard shoulder seam and slit style set-in armhole.

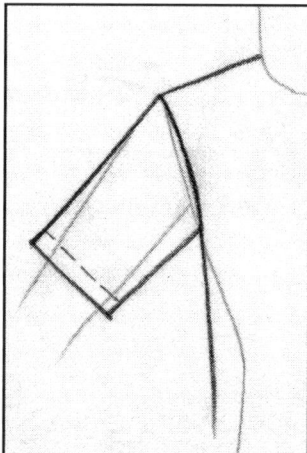

Semi fitted T-shirt with short shoulder seam.

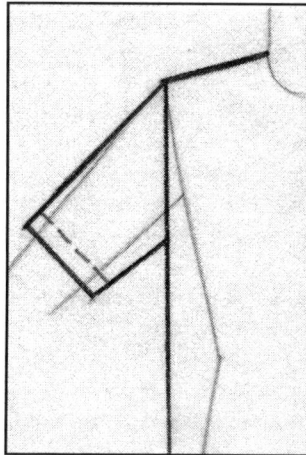

Semi-fitted T-shirt with standard shoulder seam and curved set-in armhole.

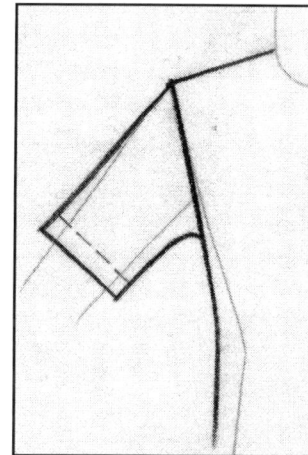

Not fitted T-shirt with relaxing or dropped shoulder seam and curved set-in armhole.

Semi fitted T-shirt with standard shoulder seam, slit style set-in armhole and curved sleeve inseam.

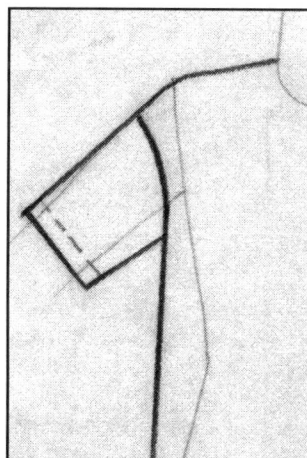

43

How to draw zippers

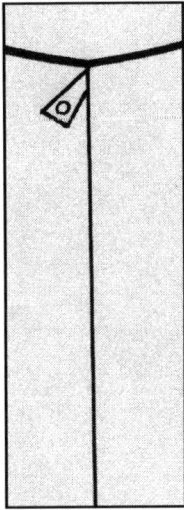

Invisible zipper
(always without topstitching).

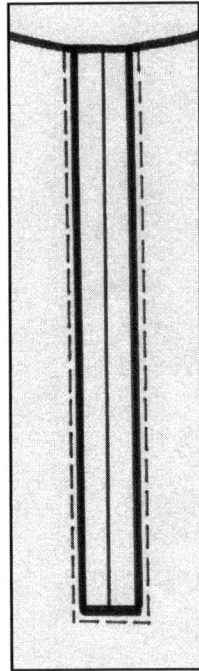

Welt zipper
with topstitching.

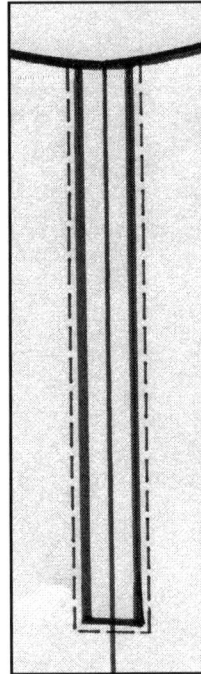

Welt zipper
(placed inside seam)
with topstitching.

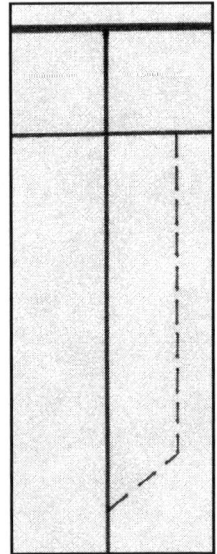

Side zipper
(always with topstitching on the side).

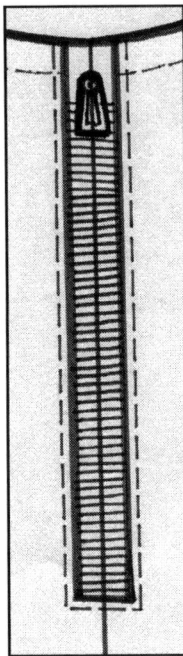

Exposed zipper
with topstitching.

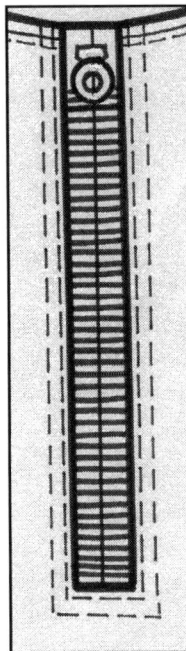

Exposed zipper
with double topstitching.

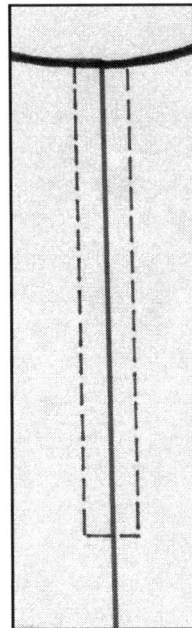

Center zipper
(always with topstitching and always placed inside seam).

44

Gallery of details for T-shirts
(necklines with zippers)

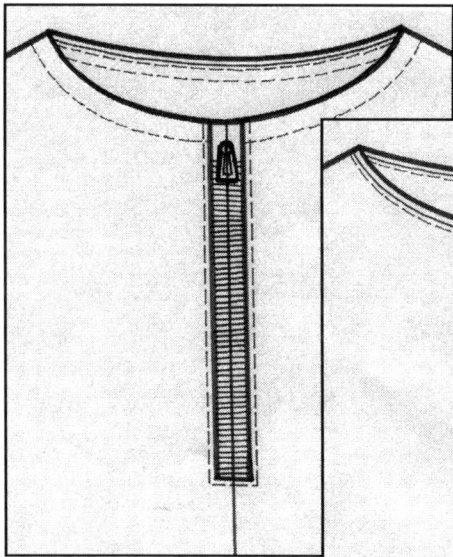

Exposed zipper with topstitching (zipper is placed inside a center seam).

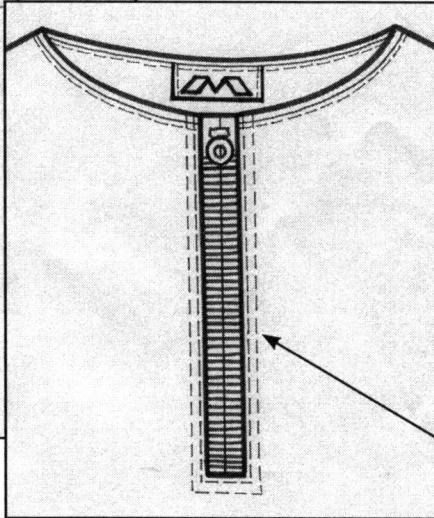

Exposed zipper with double topstitching.

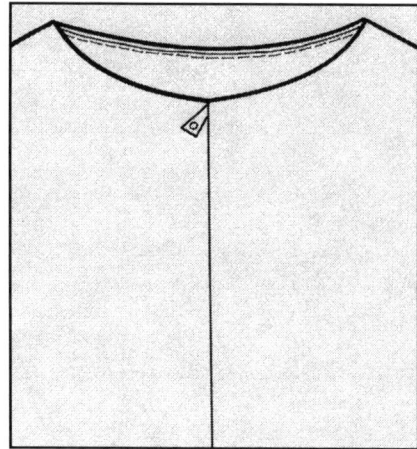

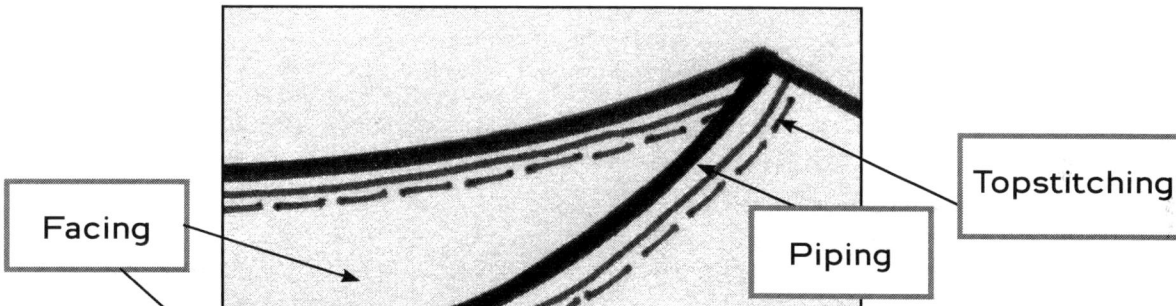

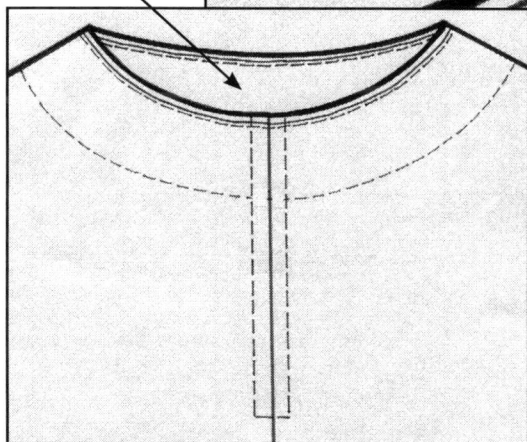

Invisible zipper (always without topstitching).

Double topstitching

Facing

Topstitching

Piping

Center zipper with double topstitching around neckline.

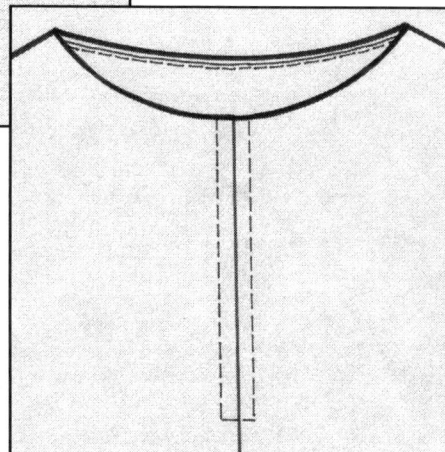

Center zipper (always with topstitching and always placed inside seam).

Underststitching

Facing

Understitching

Facing

Structure of seam with facing for clean finish neckline.

Welt zipper
with double topstitching.

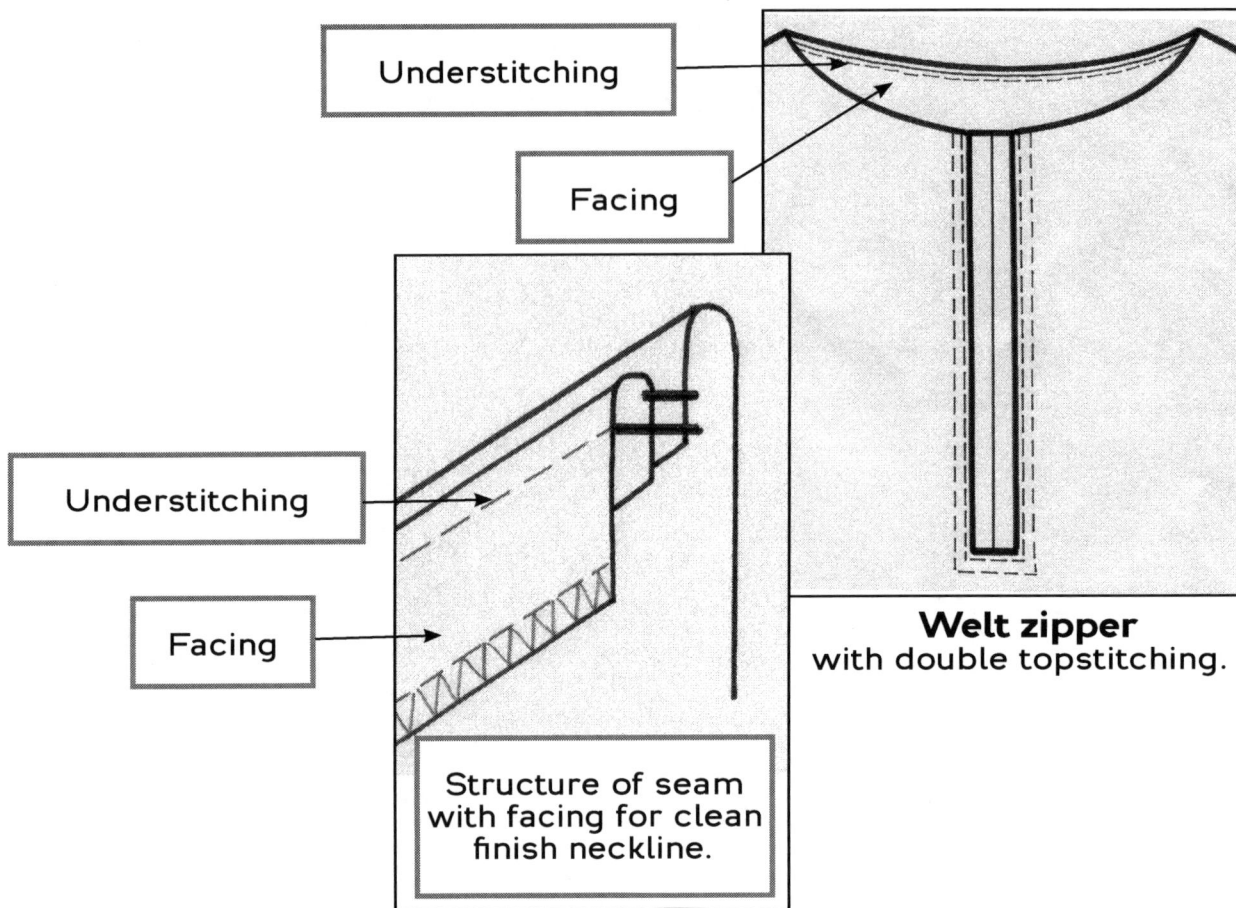

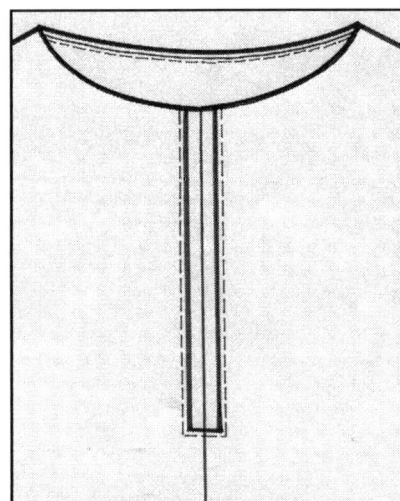

- **Facing** is a piece of fabric which is used to clean finish raw edges of a garment (necklines, armholes, hemlines, etc.).
- **Understitching** is a seam which is used to keep facing inside a garment. Facing and understitching could be seen only from inside of a garment.
- **Topstitching** is an extra seam on right side of a garment which is used as a decorative element and sometimes for reinforcement and flattening of a seam.

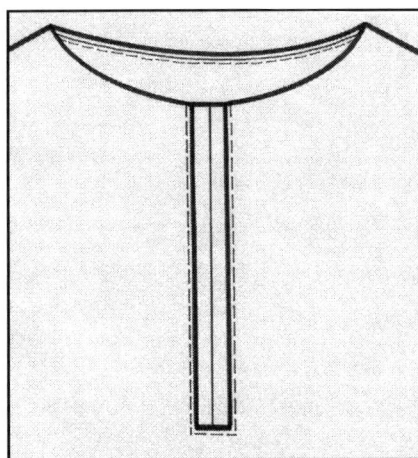

Welt zipper
with topstitching.

Welt zipper
with topstitching (zipper is placed inside a seam).

Understitching

Facing

Topstitching for neckline

Topstitching for zipper

Piping
(to cover zipper)

Understitching

Facing

Structure of seam with topstitching and facing for clean finish neckline.

Topstitching for neckline

Center seam

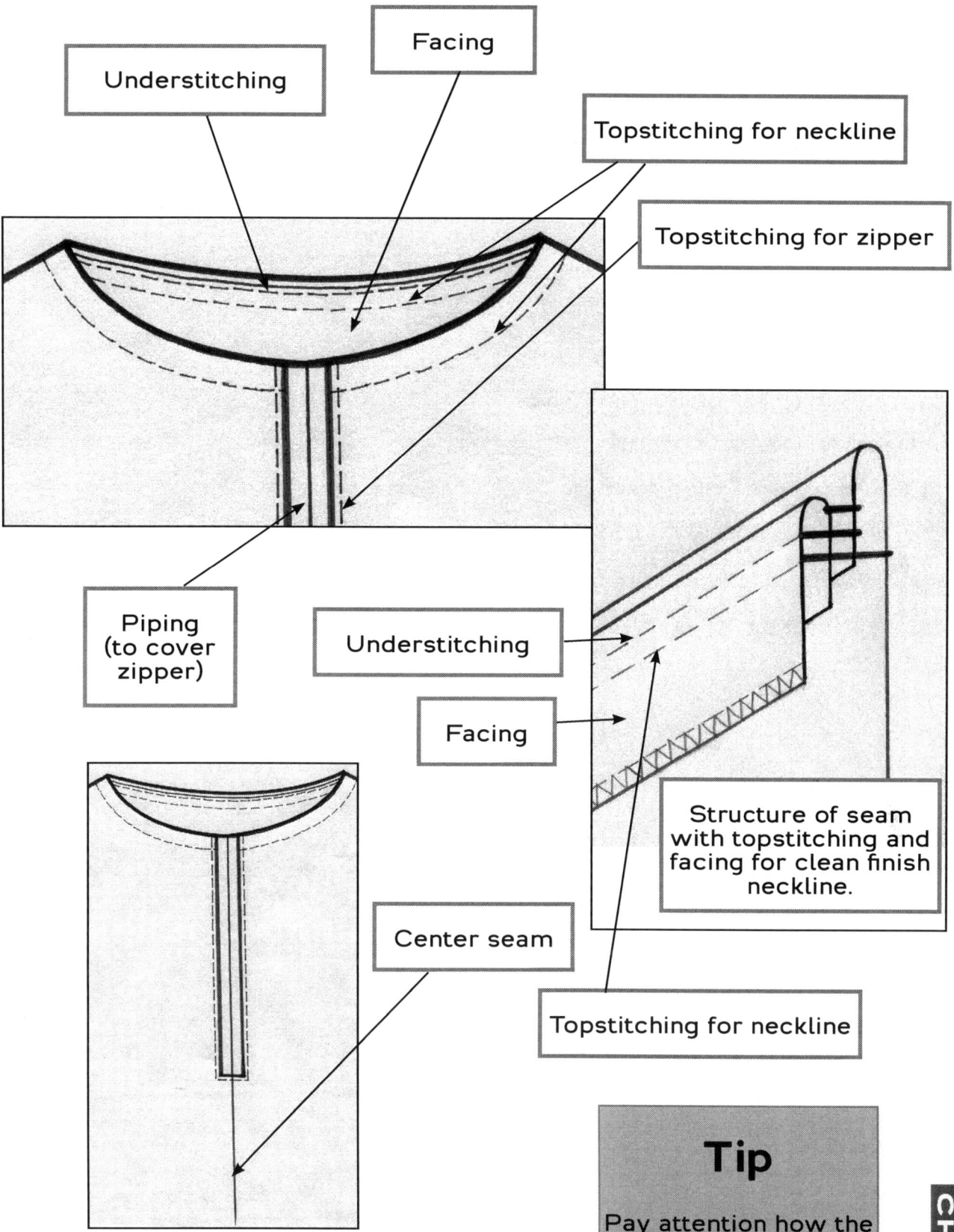

Welt zipper
with topstitching around zipper and neckline (zipper is placed inside a seam).

Tip

Pay attention how the edges of a garment are clean finished.

Gallery of details for T-shirts (plackets)

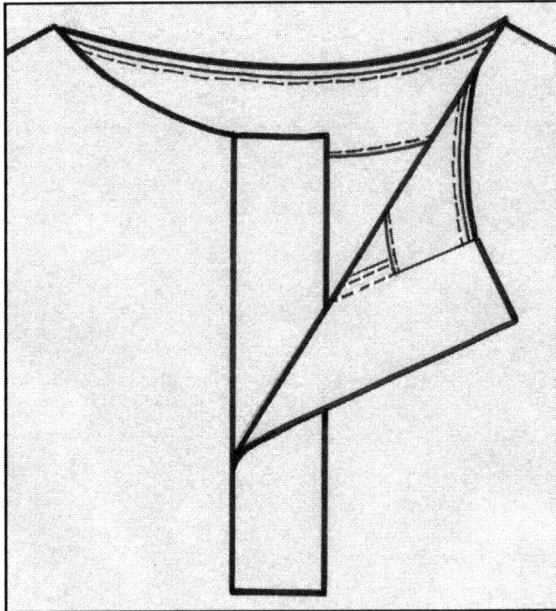

Placket without buttons. Neckline is clean finished with facing.

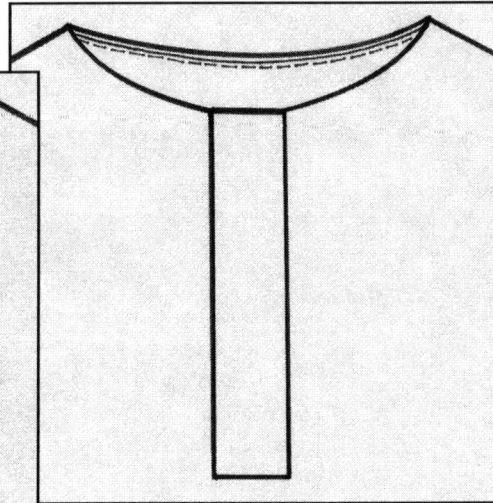

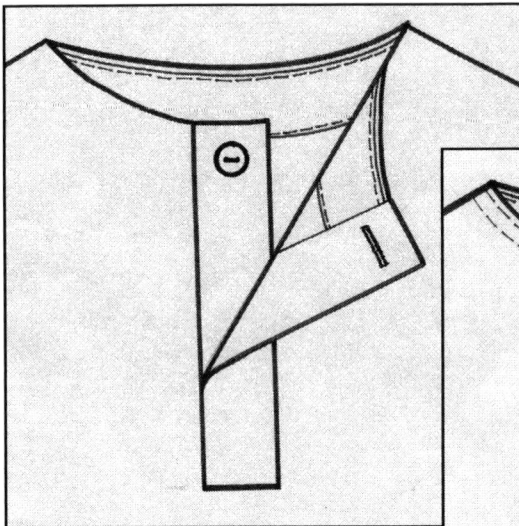

Placket with one button. Neckline is clean finished with facing.

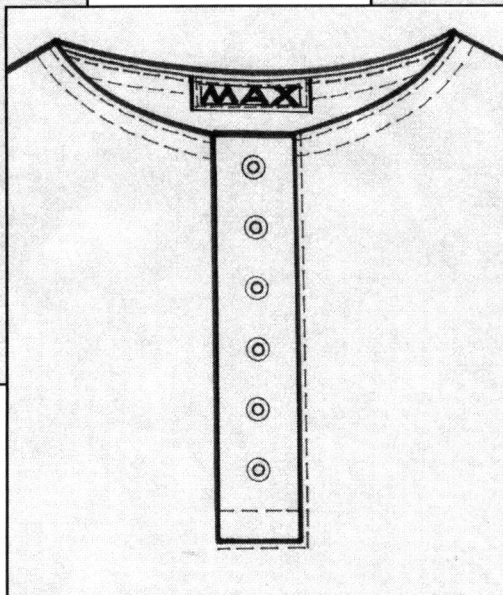

Placket with 6 snaps. Neckline is clean finished with facing and double topstitching around the neckline.

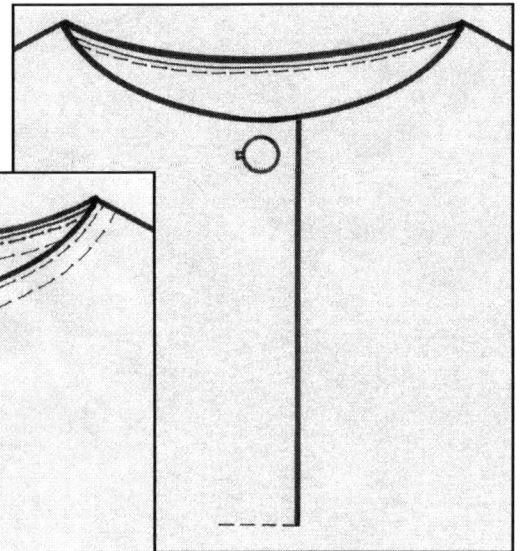

Placket with one button. Neckline is clean finished with facing.

The placket is a piece of fabric which is used to clean finish any opening of a garment. Placket could be used with buttons, snaps, or zippers.

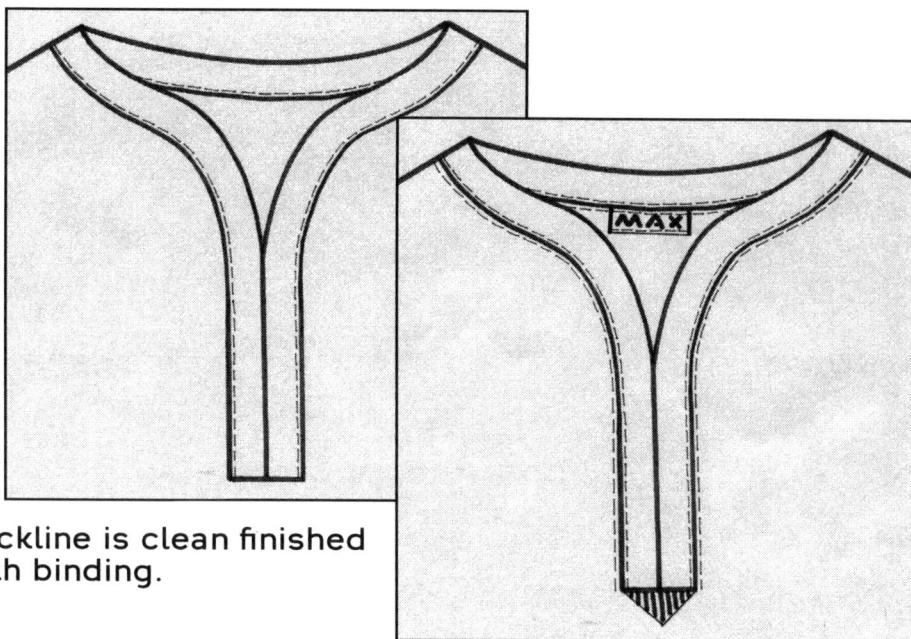

Neckline is clean finished
with binding.

Binding is a piece of fabric which is used to clean finish raw edges of a garment (necklines, armholes, hemlines, etc.). Binding could be seen from both sides (outside and inside) of a garment.

Basic binding variations

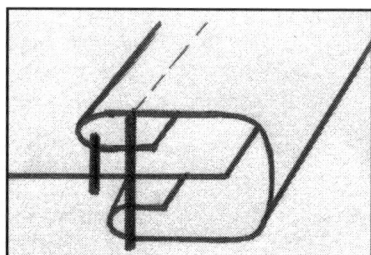

Single binding is folded from both sides to keep both sides clean finish.

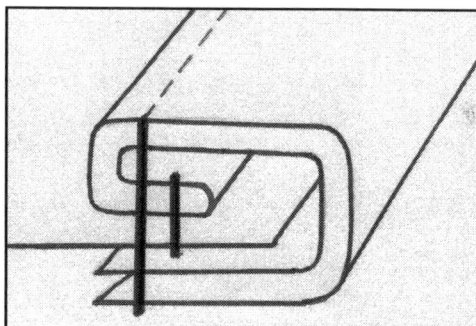

Double binding to keep the only right side of a garment clean finish. The wrong side of binding requires a finished edge serge seam.

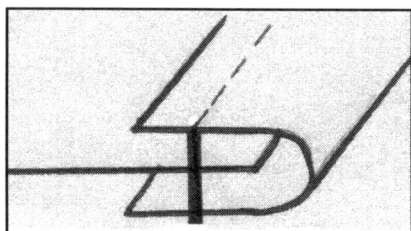

Single binding with ready to use tape.

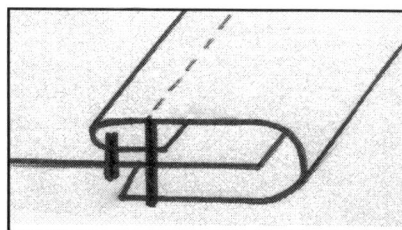

Single binding to keep the only right side of a garment clean finish. The wrong side of binding requires a finished edge serge seam.

Chapter 4

Pants

Terminology of pants

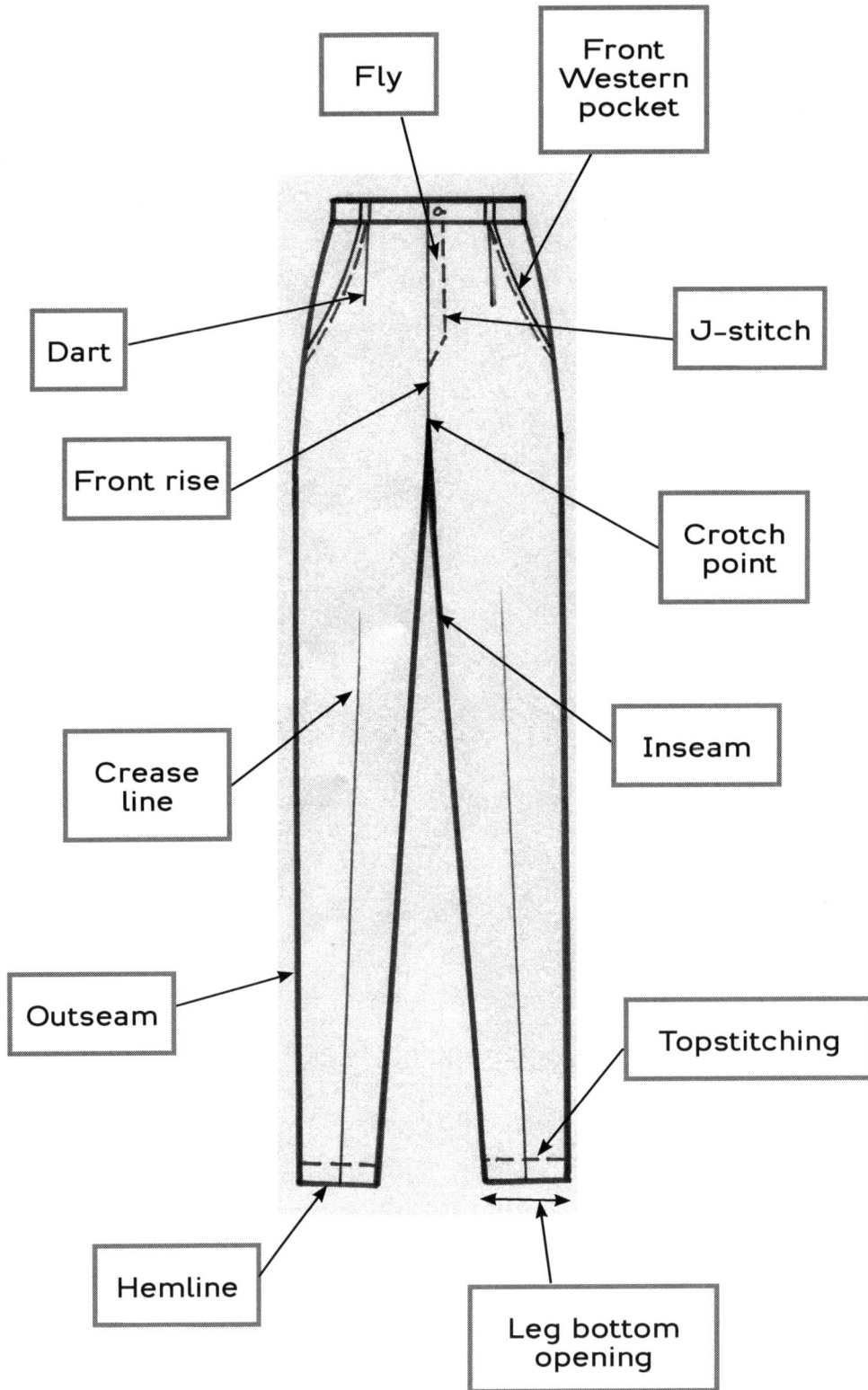

Fly

Front Western pocket

Dart

J-stitch

Front rise

Crotch point

Crease line

Inseam

Outseam

Topstitching

Hemline

Leg bottom opening

Front view

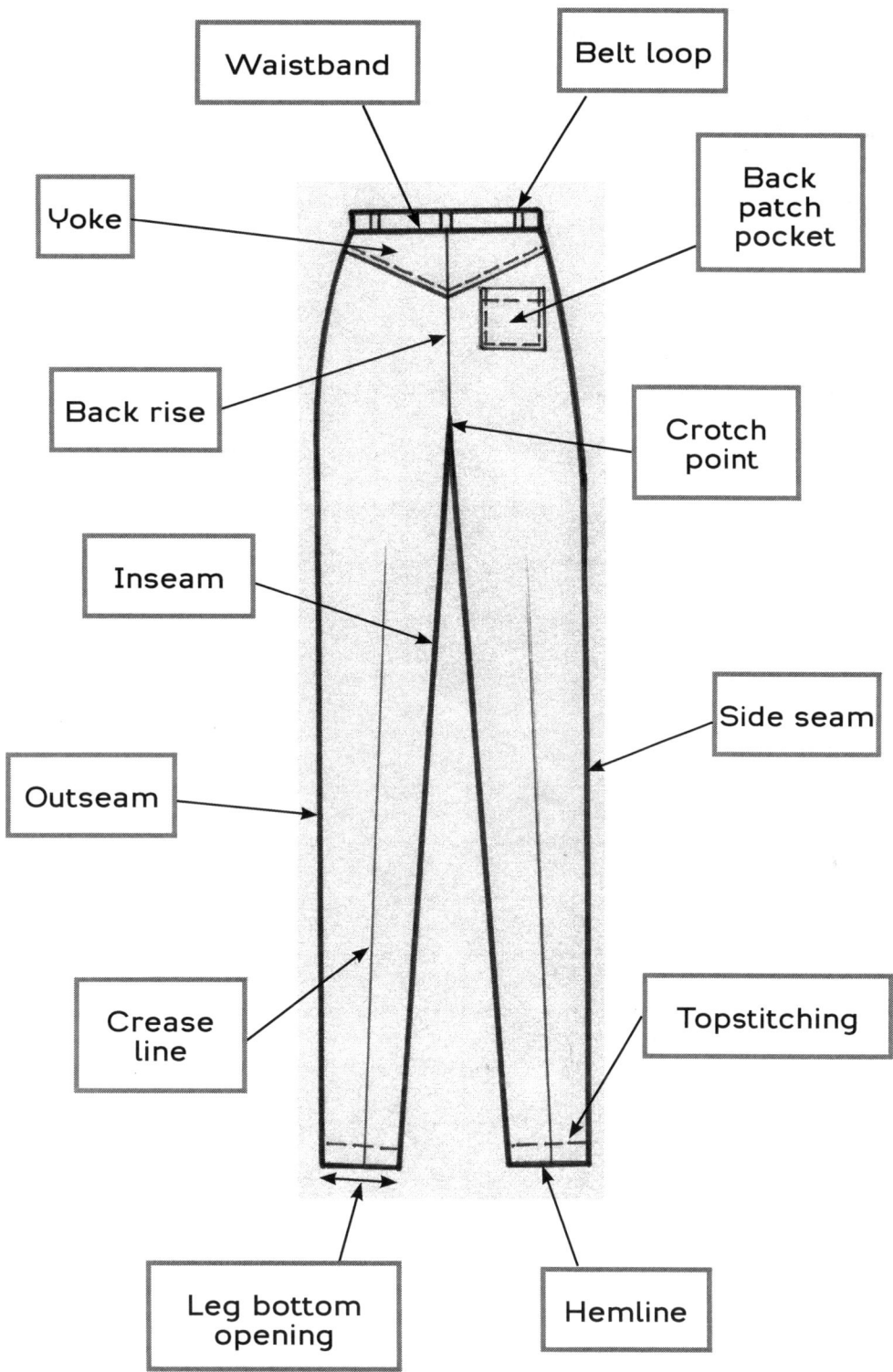

Waistband

Belt loop

Back patch pocket

Yoke

Back rise

Crotch point

Inseam

Side seam

Outseam

Crease line

Topstitching

Leg bottom opening

Hemline

Back view

Pants: basic shapes

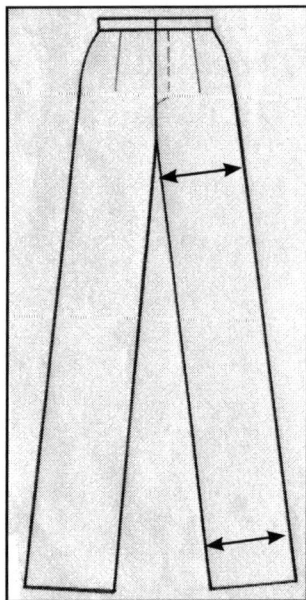

Straight pants
(width of the pants in hip and hem areas are the same).

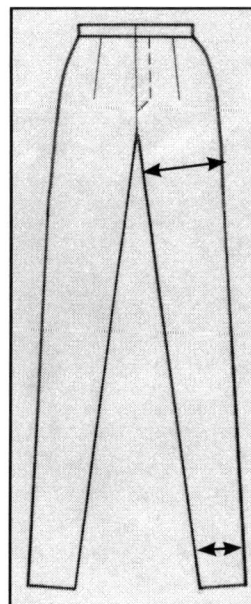

Tapered pants
(width of the pants in hip area are bigger than width of the pants in the hem).

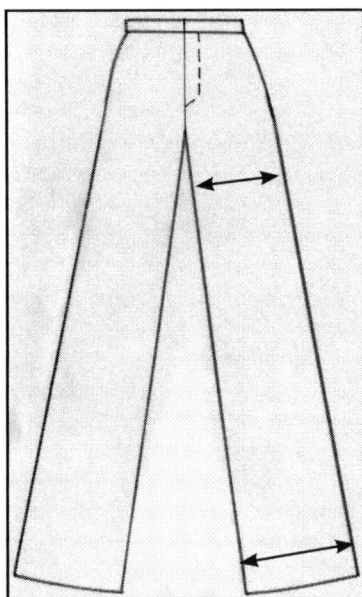

Flared pants
(width of the pants in hip area are smaller than width of the pants in the hem).

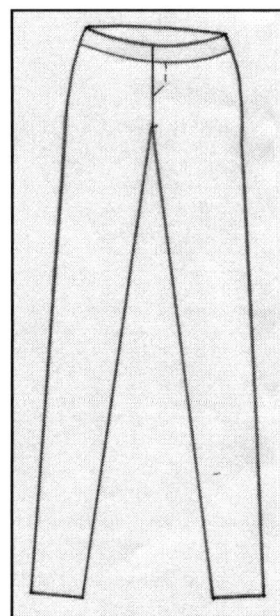

Tapered pants
with low waist band.

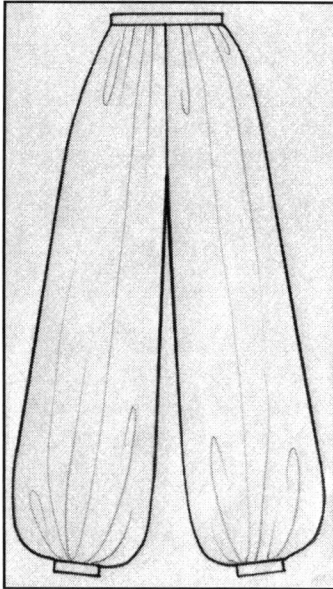

Harem
(extremely wide and gathered hem).

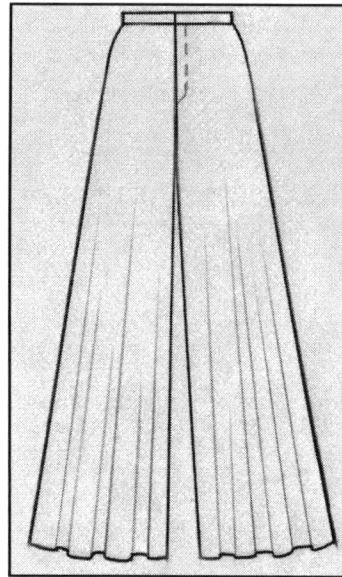

Palazzo
(extremely wide hem).

Basic hem styles in drawing flats for pants and shorts

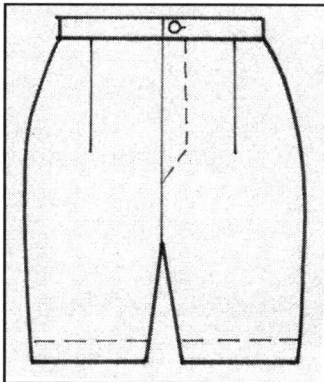

Standard hem with stitches.

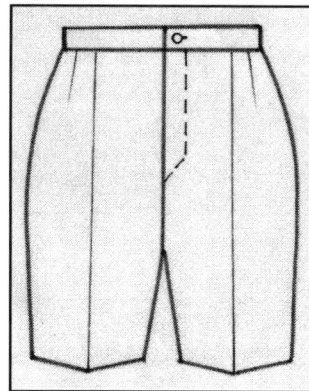

Hem with blind stitching (not visible from outside view) and with creases.

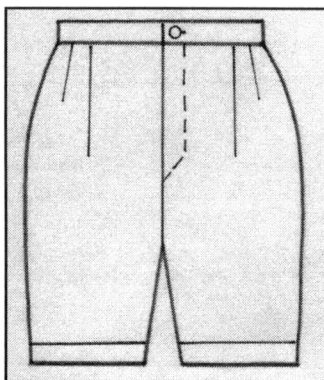

Hem with attached cuffs.

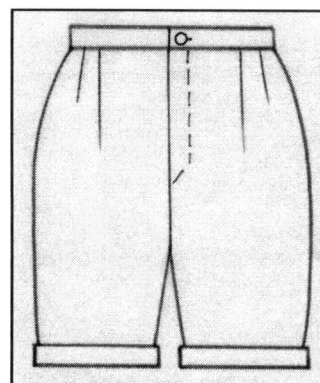

Rolled up cuffs.

Use a temporary guide line for a perfect drawing of flared pants hem.

90   **90**

Pay attention how side seams connected with hemlines. It should be 90 degree angles between these two lines.

There are no 90 degree angles between side seams and hemlines.

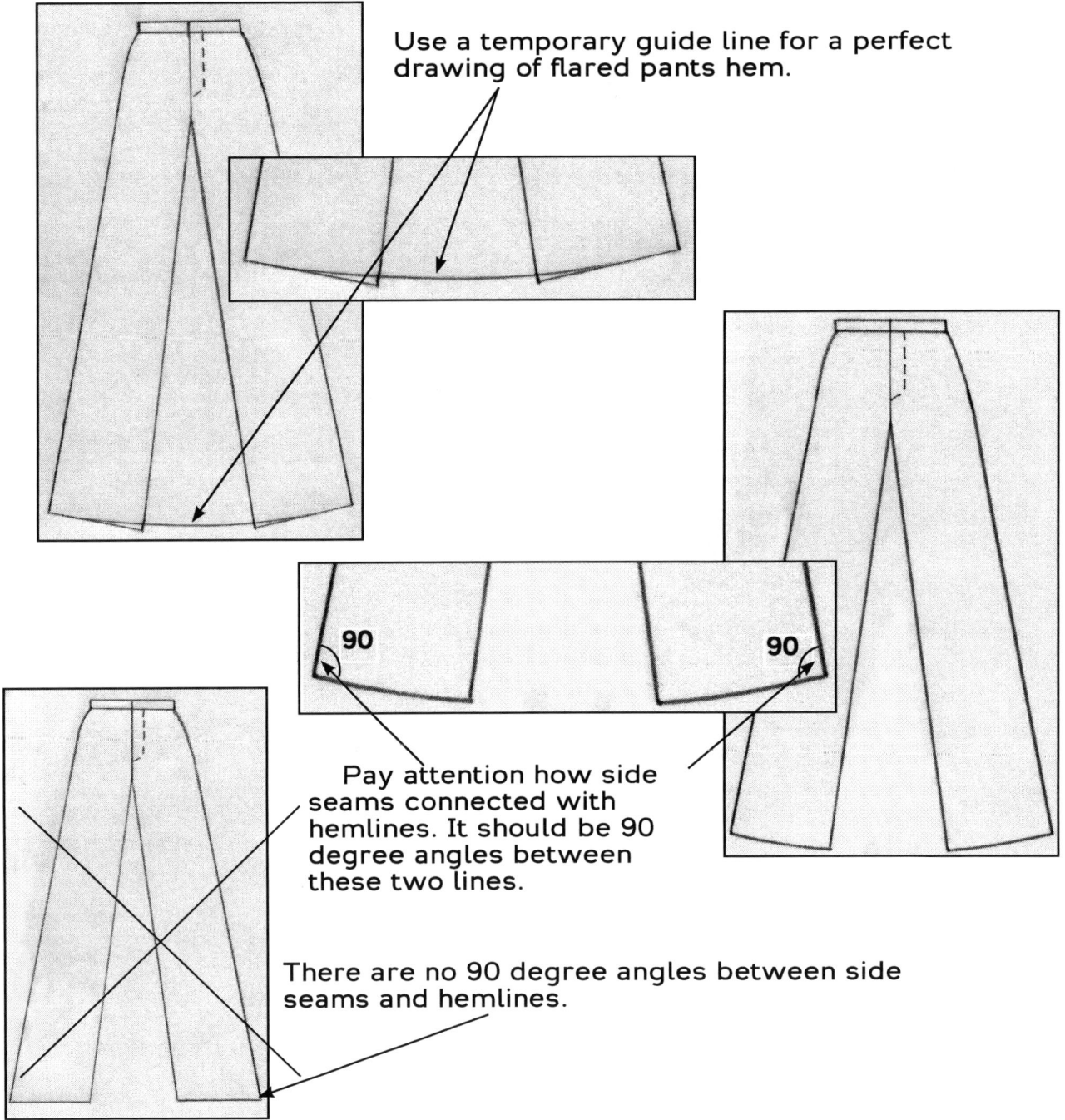

Basic waistline styles in drawing flats for pants

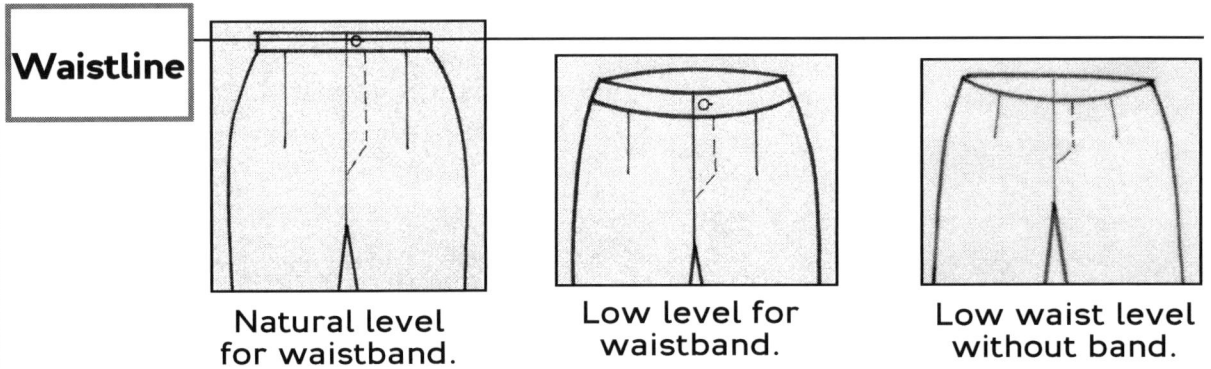

Waistline

Natural level for waistband.

Low level for waistband.

Low waist level without band.

56

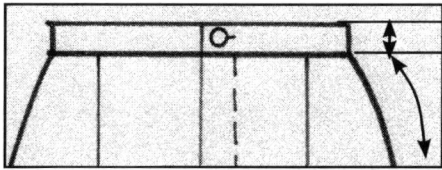

For **natural level of waistband** use
–rectangular shape for waistband,
–different outlining for pants side seam
and waistband side line.

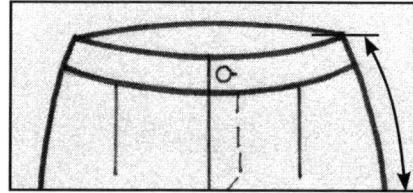

For **low level waistband** use
–curved shape for waistband,
–the same outlining for pants side
seam and waistband side line.

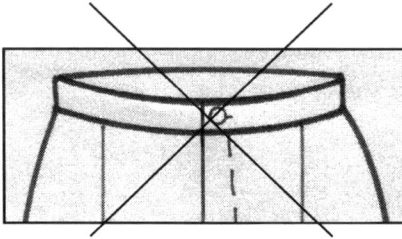

It is not natural level for the waistband neither a
low level for the waistband.
It is not natural level for the waistband because
the band is curved.
It is not a low level for the waistband because
outlining for pants side seam and waistband side
line are different.

Why we do not need darts for jeans

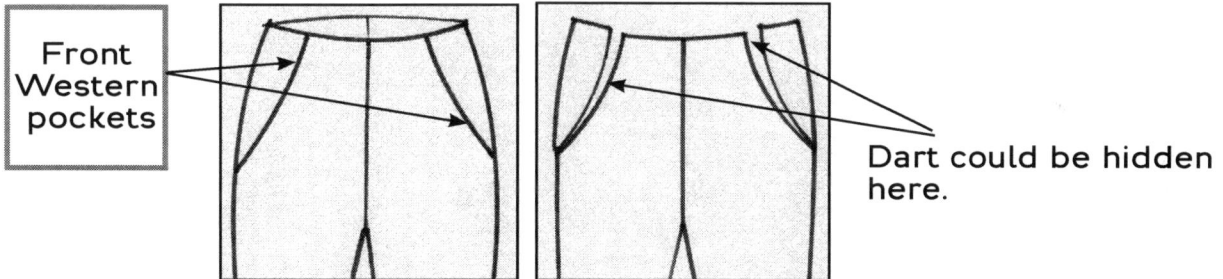

Front
Western
pockets

Dart could be hidden
here.

There is no need to do darts for pants with front Western pockets.

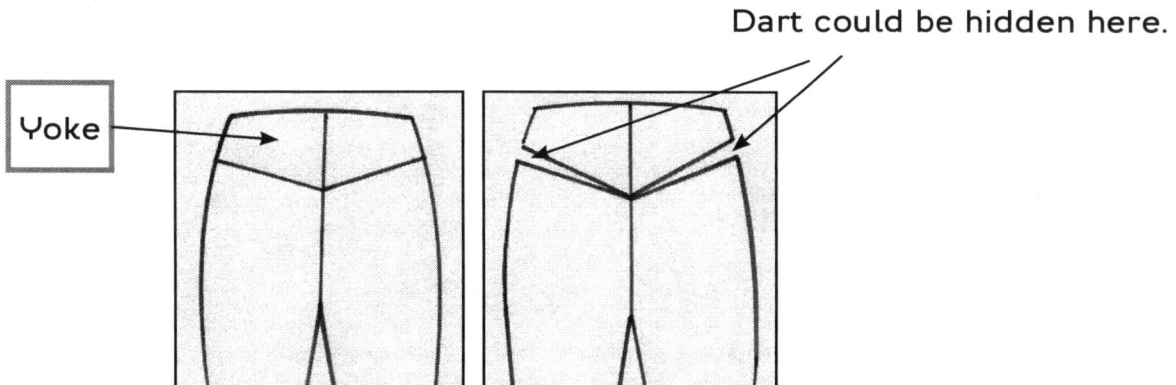

Dart could be hidden here.

Yoke

There is no need to do darts for pants with yoke.

Pants

How to draw front view flat for pants
(simple pencil line)

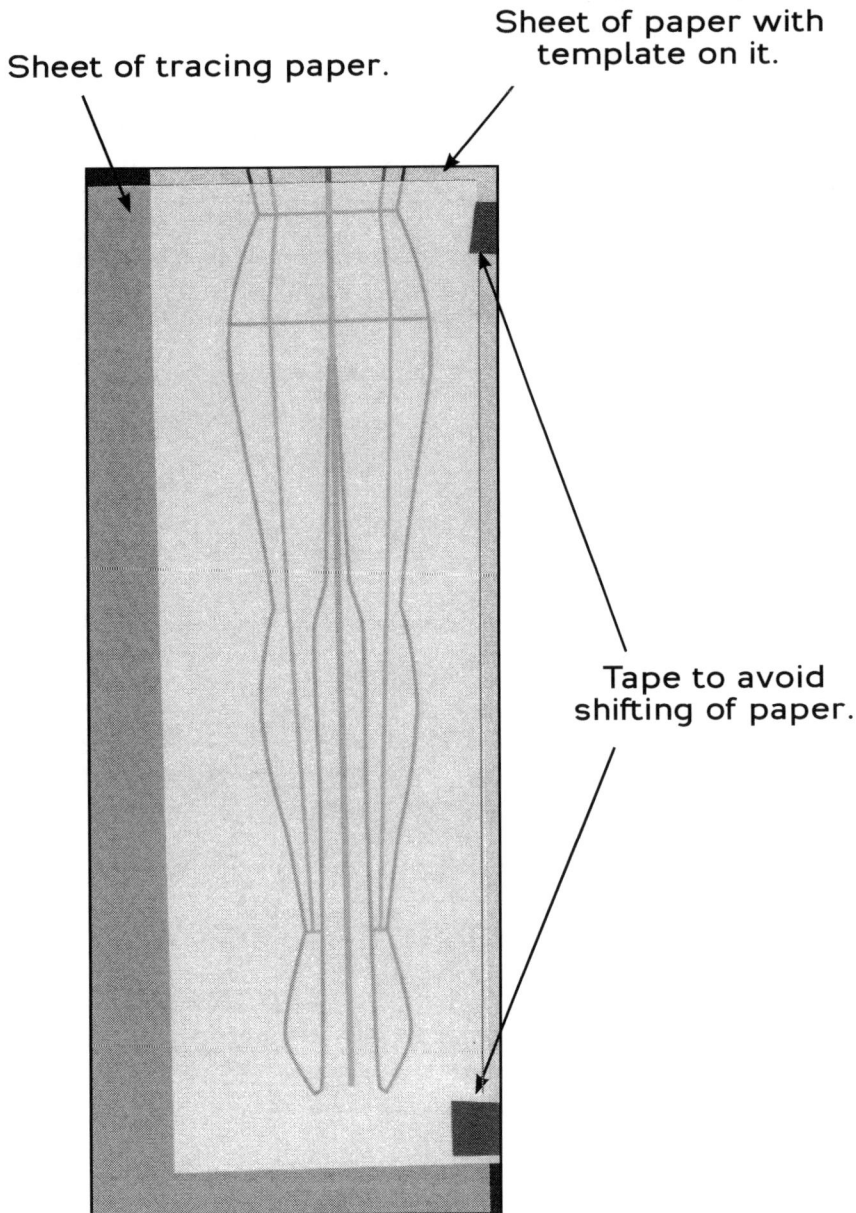

Sheet of tracing paper.

Sheet of paper with template on it.

Tape to avoid shifting of paper.

Step #1

Cover template with tracing paper and tape it to avoid shifting.

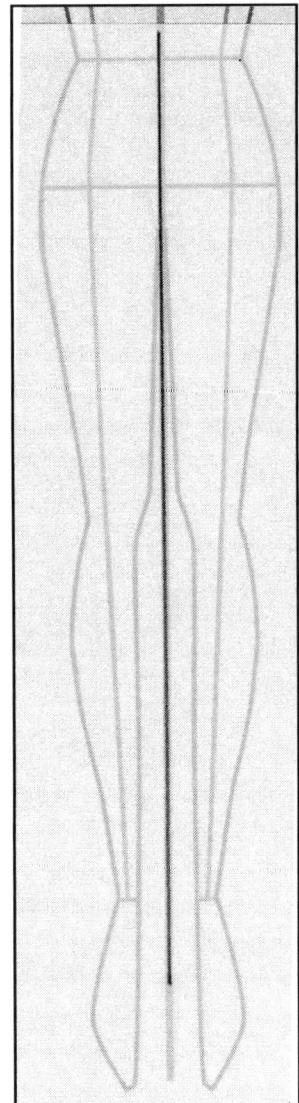

Step #2

Draw center line.

Tip

For a natural level of waistband keep croquis waistline in the middle of a flat waistband.

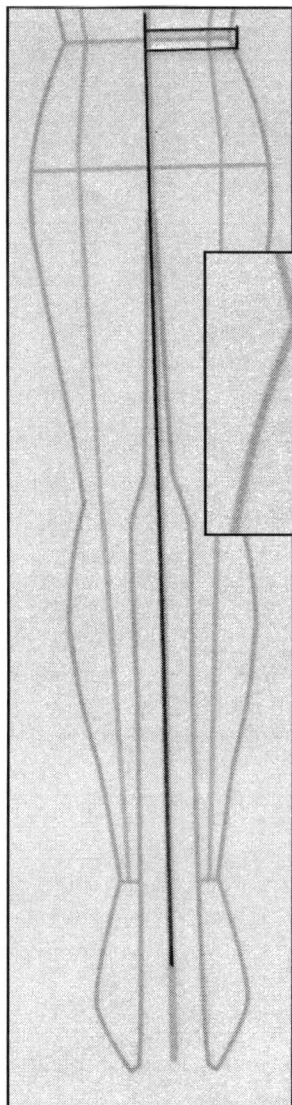

Step #3

Draw waistband.

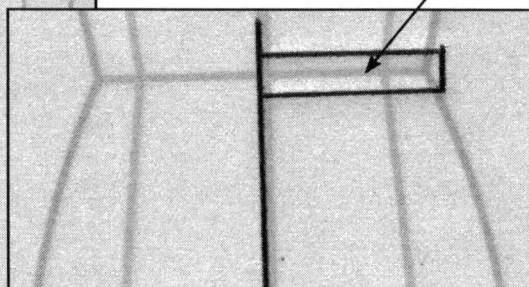

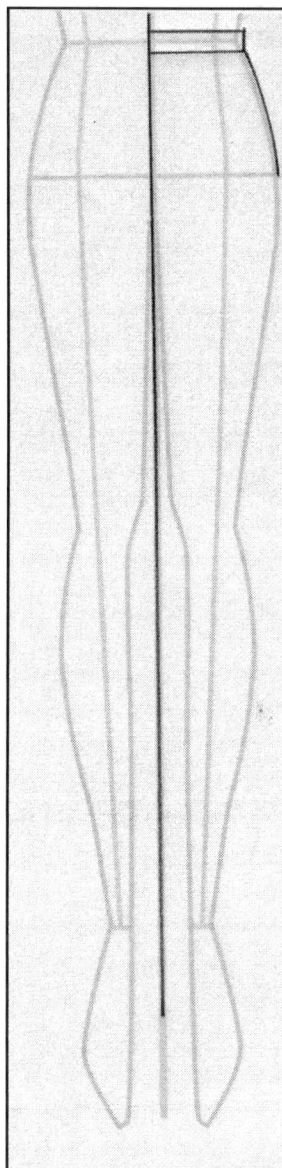

Tip

Use French curve for side seam above hip line and a ruler below hip line.

Step #4

Show side seam between waistband and hip level.

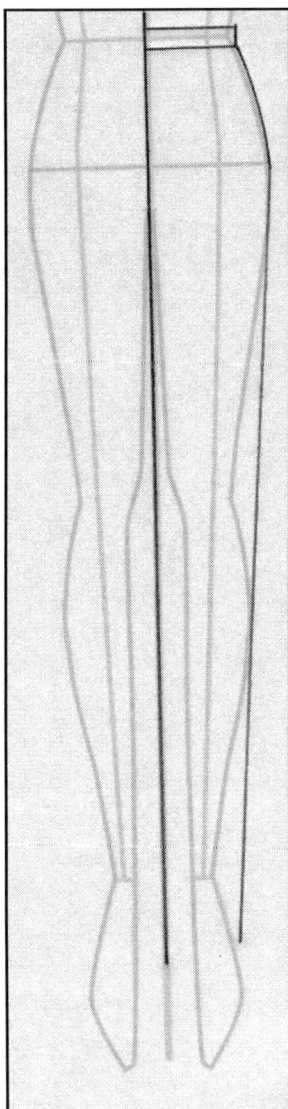

Tip

Keep inseam as close as you can to crotch point for fitted pants and far away from crotch point for lose fitted pants.

Crotch point

Inseam

Step #5

Using ruler, show outlining of side seam from hip area down to hem level.

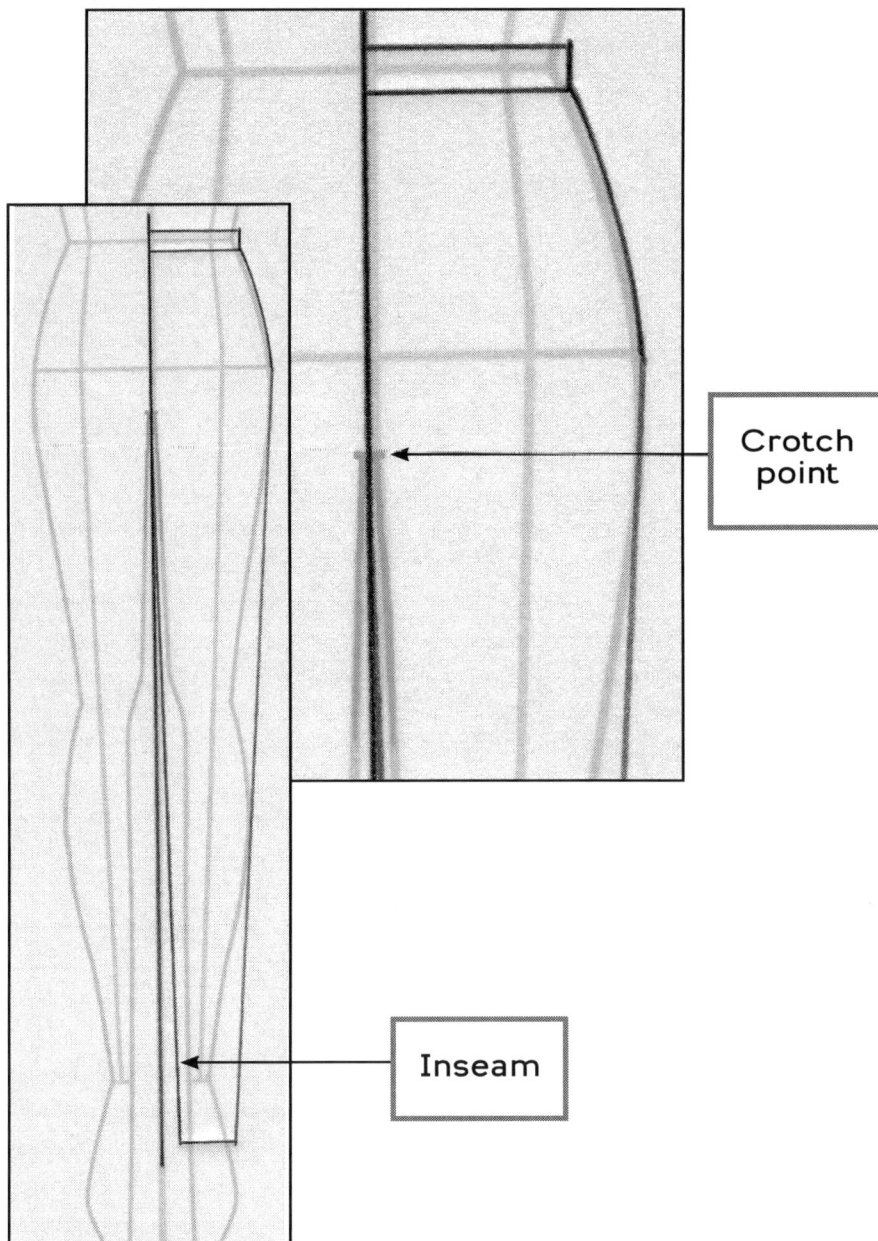

Step #6

Show hem line and inseam.

Tip

Always keep topstitching parallel to seams or edges of a garment.

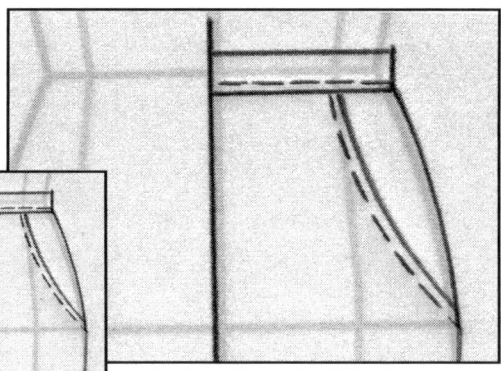

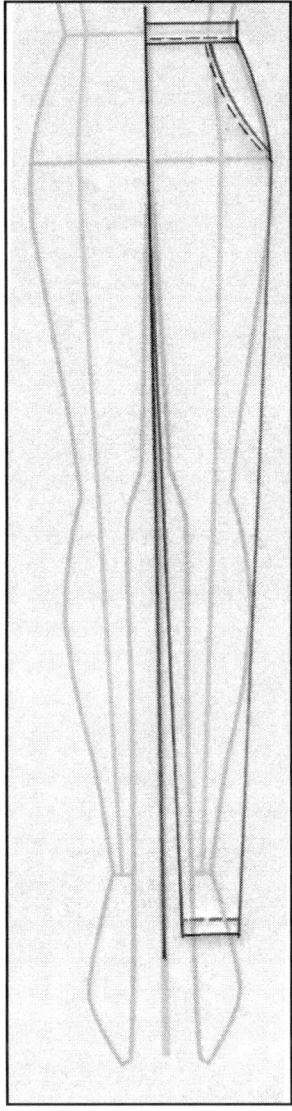

Step #7

Show Western pocket and topstitching for hem, waistband, and pocket.

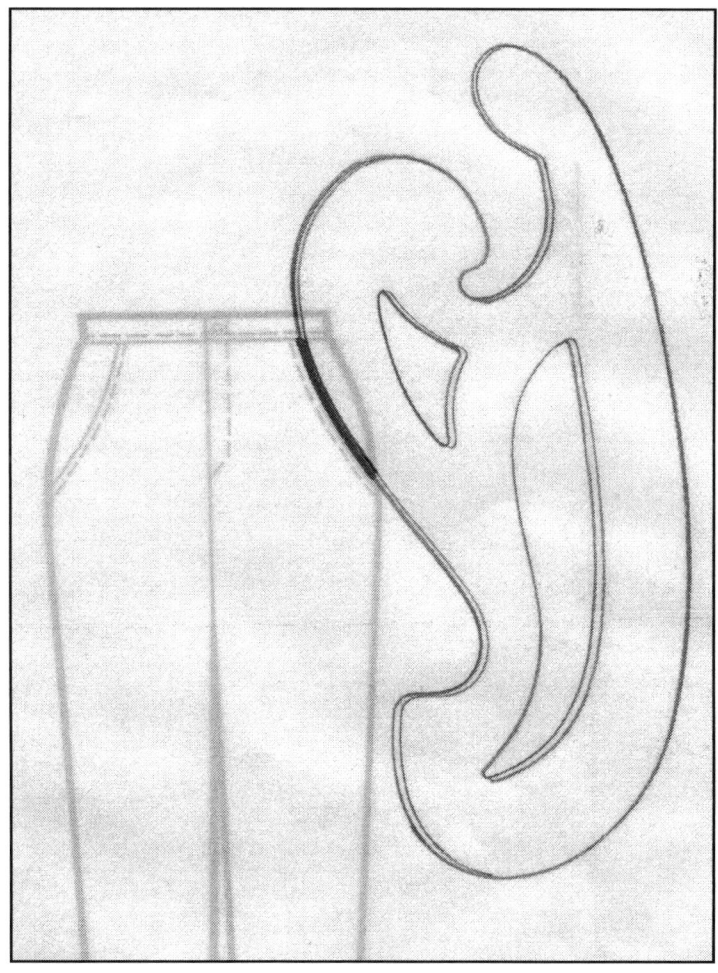

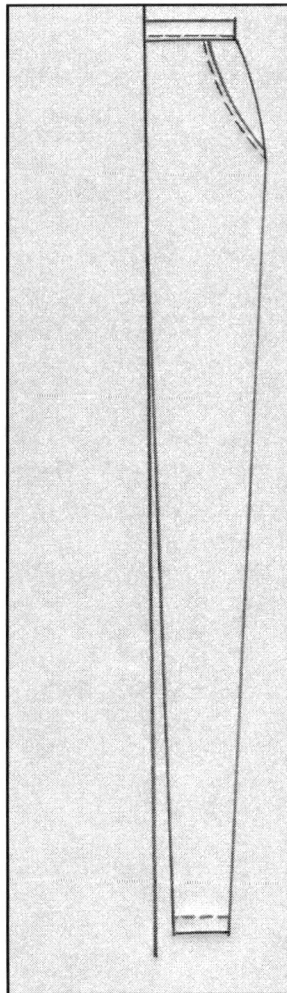

Step #8

So, the half of the flat is completed!

Now we should trace second half of the flat.

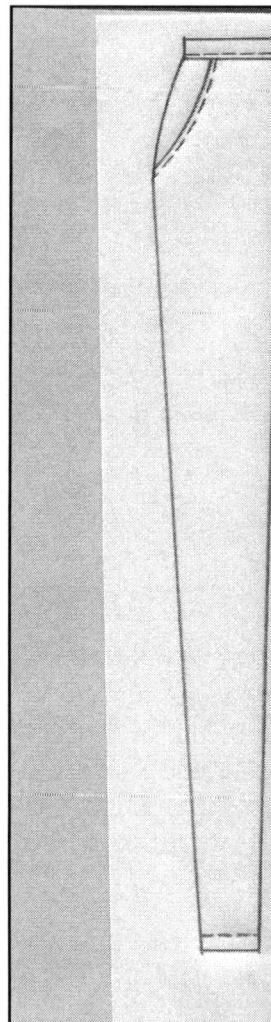

Step #9

Fold your flat along the center line and trace second half.

Tip

Always draw only one side of flat and trace the second side to make sure the garment is symmetrical.

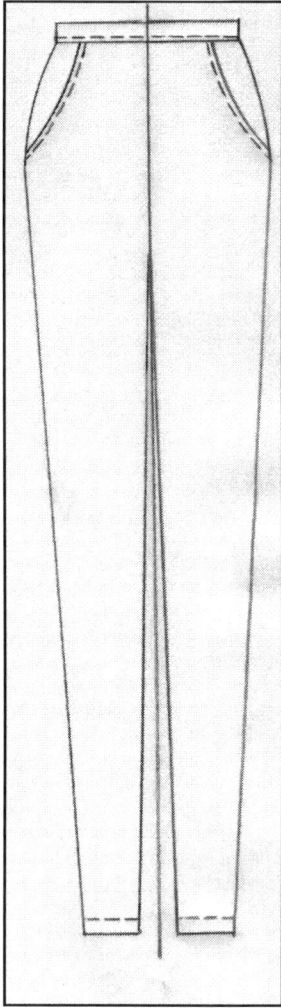

Tip

See more details for pants on pages 68-73.

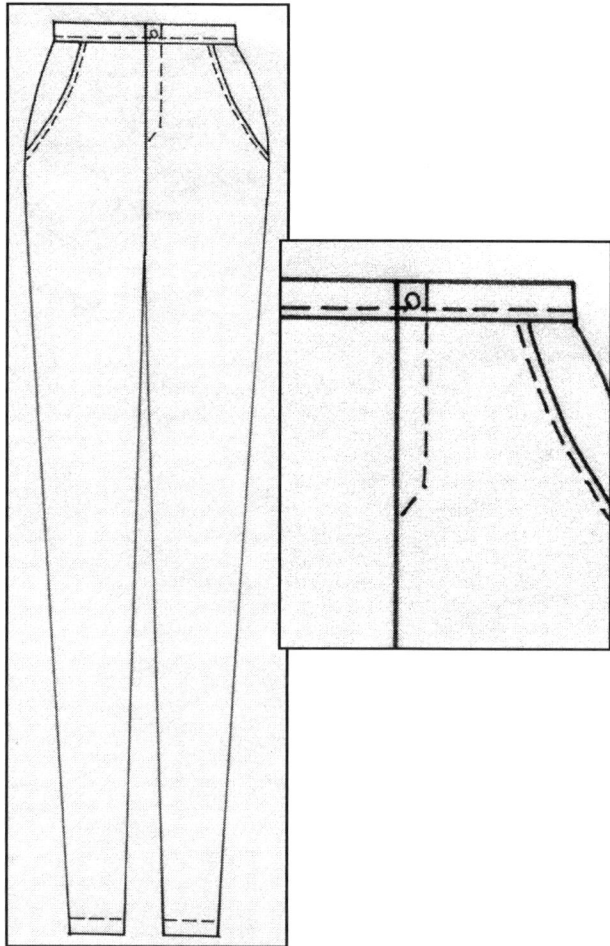

Step #10

So, basic outlining of the front view of the flat is completed!

Step #11

Show fly and button.

So, front view of the flat is completed! It is time to do corrections if needed.

Now we are ready to back view flat.

How to draw back view flat for pants
(simple pencil line)

Sheet of tracing paper (on the top).

Sheet of tracing paper with front view flat drawing of pants (underneath).

Tape to avoid shifting.

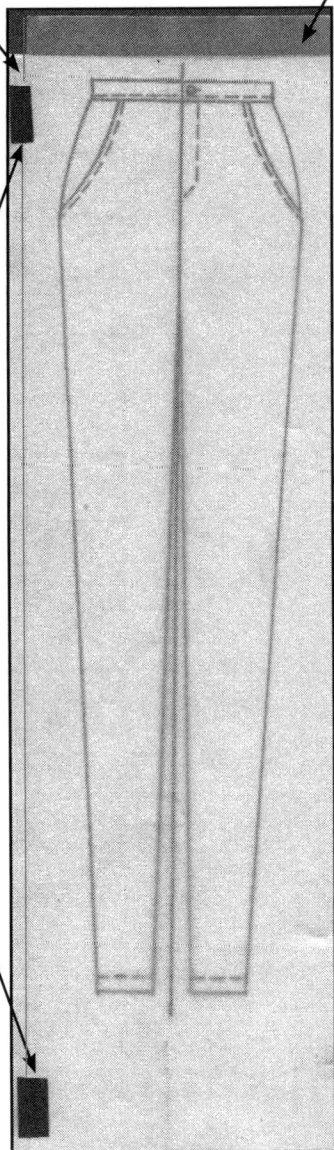

Step #12

Cover the front view flat with a new sheet of tracing paper.

Use tape to avoid shifting.

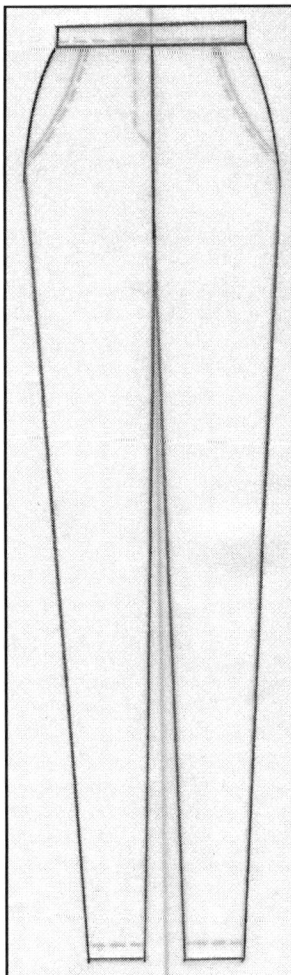

Step #13

Outline basic shape of the pants and details related to the back view.

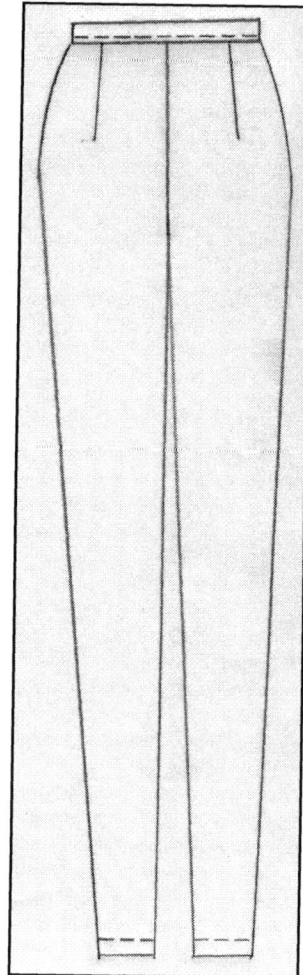

Step #14

Show darts and topstitching for hem lines and waistband.

So, back view of the pants is ready!

How to draw final front view of flats for pants (marker line)

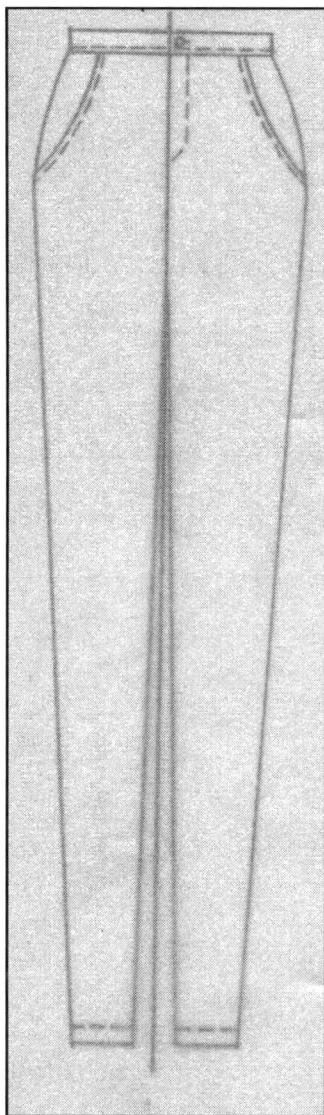

Step #15

A   **B**

Step #16

To draw a front view flat with black marker line use a front view flat with simple pencil line.

Cover your simple pencil front view flat drawing with a new sheet of marker paper. Use tape to avoid shifting.

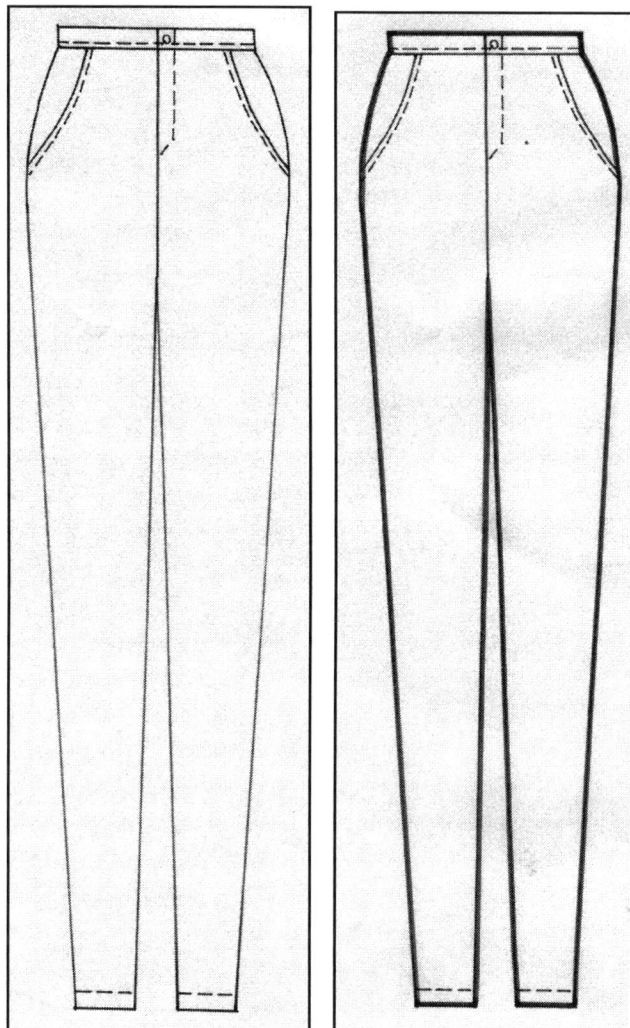

For final outlining you can use only one marker (A) or a few different markers (B) to show a thicker line for the basic shape and skinnier lines for details and topstitching.

The most preferred method is the contrast technique with thick garment outlining and a thin line for inner details.

How to draw final back view of flats for pants (marker line)

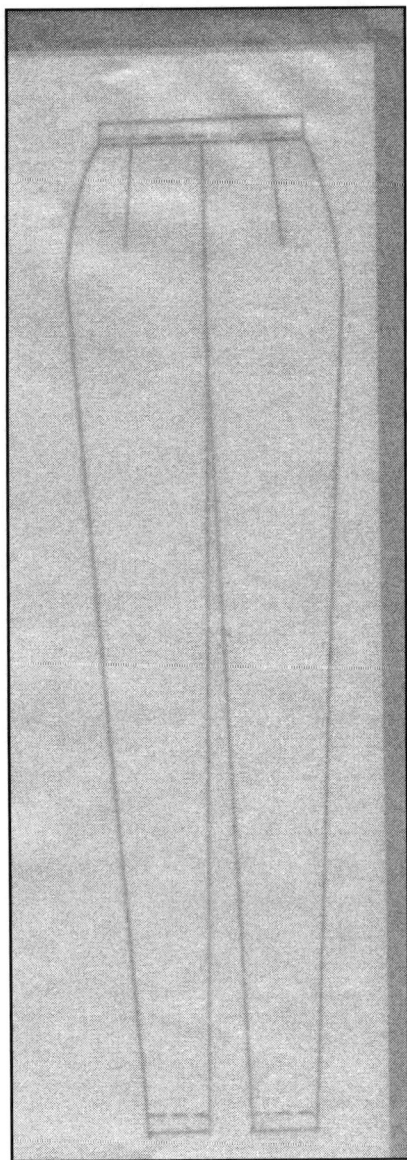

Step #17

To draw a back view flat with black marker line use a back view flat with simple pencil line.

Cover your simple pencil back view flat with a new sheet of marker paper.
Use tape to avoid shifting.

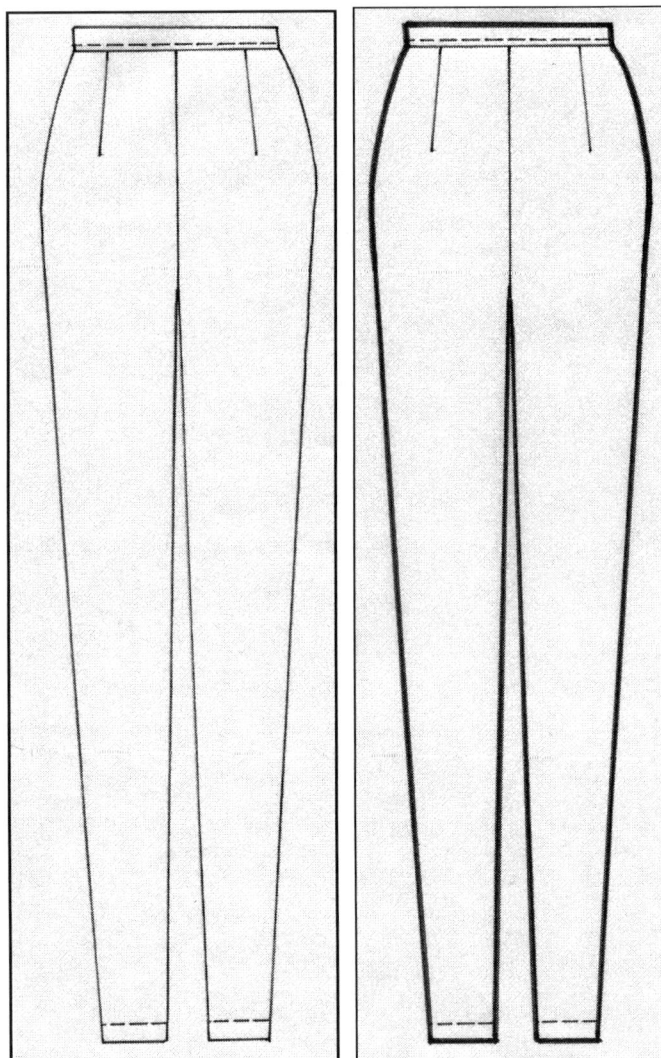

A

B

Step #18

For final outlining you can use only one marker (A) or a few different markers (B) to show a thicker line for the basic shape and skinnier lines for details of the pants and topstitching.

The most preferred method is the contrast technique with thick garment outlining and a thin line for inner details.

66

How to draw fly

Tip

Do not draw fly for pants too long. Always keep a distance between fly and crotch point.

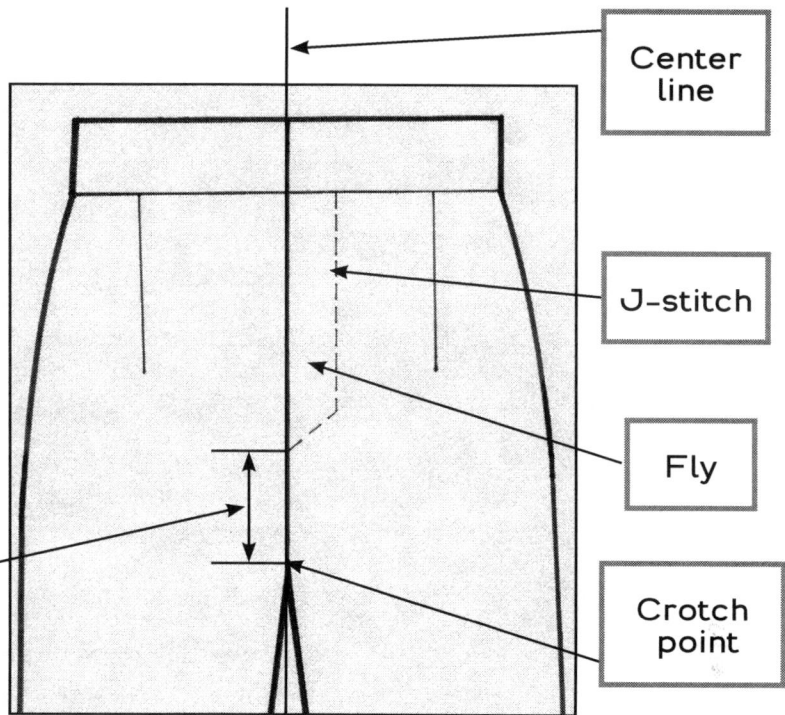

Center line

J-stitch

Fly

Crotch point

Distance between fly and crotch point

Tip

For loose fitting of pants keep longer distance between crotch point on the pants and crotch point on the body. For tight fitting of pants keep crotch points for the pants and the body on the same level.

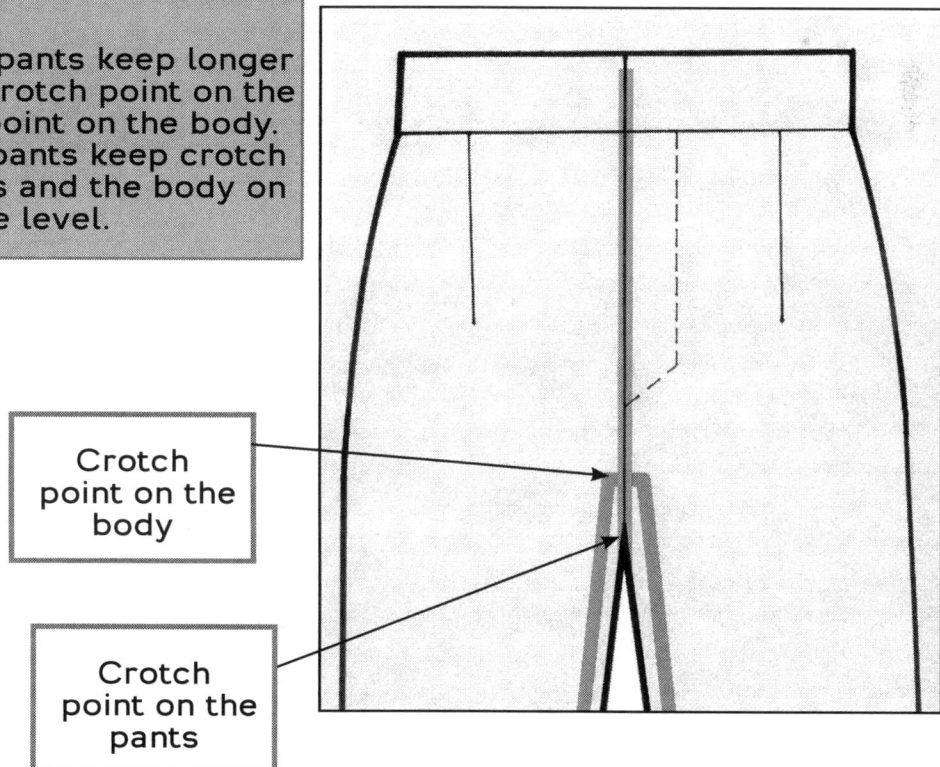

Crotch point on the body

Crotch point on the pants

Gallery of closures for pants

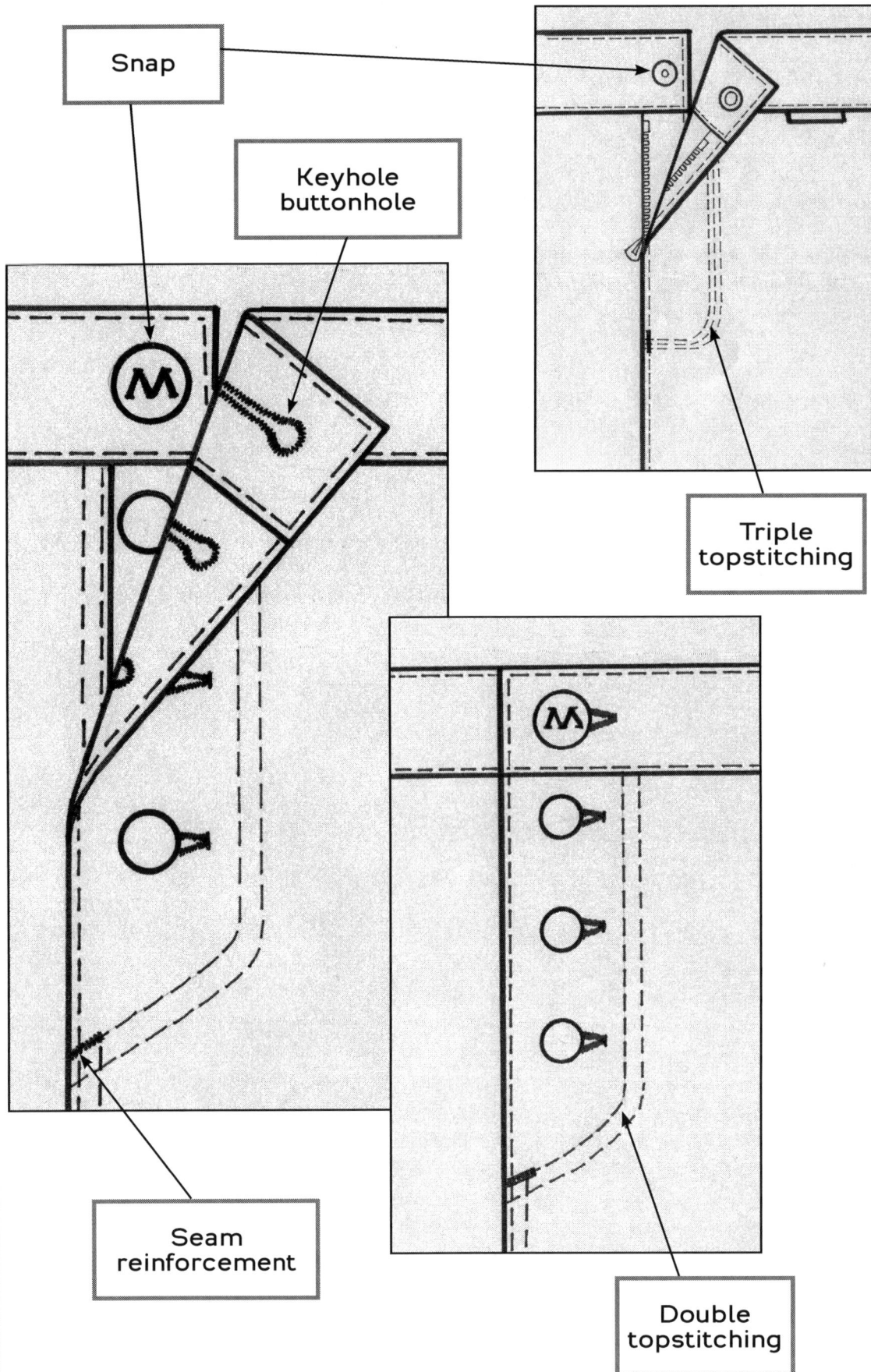

Snap

Keyhole buttonhole

Triple topstitching

Seam reinforcement

Double topstitching

© 2016 Irina V. Ivanova

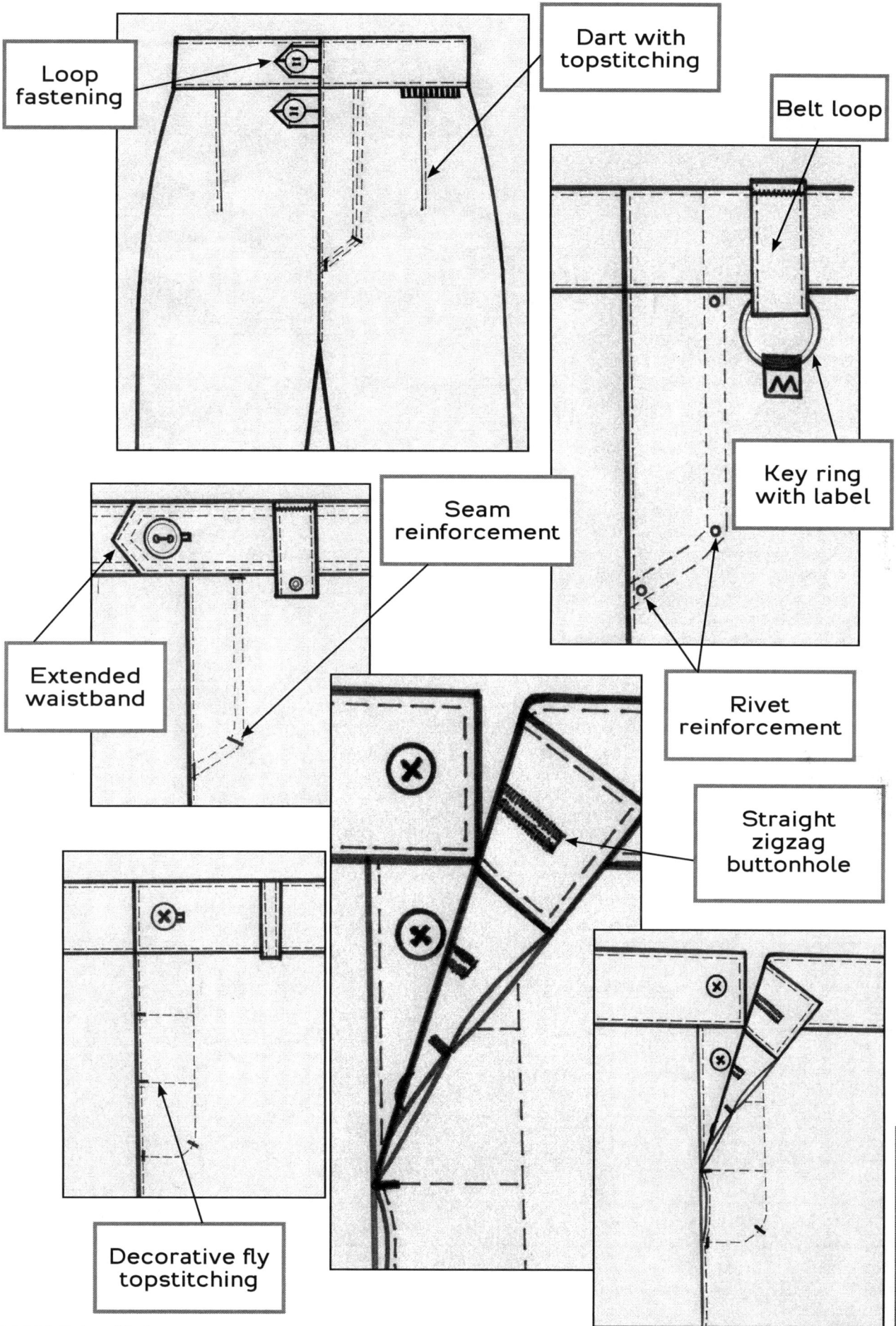

Loop
fastening

Dart with
topstitching

Belt loop

Key ring
with label

Seam
reinforcement

Extended
waistband

Rivet
reinforcement

Straight
zigzag
buttonhole

Decorative fly
topstitching

How to Draw Fashion Flats A practical guide to fashion technical drawing by Irina V. Ivanova

Gallery of pockets for pants
Family of pockets:

- Patch pockets
- Western style (seam-to-seam) pockets
- In-seam pockets
- Slash pockets

Patch pockets

Patch pocket is a piece of fabric attached to a garment.
Patch pockets are easy to add and remove from a garment.

Tip

Do not forget to show how you want to attach patch pocket to garment :
- with single topstitching
- with double topstitching

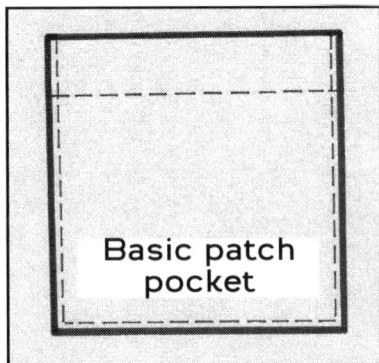

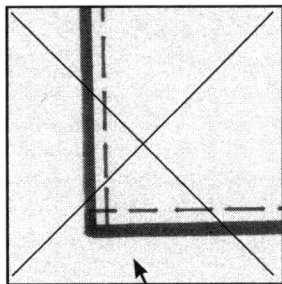

Basic patch pocket

Do not overlap topstitching in the bottom corners of a pocket.

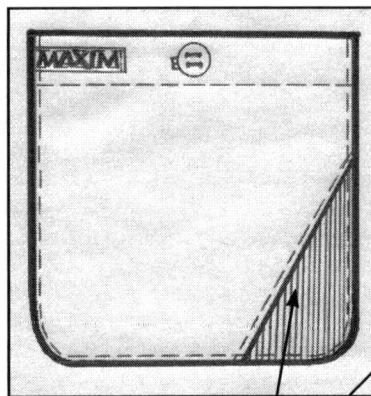

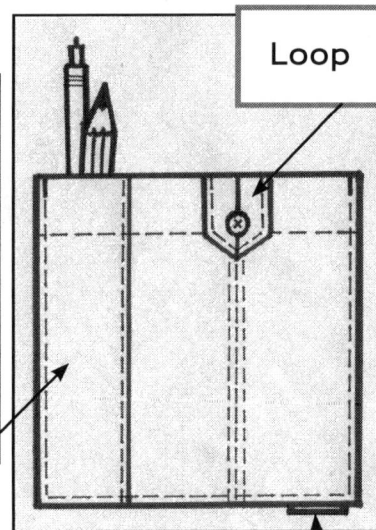

Loop

Pocket insert

Label

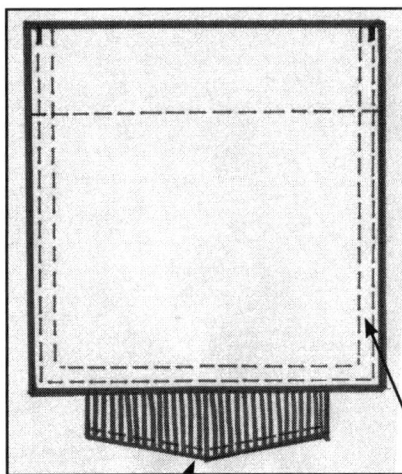

Decorative element

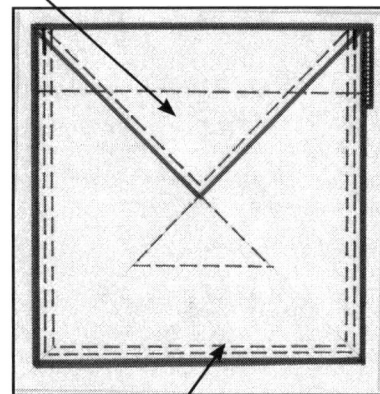

Double topstitching

How to Draw Fashion Flats A practical guide to fashion technical drawing by Irina V. Ivanova

CHAPTER 4

Western pockets

Western (seam to seam) pocket is a pocket set in a garment with an opening between two seams, usually between waistline seam and side seam.

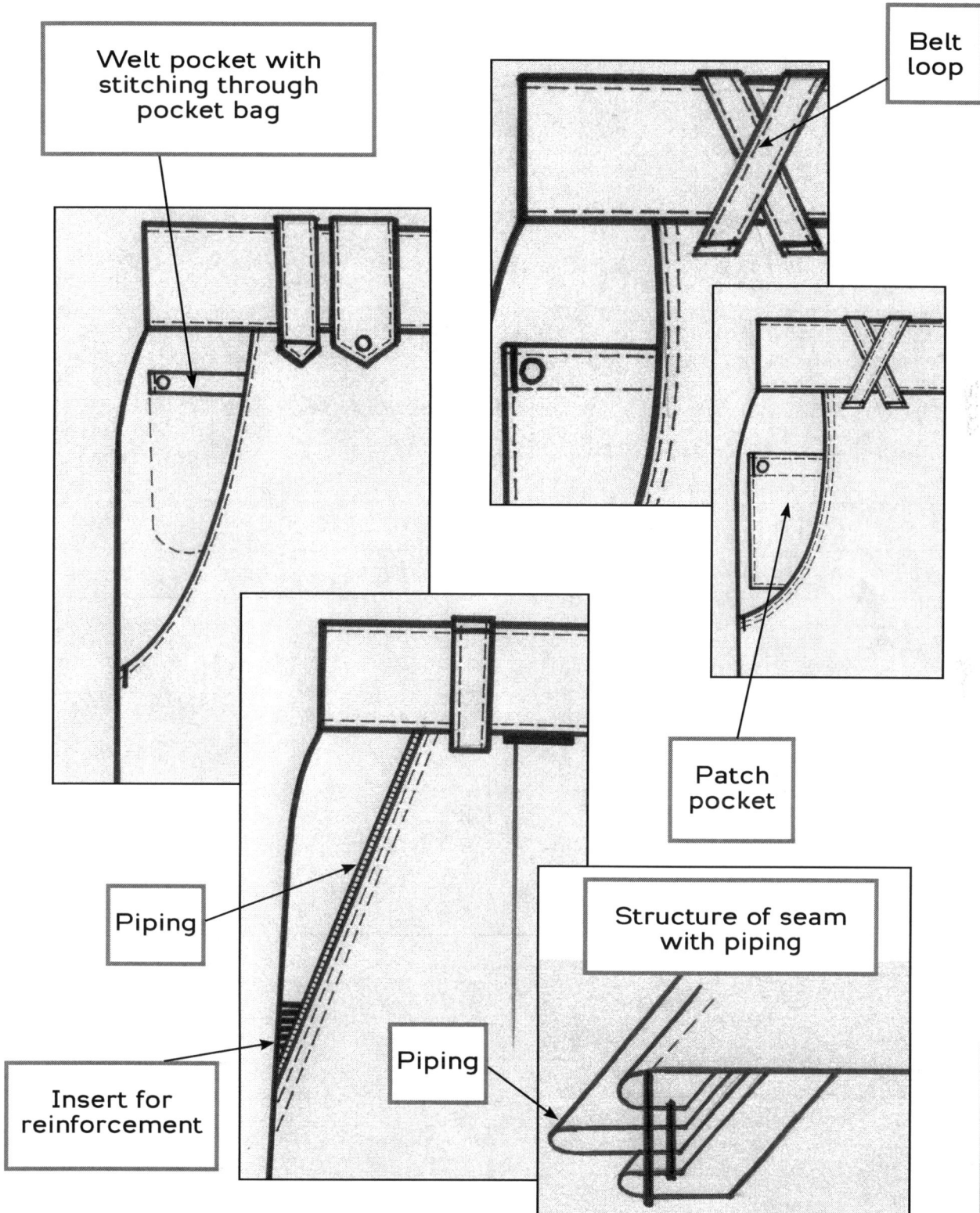

Welt pocket with stitching through pocket bag

Belt loop

Patch pocket

Piping

Insert for reinforcement

Piping

Structure of seam with piping

In-seam pockets

In-seam pocket is a pocket hidden inside the garment and sewn with an opening in the seam of a garment.

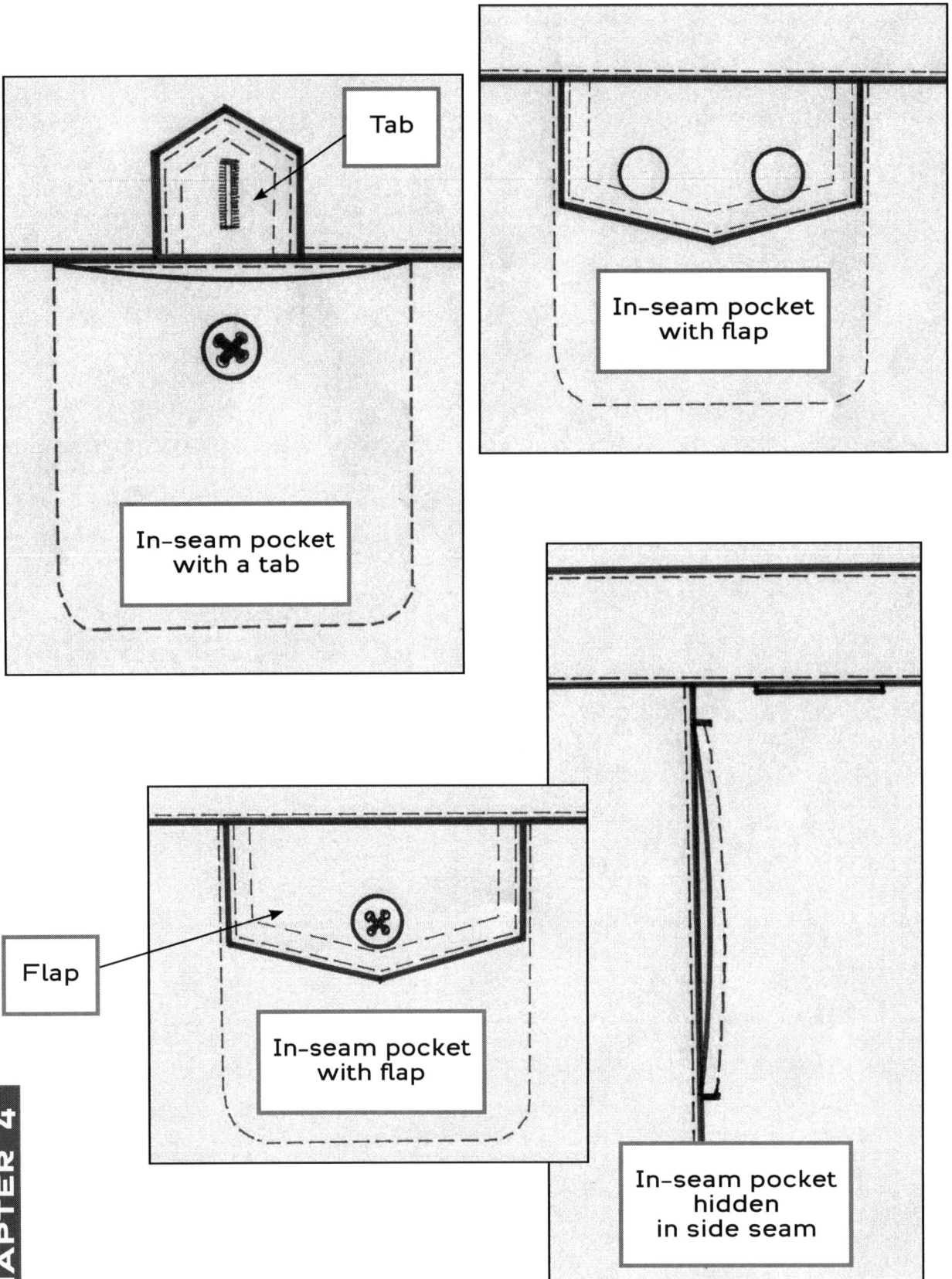

Tab

In-seam pocket
with a tab

In-seam pocket
with flap

Flap

In-seam pocket
with flap

In-seam pocket
hidden
in side seam

72

Slash pockets

Slash pocket is a pocket set in a garment with a slit for the opening. Slash pockets are impossible to remove without of ruining of a garment. There are two basic types of slash pockets: **piped** pockets and **welt pockets**. Other names for piped pockets are **buttonhole**, **besom** or **bound** pockets.

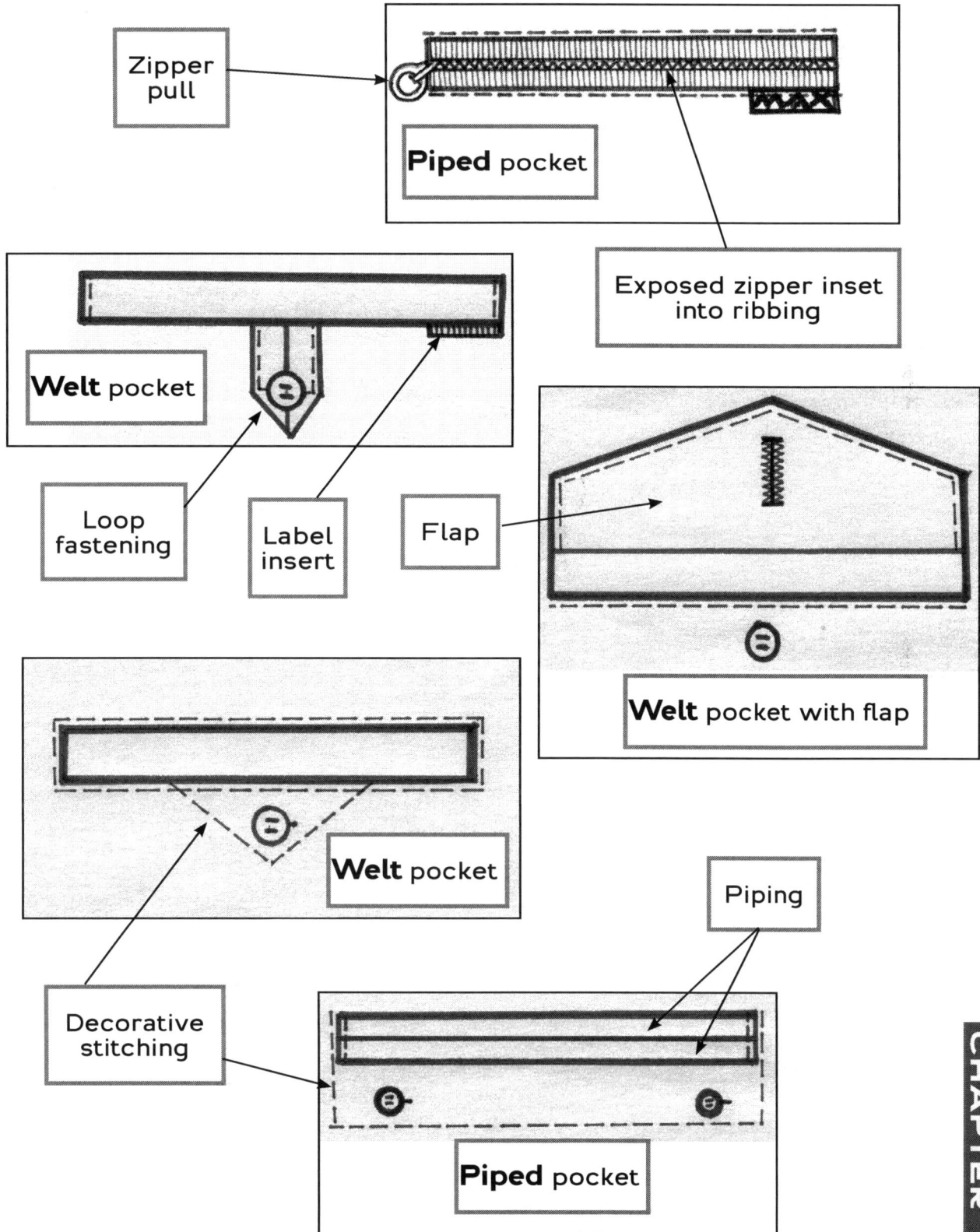

Zipper pull

Piped pocket

Exposed zipper inset into ribbing

Welt pocket

Loop fastening

Label insert

Flap

Welt pocket with flap

Decorative stitching

Welt pocket

Piping

Piped pocket

Chapter 5

Dresses and skirts

Terminology of dress

Tip

Direct dart toward apex.

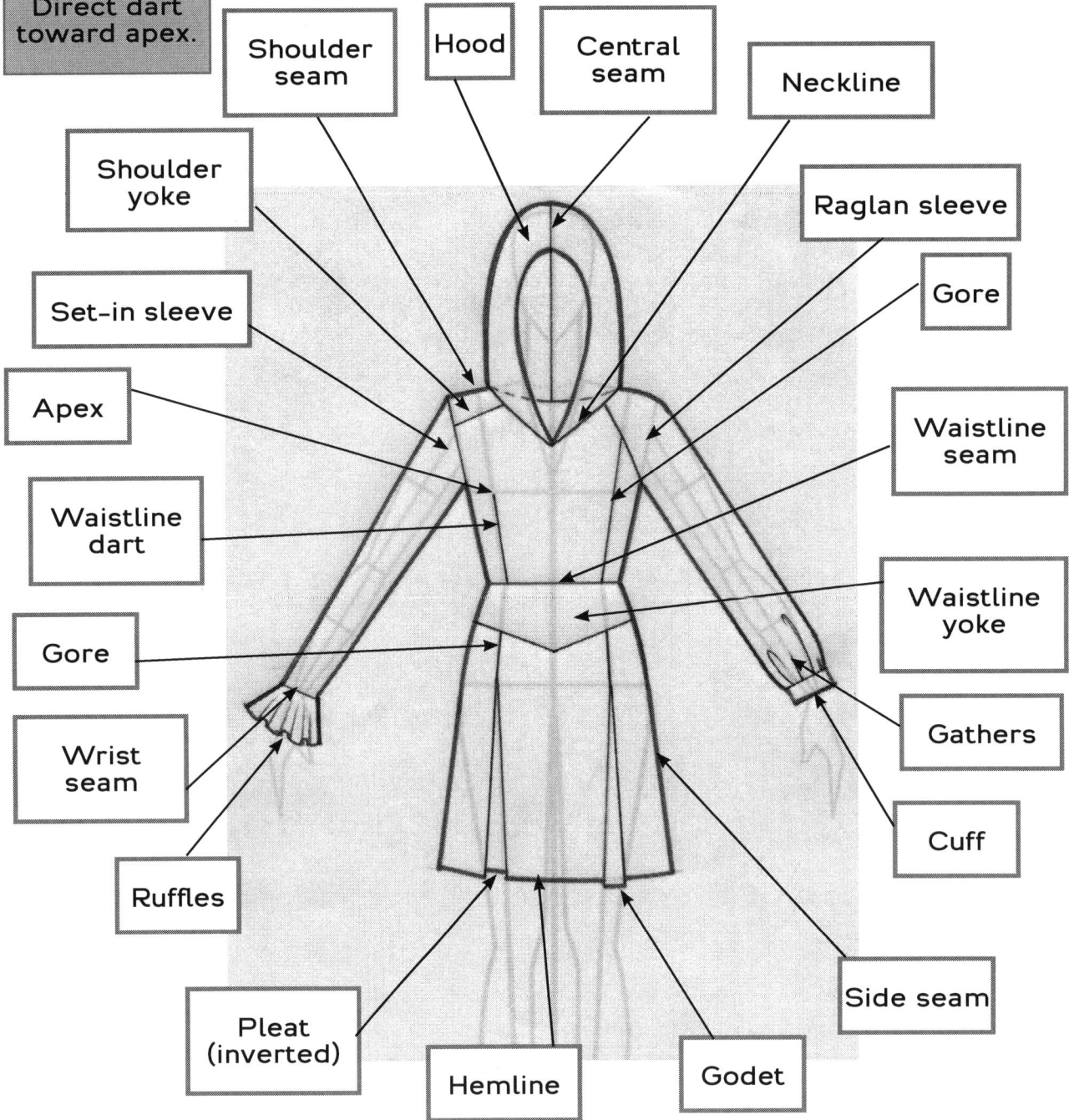

Shoulder seam

Hood

Central seam

Neckline

Shoulder yoke

Raglan sleeve

Gore

Set-in sleeve

Apex

Waistline seam

Waistline dart

Waistline yoke

Gore

Gathers

Wrist seam

Cuff

Ruffles

Side seam

Pleat (inverted)

Hemline

Godet

Tip

Keep hemline shorter inside pleat.

Tip

Keep hemline longer inside godet.

Apex – is highest point of breast. It is a point of intersection between bust line and princess line.

Godet – is an extra piece of fabric in hem area inserted as a rule inside the gores.

Yoke is an extra piece of fabric in shoulder or hip areas inserted for decorative or/and fitting purposes.

Ruffles is an extra piece of gathered, pleated, or/and flared fabric used for decoration.

Set-in sleeves have an armhole seam between armpit point and the end of the shoulder seam.

Raglan sleeves have an armhole seam between armpit point and the neckline.

Darts and gores are fundamental elements of garment construction because they allow flat fabric to take a shape of the body.

Darts are sewn folds in garment which help to fit fabric to the body.

Gores are seams in garment which help to fit fabric to the body.

How to draw fitted garment

One silhouette and three different ways to fit garment

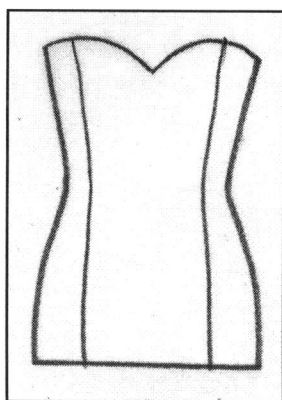

| Top fitted with gores | Top fitted with darts | Top fitted with elastic |

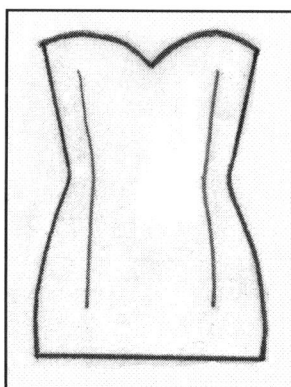

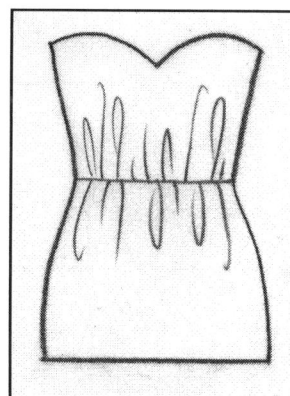

Waistline level for dresses

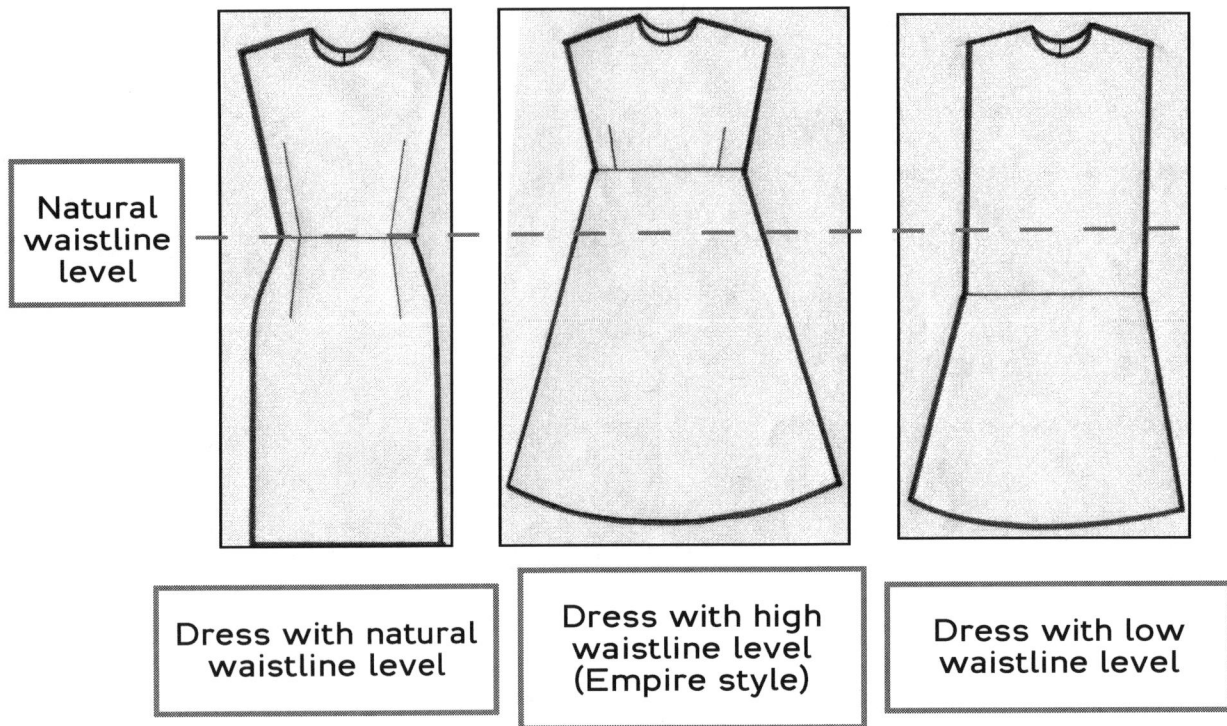

Natural waistline level

Dress with natural waistline level

Dress with high waistline level (Empire style)

Dress with low waistline level

Gallery of silhouettes for dresses

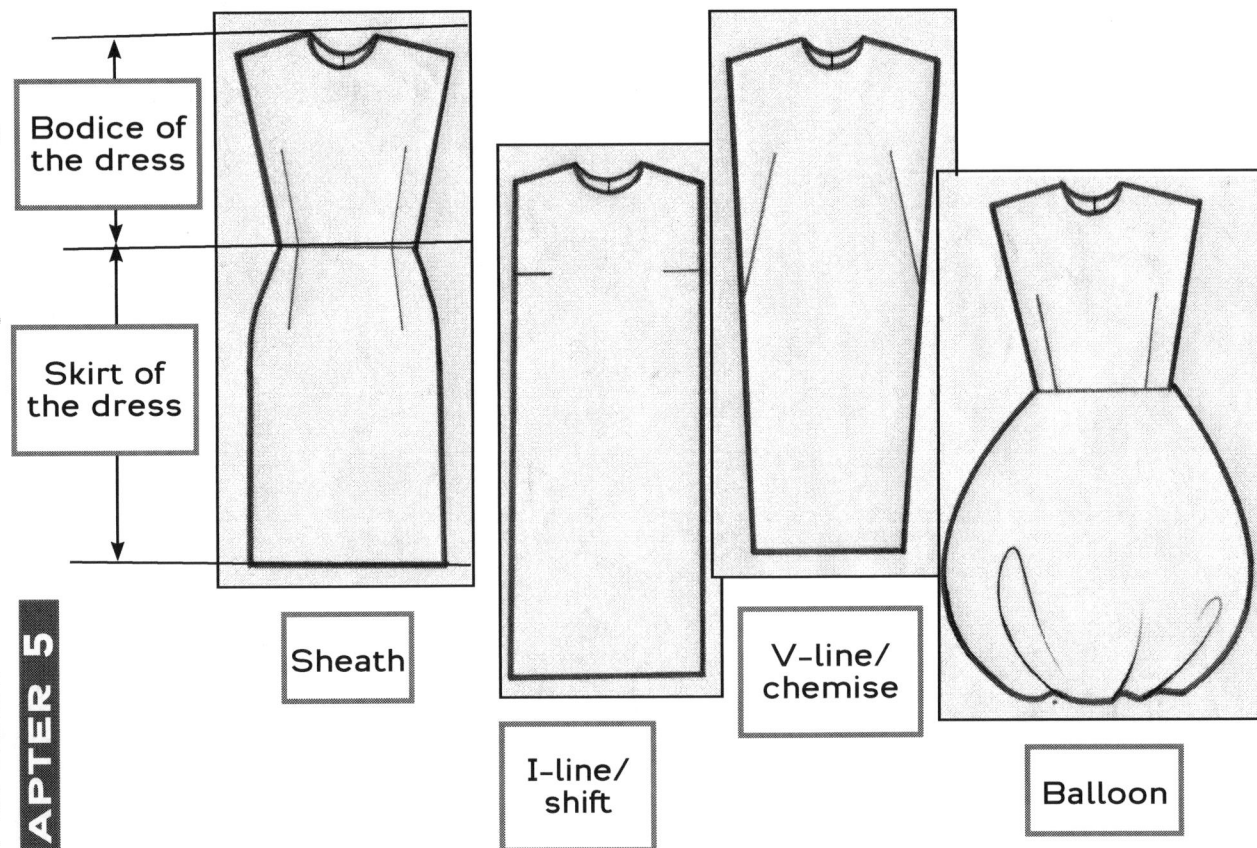

Bodice of the dress

Skirt of the dress

Sheath

I-line/ shift

V-line/ chemise

Balloon

78

For full, **volume silhouettes**, flaring, gathering, or drapery must be depicted. Otherwise, it is not clear how the volume of a garment was achieved.

For **fitted silhouettes,** darts and gores must be depicted (unless it is stretchy fabric). Otherwise, it is not clear how fitting was achieved.

Bell

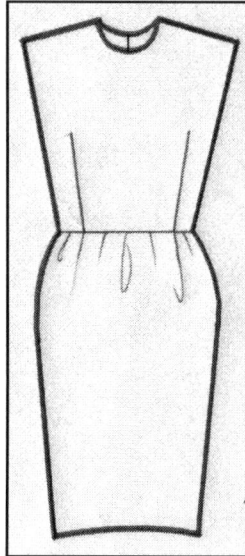

Pegged

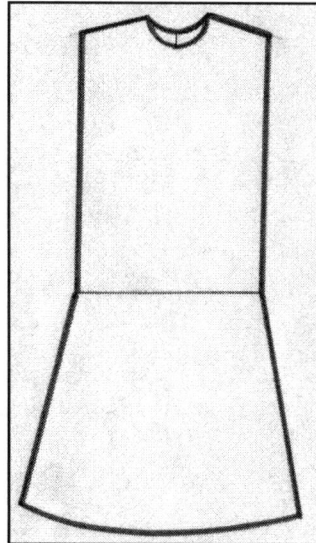

Low waist

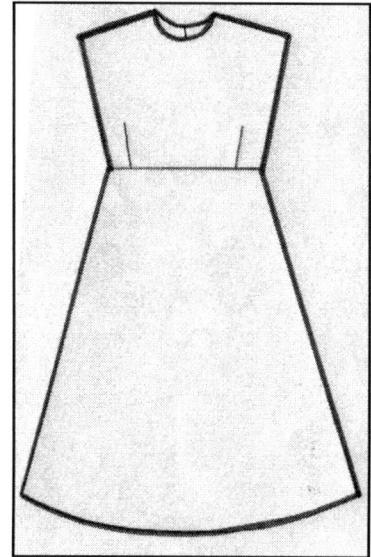

Empire style

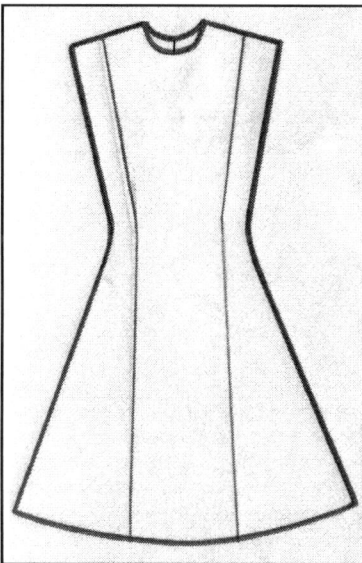

Princess style

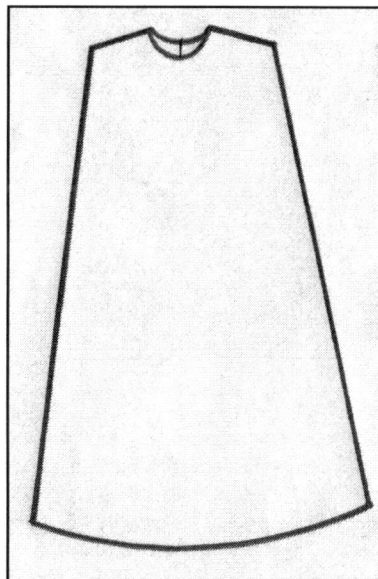

Trapezoid

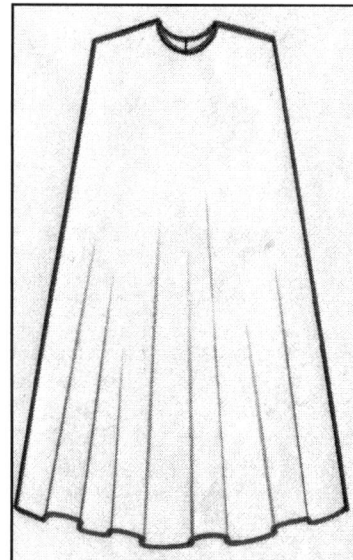

Tent

Terminology for basic waistline levels

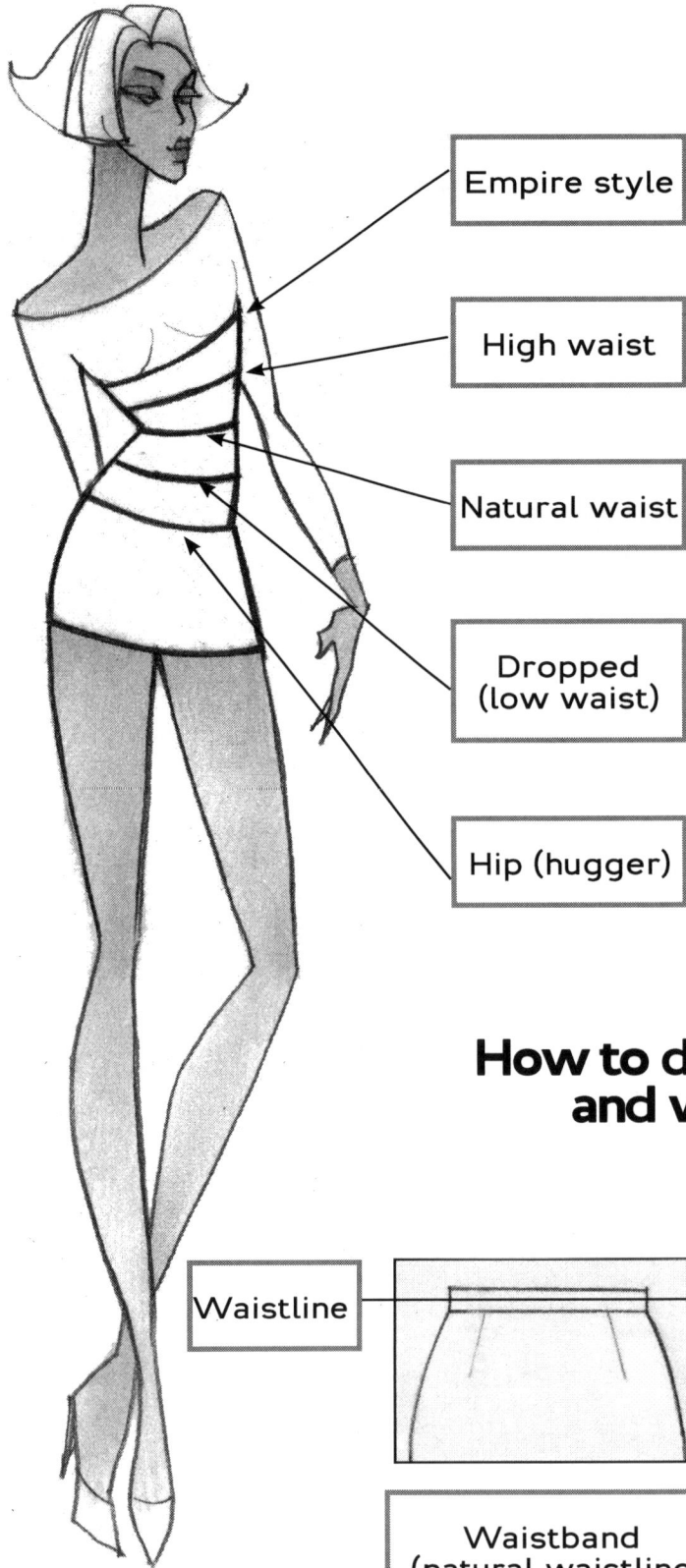

Empire style

High waist

Natural waist

Dropped
(low waist)

Hip (hugger)

How to draw waistlines
and waistbands

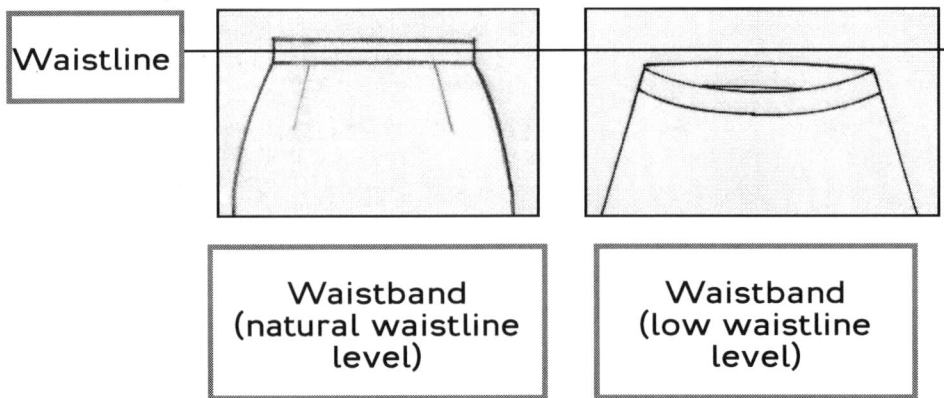

Waistline

Waistband
(natural waistline
level)

Waistband
(low waistline
level)

© 2016 Irina V. Ivanova

Basic waistline styles

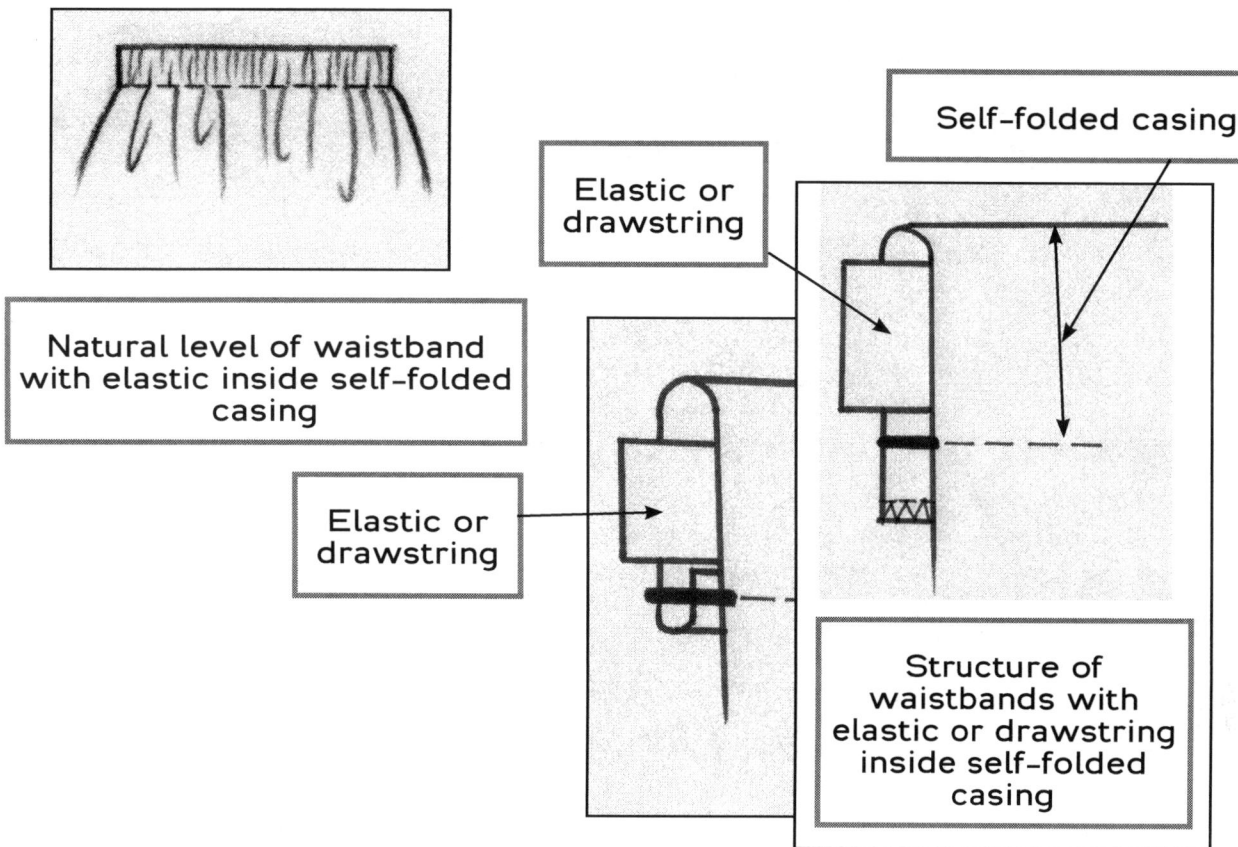

Natural level of waistband with elastic inside self-folded casing

Self-folded casing

Elastic or drawstring

Elastic or drawstring

Structure of waistbands with elastic or drawstring inside self-folded casing

Self-folded casing is an extension of a garment folded inside to create room for elastic or drawstring.

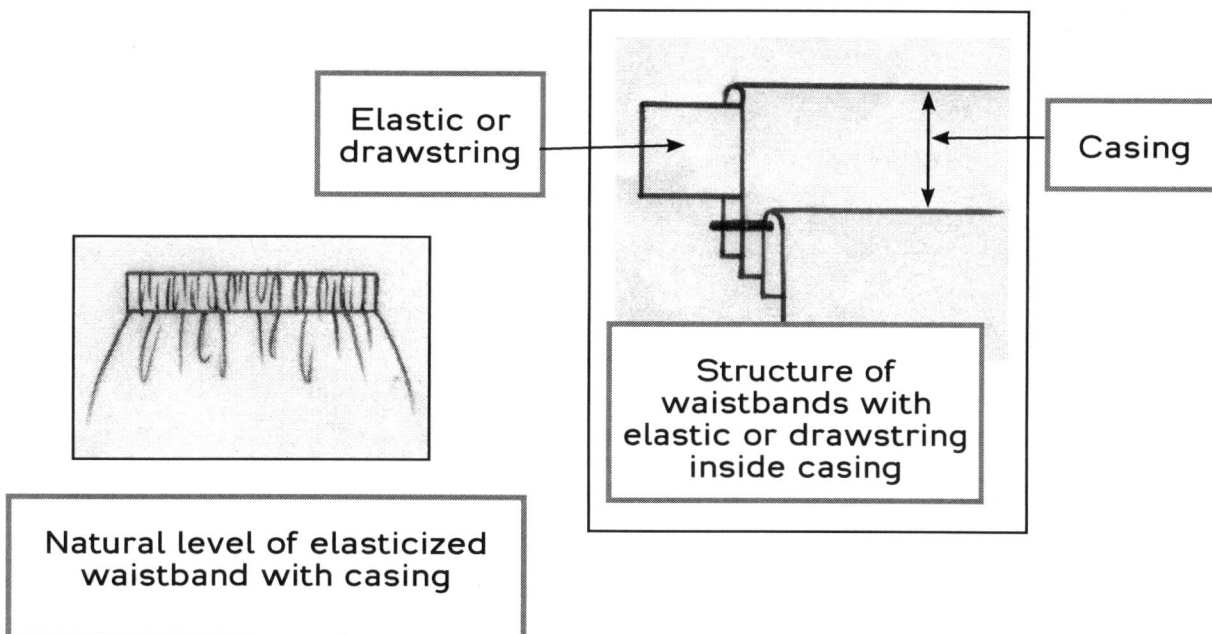

Elastic or drawstring

Casing

Structure of waistbands with elastic or drawstring inside casing

Natural level of elasticized waistband with casing

Casing is an extra piece of fabric attached to a garment to create room for elastic or drawstring.

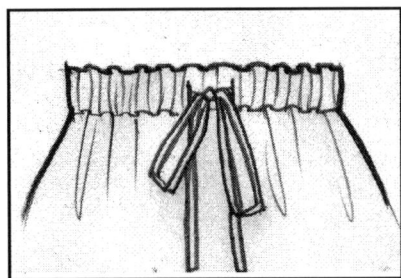

Natural level of
waistband with
drawstring

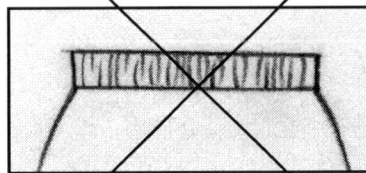

Do not forget to show
gathers for elasticized
waistband.

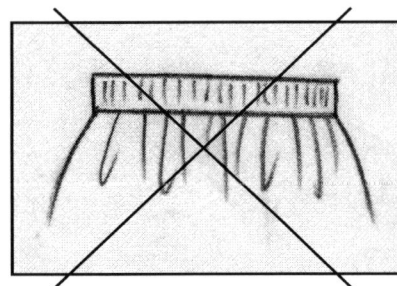

Make sure you have
wrinkles to show
gathers for elasticized
waistband.

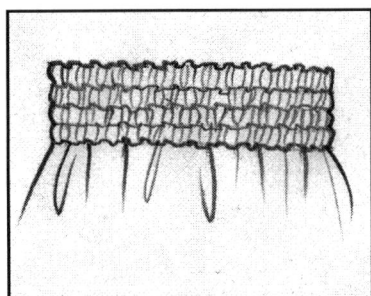

Natural level of
waistband with
shirring

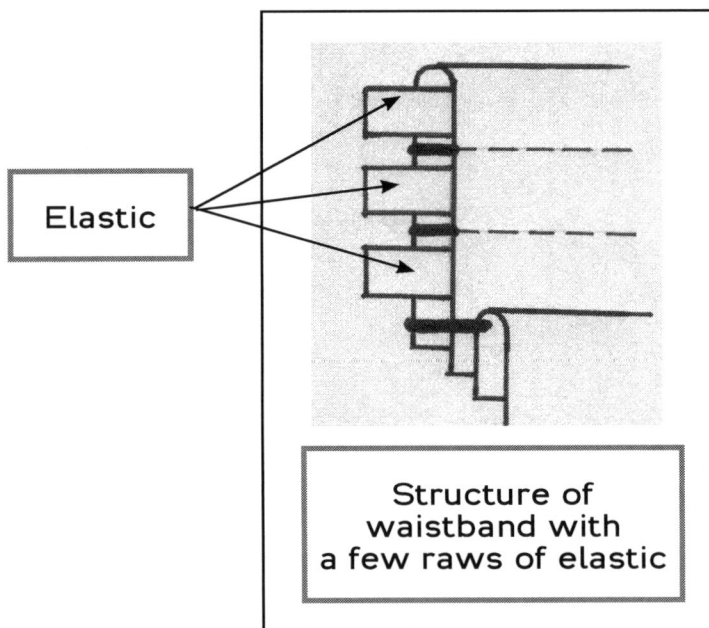

Elastic

Structure of
waistband with
a few raws of elastic

Shirring is a few rows of gathering in a garment.

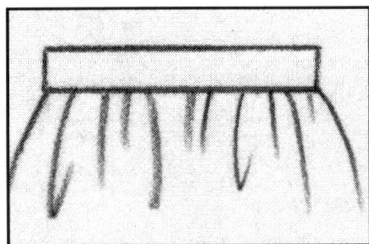

Natural level of
hard waistband with
gathers

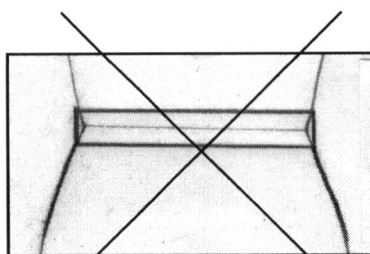

Do not forget to show
darts, gores, or gathers
for fitting.

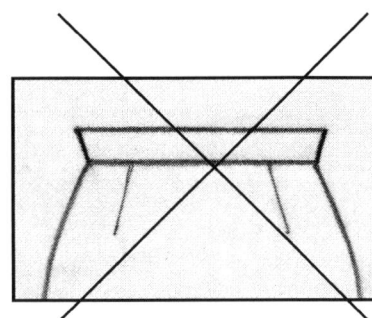

Keep rectangular
shape for natural
level waistband.

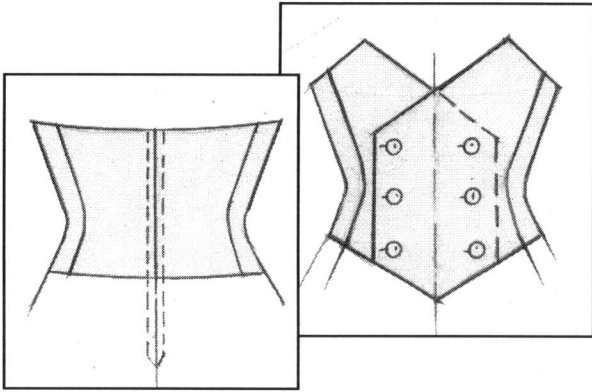

High waistband connected with yoke (front and back views)

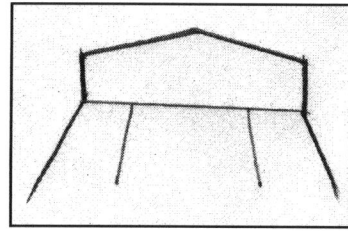

Pointed (shaped) waistband

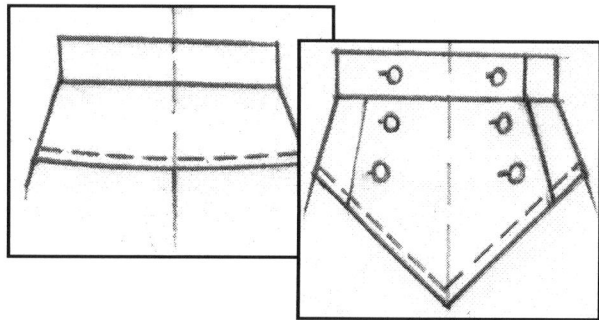

Natural level waistband and yoke (front and back views)

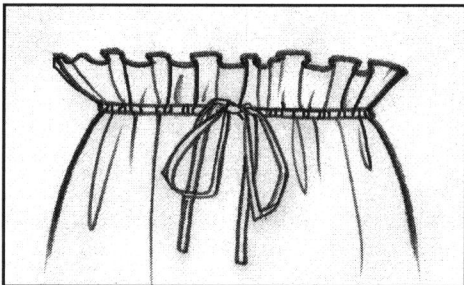

Paper bag style with drawstring

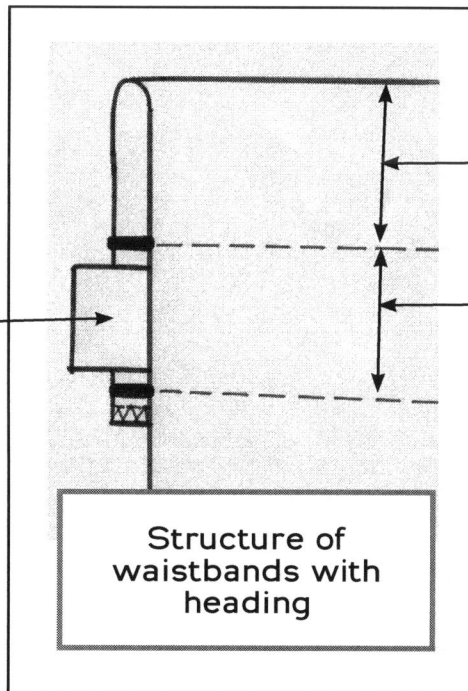

Elastic or drawstring

Heading

Casing

Structure of waistbands with heading

Sleeves
Family of sleeves:

- **Set-in sleeves**
- **Cut in one-piece-with-bodice sleeves** (kimono, batwing, dolman)
- **Raglan sleeves**

Terminology of set-in sleeve

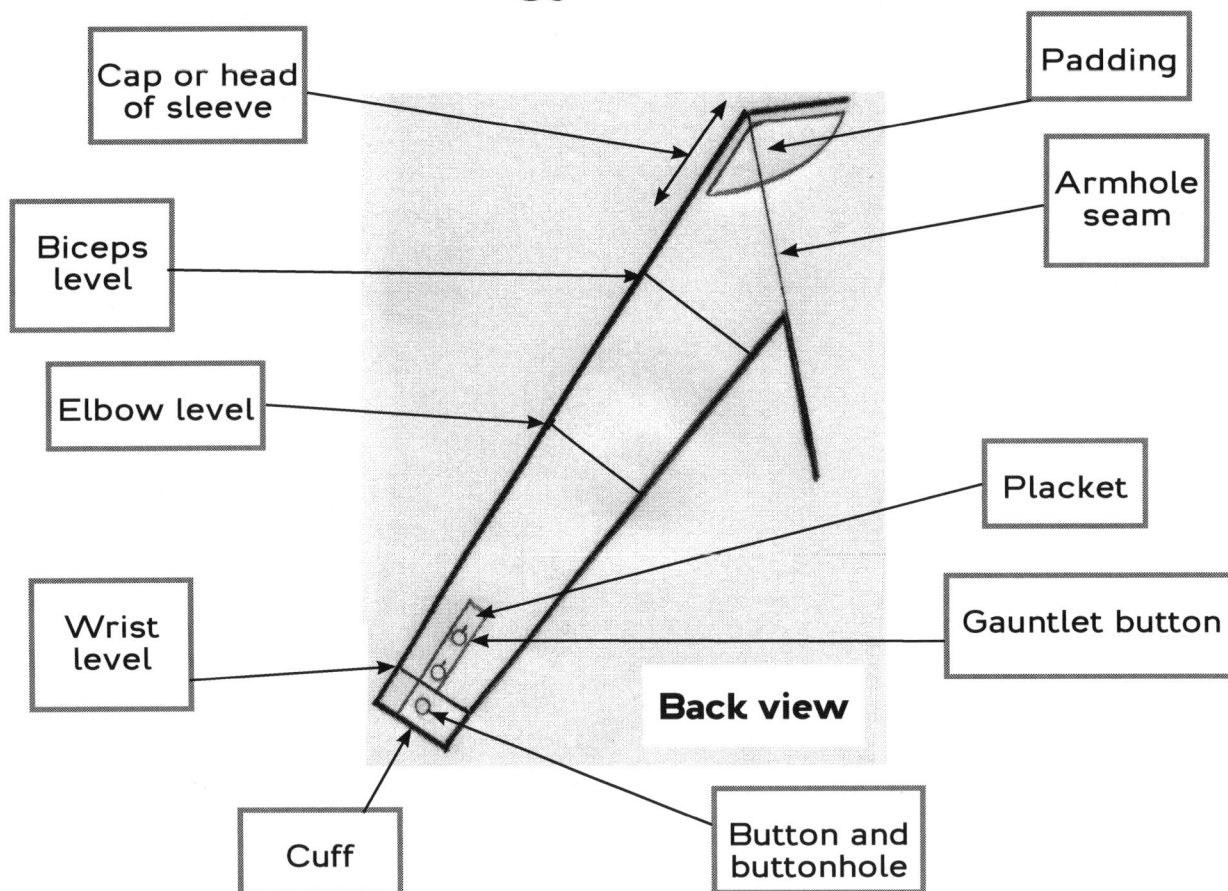

Cap or head of sleeve

Padding

Biceps level

Armhole seam

Elbow level

Placket

Wrist level

Gauntlet button

Back view

Cuff

Button and buttonhole

Padding is additional material used to extend or support a shoulder seam and head of the sleeve.

Cap or head of sleeve is upper part of the sleeve.

Biceps level is in the middle between elbow and shoulder seam.

Elbow level is elbow level (middle of arm).

Wrist level is a seam between cuff and sleeve on the wrist level.

Gauntlet button is placket button.

Armhole seam is seam between sleeve and bodice of garment.

Placket is extra piece of fabric used for finishing of garment opening.

Cuff is extra piece of fabric used for finishing of sleeve hem.

Basic set-in sleeves

All **set-in sleeves** are started in the end of the shoulder seam.

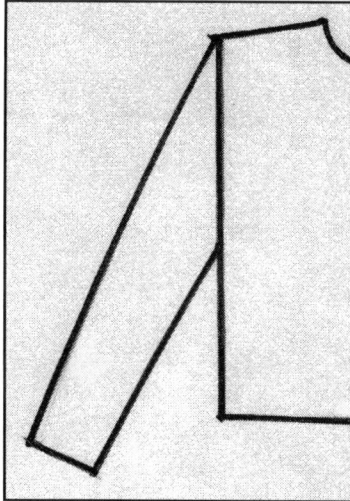

Standard set-in sleeve

- Has standard length shoulder seam.
- Most popular sleeve.

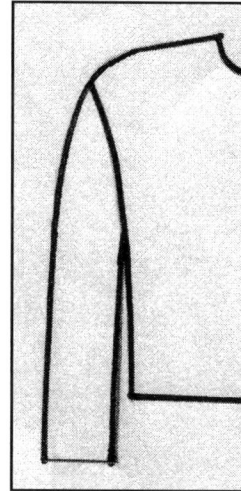

Relaxed set-in sleeve

- Shoulder seam are longer than standard shoulder seam.
- Sleeve is never fitted to arm.
- Often used in T-shirt.

Ease is extra fabric which is distributed over the seam without gathering.

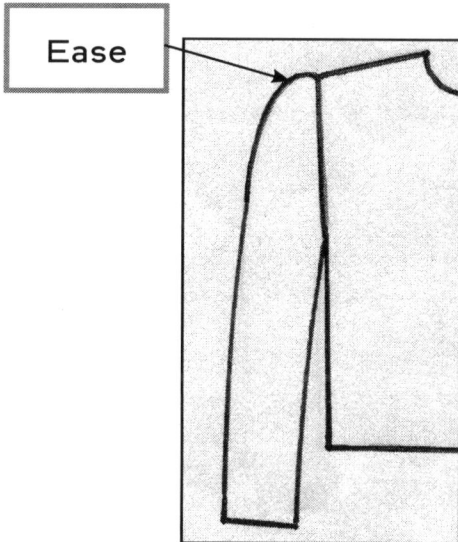

Ease

Tailored set-in sleeve

- Tailored (shaped to natural arm form).
- Sleeve has an ease in the cap area.
- Padding (inner supporting structure).
- Used mostly for jackets and coats.

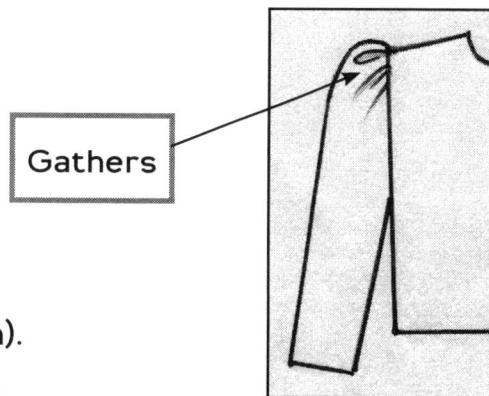

Gathers

Set-in sleeve with gathers in the head of the sleeve.

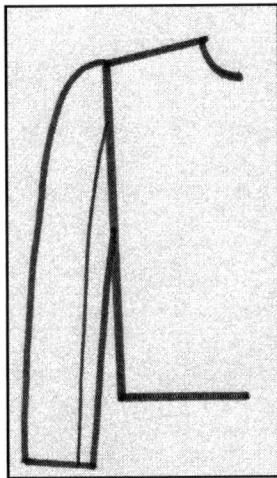

Tailored set-in sleeve (back view) with extra seam for better arm fitting.

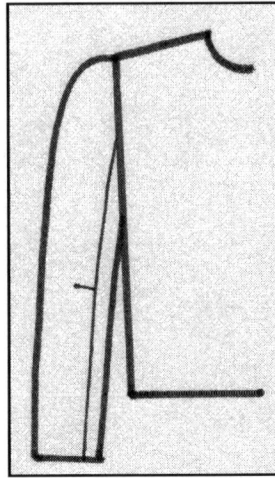

Tailored set-in sleeve (back view) with extra seam and dart for better arm fitting.

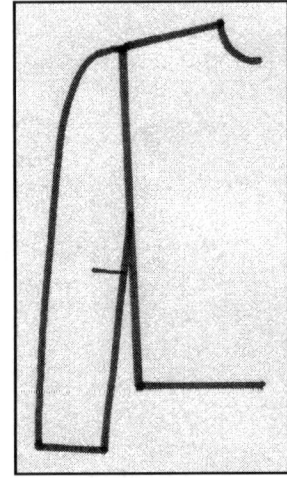

Tailored set-in sleeve (back view) with dart for better arm fitting.

Gallery of set-in sleeves

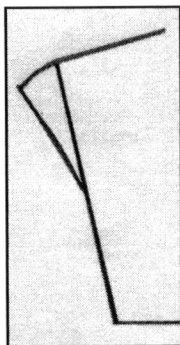

Melon/lantern

Two pieces set-in sleeve with horizontal seam.

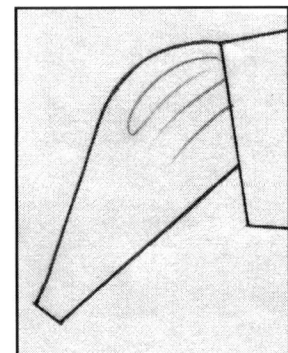

Cap

Extremely short set-in sleeve.

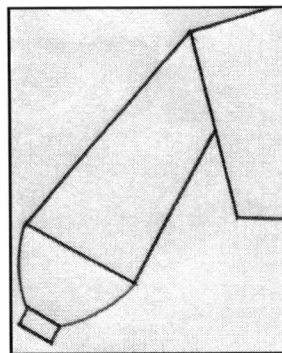

Leg-o-mutton/ Gigot

Sleeve with a lot of gathers or pleats in armhole and tight fitting in wrist seam.

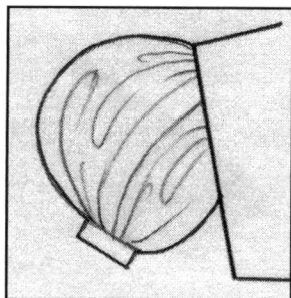

Puff

Super big and puffy set-in sleeve with a lot of gathering.

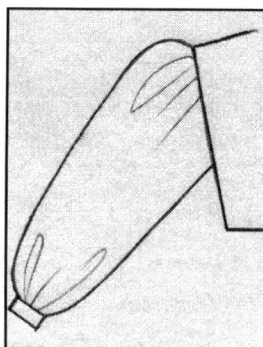

Peasant

Always with gathering in wrist seam and armhole.

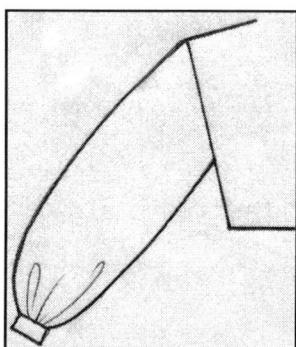

Bishop

Always with gathering in wrist seam.

Petal

Two pieces set-in sleeve. The pieces could be connected or not.

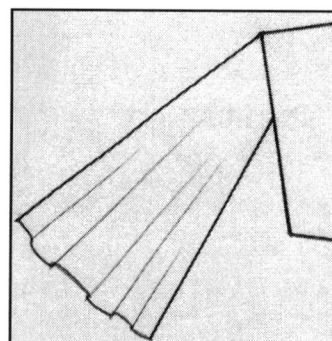

Bell/ angel

Set-in sleeve with wide flared hem.

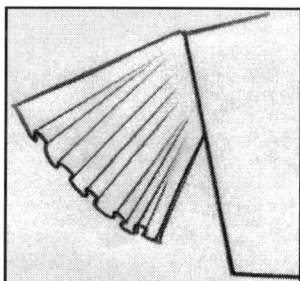

Circular

Set-in sleeve with extremely wide flared hem.

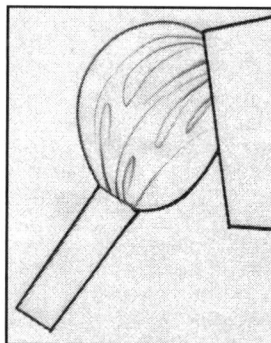

Juliet

Two pieces set-in sleeve. Upper part is big and puffy with a lot of gathering and bottom part is fitted and narrow with horizontal seam.

Gallery of raglan sleeves

All **raglan sleeves** are started on the neckline or close to it.

HPS (high point shoulder)

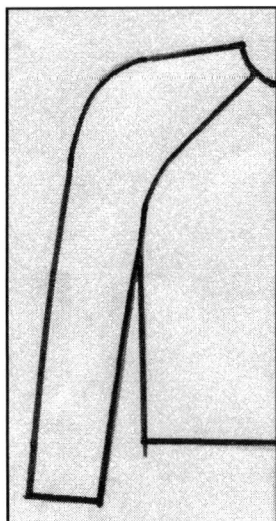

Standard raglan sleeve (started from neckline) with almost straight raglan seam.

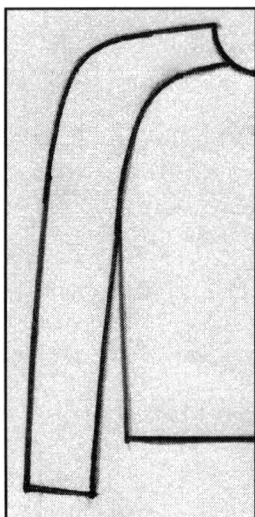

Standard raglan sleeve (started from neckline) with slightly curved raglan seam.

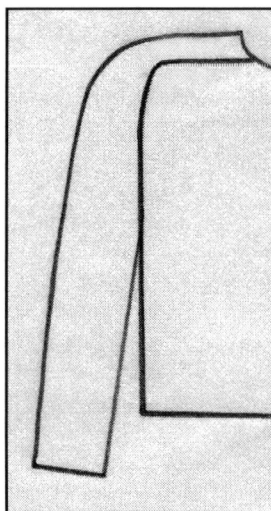

Saddle sleeve (raglan seam is angular).

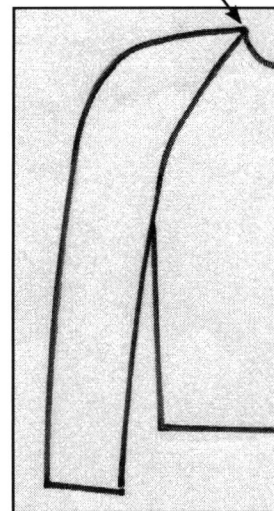

Zero-raglan sleeve (started from high point shoulder HPS).

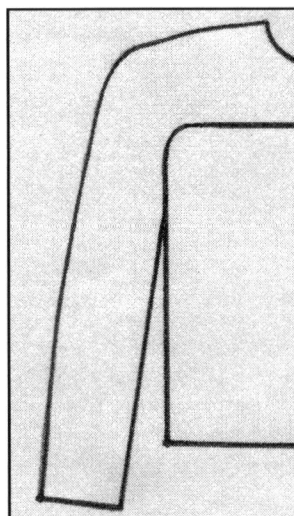

Raglan-yoke sleeve (combination of raglan sleeve and yoke).

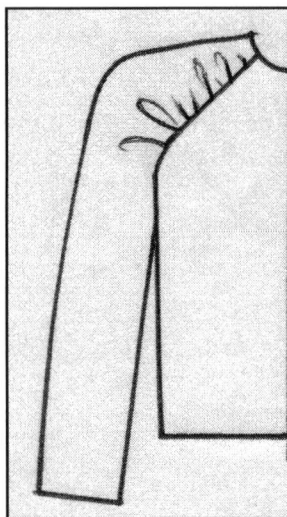

Raglan sleeve gathered in raglan seam.

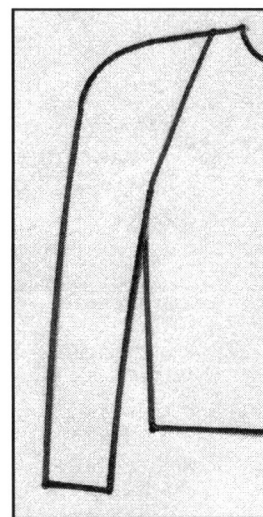

Semi-raglan sleeve (started from shoulder seam but close to neckline).

Gallery of one-piece-with-bodice sleeves

All **one-piece-with-bodice sleeves** have no armholes or seams between sleeves and bodies.

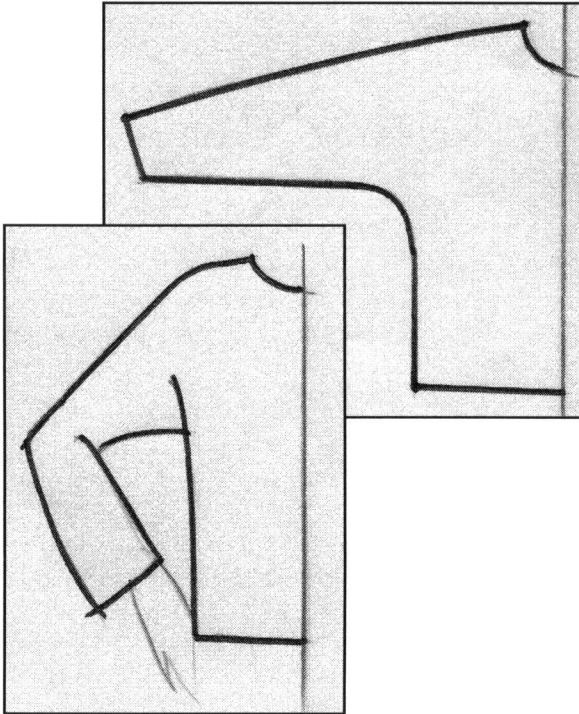

Kimono sleeves
(armhole is more fitted).

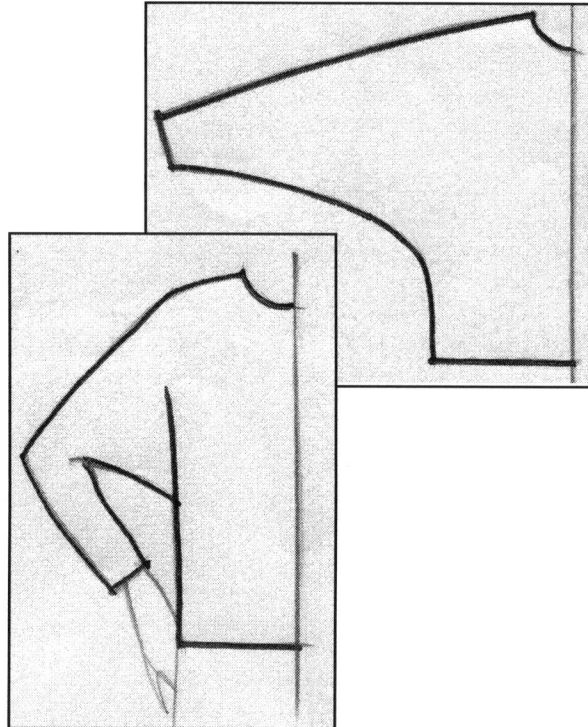

Dolman or batwing sleeves
(armhole is less fitted).

Kimono sleeves may have a **gusset** (extra piece of fabric in armpit area). Gusset could be used as a decorative element or for fitting purposes.

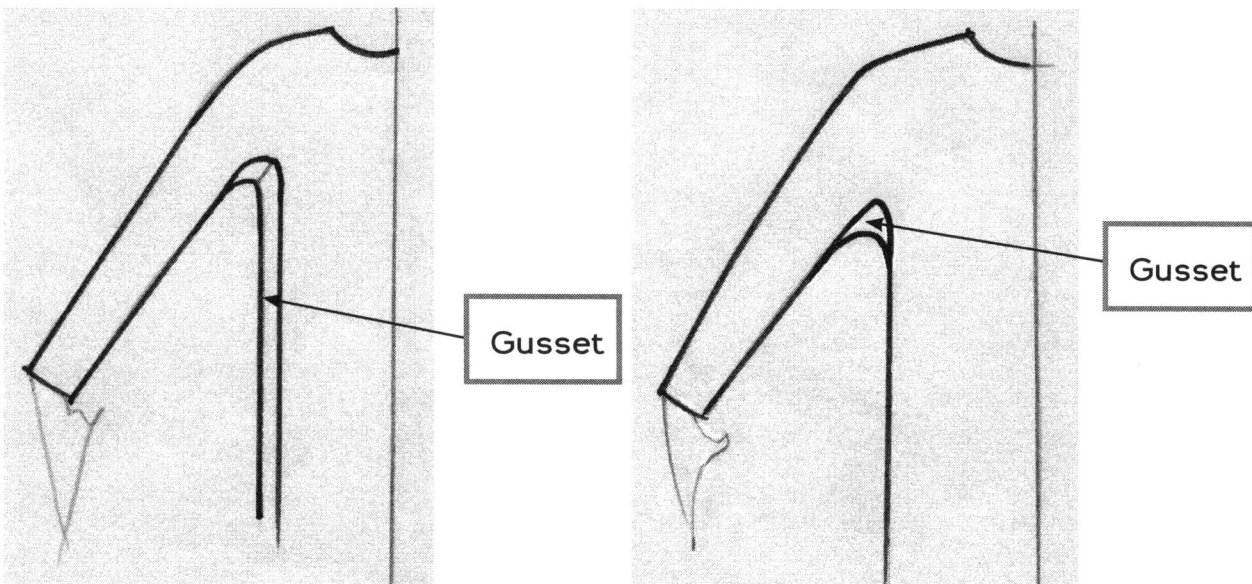

Gusset

Gusset

Kimono sleeves with different styles of gussets.

Terminology for hemline levels

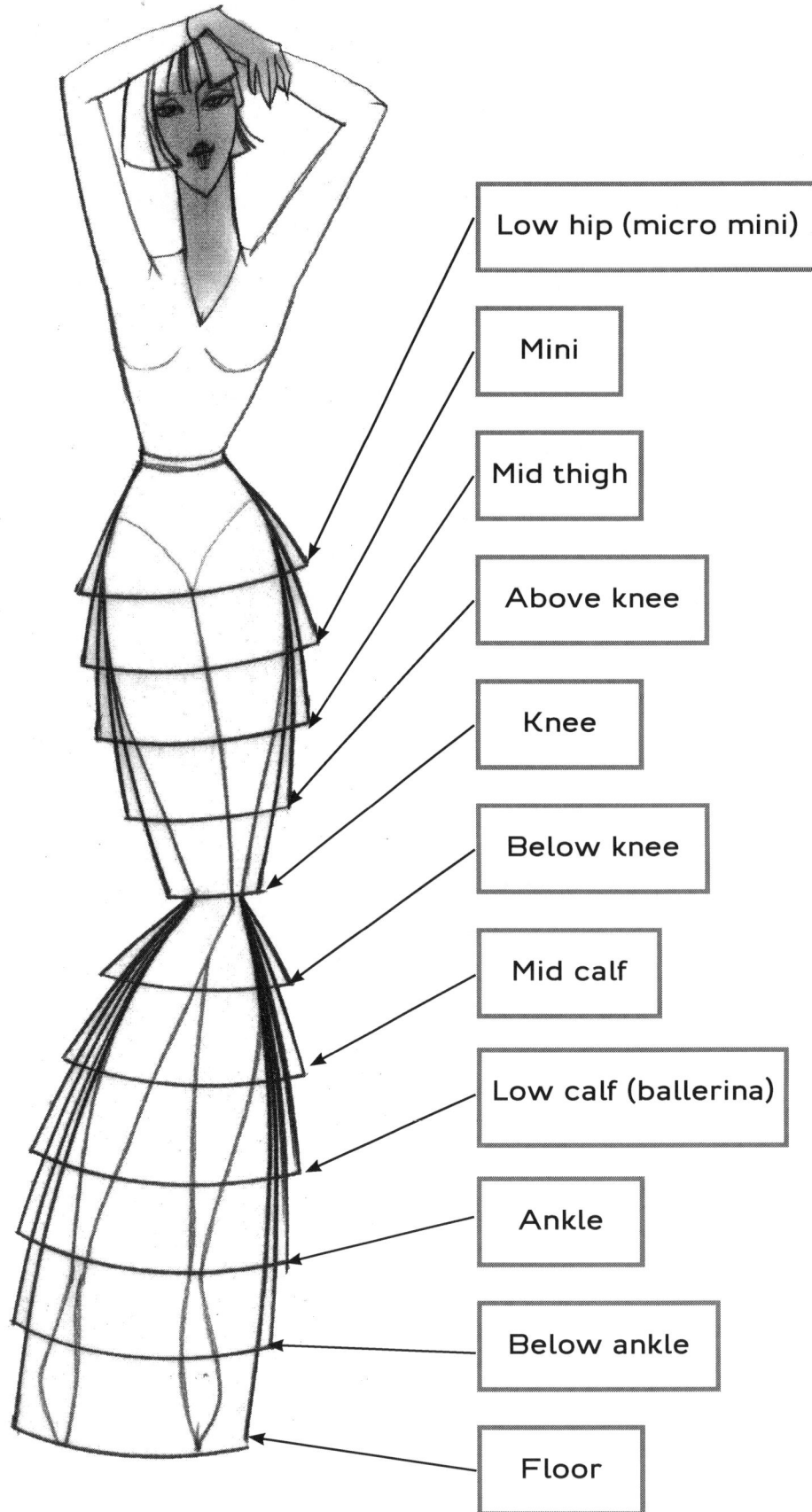

Low hip (micro mini)

Mini

Mid thigh

Above knee

Knee

Below knee

Mid calf

Low calf (ballerina)

Ankle

Below ankle

Floor

Skirts

Family of skirts:

- **Straight skirts**
- **Flared skirts**
- **Draped skirts**
- **Circle skirts**

How to draw basic straight skirt

A **straight skirt** has the same width for hip and hem levels. This skirt does require darts, gores, or gathers for fitting around waist.

Based on straight skirt you can create a variety of skirts with different details and elements (see a gallery of details for dresses and skirts on pages 106–113).

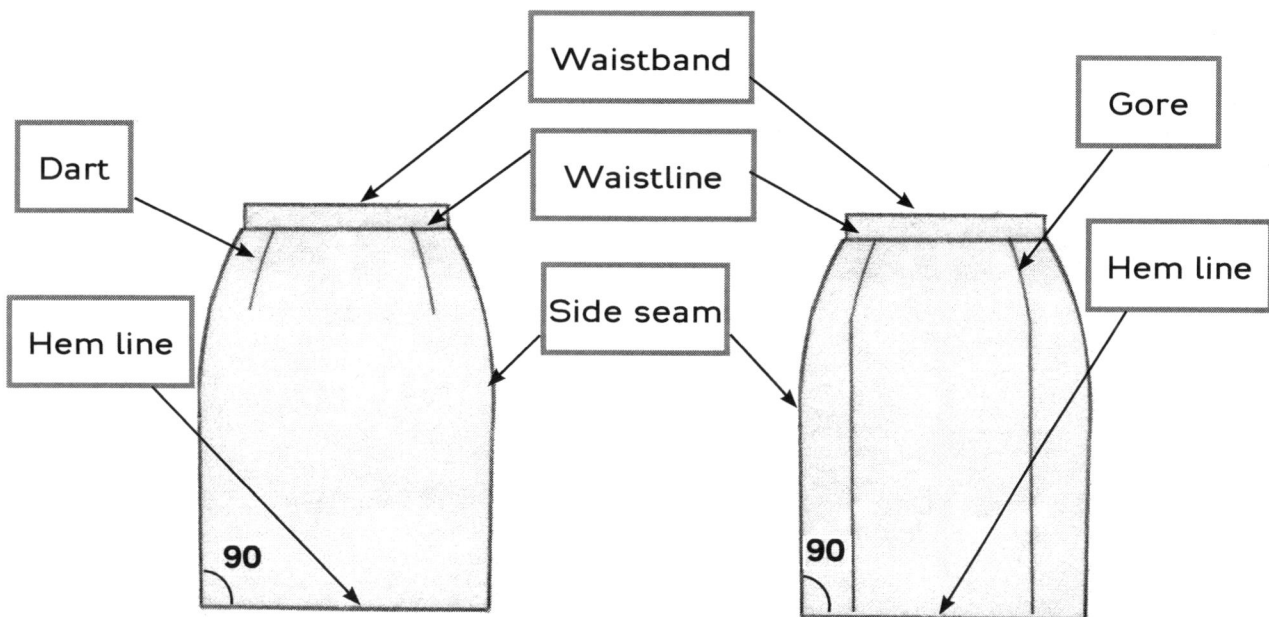

Straight skirt fitted with **darts.**   Straight skirt fitted with **gores.**

For the back view you could use a vent or slit for ease of movement.

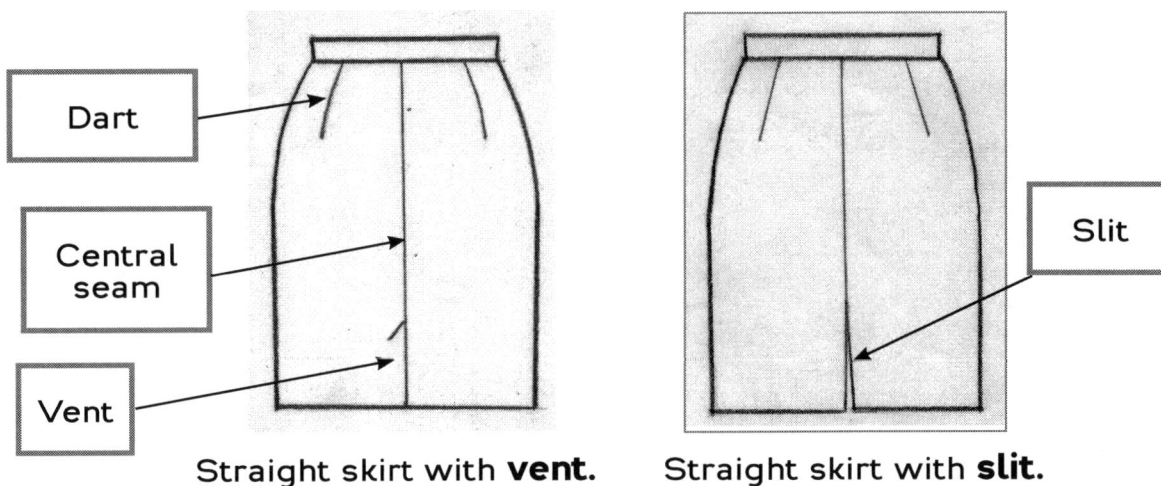

| Dart |
| Central seam |
| Vent |

Straight skirt with **vent.**

| Slit |

Straight skirt with **slit.**

Tip

A vent is always placed in the end of the seam.

A **slit** is a long, narrow opening in the hem area of garment, generally to allow for ease of movement. A slit placed as a rule in the end of a seam.

A **vent** is a open pleat in the hem area of garment, generally to allow for ease of movement.

Patterns for basic straight skirt

Tip

Darts for front skirt are always shorter than darts for back.

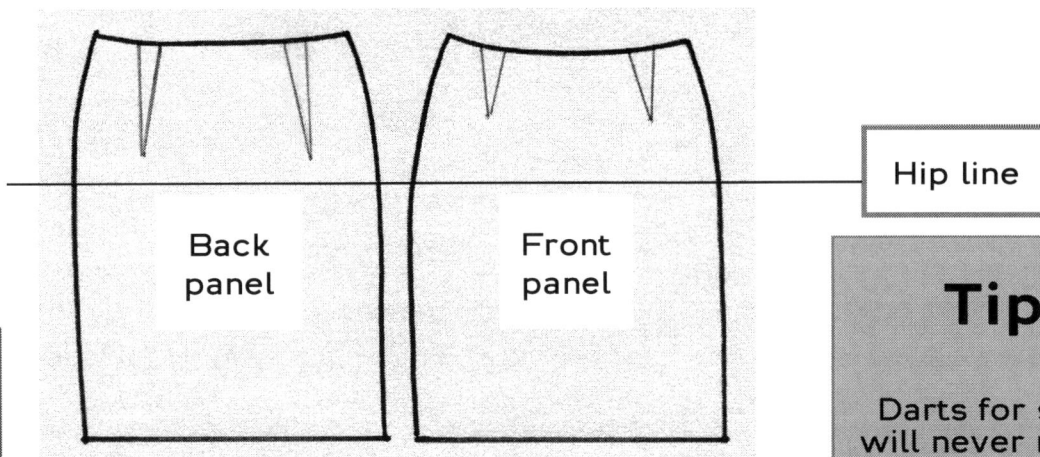

| Hip line |

Back panel

Front panel

Tip

Darts for skirt will never reach hip line.

Patterns for straight skirt fitted with **darts.**

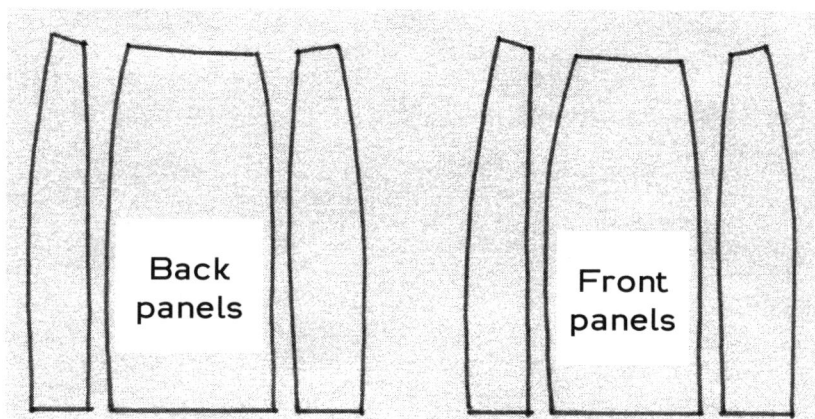

Patterns for straight skirt fitted with **gores**.

Common mistakes in drawing basic straight skirt

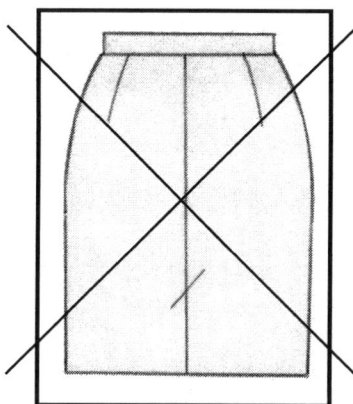

Do not show vent seam crossing central back seam.

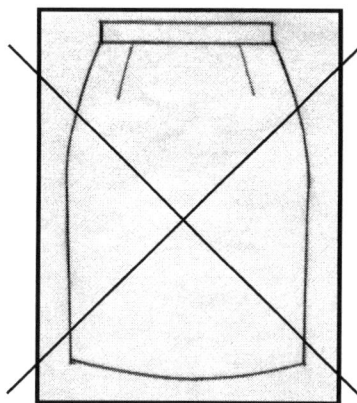

Do not curve hem line for straight skirt. Keep it true to patternmaking.

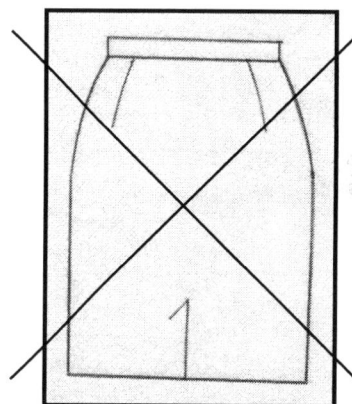

Do not draw vent without central seam.

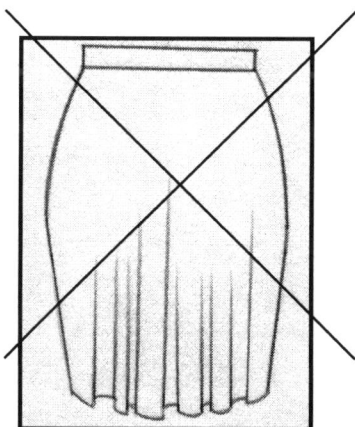

Do not show skirt fitted (narrower) and flared (wider) in hem area at the same time. It is impossible in one skirt.

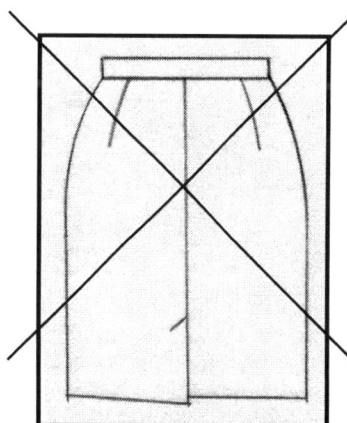

Do not draw vent longer in the hem area, because it is a sign of a mistake in sewing or patternmaking.

How to draw basic flared skirt

A **flared skirt** has wider width for hem than for hip levels. This skirt does not require darts or gores.

A **circle skirt** is a flared skirt which is formed from a circular shape of patters.

Based on flared skirt you can create a variety skirts with different details and elements (see a gallery of details for dresses and skirts on pages 106–113).

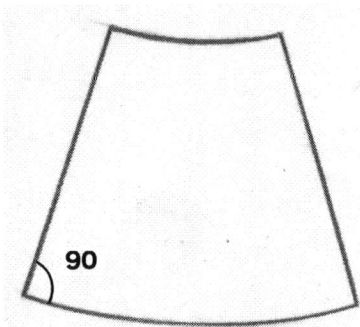

90

Patterns (front and back) for basic flared skirt.

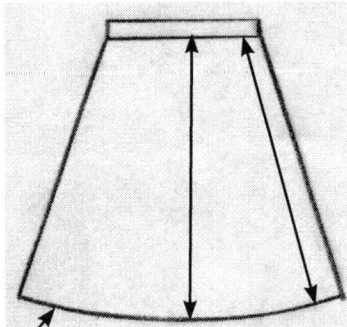

Flared skirt

Tip

Make sure the skirt has the same length for side and center lines.

Tip

Always show curve hem line for flared garment or flared garment details.

Tip

Length of hemline and amount of flare lines are related (see A and B below).

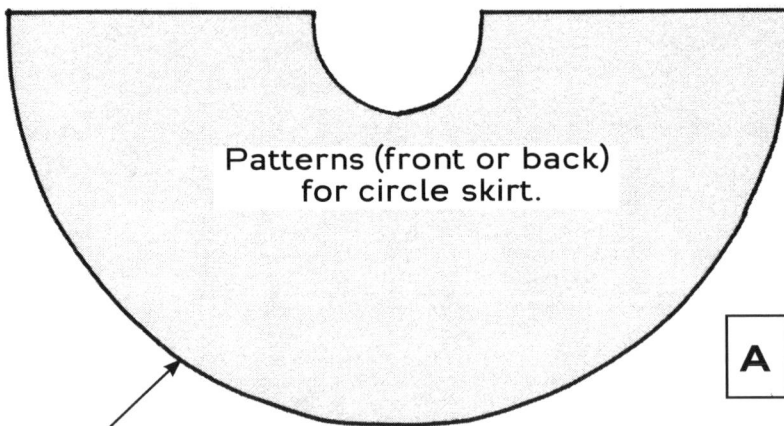

Patterns (front or back) for circle skirt.

Hemline is long.

A

Use more flare lines for skirt flat drawing if skirt has long hemline (for example circle skirt).

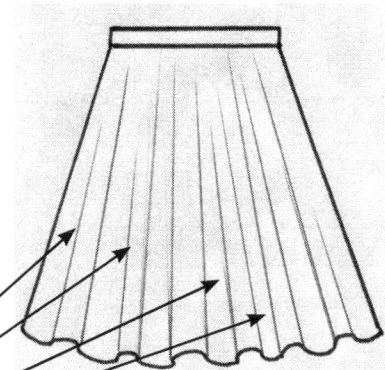

Flat (front or back) for basic flared skirt.

Patterns (front or back)
for flared skirt.

Hemline is shorter.

B

Flat (front or back)
for basic flared skirt.

Use less flare lines for
skirt flat drawing if skirt
has shorter hemline.

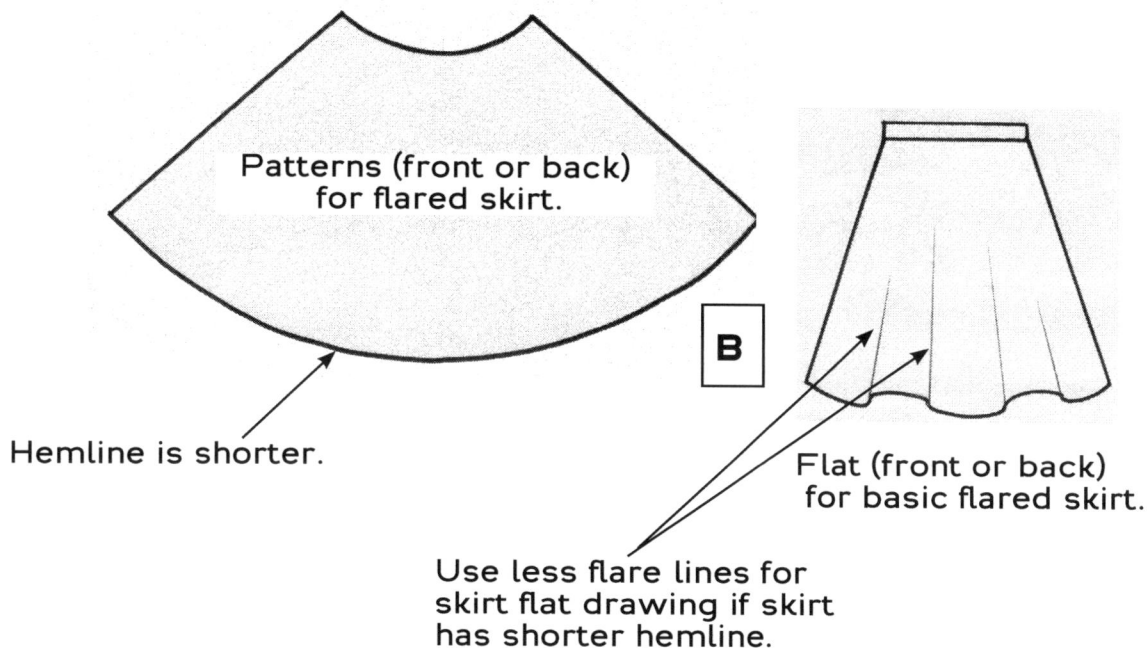

Comparison of different skirt silhouettes

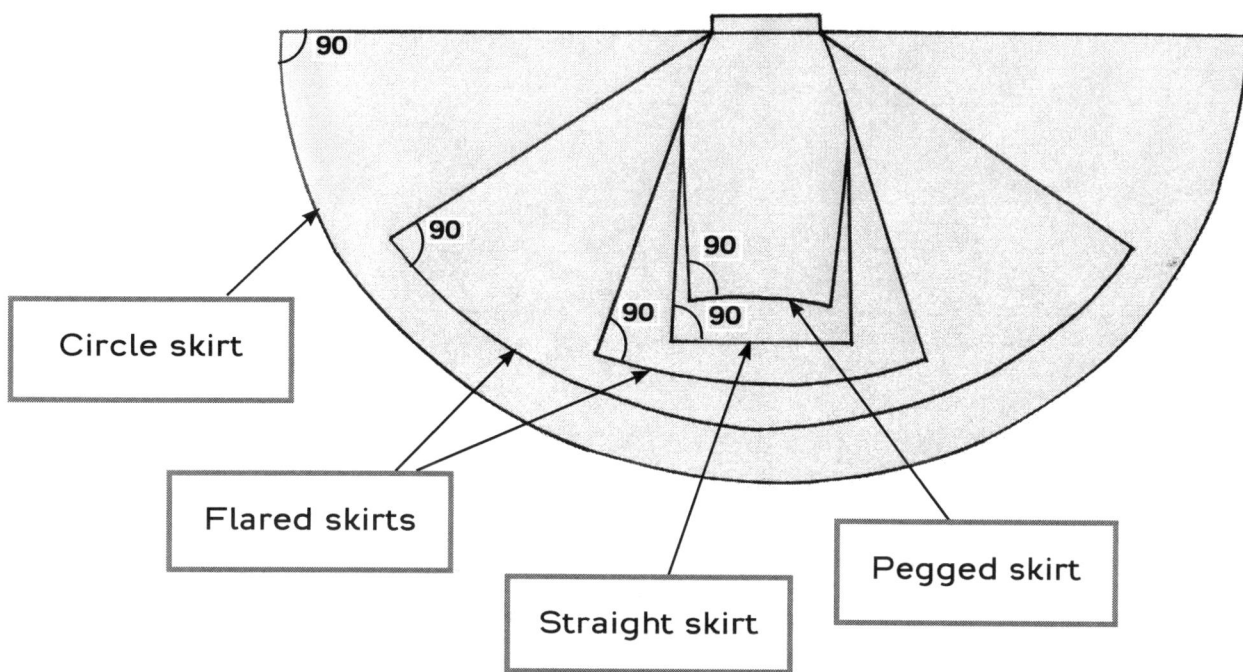

90
90
90
90
90

Circle skirt

Flared skirts

Straight skirt

Pegged skirt

Tip

Always keep 90 degrees (right) angle between
hemline and side seam for all garments and garment
details for smooth blending from front hem to back hem views.

How to Draw Fashion Flats A practical guide to fashion technical drawing by Irina V. Ivanova

CHAPTER 5

Common mistakes in drawing basic flared skirt

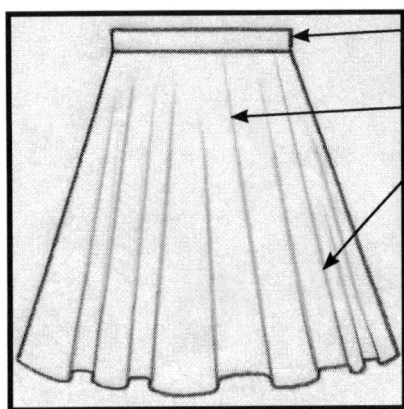

Natural waistline level for waistband.

Flare lines

Flared skirt

There is no need for darts or gores for fitting purposes in flared skirts.

Do not depict any flare lines towards the side seams.

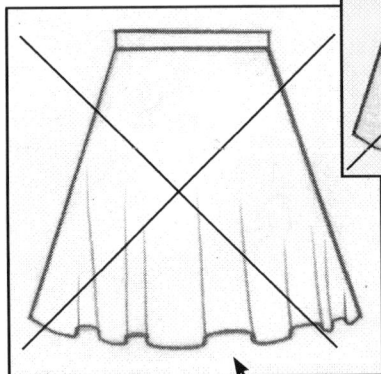

Tip

Start flare lines from hemline up and move them toward any upper seam (for example waistline).

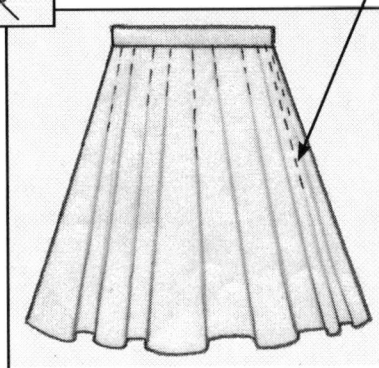

Flared lines are too parallel to each other and not all of them are directed toward waistline.

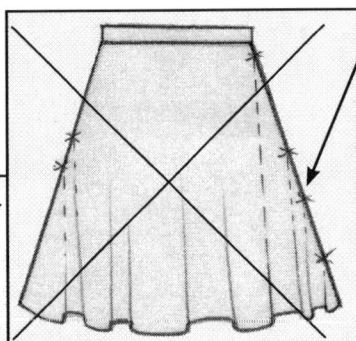

Tip

Do not depict straight hemline for flared skirt and make sure you have 90 degrees (right) angle between hemline and side seam.

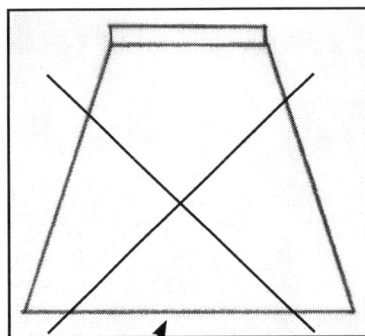

90

Hemline is not supposed to be straight for flared skirt.

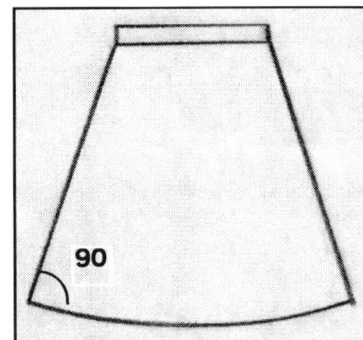

Hemline for flared skirt is always curved.

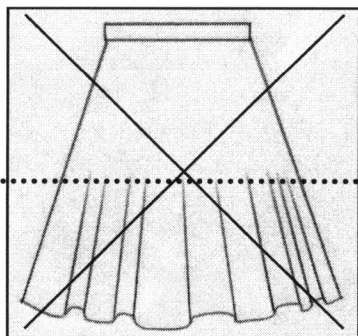

Do not use
one upper
level for all
flared lines.

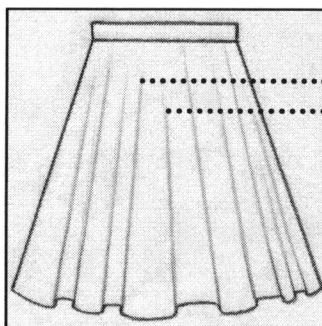

Always use
more than one
upper levels for
flared lines.

Tip

Do not keep the flare lines on the
same level from hemline up.

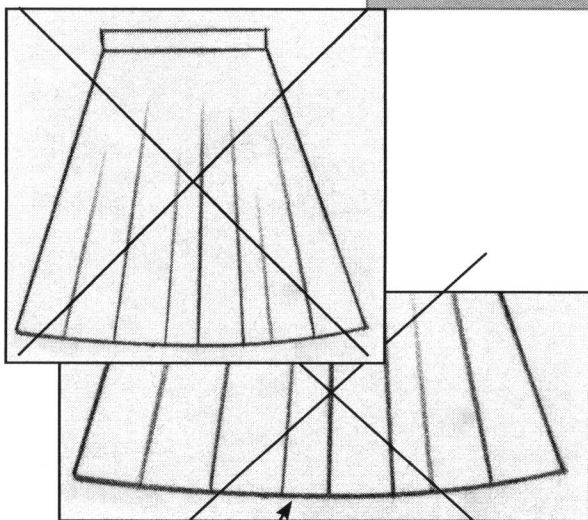

Tip

Do not forget to
finalize hemline.

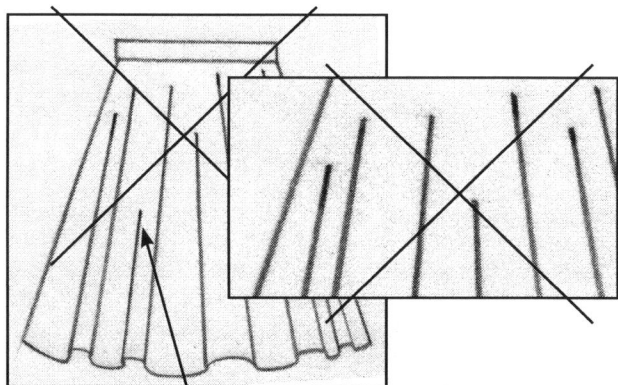

Hemline is not finalized yet.

Hemline is finalized.

Tip

To avoid heavy flare lines start them
from hemline up.

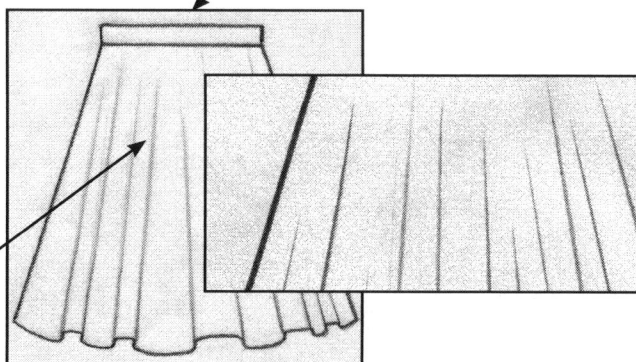

Flare lines are too heavy.

Flare lines are very light.

97

Tip

Always connect or overlap **gathers** and **flare** in the same detail.

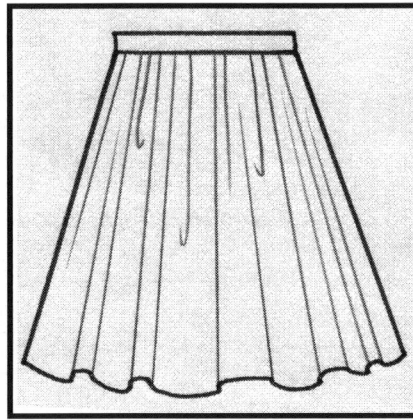

Flared skirt with gathers

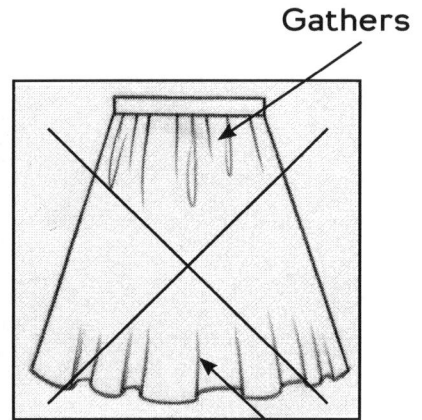

Gathers

Flare

Gathers and flare lines are not connected.

How to draw flared hem

Flare lines outside

Keep the same direction for outside and inside flare lines.

Flared skirt with extra flare in the hem area

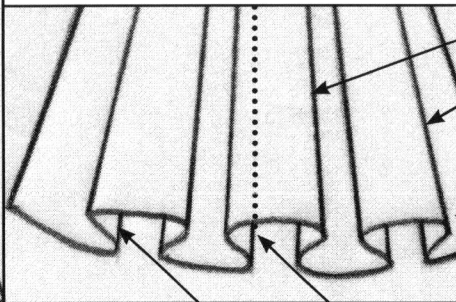

Flare lines inside

Directions for outside and inside flare lines are different.

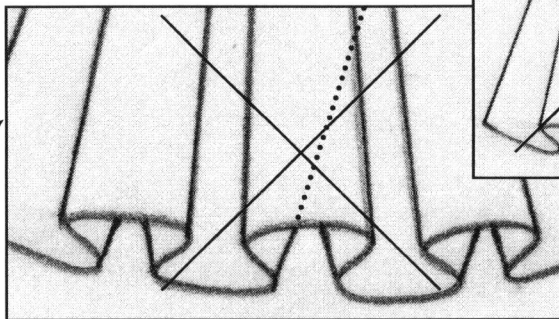

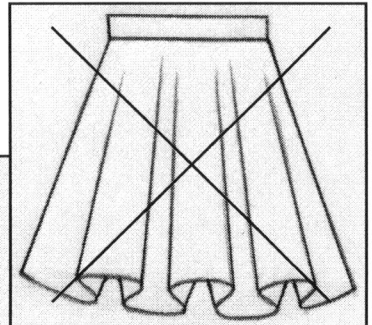

Tip

Always show outside and inside flare lines in the same direction toward upper seam.

How to draw gathers

Gathers

Tip

To show **gathers** always start them from a seam above.

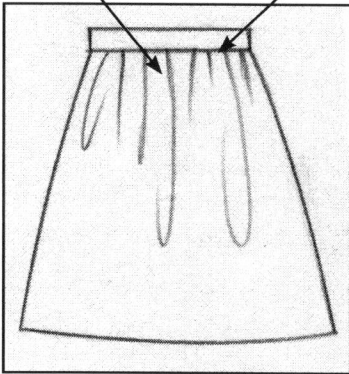

Flared skirt with gathers

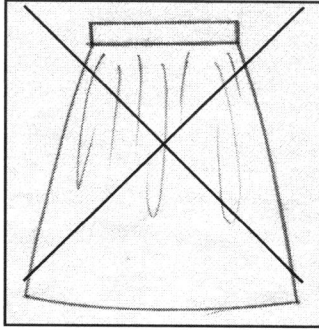

Start gathers from a seam above.

Do not start gathers from side seam.

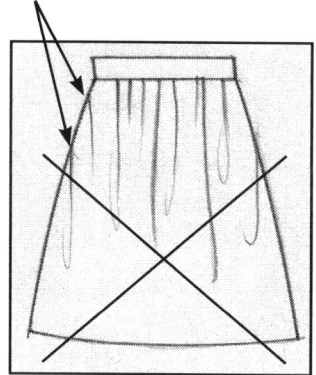

How to draw pleats

Side pleats

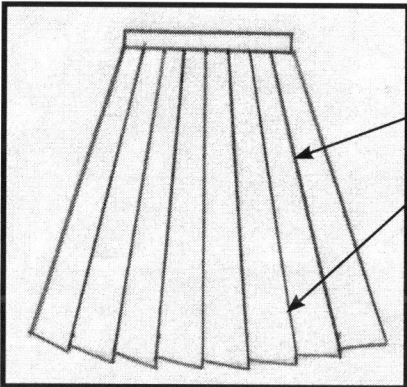

Pleated skirt

Tip

Always start pleats from seams above.

Pleats should start from a seam above.

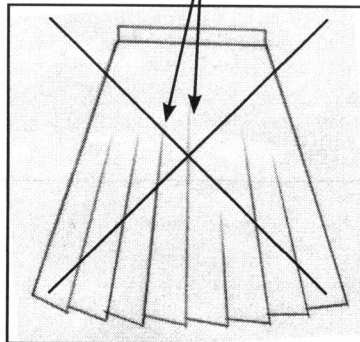

Do not start pleats from side seam.

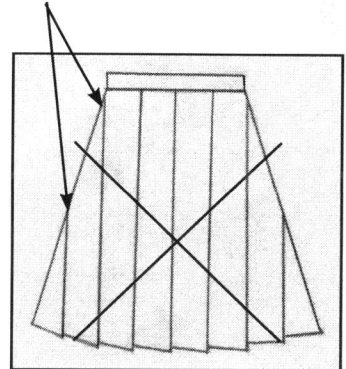

Basic pleat styles

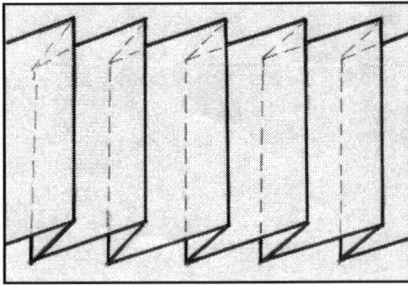

Side pleats

Accordion pleats

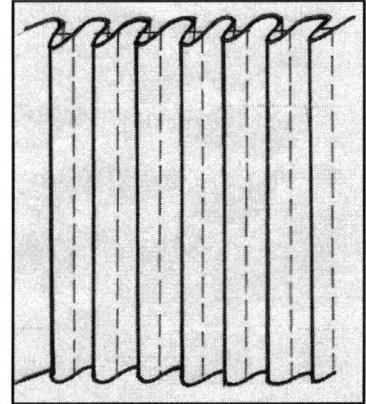

Tucks
(very narrow stitched pleats)

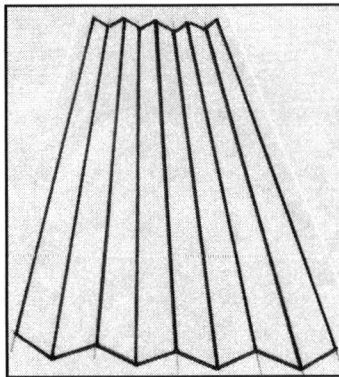

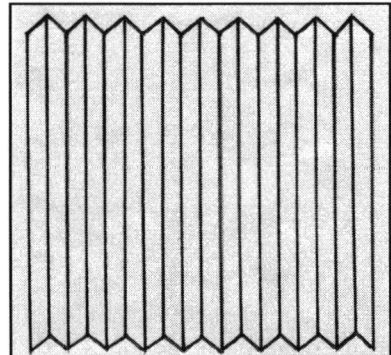

Sunburst pleats

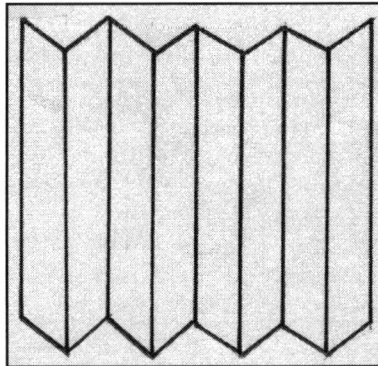

Crystal pleats
(very narrow accordion pleats)

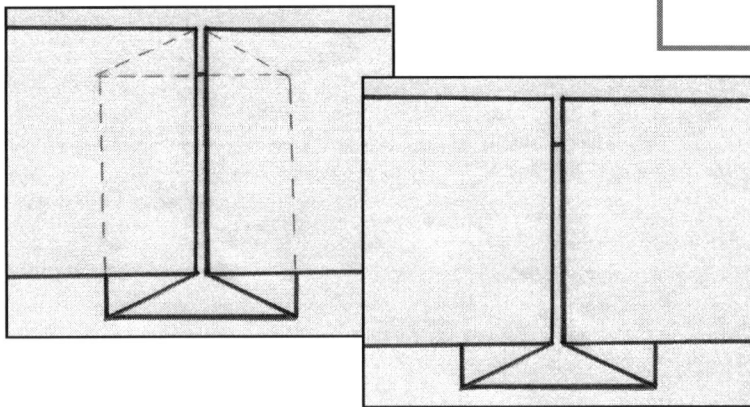

Inverted pleats
(opposite to box pleats)

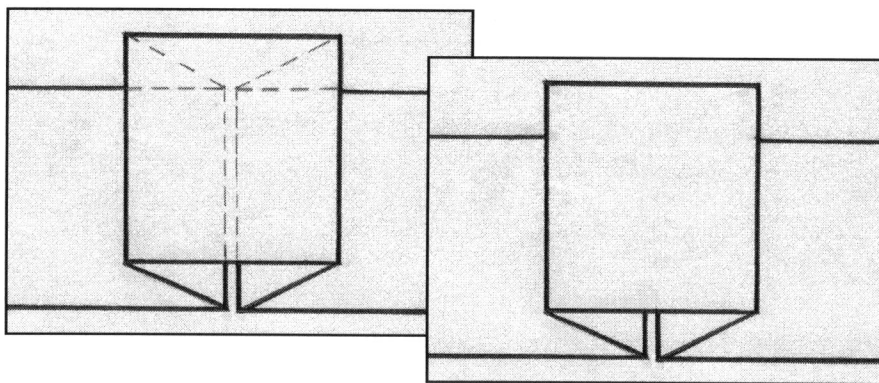

Box pleats
(opposite to inverted pleats)

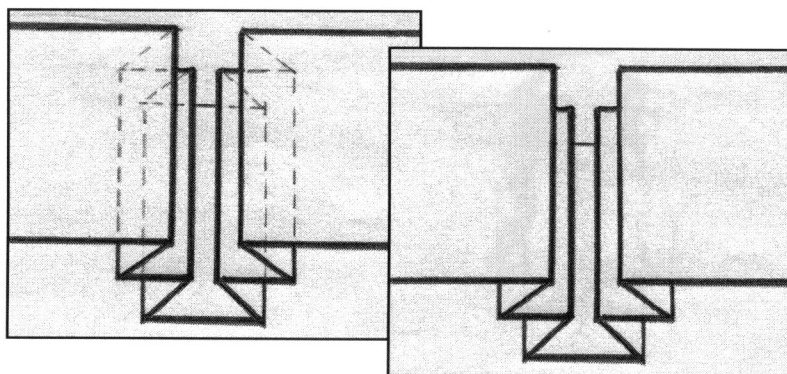

Cluster pleats
(combination of pleats)

How to draw drapery

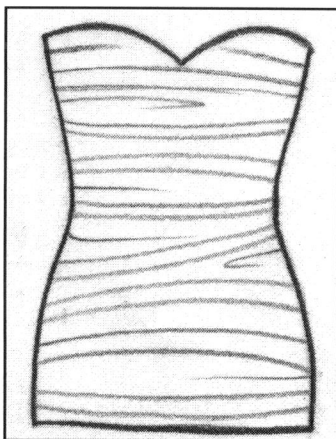

Step # 1

Show directions and placement for drapery.

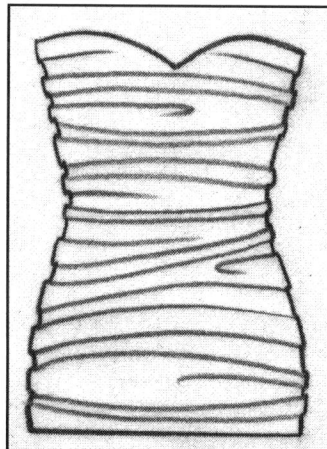

Step # 2

Finalize side seams to show extra fabric in wrinkles.

Skirts

How to draw front view flat for low waisted skirt (simple pencil line)

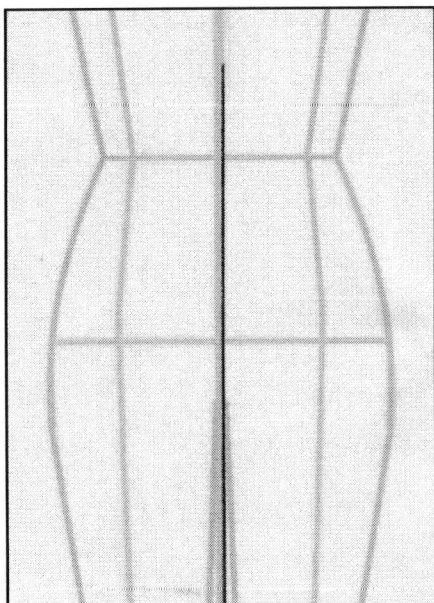

Step #1

Cover template with tracing paper and tape it to avoid shifting.
Draw central line.

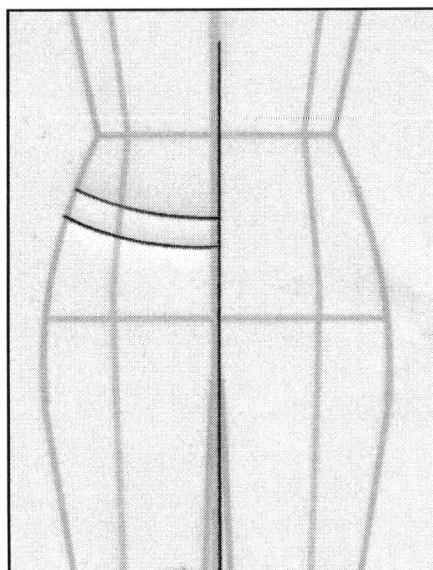

Step #2

Draw front waistband.

Tip

Always draw only one side of flat and trace the second side to make sure the garment is symmetrical.

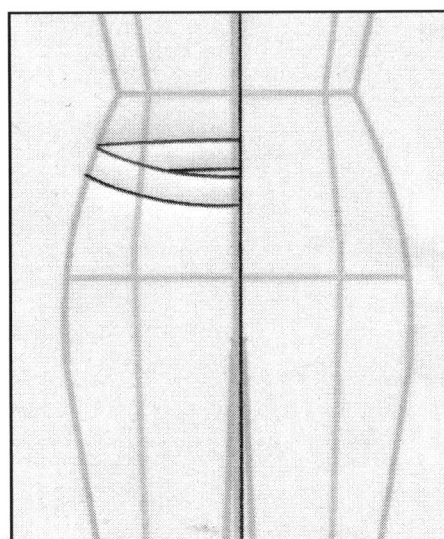

Step #3

Draw back waistband.

102

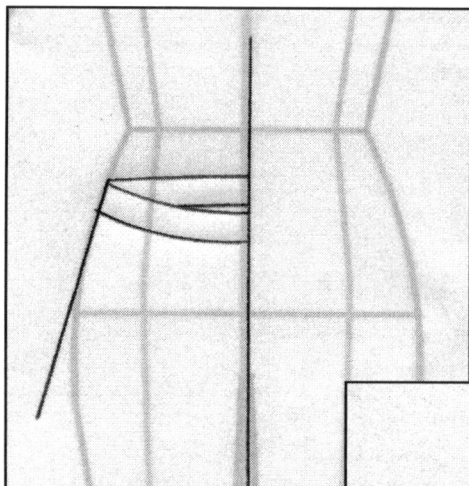

Step #4

Draw side seam.

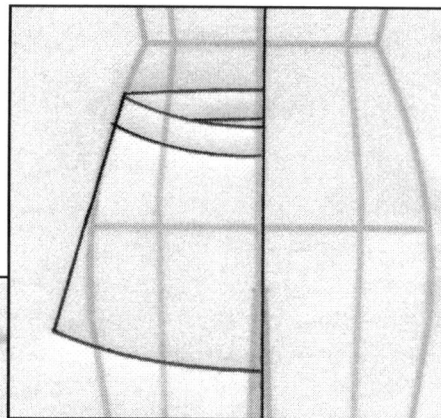

Step #5

Draw hemline.
So, the half of the flat is completed!

Now we should trace second half of the flat.

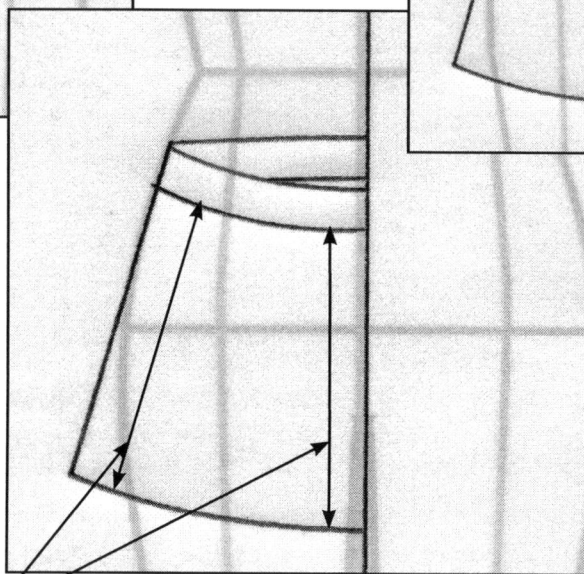

Make sure the skirt has the same length for side and central lines.

Tip

Keep 90 degrees (right) angle between hemline and side seam.

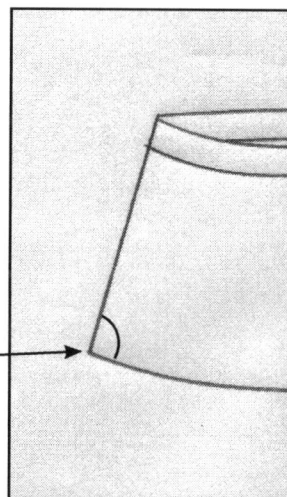

Step #6

Fold your flat along the center line and trace second half.
So, basic outlining of the front view of the flat is completed!

How to draw back view flat for skirts (simple pencil line)

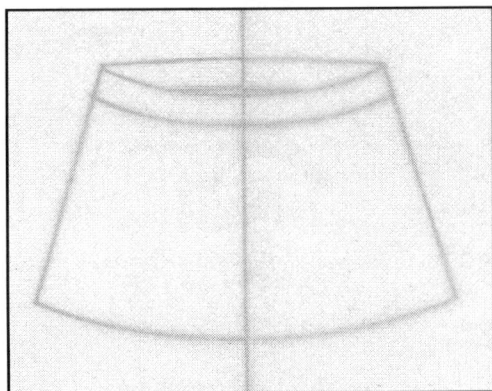

Step #7

Cover the front view flat with a new sheet of tracing paper.

Use tape to avoid shifting.

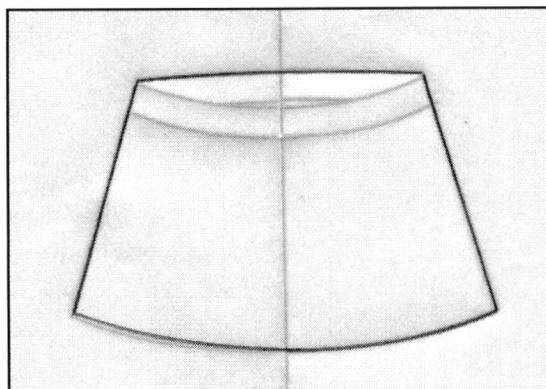

Step #8

Outline the basic shape of the skirt.

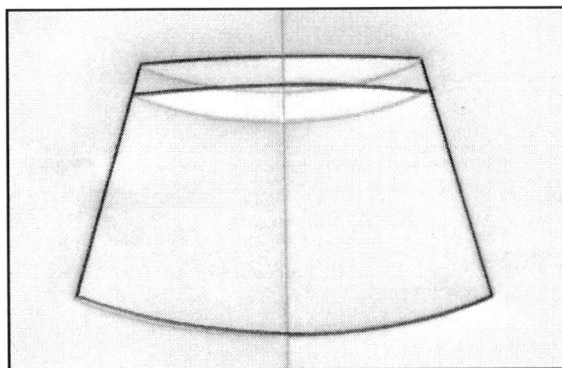

Step #9

Outline back waistband.

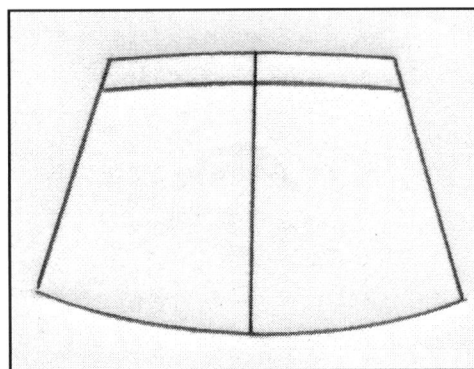

Step #10

Show central seam.
So, back view of the skirt is ready!

How to draw final front and back views of flats for skirts (marker line)

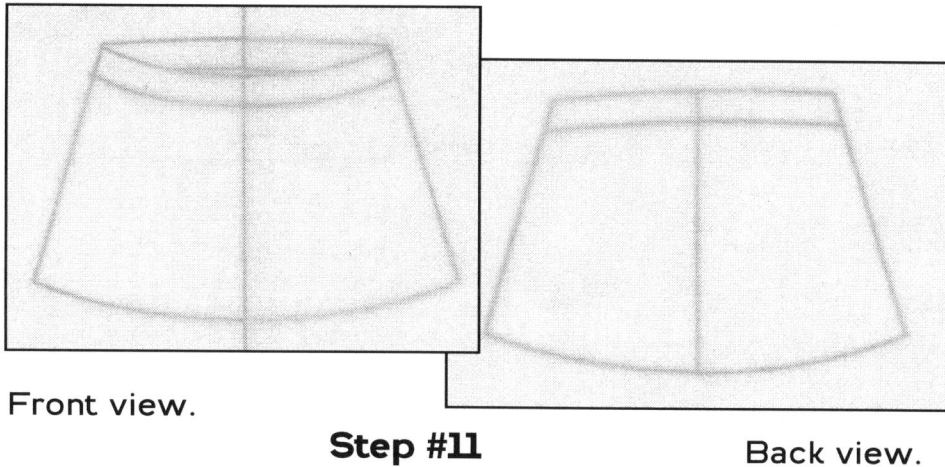

Front view.

Step #11

Back view.

To draw flats with black marker line use flats with simple pencil line.

Cover your simple pencil flat drawings with new sheets of marker paper. Use tape to avoid shifting.

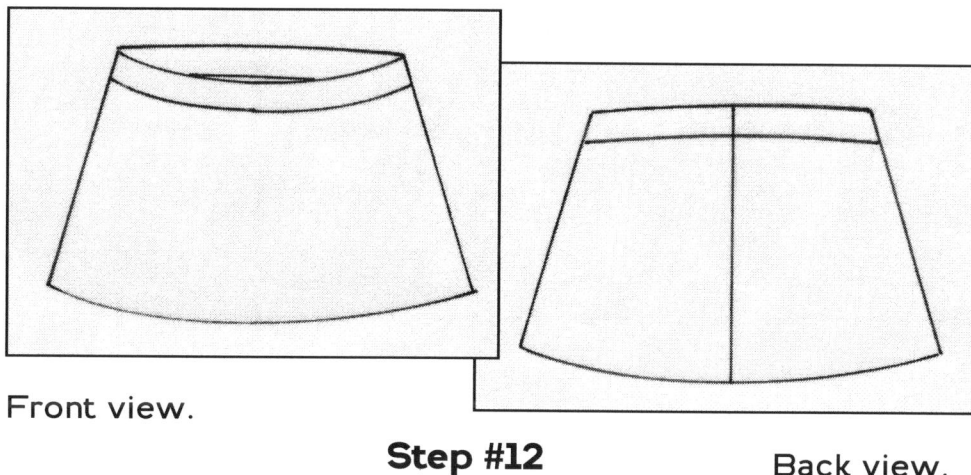

Front view.

Step #12

Back view.

Outline the front and back views simple pencil line flats with marker.

Tip

Use double sided inking edge French curve or ruler for perfect marker outlining (see page 14-15).

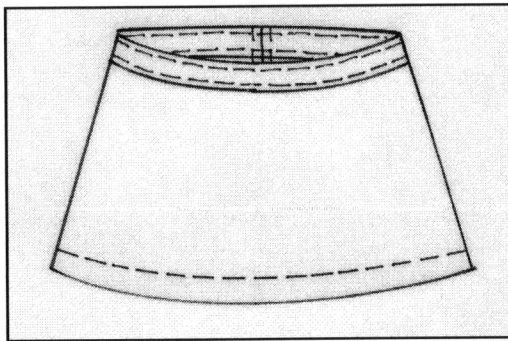

Front view. **Step #13** Back view.

Add all necessary details and topstitching.

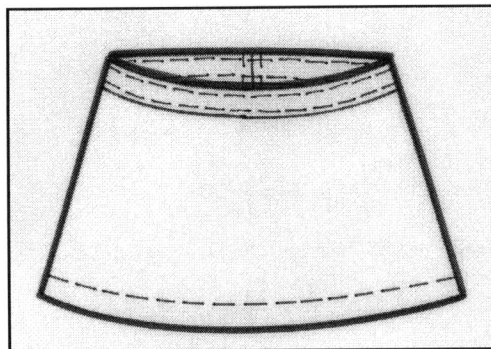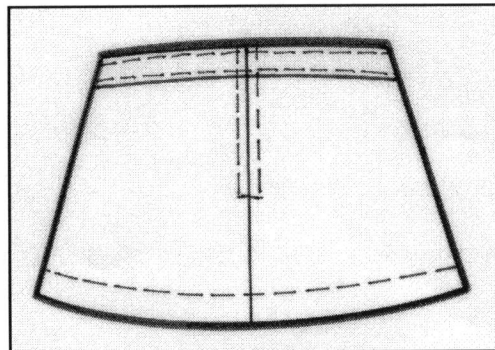

Front view. **Step #14** Back view.

For final outlining you can use a thicker line for the basic shape and skinnier lines for details and topstitching.

The most preferred method is the contrast technique with thick garment outlining and a thin line for inner details.

Gallery of details for dresses and skirts

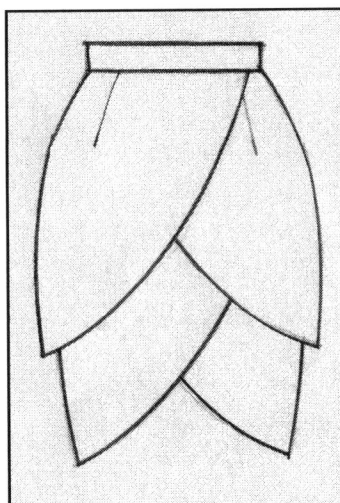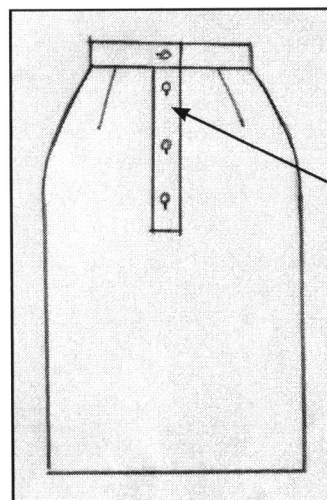

Placket

Petal style skirt.   Fitted straight skirt.

106

Gore

Godet "handkerchief" style

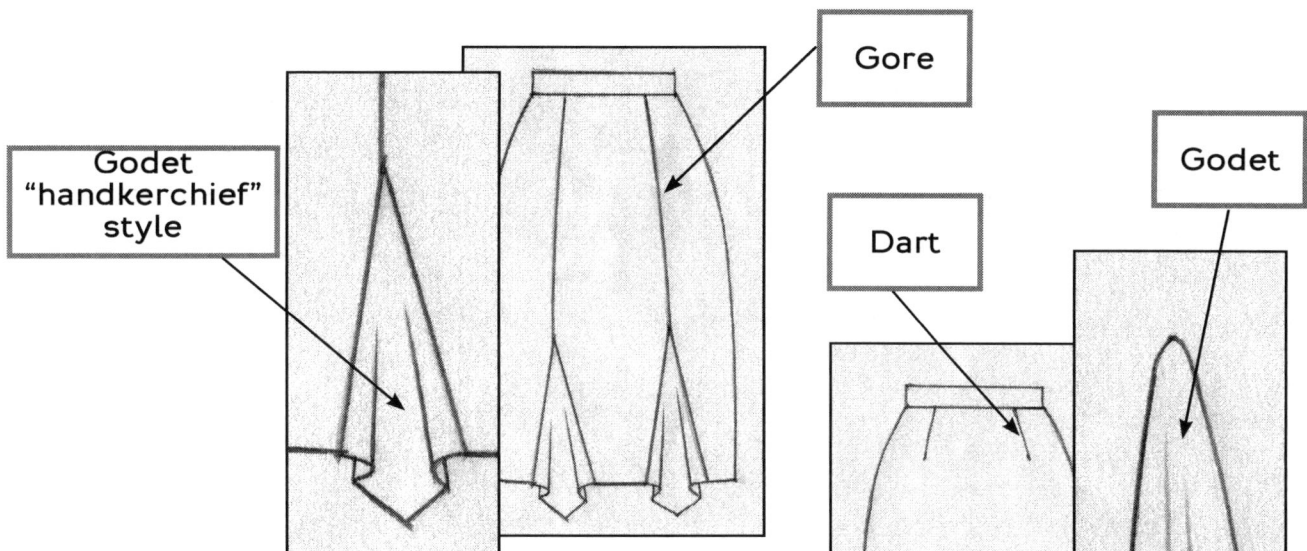

Straight skirt fitted with gores.

Godet

Dart

Straight skirt fitted with darts.

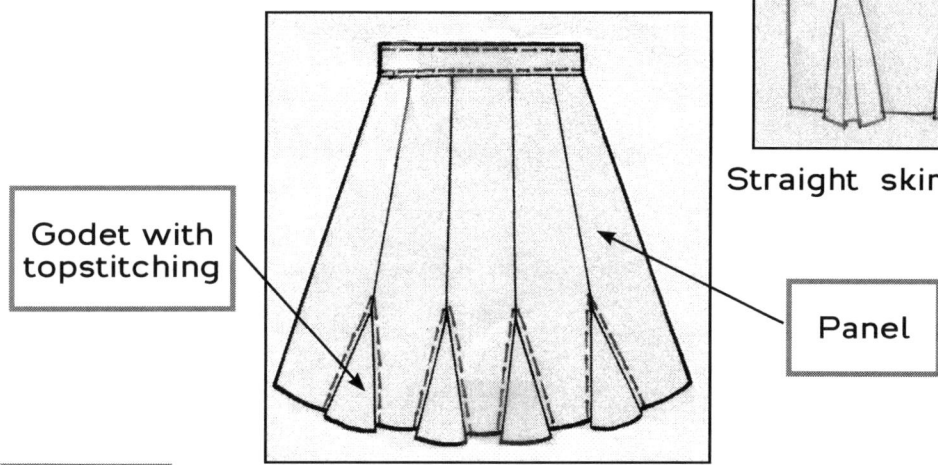

Godet with topstitching

Panel

Flared skirt with 5 panels on the front.

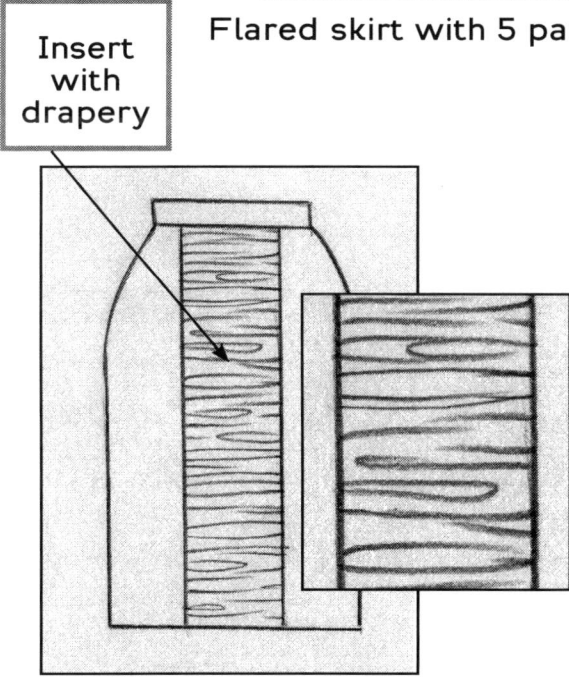

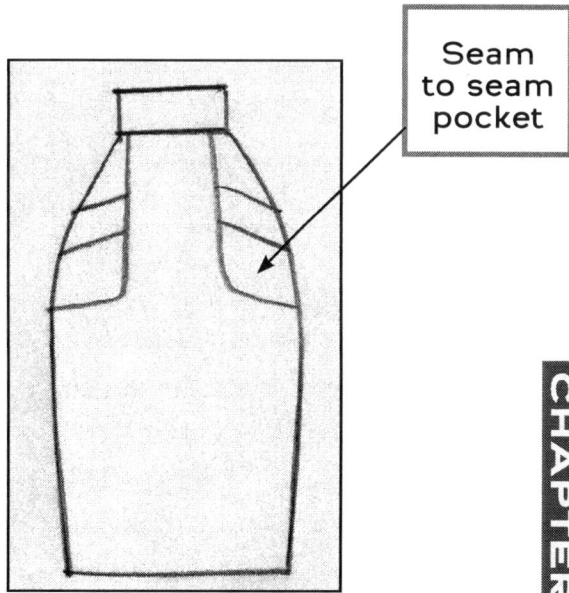

Insert with drapery

Seam to seam pocket

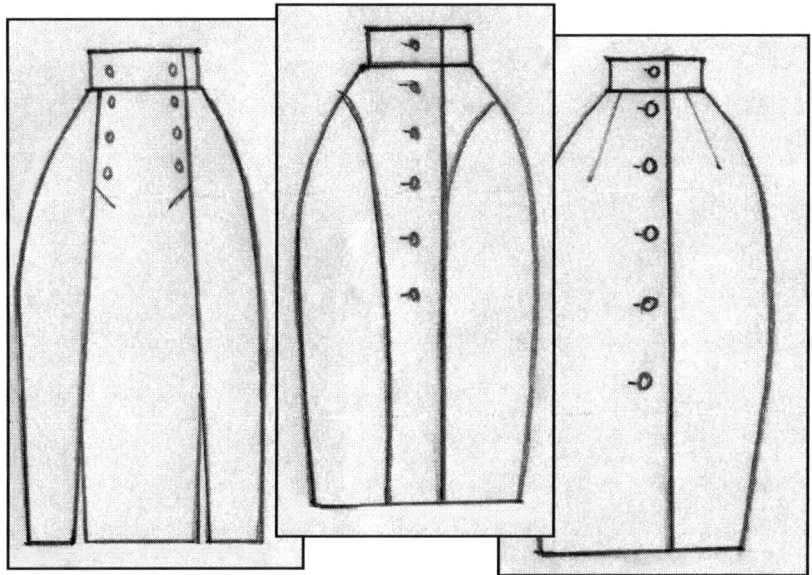

Straight skirts with front closures.

Pleats

Handkerchief skirt.

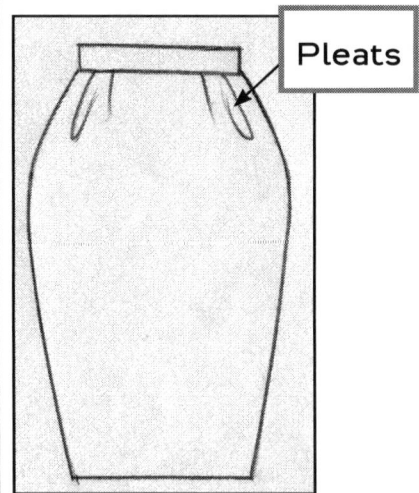

Pegged skirt fitted with soft pleats.

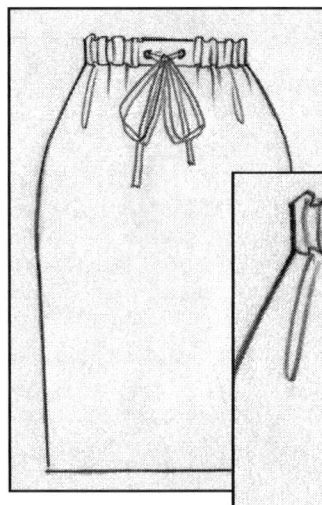

Drawstring

Straight skirt (dirndl).

108

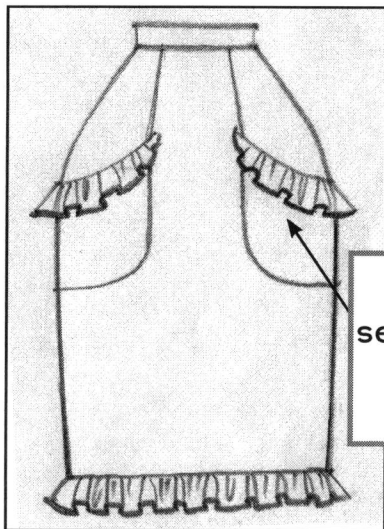

Seam to seam pocket with ruffles

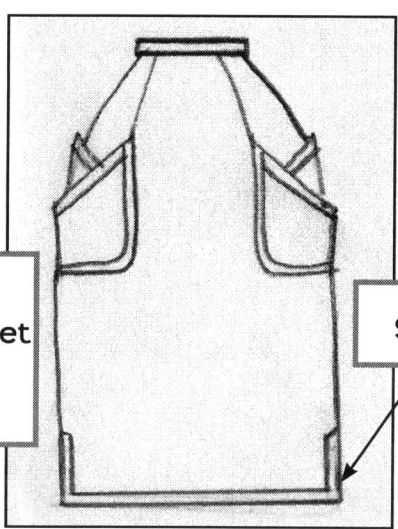

Slit

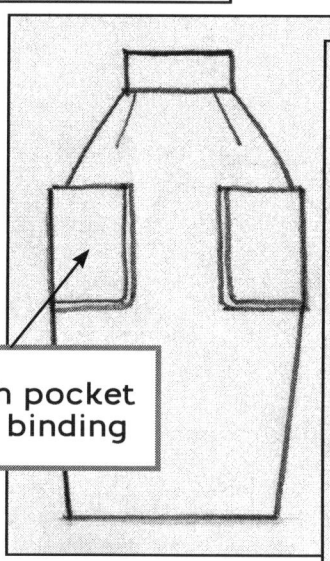

Patch pocket with binding

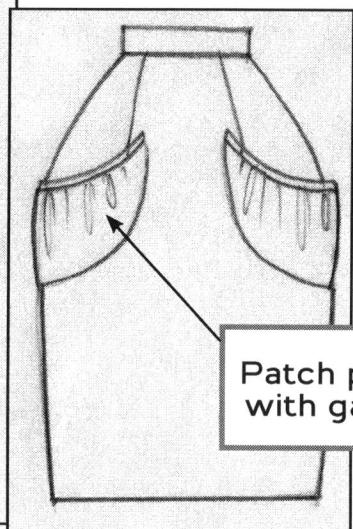

Patch pocket with gathers

Skirts with patch pockets.

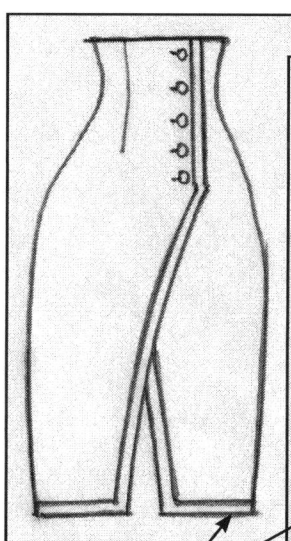

Ruffles

Binding

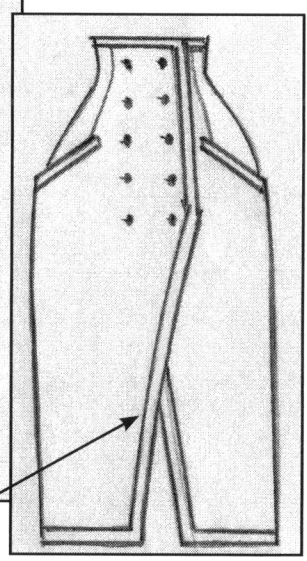

Straight skirts with binding.

Patch pocket with ruffles.

Skirts with asymmetrical drapery and details

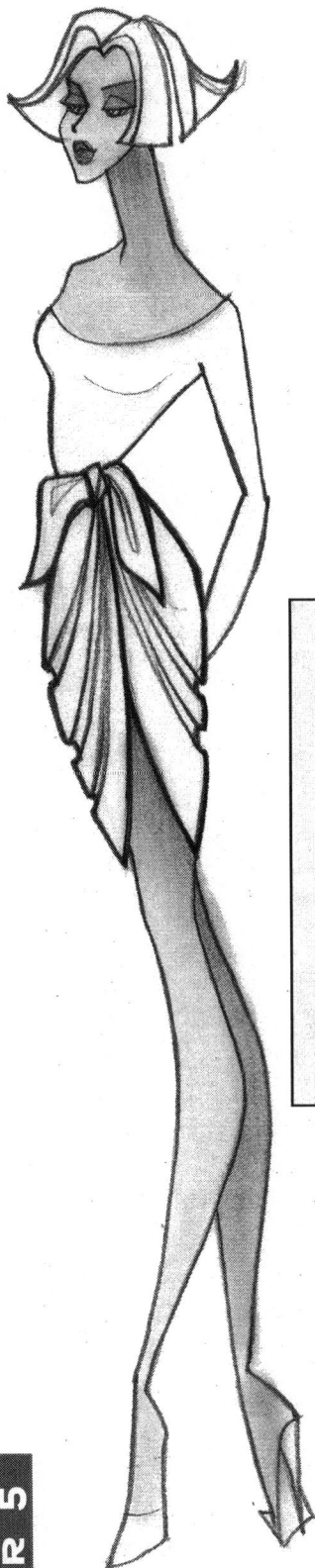

Asymmetrical draped closure

Patch pocket with bow

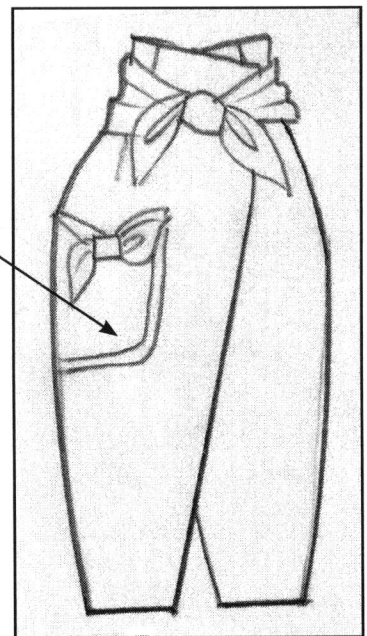

Wrap skirt with bow on draped waistband.

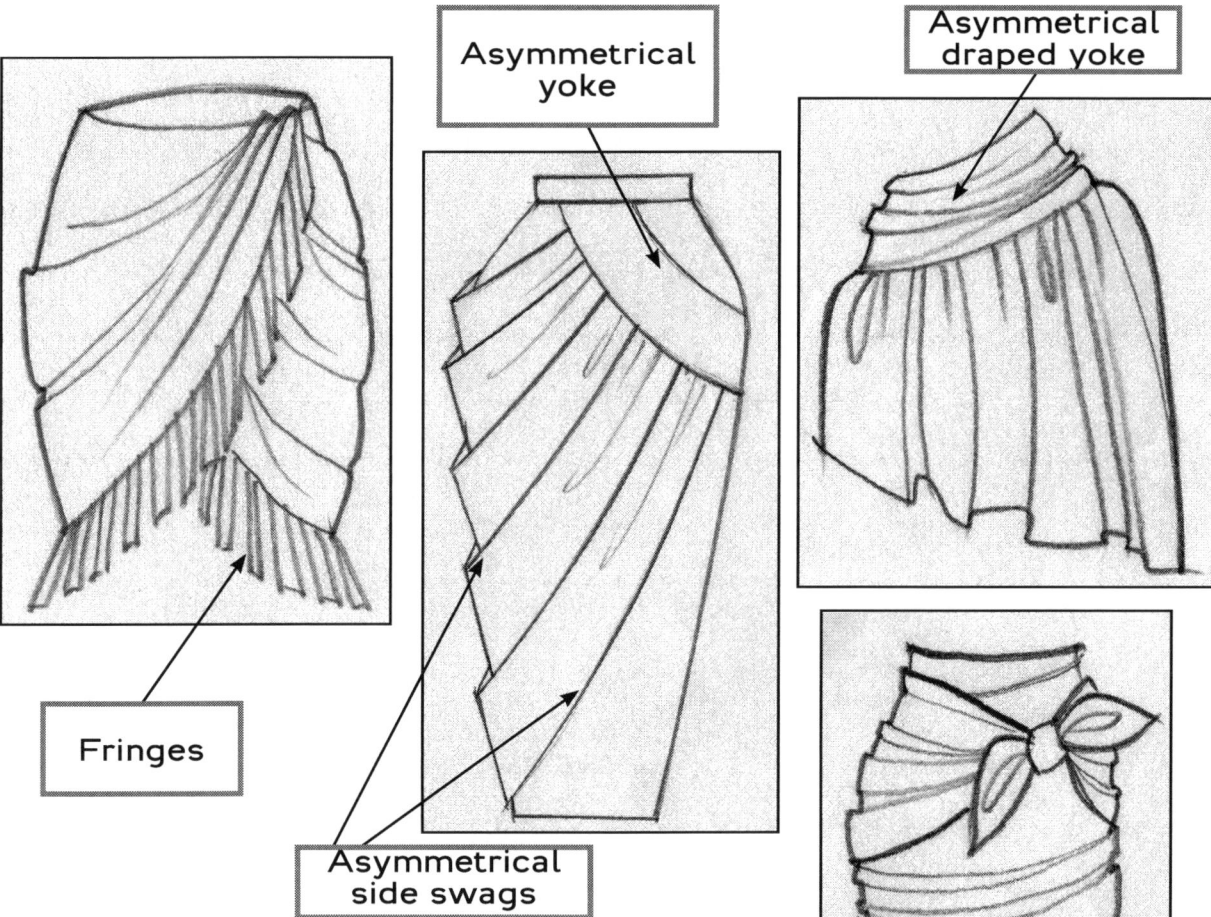

Asymmetrical yoke

Asymmetrical draped yoke

Fringes

Asymmetrical side swags

Draped skirt with asymmetrical bow.

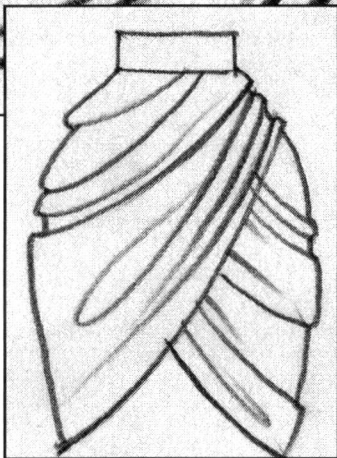

Wrap skirt with drapery.

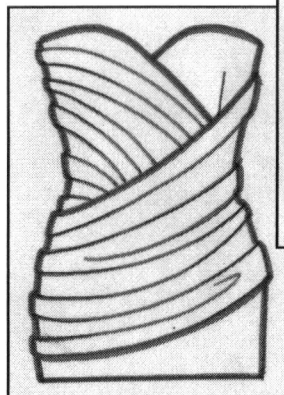

Dresses with asymmetrical drapery.

Skirts and dresses with symmetrical drapery, flares and details

Scalloped edge yoke

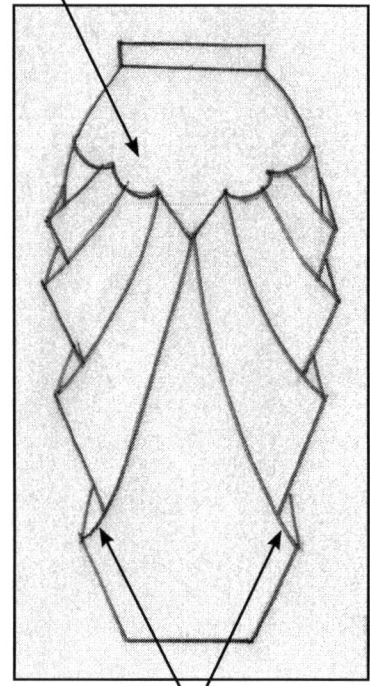

Symmetrical side swags

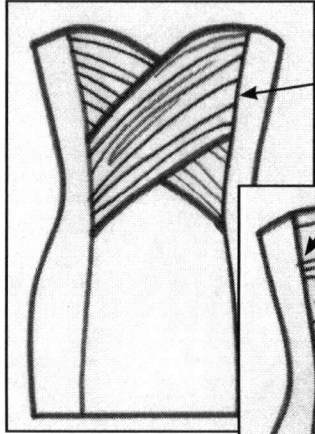

Gore

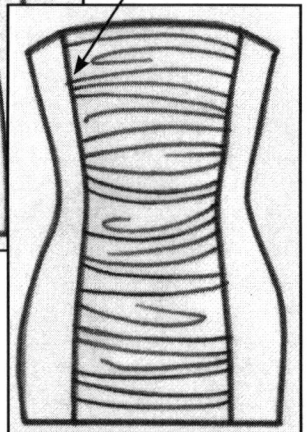

Dresses with drapery between gores.

112

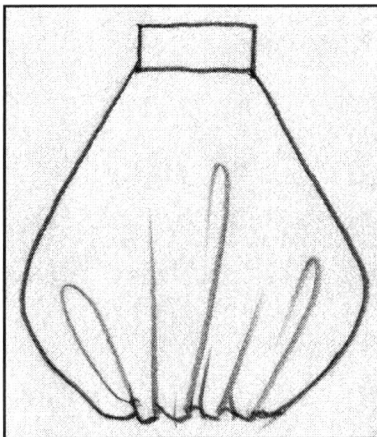

Pouf skirt.

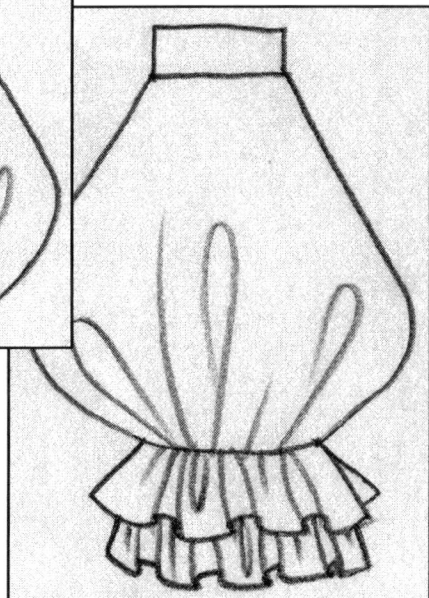

Pouf skirt with ruffles.

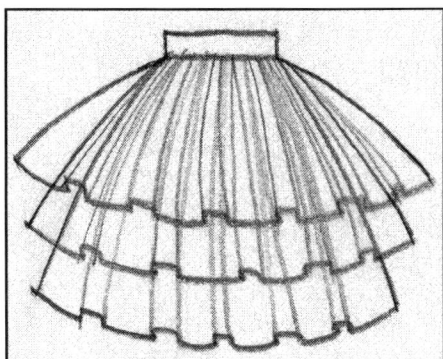

Layered skirt from transparent fabric.

Symmetrical side swags

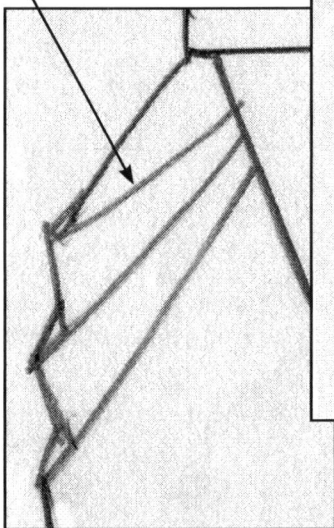

Center insert

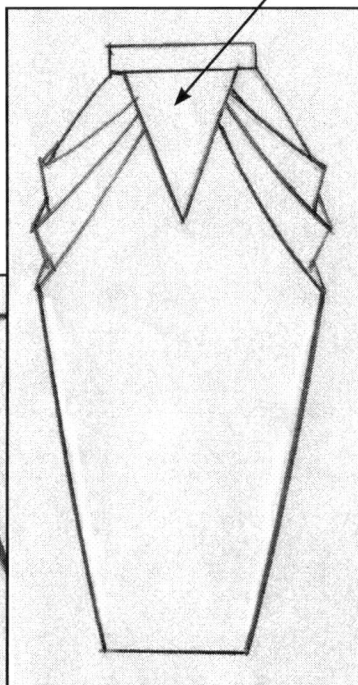

Chapter 6

Jackets, vests and shirts

Terminology of jacket

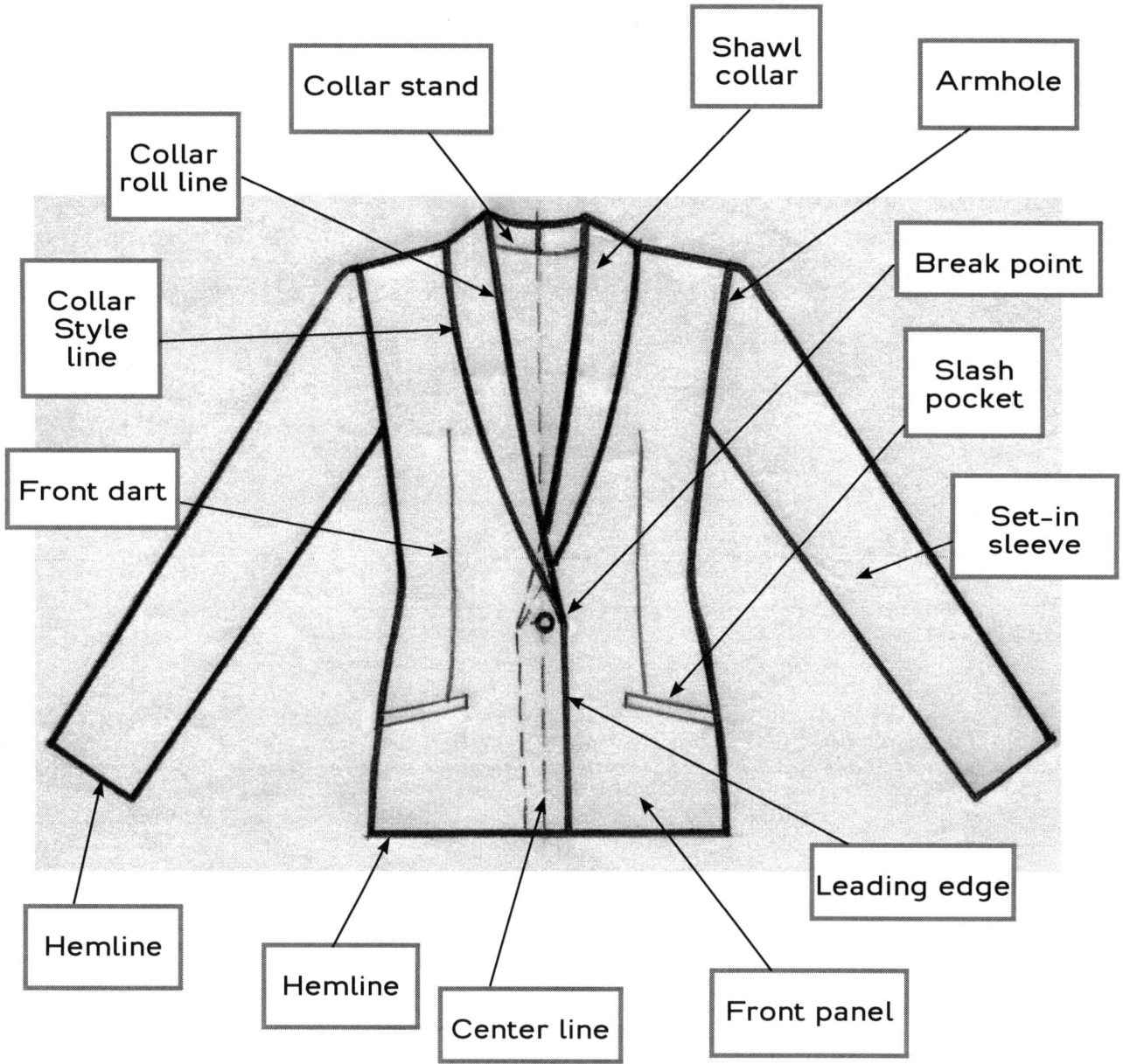

Collar stand

Shawl collar

Armhole

Collar roll line

Collar Style line

Break point

Slash pocket

Front dart

Set-in sleeve

Leading edge

Hemline

Hemline

Center line

Front panel

Front view

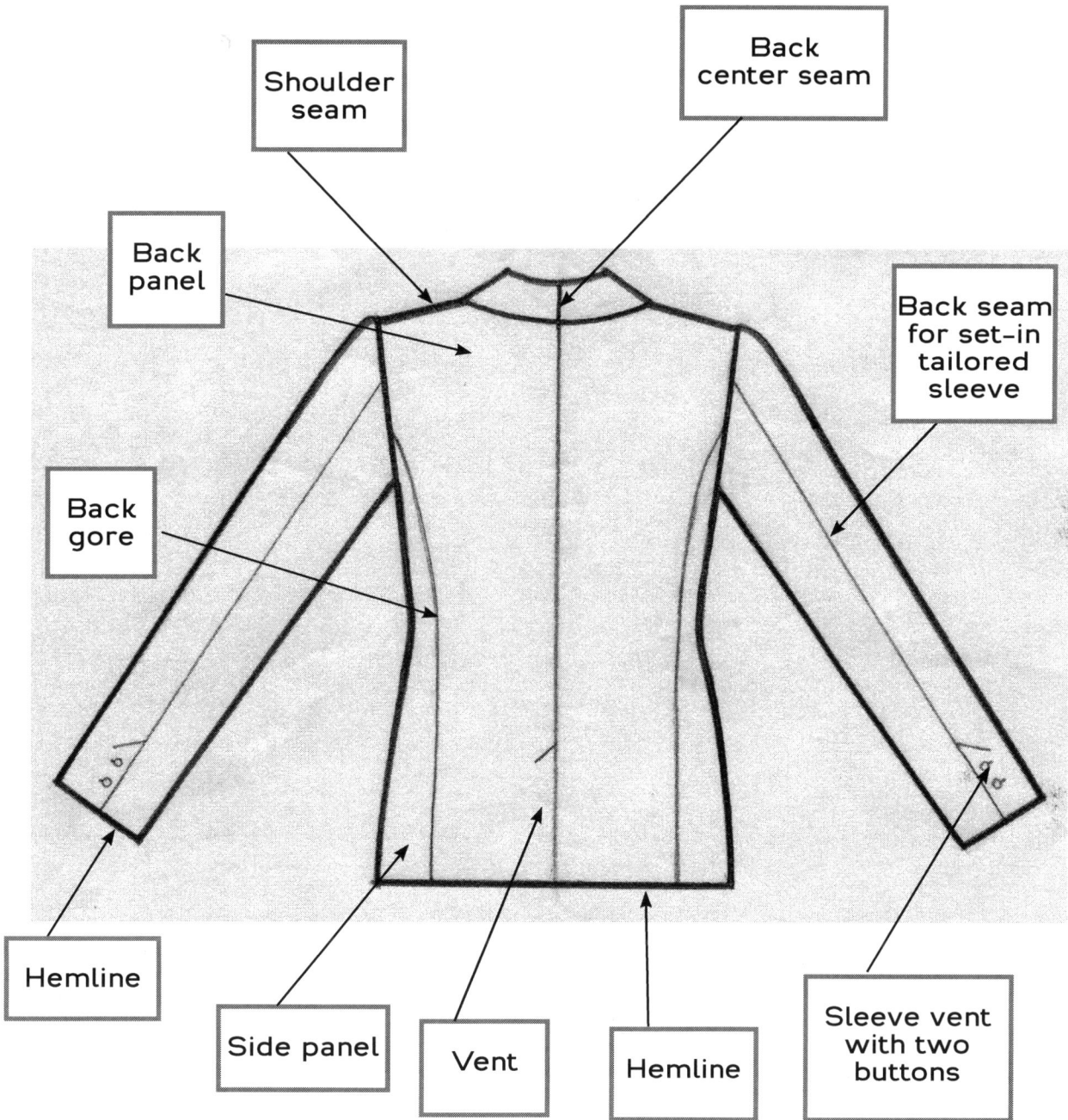

Shoulder seam

Back center seam

Back panel

Back seam for set-in tailored sleeve

Back gore

Hemline

Side panel

Vent

Hemline

Sleeve vent with two buttons

Back view

117

Jacket

How to draw front view flat for jacket (simple pencil line)

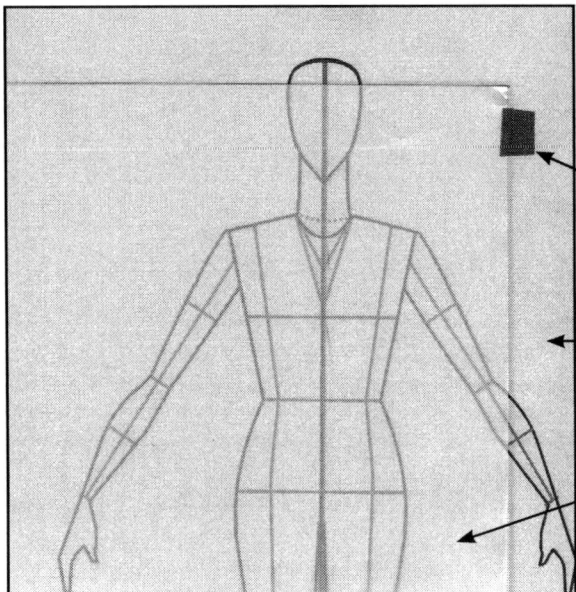

Cover template with tracing paper and tape it to avoid shifting.

Tape.

Sheet of paper with template on it.

Sheet of tracing paper.

Step # 1

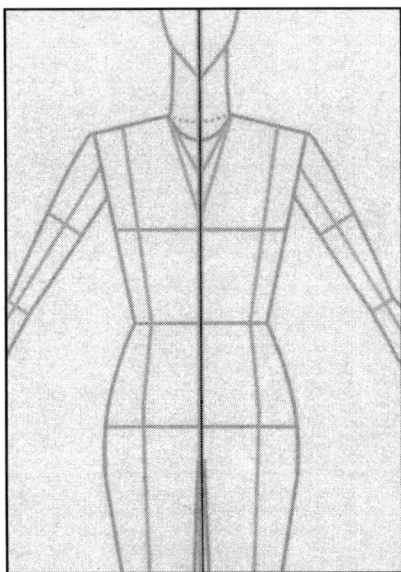

Step # 2

Draw center line.

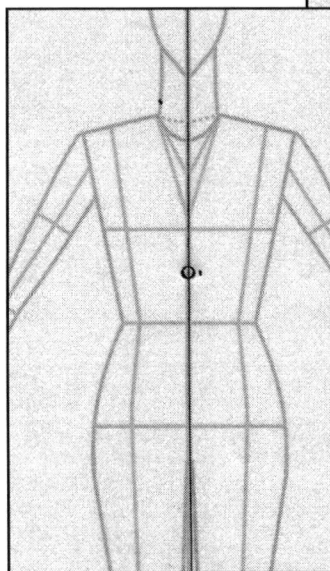

Step # 3

Draw the first upper button on the center line.

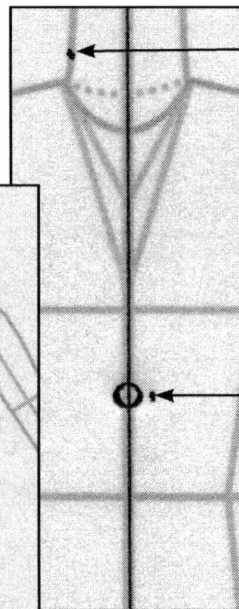

Desirable level for collar stand

Break point

118

Tip

Always draw only one side of flat and trace the second side to make sure the garment is symmetrical.

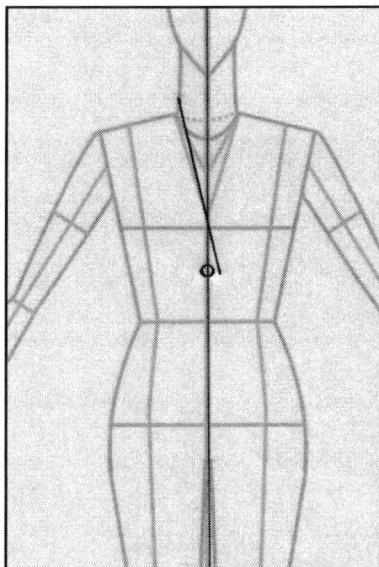

Step # 4

Draw roll line from break point till stand level.

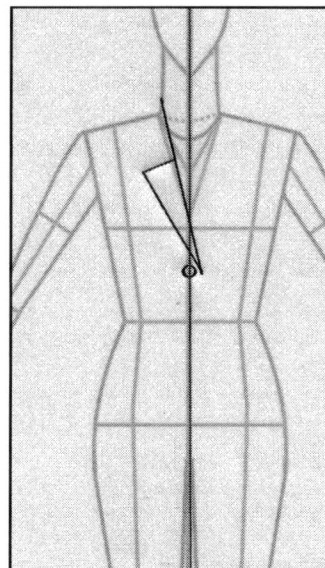

Step # 5

Draw lapel on the roll line.

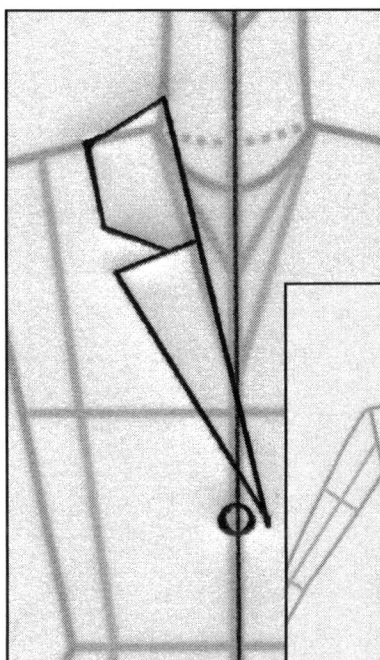

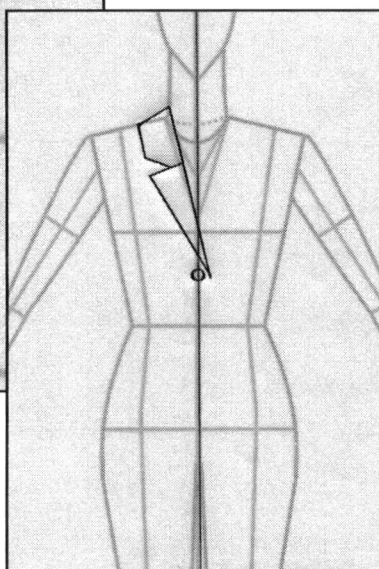

Step # 6

Draw upper collar.

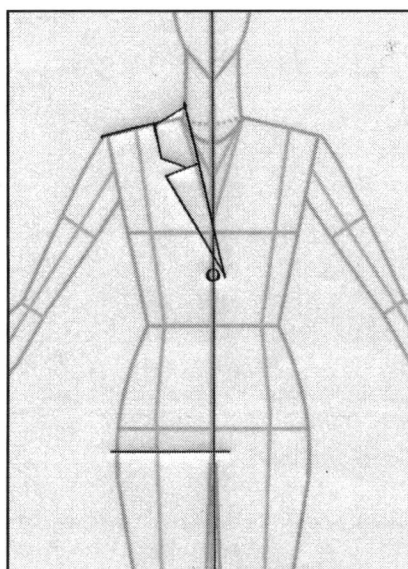

Step # 7

Draw shoulder and hemline.

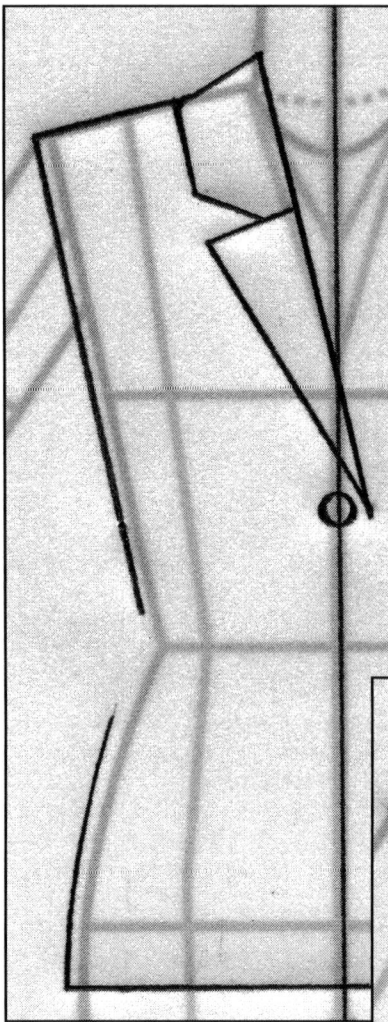

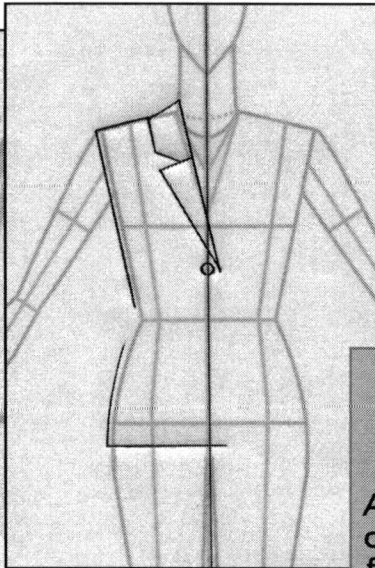

Draw upper part of side seam using ruler and lower part of side seam using French curve.

Step # 8

Tip

Allow for **garment ease** when drawing flats. Use bigger ease for outer garment and smaller ease for underwear.

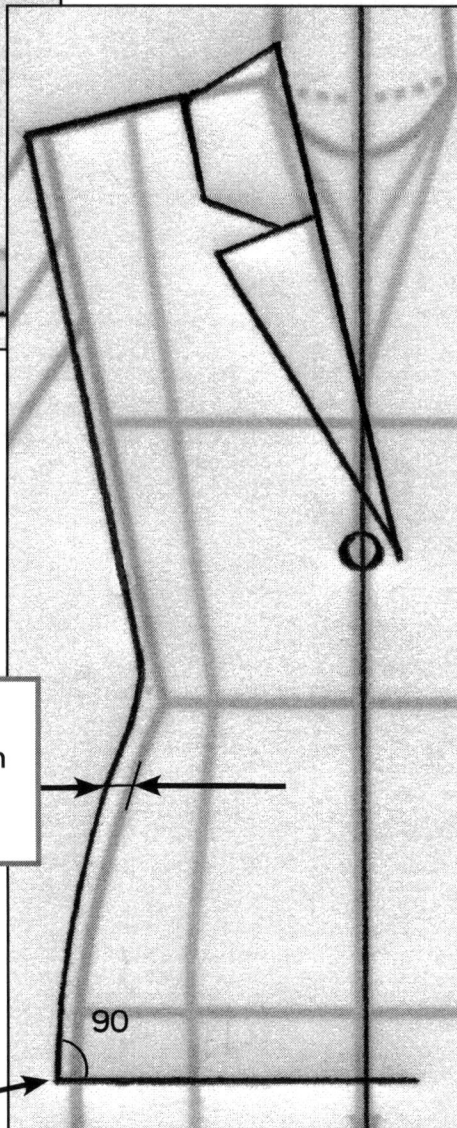

Ease
(the distance between garment and body)

90 degree angle between side and hem lines

90

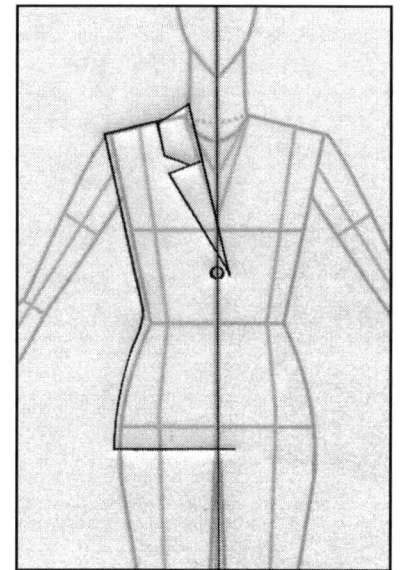

Step # 9

Connect upper and lower parts of side seam.

Use French curve or do it by hand drawing.

Step # 10

Start the sleeve outlining from shoulder seam down toward hemline.

Make sure you have 90 degree angle between center line of sleeve and hemlines.

90 degree angle between sleeve center line and hem

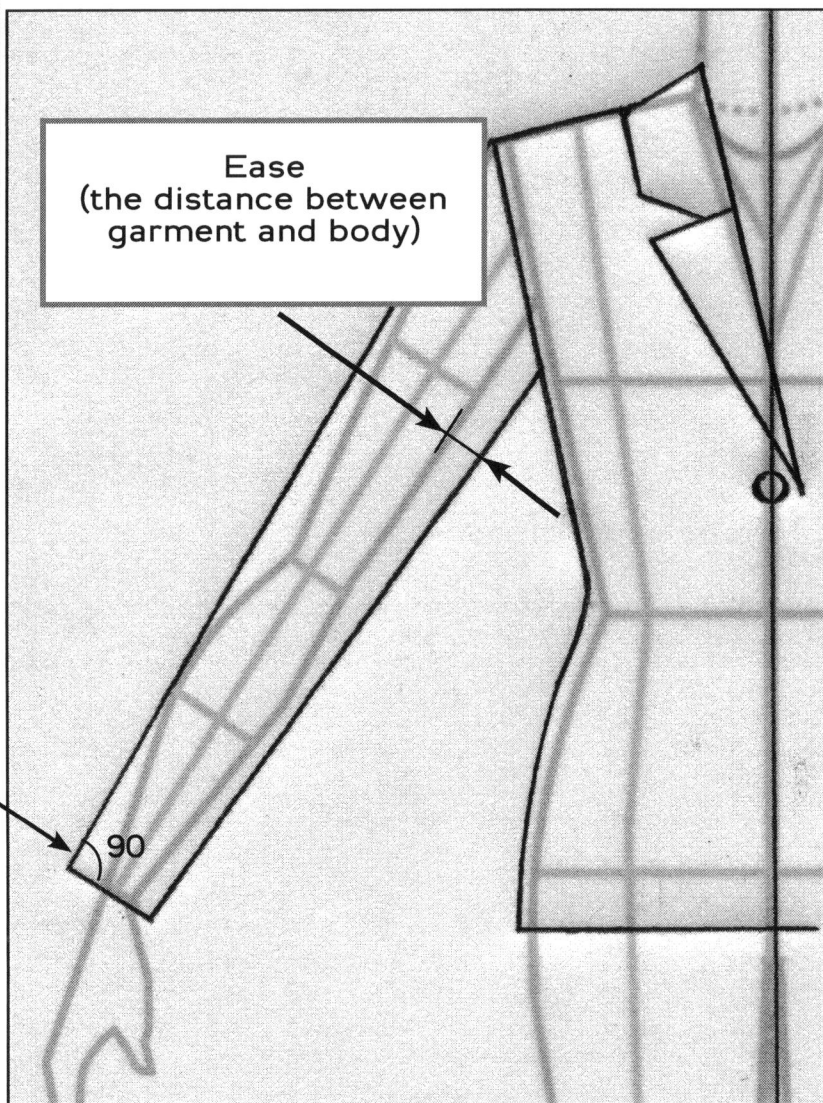

Step # 11

Draw inseam for sleeve.

Tip

Do not draw the sleeve too close to arm and armpit. Allow for **ease** in armpit area for comfortable fit.

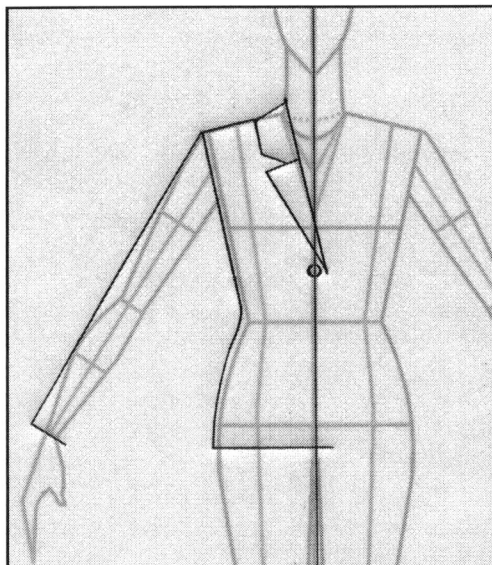

Ease
(the distance between garment and body)

90

Tip

Make sure the sleeve hem area is wide enough for hand to go through.

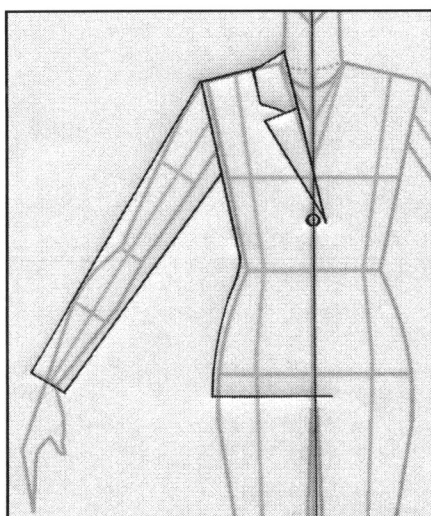

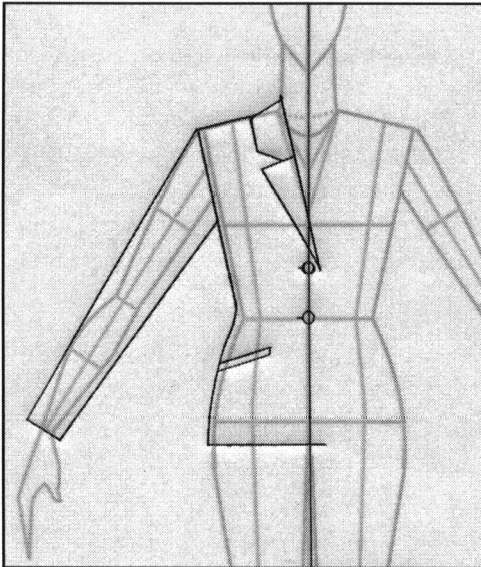

Step # 12

Draw slash pocket and
more buttons if necessary.

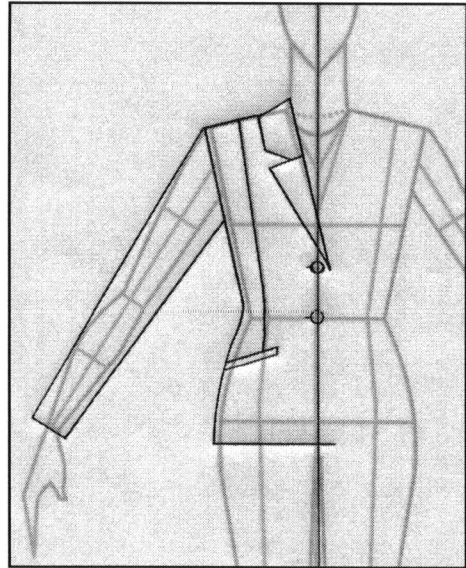

Step # 13

Show dart using princess line on the
template as a guide.

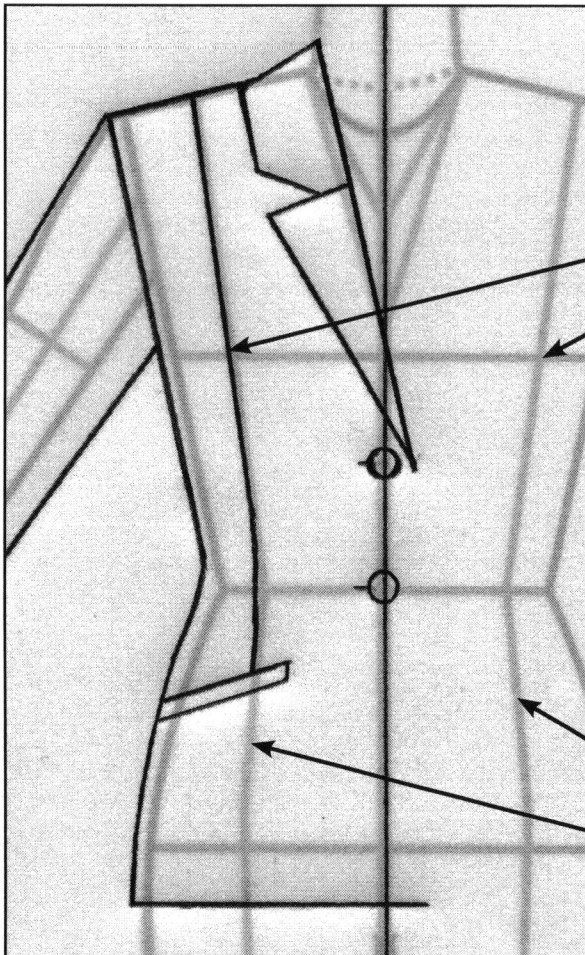

Apex

Tip

Draw darts pointed to apex
and gores through apex for
a fitted garment.

Princess line

122

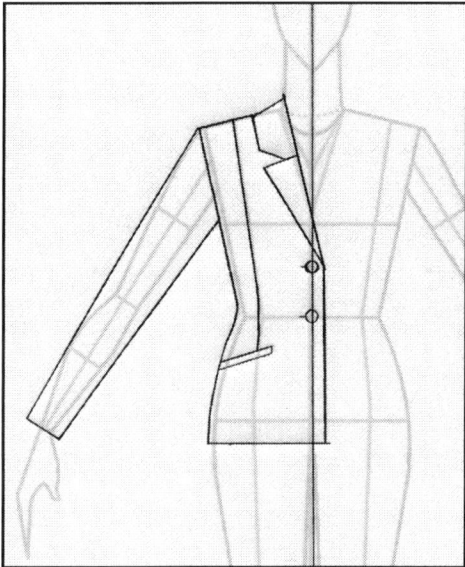

Step # 14

Draw leading edge. So, the half of the flat is almost completed! Now we should trace second half of the flat.

Tip

Keep leading edge parallel to central line.

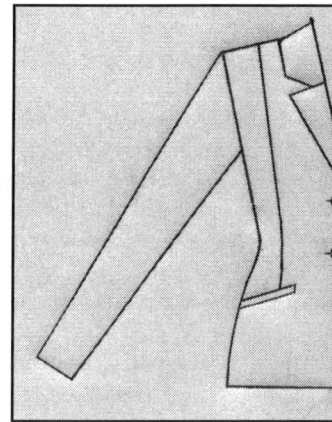

Step # 15

Fold your flat along the center line and trace second half.

Step # 16

So, basic outlining of the front view of the flat is almost completed!

Step # 17

Show back part (stand) of the collar.

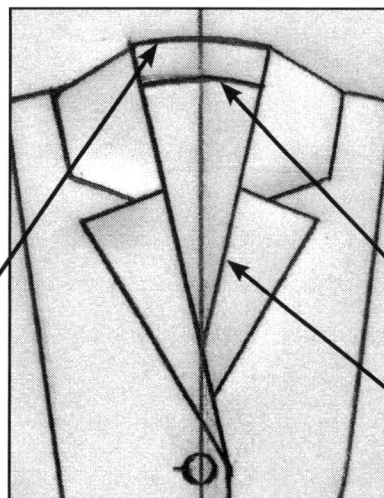

Tip

Keep roll line for back collar always parallel to neckline seam.

Roll line for back collar

Neckline seam

Roll line for front collar

How to draw back view flat for jacket (simple pencil line)

Step # 18

Cover the front view flat with a new sheet of tracing paper. Use tape to avoid shifting.

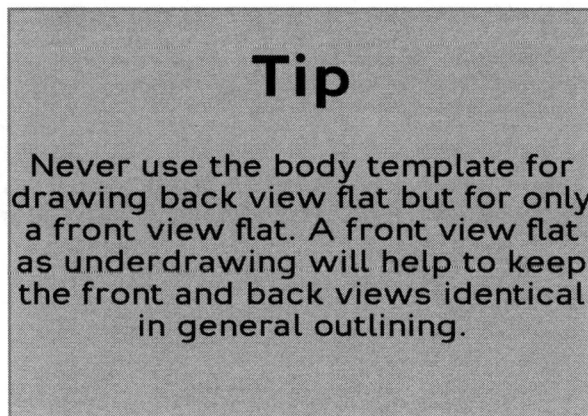

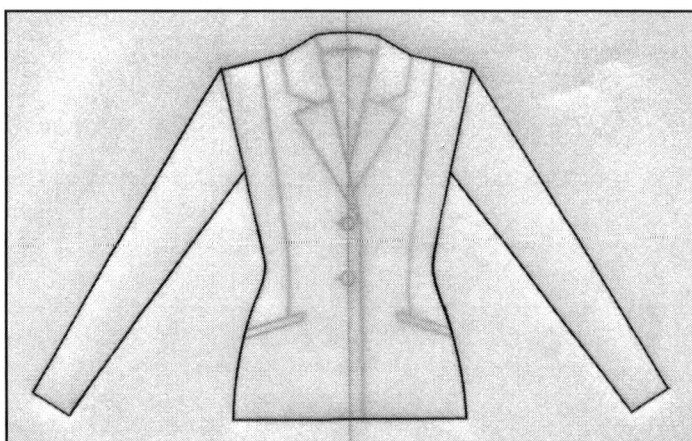

Tip

Never use the body template for drawing back view flat but for only a front view flat. A front view flat as underdrawing will help to keep the front and back views identical in general outlining.

Step # 19

Outline basic shape of the jacket.

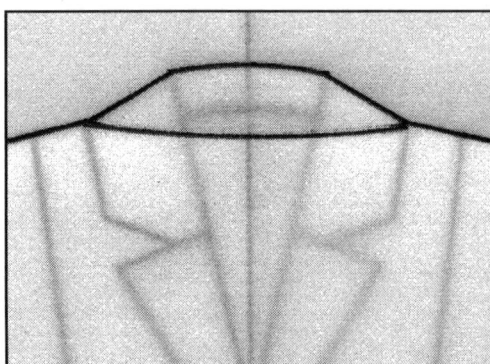

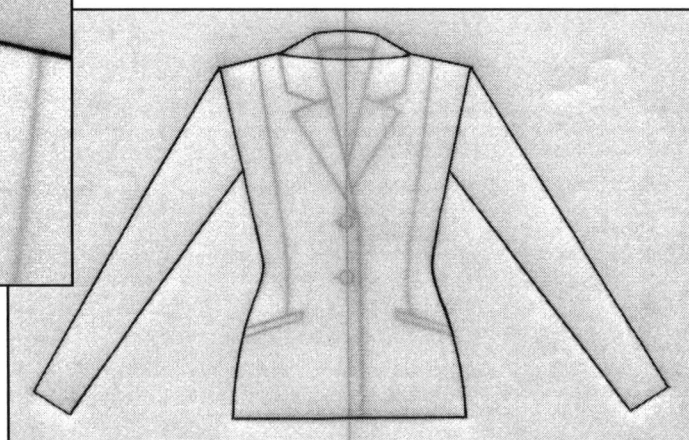

Step # 20

Show back neckline.

How to Draw Fashion Flats A practical guide to fashion technical drawing by Irina V. Ivanova

CHAPTER 6

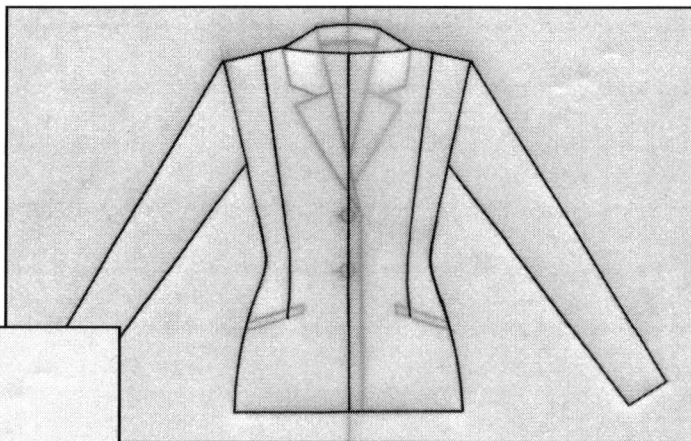

Step # 21

Show darts and center seam.

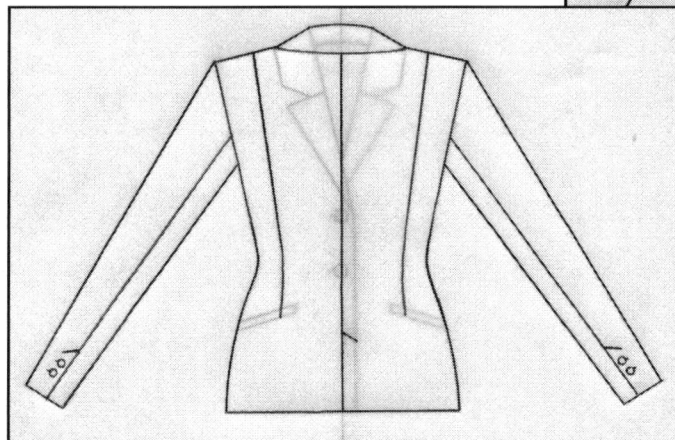

Tip

Show back seam for tailored set-in sleeves.

Step # 22

Add back seams with double buttoned vents on the sleeves.
So, the back view of the flat in simple pencil line is completed!

Tip

Always draw vent on the seam.

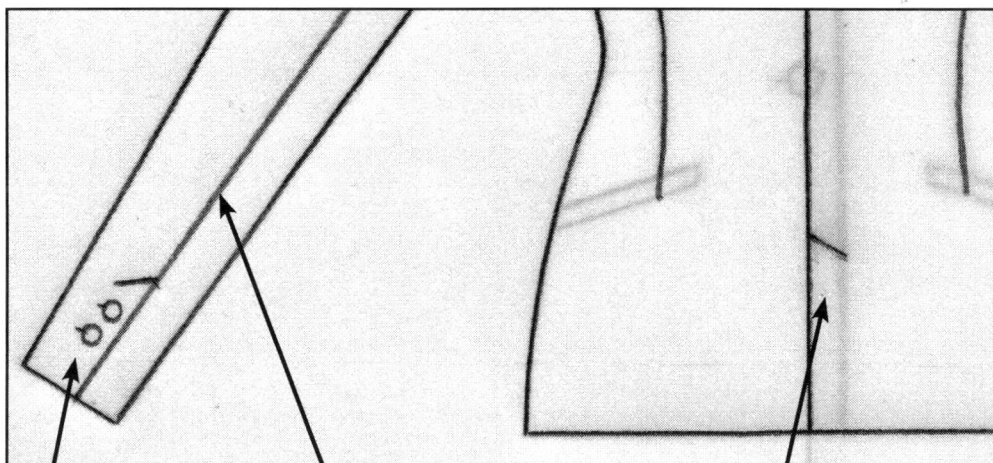

Double buttoned sleeve vent

Sleeve back seam

Vent on the center seam

How to draw final front and back views of flats for jacket (marker line)

Step # 23

To draw a front view flat with black marker line use a front view flat with simple pencil line.

Cover your simple pencil front view flat with a new sheet of marker paper.

Use tape to avoid shifting.

Step # 24

Outlining of front view of jacket with marker line.

Step # 25

To draw a back view flat with black marker line use a back view flat with simple pencil line.

Cover your simple pencil back view flat with a new sheet of marker paper.

Use tape to avoid shifting.

126

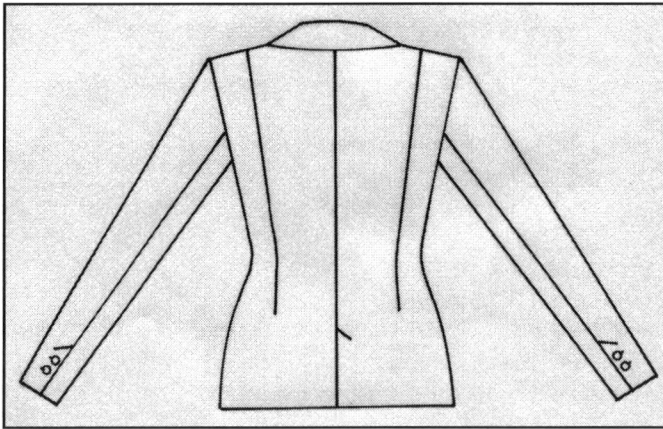

Step # 26

Outlining of back view of jacket with marker line.

Tip

Use double sided inking edge French curve or ruler for perfect marker outlining (see page 13).

Step # 27

You can use for final outlining two different markers.
A thicker marker line could be used for the basic shape, and main details.
A thinner marker line could be used for inner seams.

Step # 28

You can use for final outlining two different markers.
A thicker marker line could be used for the basic shape, and main details.
A thinner marker line could be used for inner seams.

Terminology for notched collar
Single breasted closure

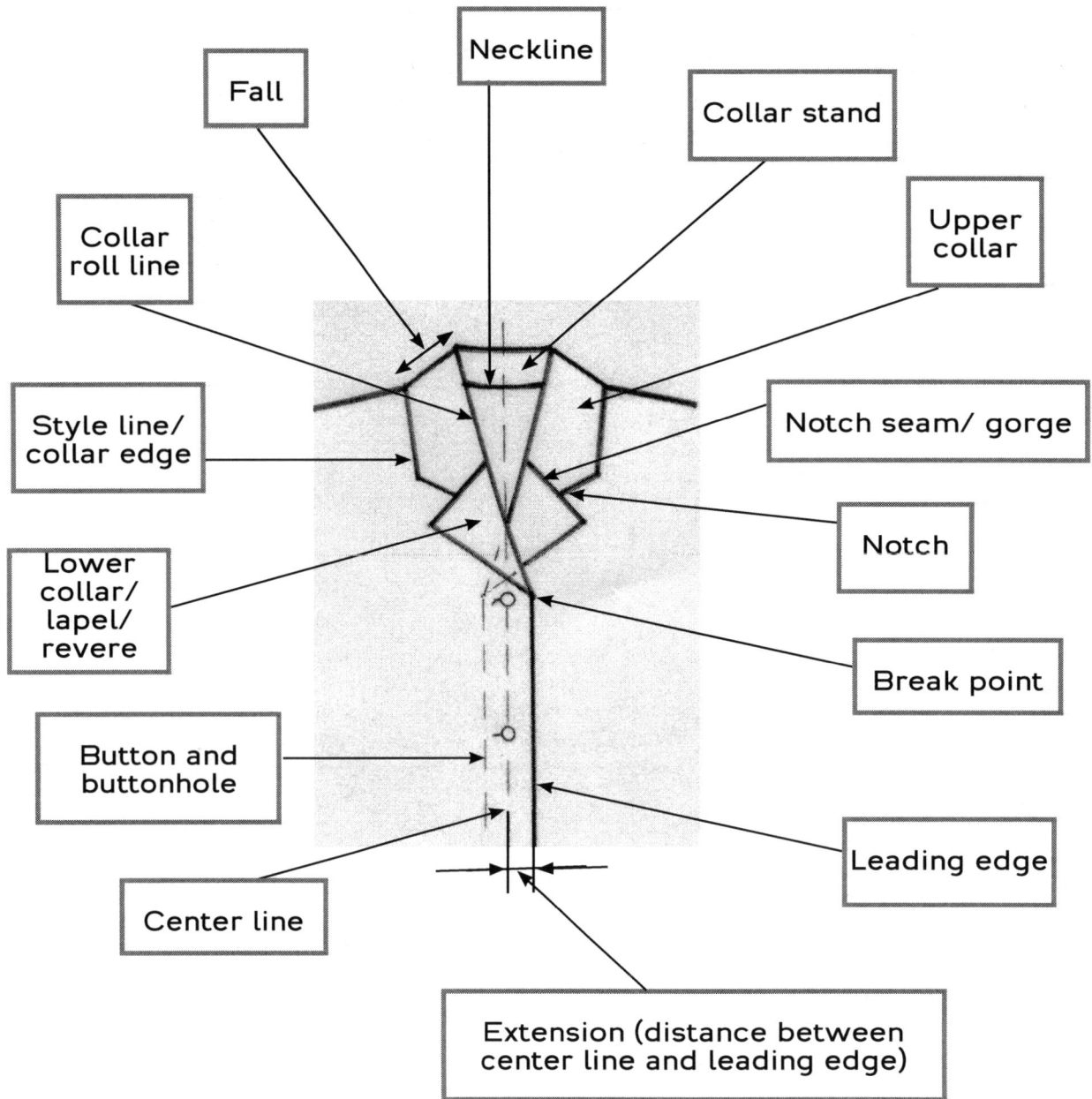

Neckline

Fall

Collar stand

Collar roll line

Upper collar

Style line/ collar edge

Notch seam/ gorge

Notch

Lower collar/ lapel/ revere

Break point

Button and buttonhole

Leading edge

Center line

Extension (distance between center line and leading edge)

128

© 2016 Irina V. Ivanova

Terminology for notched collar
Double breasted closure

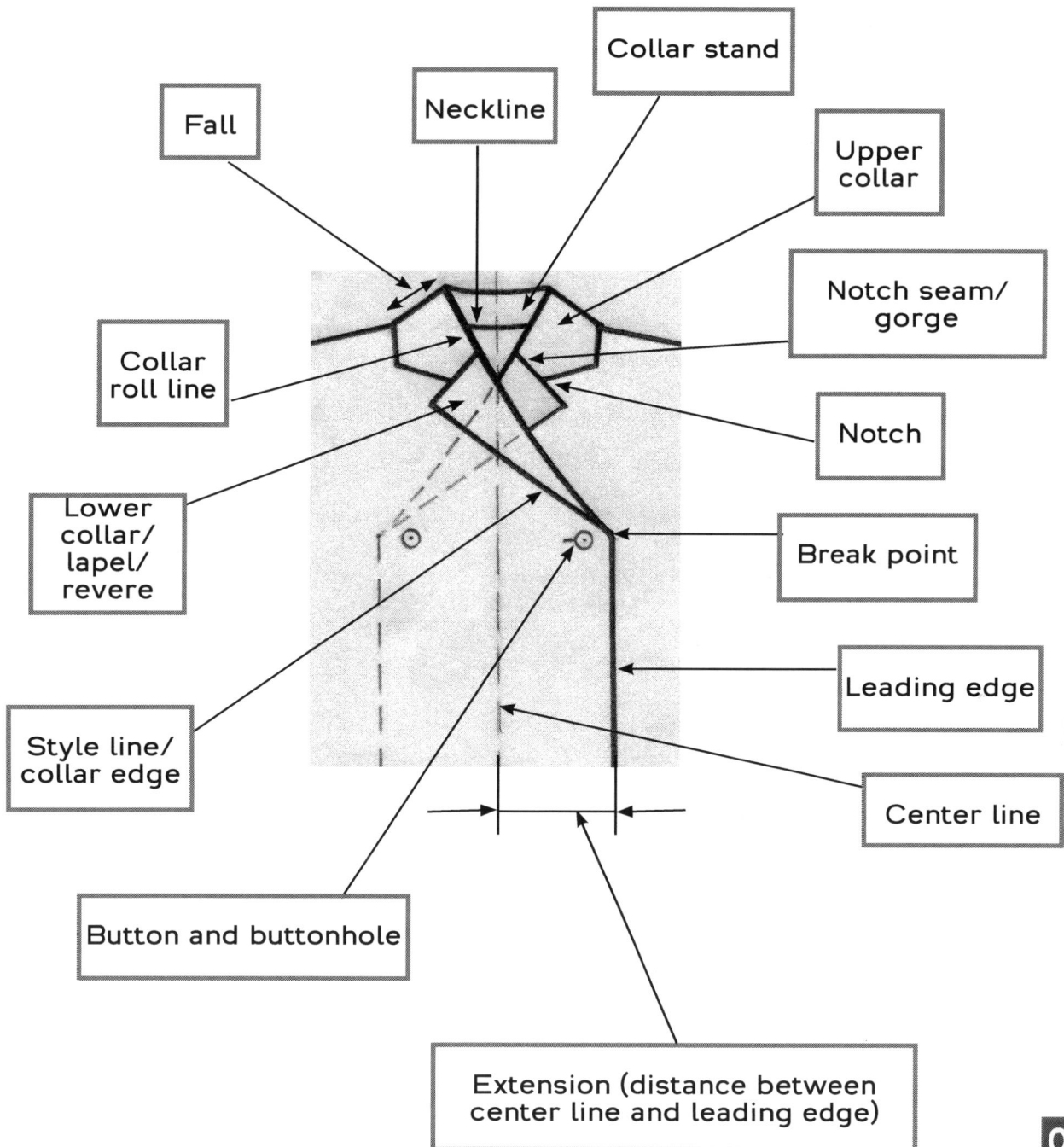

Collar stand

Neckline

Fall

Upper collar

Notch seam/ gorge

Collar roll line

Notch

Lower collar/ lapel/ revere

Break point

Leading edge

Style line/ collar edge

Center line

Button and buttonhole

Extension (distance between center line and leading edge)

How to draw buttoned closures

- For all **single breasted closures**, the buttons are precisely on the center line of the garment.
- For all **double breasted closures**, the center line of the garment is between the buttons.
- Space between buttons on the garment must be **equally distributed**.
- **Buttonholes** on the garment must be depicted.
- **Leading edge** must have an **extension** from the line of buttons.
- The size of the **buttonhole must be correlated** with the size of the button.

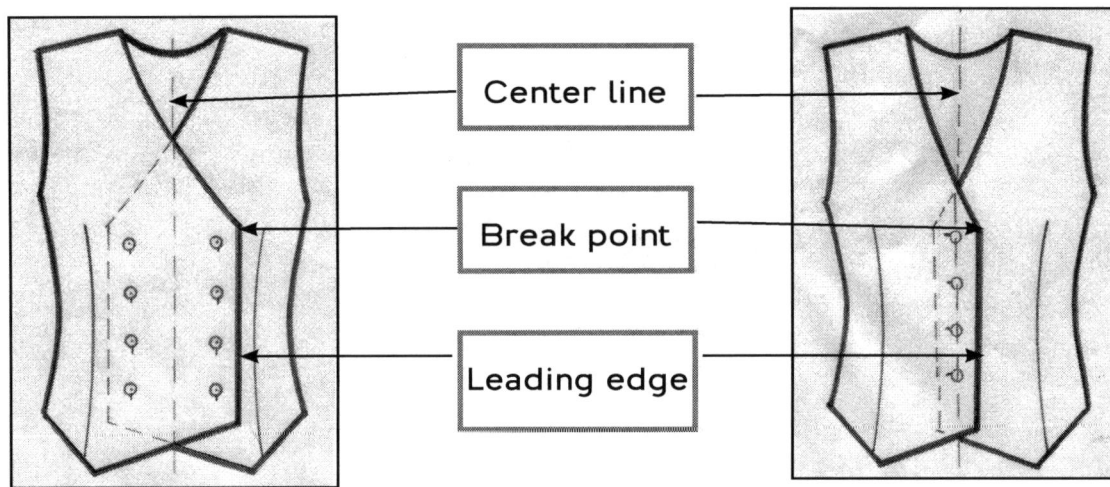

Center line

Break point

Leading edge

Double breasted closure
(keep buttons at the same distance from the center line).

Single breasted closure
(keep buttons on the center line).

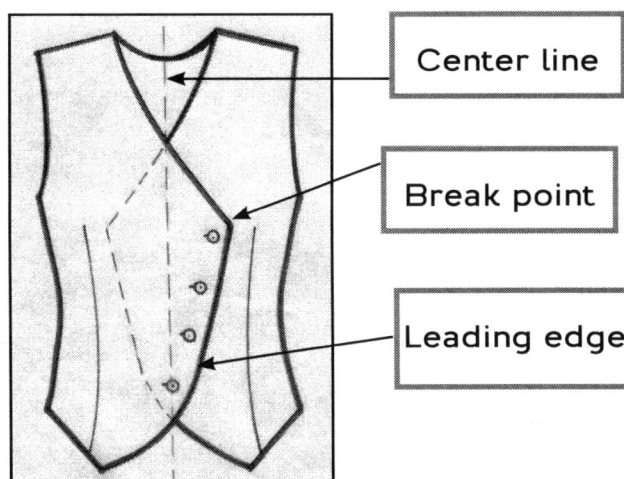

Center line

Break point

Leading edge

Asymmetrical closure
(keep at least one button on the center line).

How to draw buttons and buttonholes

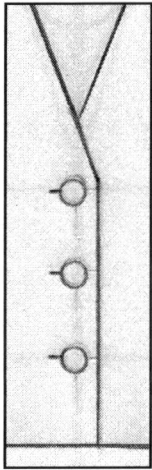

Horizontal buttonholes
for single breasted closure.

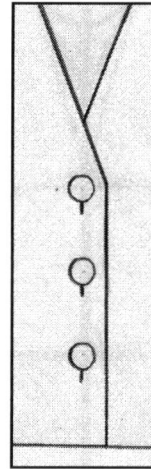

Vertical buttonholes
for single breasted closure.

Common mistakes in buttons and buttonholes drawing

Center line

Buttonholes are too close to leading edge.

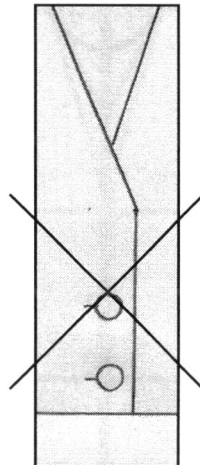

Buttonholes are too long.

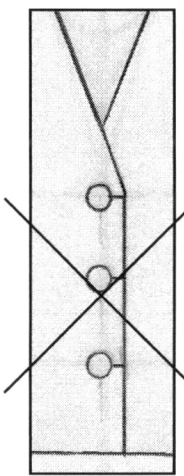

Buttons are too close to leading edge.

Buttons are too far from break point.

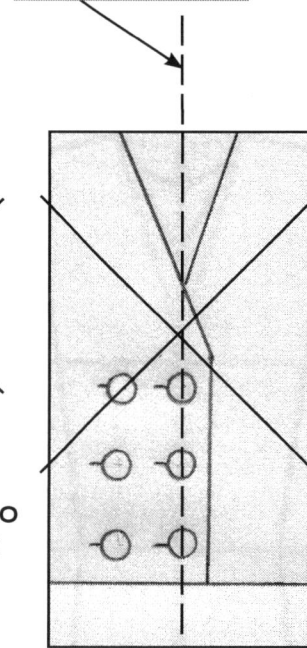

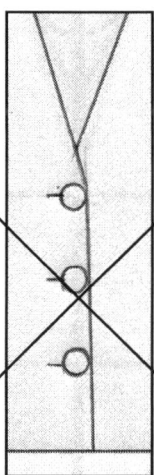

Buttons are shifted out of the center line.

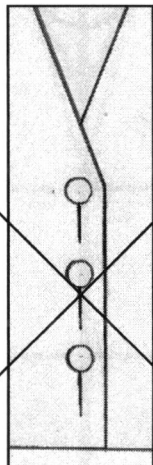

How to draw shawl collar

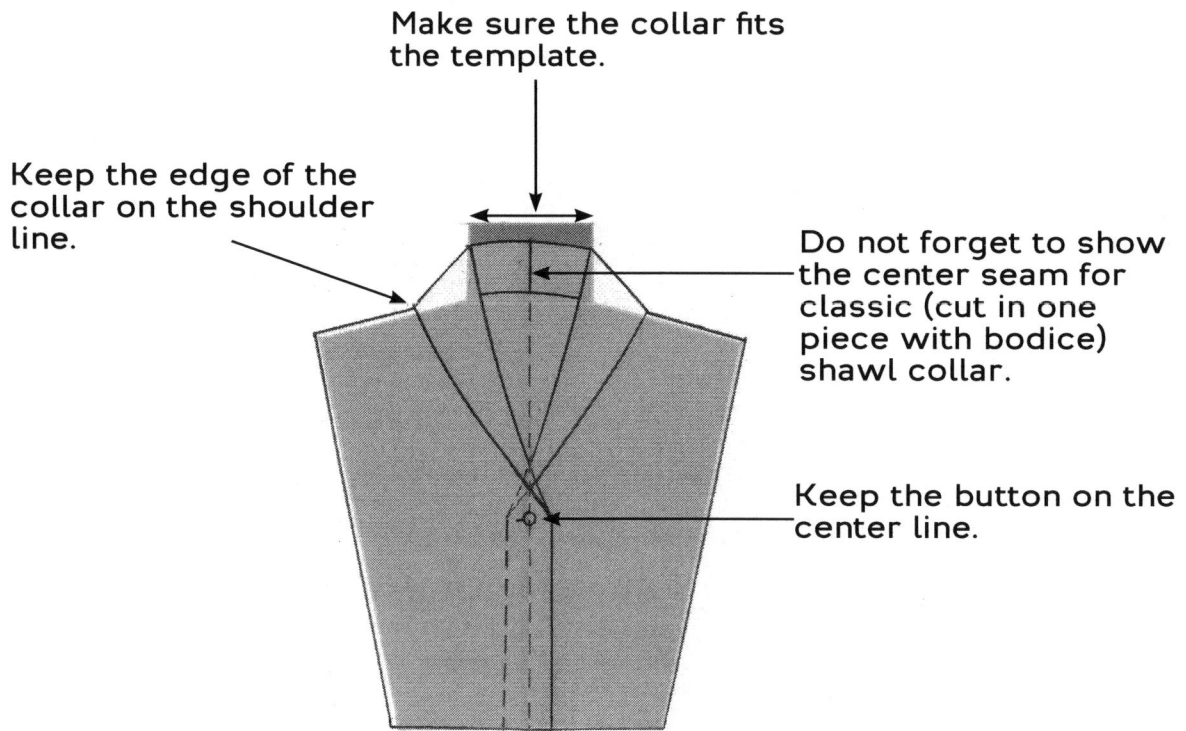

Make sure the collar fits the template.

Keep the edge of the collar on the shoulder line.

Do not forget to show the center seam for classic (cut in one piece with bodice) shawl collar.

Keep the button on the center line.

How to show thickness of fabric

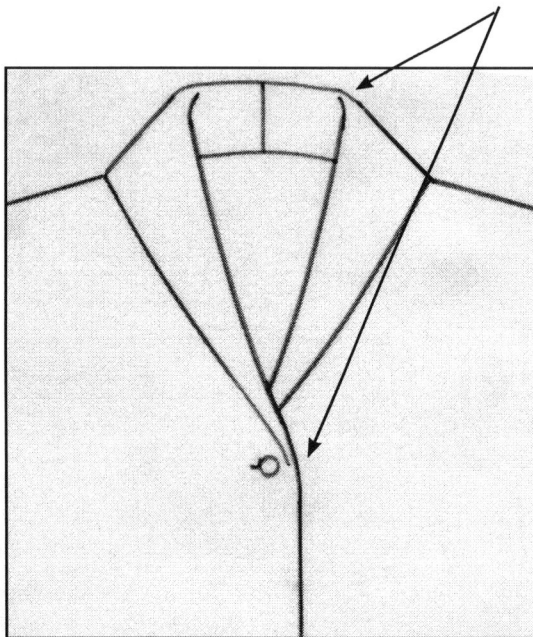

How to show thick fabric.

How to show thin fabric.

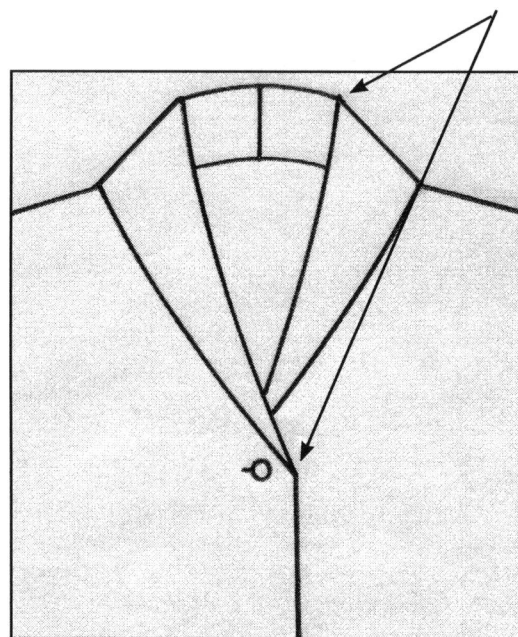

132

Show center seam on the flat for classic shawl collar (cut in one piece with bodice).

A

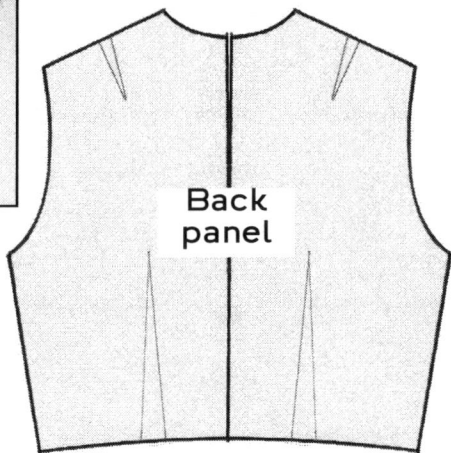

Back panel

Shawl collar.

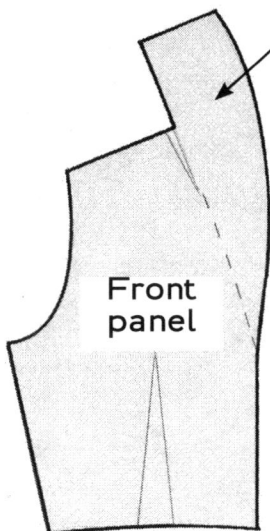

Front panel

Front panel

**Patterns for classic shawl collar
(cut in one piece with bodice).**

Do not show center seam on the flat for shawl collar cut separately from bodice.

B

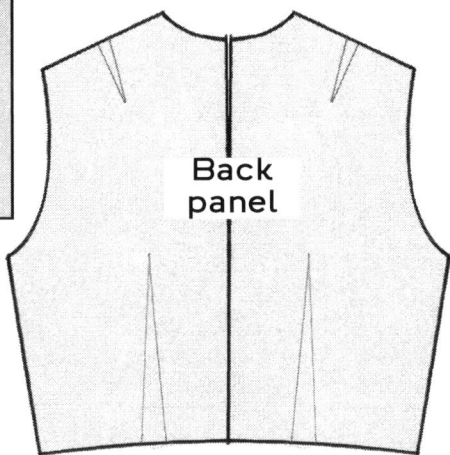

Back panel

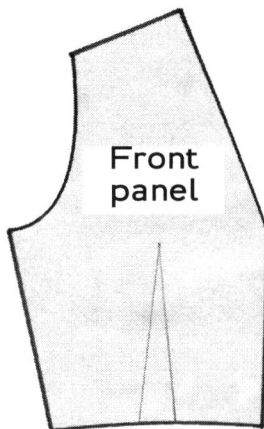

Front panel

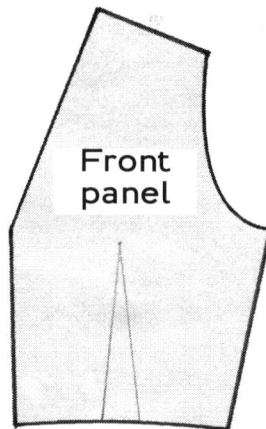

Front panel

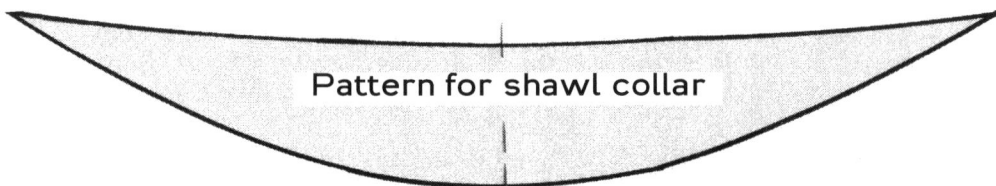

Pattern for shawl collar

**Patterns for shawl collar
(cut separately from bodice).**

Jacket: darts and gores

Two different ways to design darts

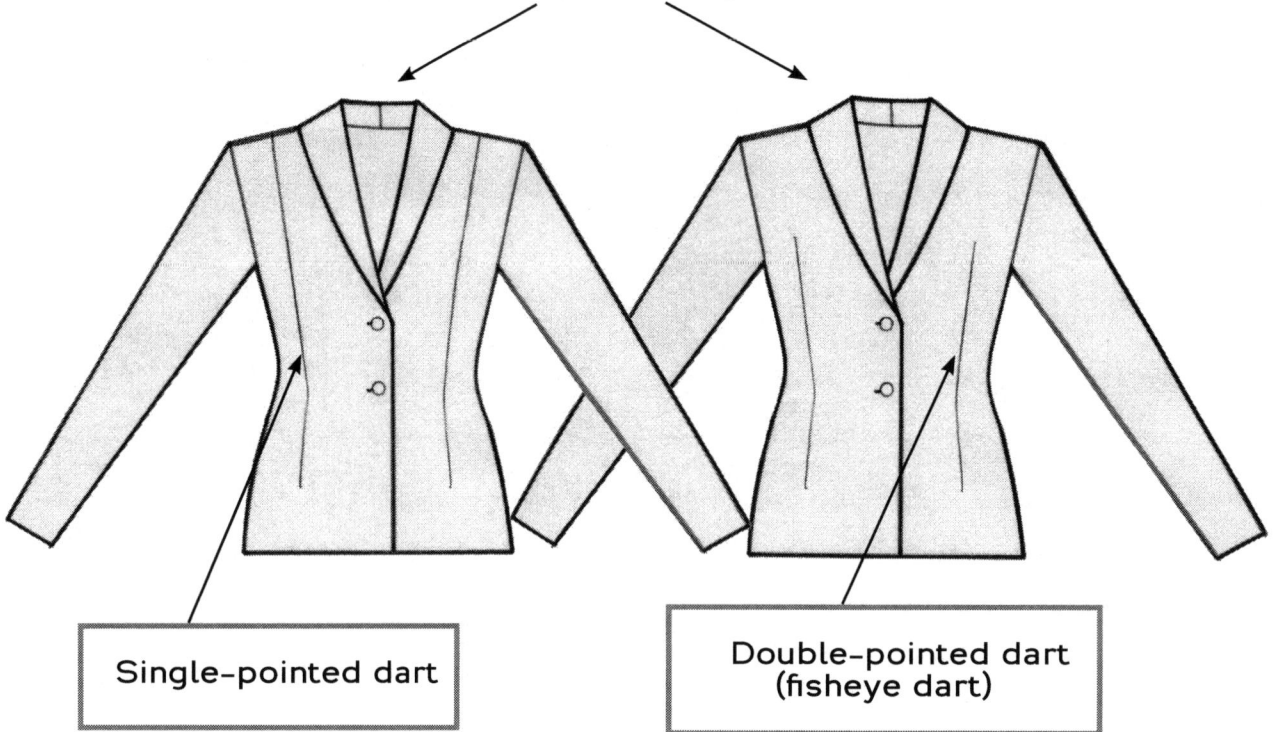

Single-pointed dart

Dart is connected with one of the garment seams (shoulder seam in this case).

Double-pointed dart (fisheye dart)

Fisheye dart (double-pointed) is only dart which has no connections with any garment seams and placed within the shape of the garment.

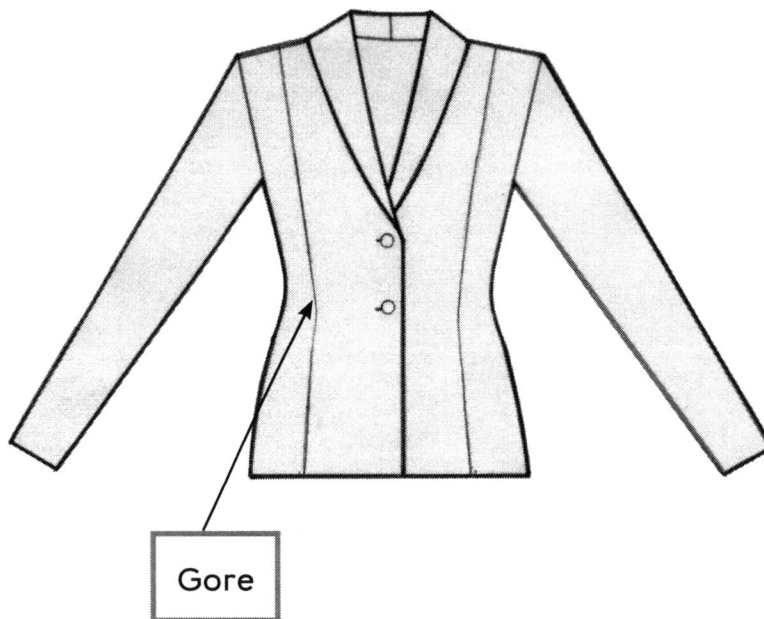

Gore

All gores are always originated and ended at seams or edge lines, which resulting in two or more panels of garment.

© 2016 Irina V. Ivanova

How to draw vest with pointed hemline

Preliminary look (inner structure) of single breasted vest.

Final look of single breasted vest.

Single breasted vest

Preliminary look (inner structure) of double breasted vest.

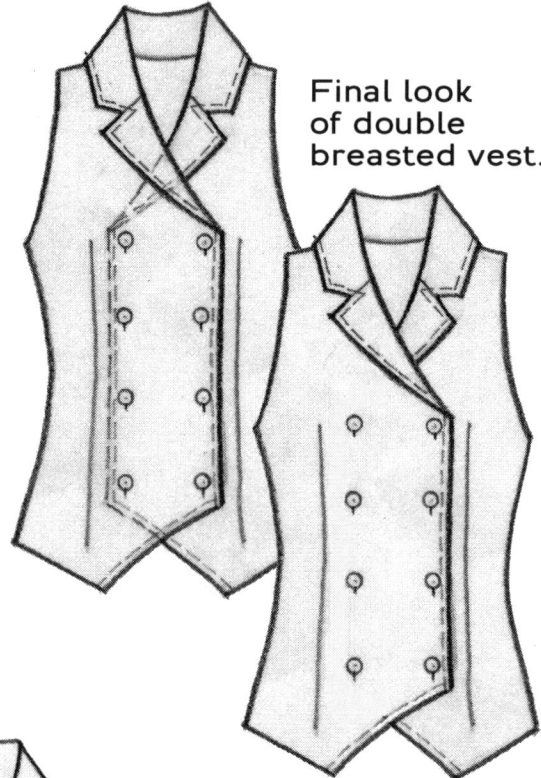

Final look of double breasted vest.

Double breasted vest

Preliminary look (inner structure) of vest with double breasted V-shaped closure.

Final look of vest with double breasted V-shaped closure.

Vest with double breasted V-shaped closure

135

Common mistakes in drawing of flats for jackets

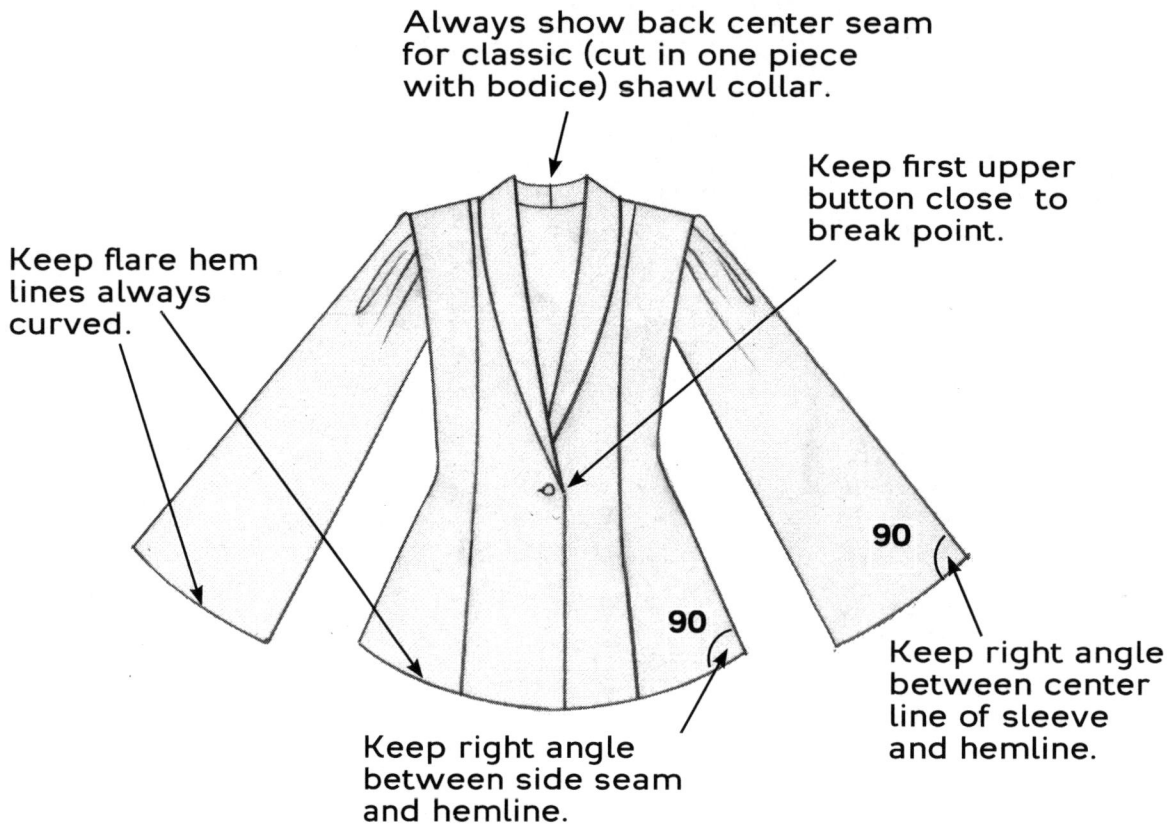

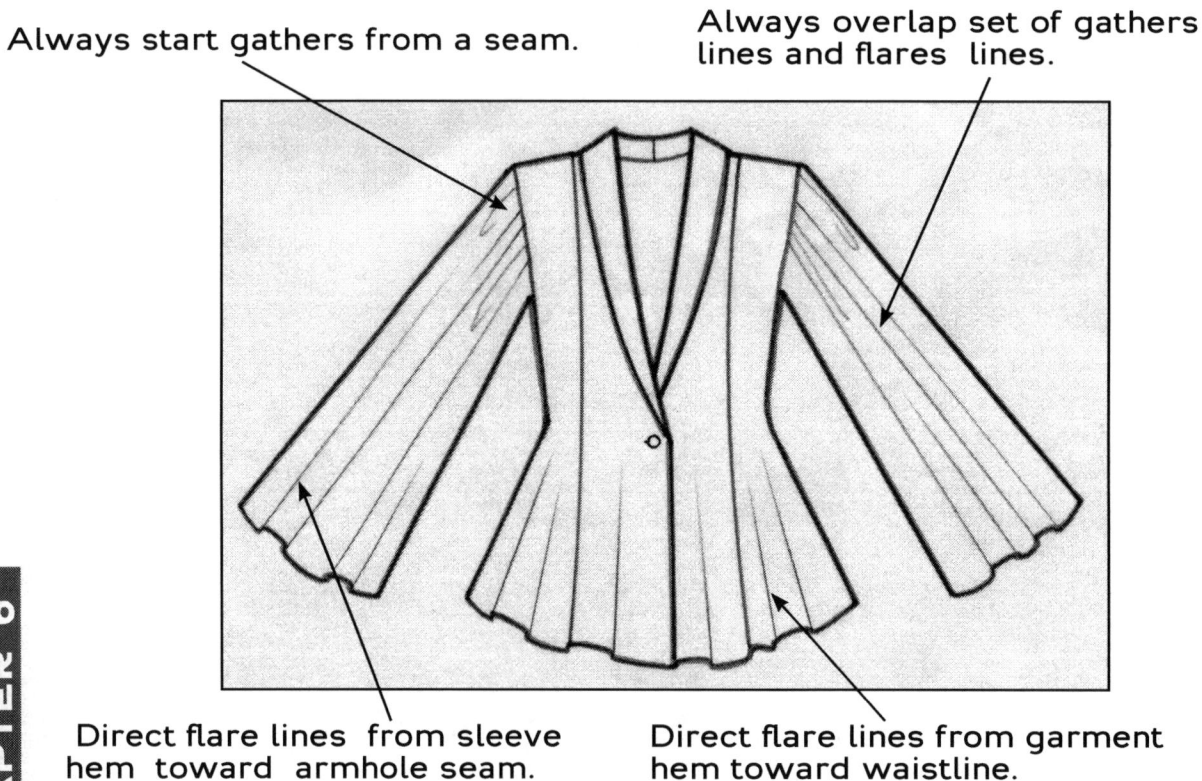

Always show back center seam for classic (cut in one piece with bodice) shawl collar.

Keep first upper button close to break point.

Keep flare hem lines always curved.

90

Keep right angle between center line of sleeve and hemline.

90

Keep right angle between side seam and hemline.

Always start gathers from a seam.

Always overlap set of gathers lines and flares lines.

Direct flare lines from sleeve hem toward armhole seam.

Direct flare lines from garment hem toward waistline.

Classic shawl collar should have center back seam.

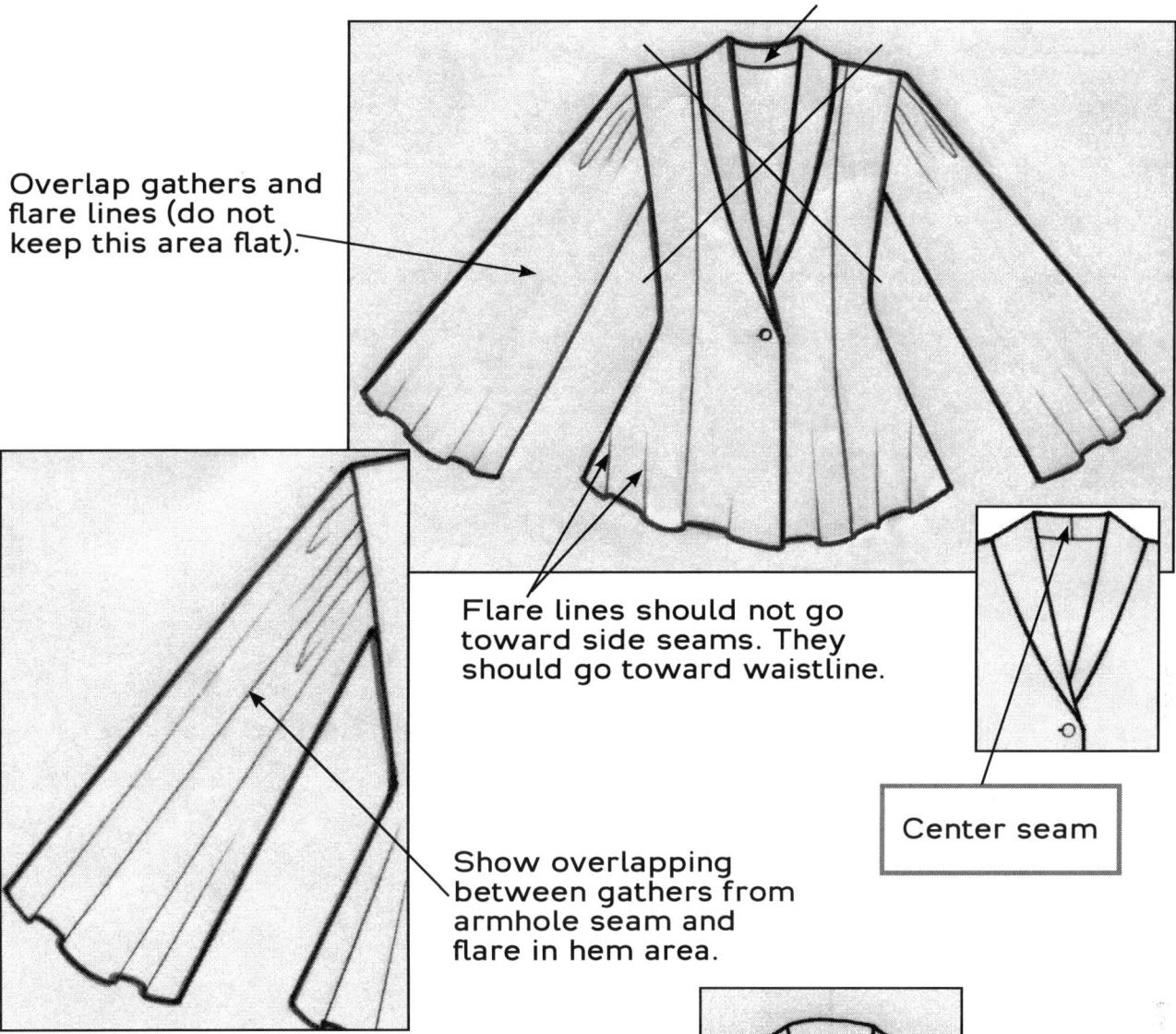

Overlap gathers and flare lines (do not keep this area flat).

Flare lines should not go toward side seams. They should go toward waistline.

Center seam

Show overlapping between gathers from armhole seam and flare in hem area.

Notched collar should have notch seam.

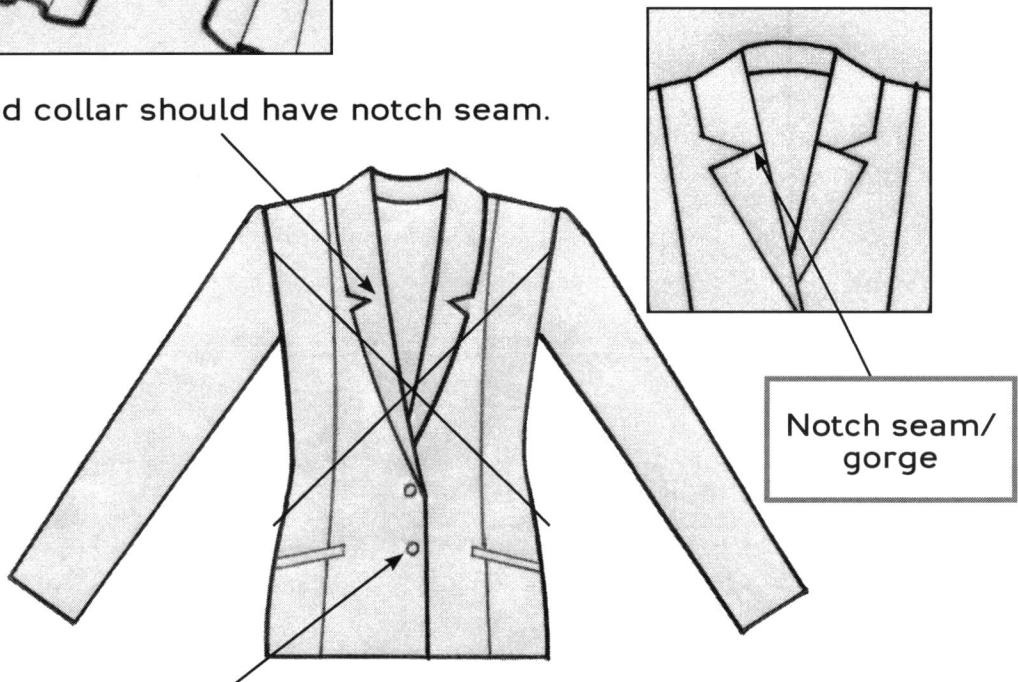

Notch seam/ gorge

Buttons should be shown with buttonholes.

Jacket fitted with gores.

Jacket fitted with darts.

Gore

Dart

Tip

Do not show fitted jackets without darts or gores.

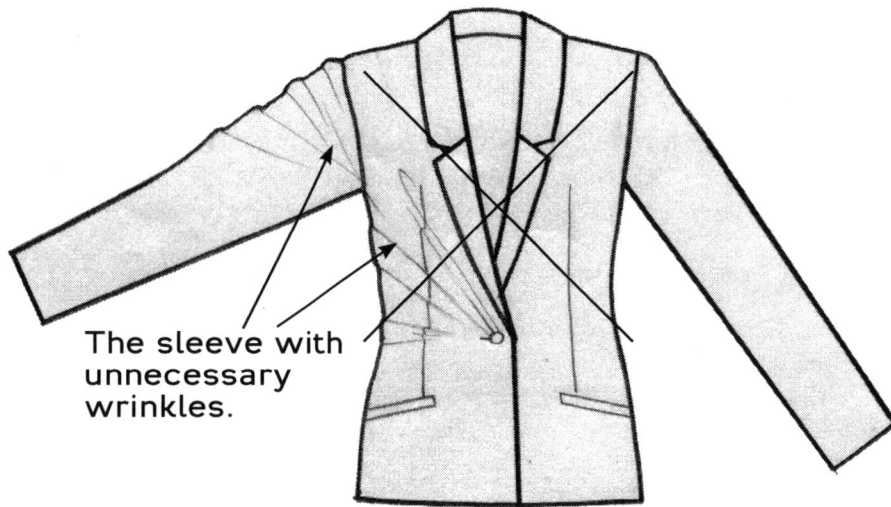

The sleeve with unnecessary wrinkles.

Pick the right template with the best arm movement to show the sleeve.

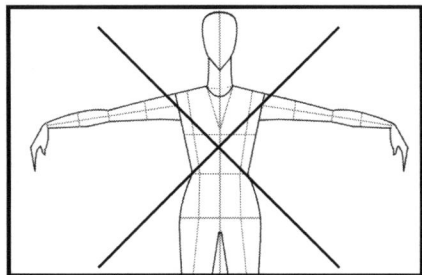

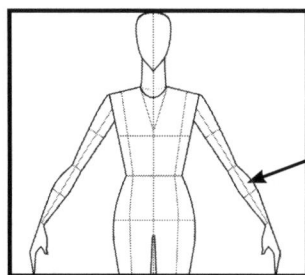

The best arm movement to show the sleeve for jacket without distortions.

138

Two different ways to draw roll line and neckline

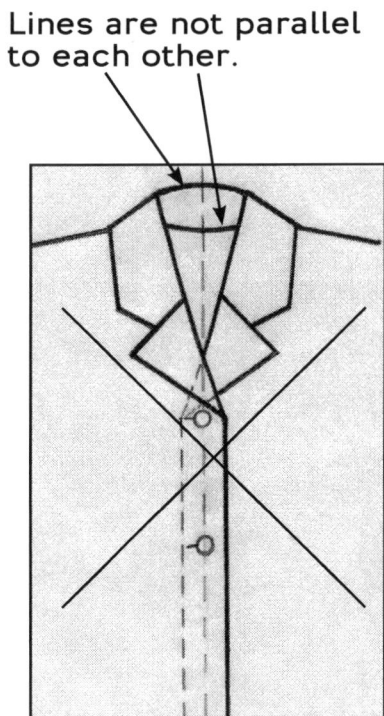

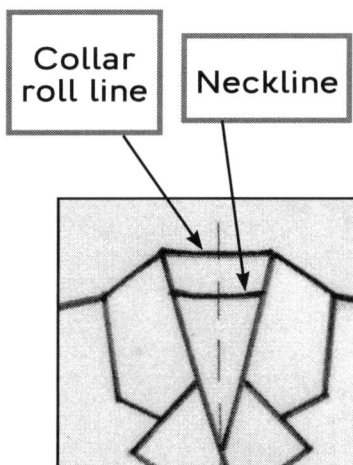

Lines are not parallel to each other.

| Collar roll line | Neckline |

Roll line and neckline are both curved down.

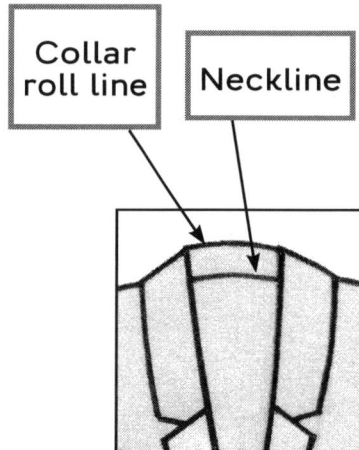

| Collar roll line | Neckline |

Roll line and neckline are both curved up.

Tip

Always keep both lines (roll line and neckline) parallel to each other.

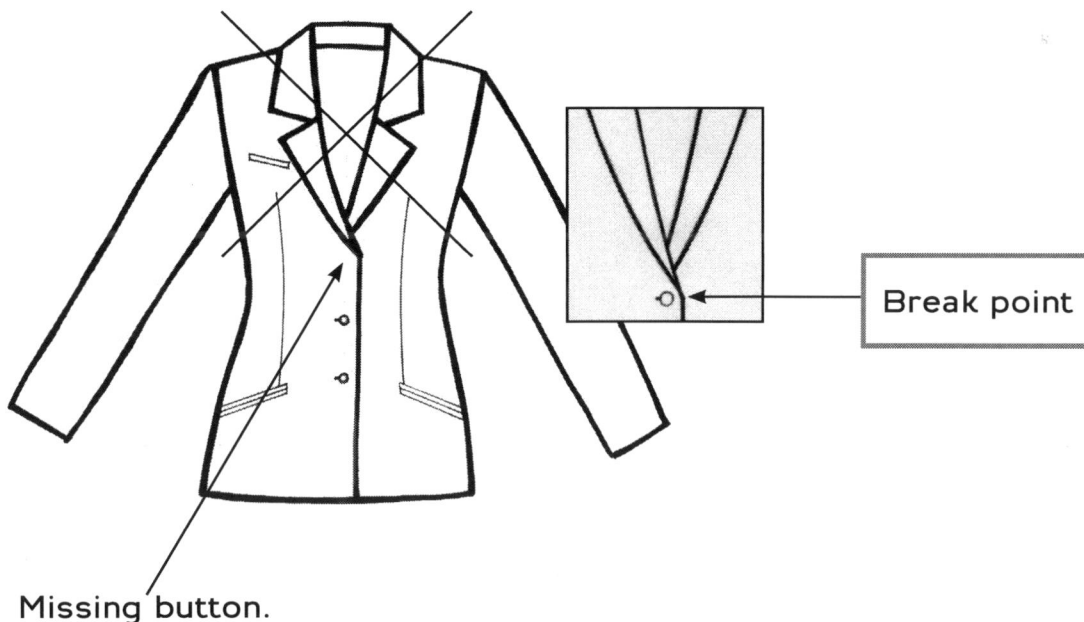

Break point

Missing button.

First button should be placed next to the break point or in the end of a lapel.

Collars

Family of collars:

- **Stand collar**
- **Flat collar**
- **Rolled collar**

Stand collars

Stand collars are started from the neckline and go up without laying on the shoulders.
Stand could be partial (only for back neckline) or complete (for front and back necklines).

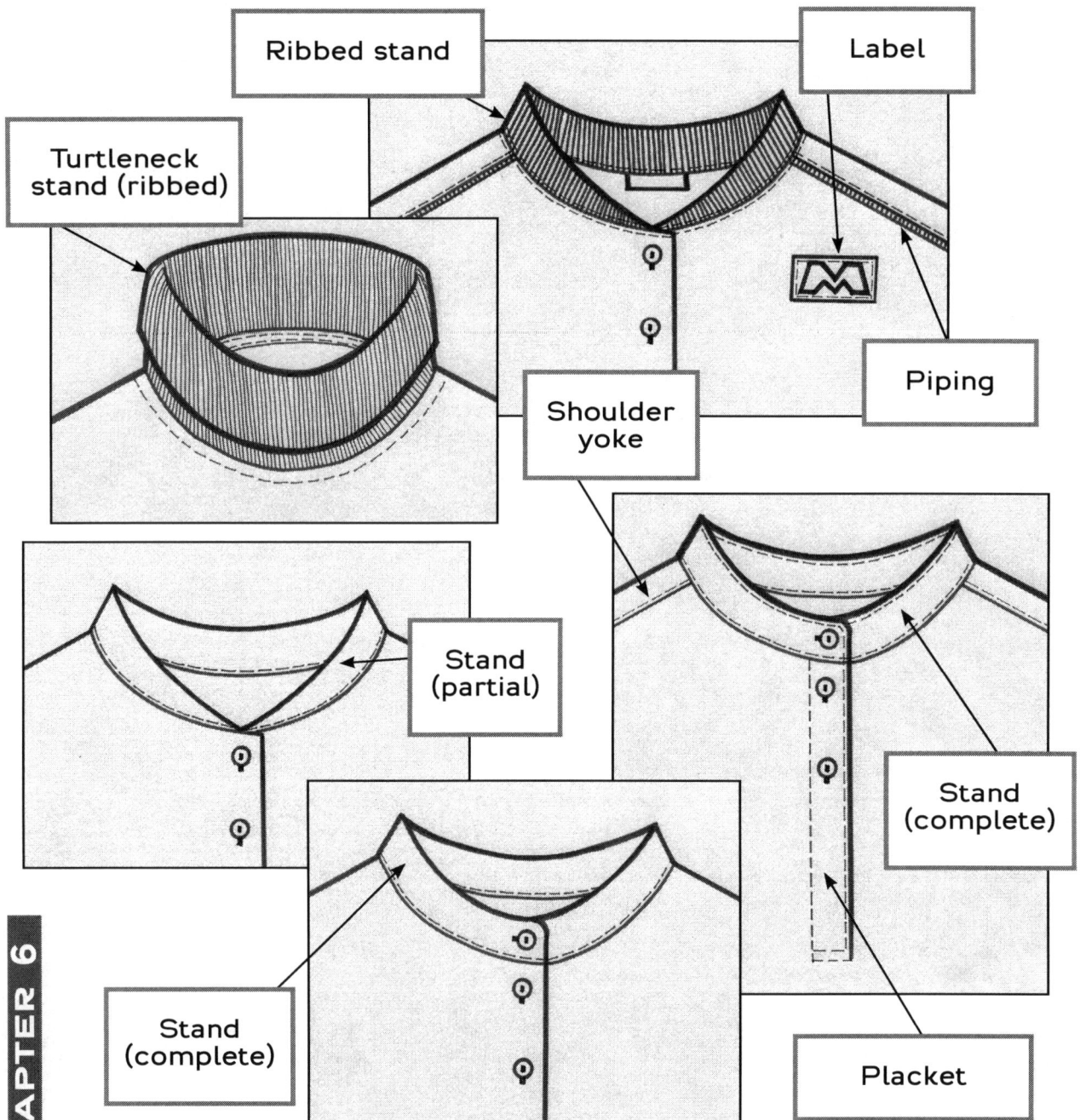

Ribbed stand

Label

Turtleneck stand (ribbed)

Piping

Shoulder yoke

Stand (partial)

Stand (complete)

Stand (complete)

Placket

Flat collars

Flat collars are started from the necklines and cover shoulder seams without rising up.

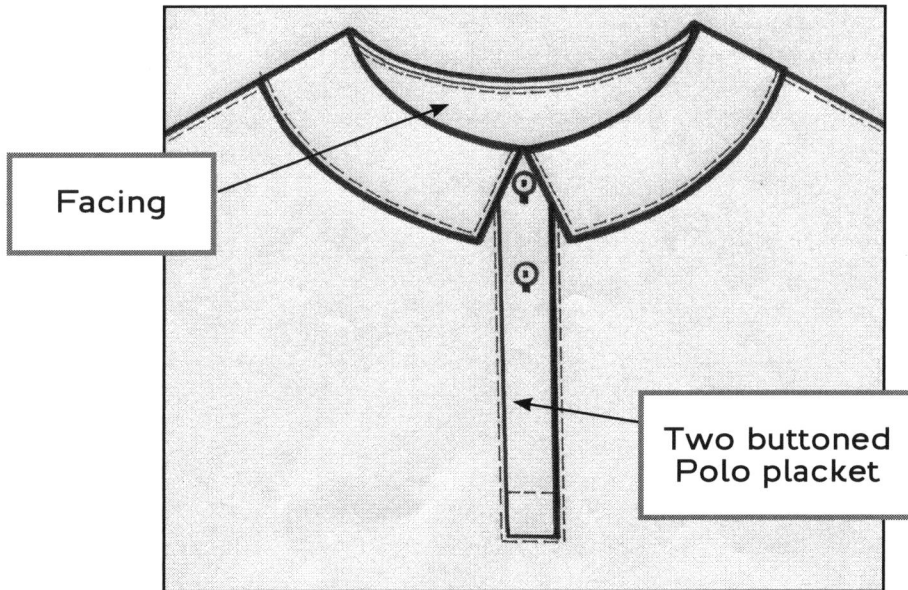

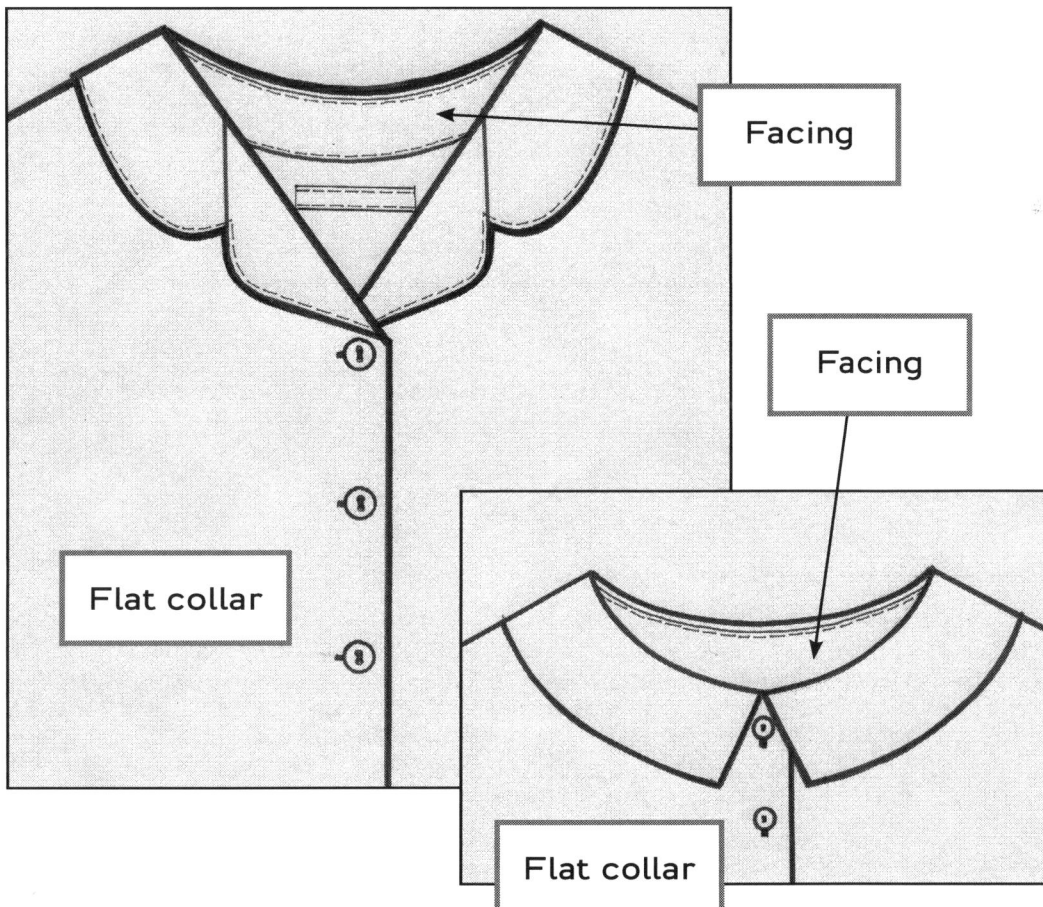

Facing

Two buttoned
Polo placket

Facing

Facing

Flat collar

Flat collar

Rolled collars

Rolled collars are started from the neckline, go up with stand, and rolled down on shoulder seams.

Stand for rolled collar could be cut separately or together with collar.

Stand could be **partial** (only for back neckline) or **complete** (for front and back necklines).

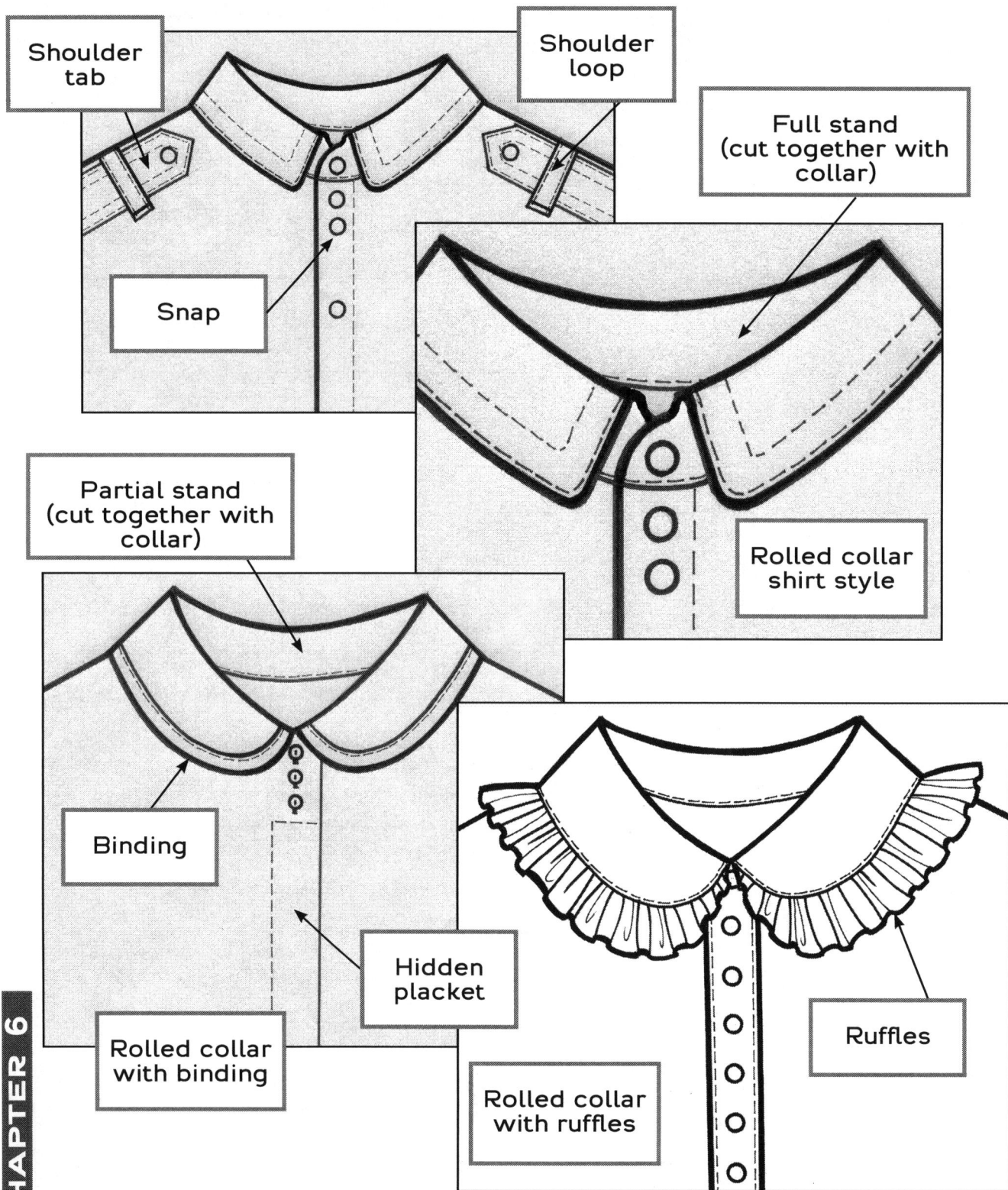

Shoulder tab

Shoulder loop

Full stand (cut together with collar)

Snap

Rolled collar shirt style

Partial stand (cut together with collar)

Binding

Hidden placket

Rolled collar with binding

Ruffles

Rolled collar with ruffles

How to Draw Fashion Flats A practical guide to fashion technical drawing **by Irina V. Ivanova**

CHAPTER 6

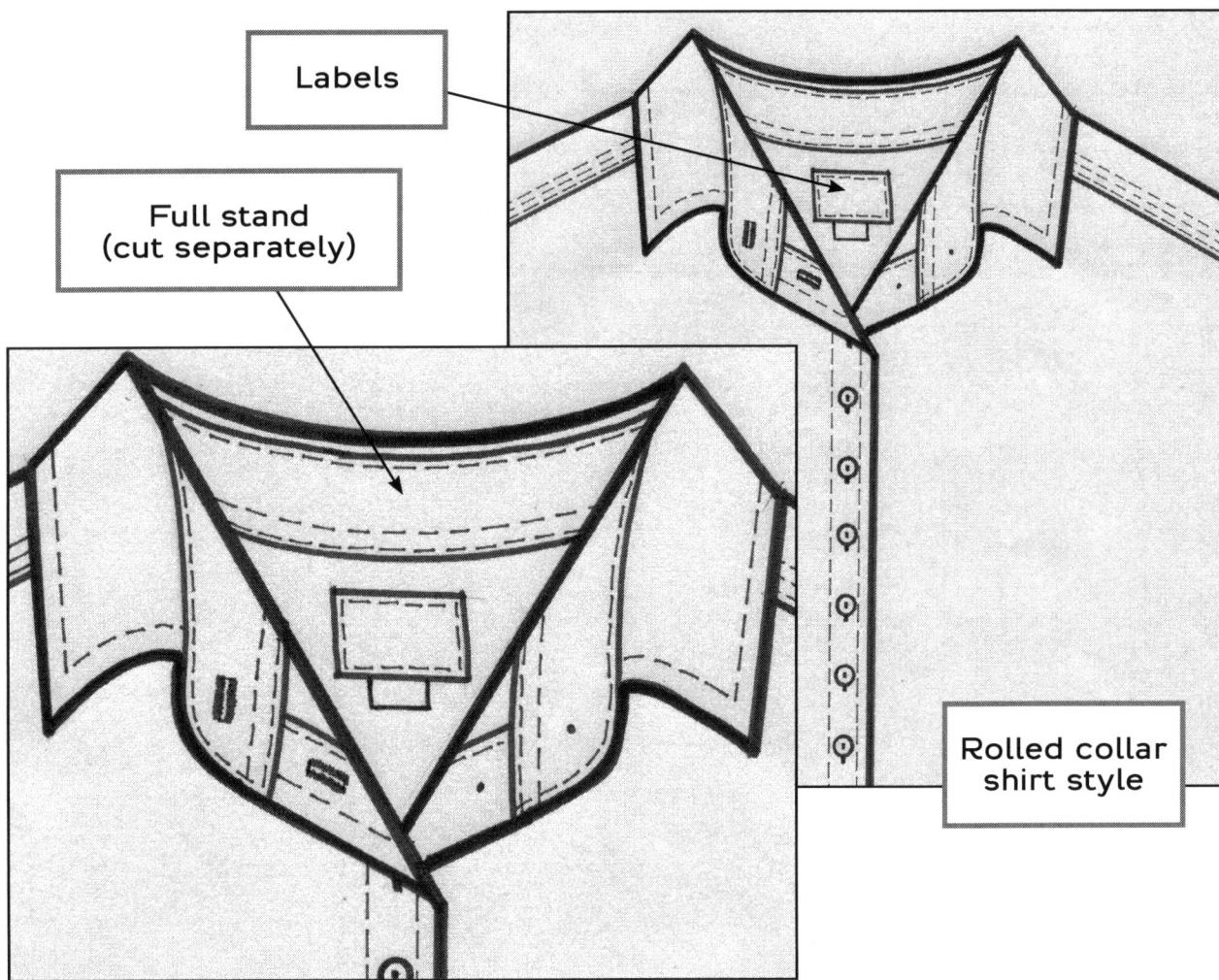

Labels

Full stand
(cut separately)

Rolled collar
shirt style

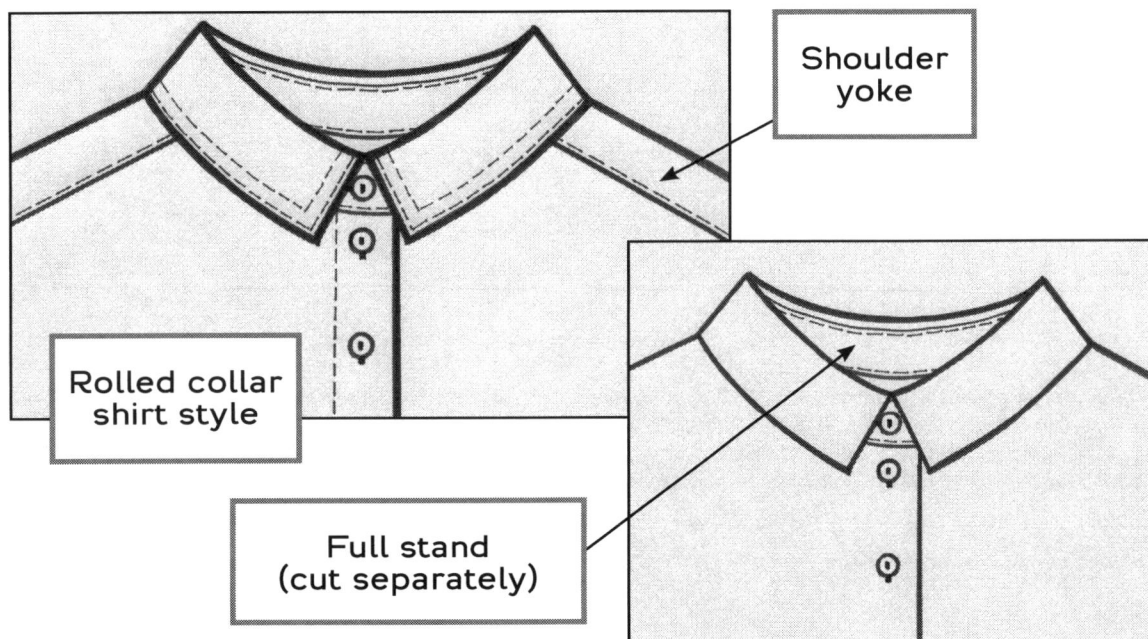

Shoulder
yoke

Rolled collar
shirt style

Full stand
(cut separately)

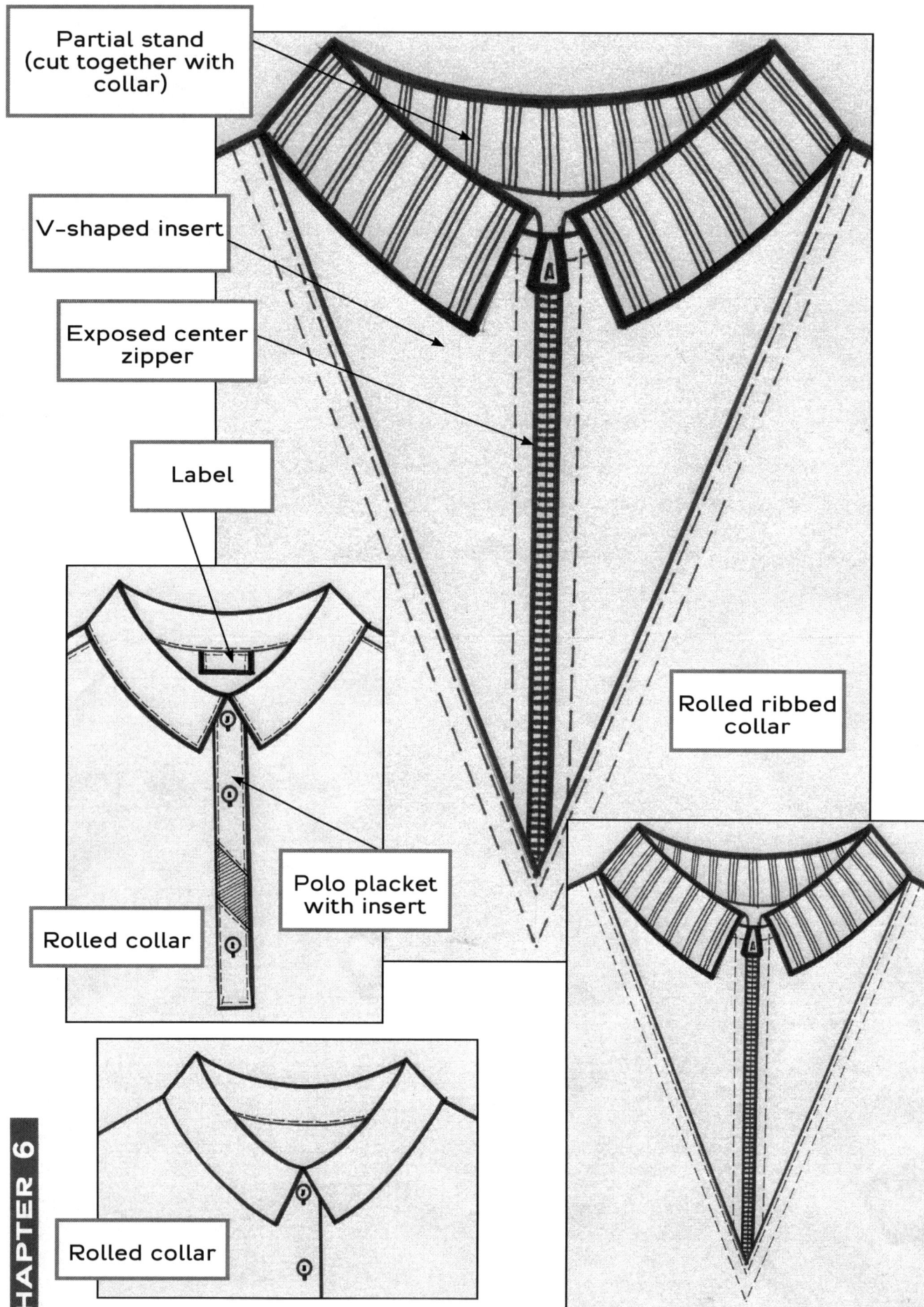

Partial stand
(cut together with
collar)

V-shaped insert

Exposed center
zipper

Label

Rolled ribbed
collar

Rolled collar

Polo placket
with insert

Rolled collar

Cuffs and plackets for sleeves

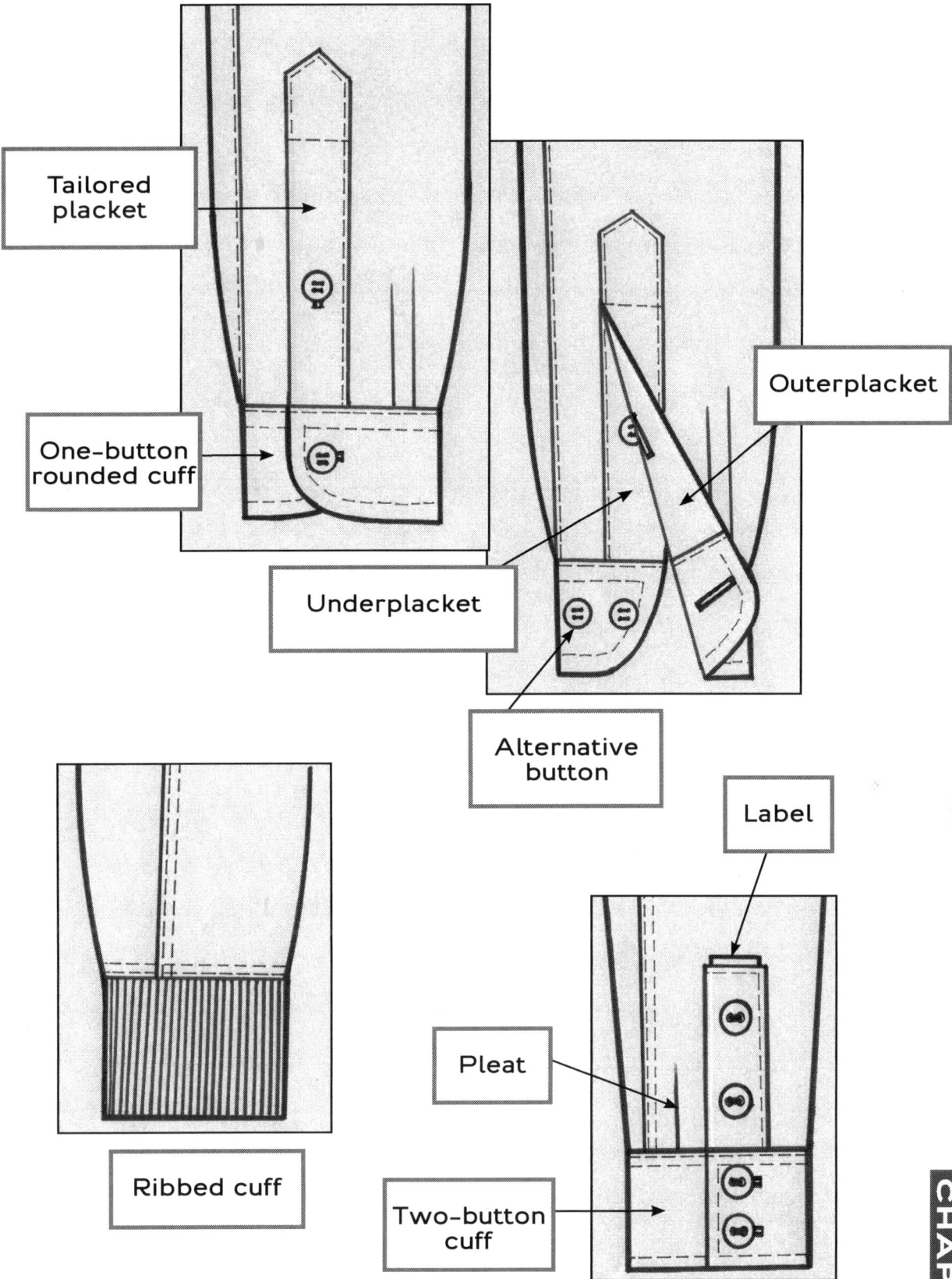

Tailored placket

One-button rounded cuff

Outerplacket

Underplacket

Alternative button

Label

Pleat

Two-button cuff

Ribbed cuff

Chapter 7

Swimwear

Swimwear

Basic shapes for bikini bra front views

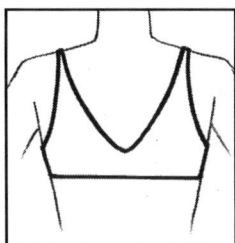

Standard
(straight up straps).

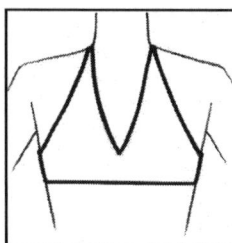

Halter style bra
(with ties behind
the neck).

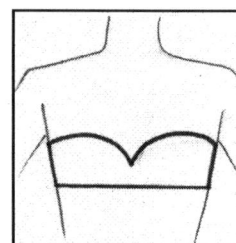

Strapless style
bra.

Basic shapes for bikini bottom back views

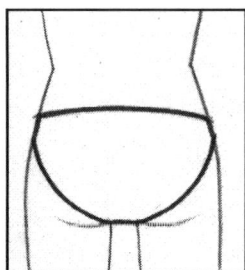

Moderate
coverage.

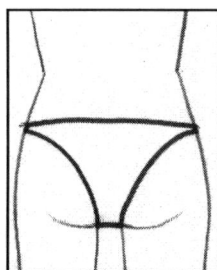

Brazilian cut
(low coverage).

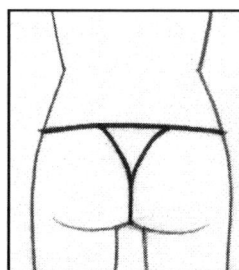

Thong (minimum
coverage).

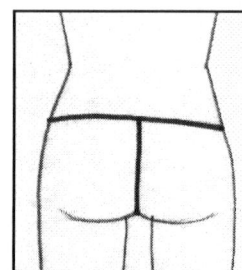

G-string
(no coverage).

Gallery of basic swimsuits

> ### Two-piece swimsuits

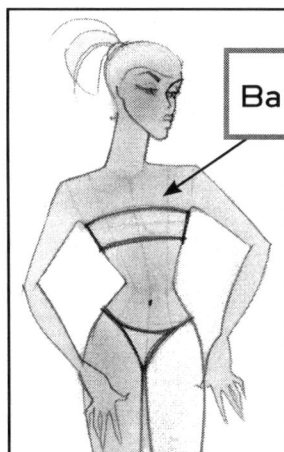

Bandeau

Bandeau is a strapless top.

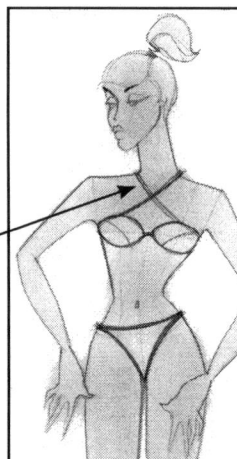

Cross
front

Cross front is
top piece with
criss-cross
straps.

Halter

Boy
shorts

Boy shorts or hot pants is a swimsuit bottom with a lower leg cut.

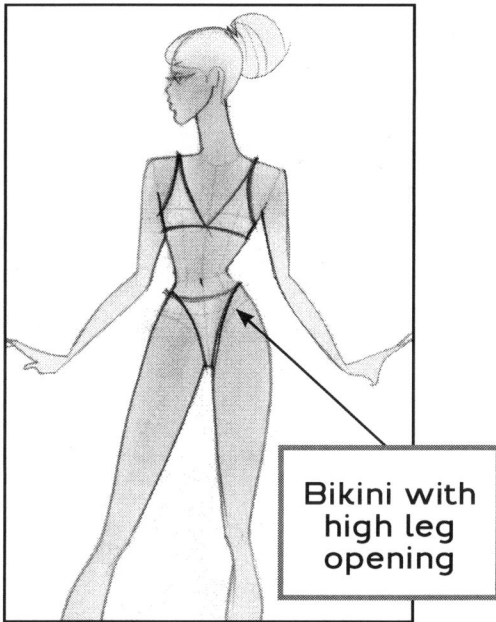

Bikini with high leg opening

Bikini is a two-piece swimsuit for women.

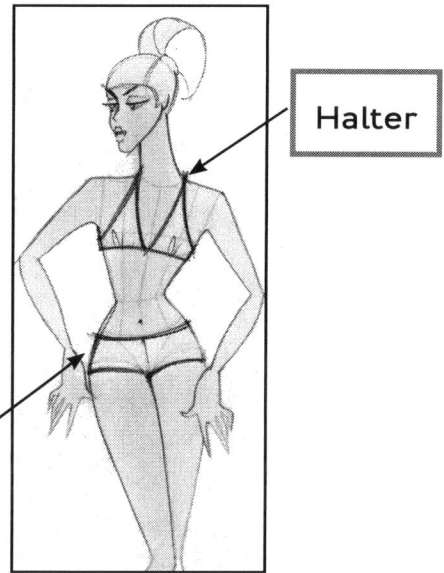

One-piece swimsuits

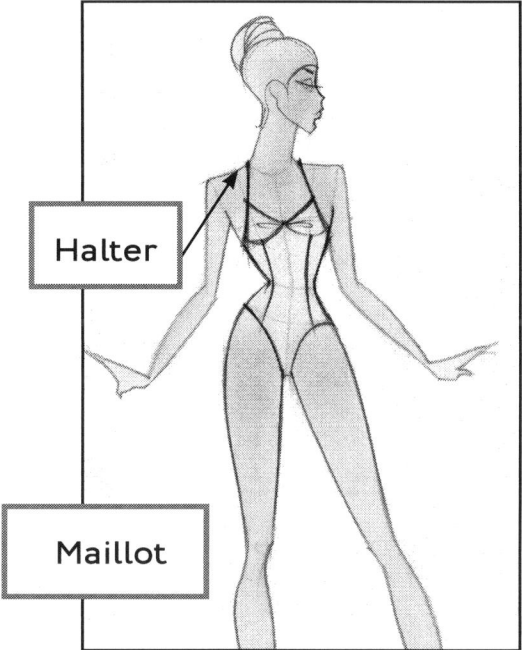

Halter

Maillot

Maillot is just another name for one-piece swimsuit.

Leotard could be designed with or without sleeves and legs.

Leotard

Leotard is a close-fitting garment made of a stretchy fabric and worn by dancers or athletes.

CHAPTER 7

How to design different bikini bottom shapes:

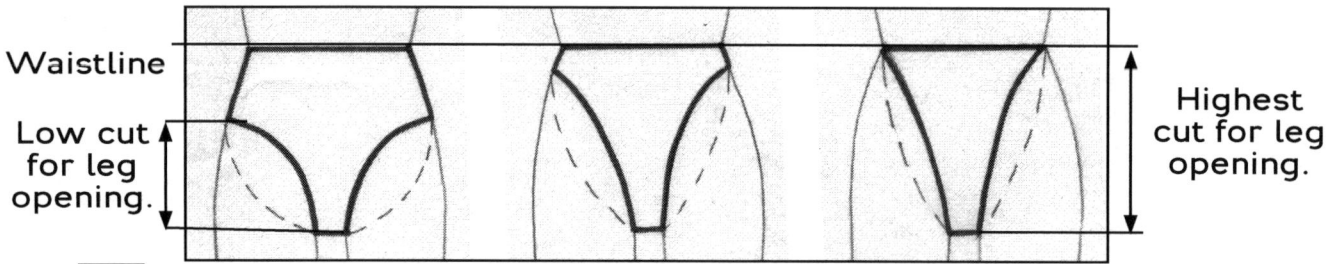

Waistline

Low cut for leg opening.

Highest cut for leg opening.

A – by moving leg cut.

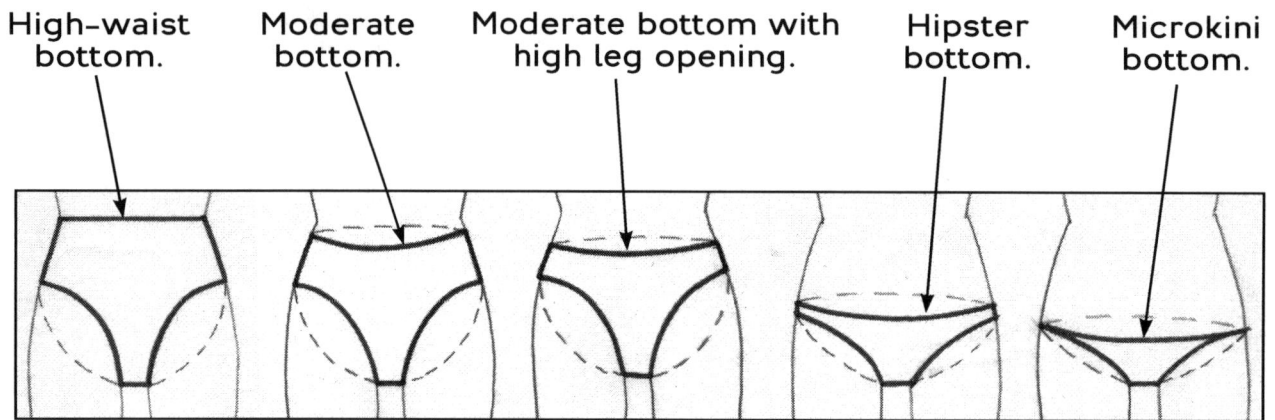

High-waist bottom.

Moderate bottom.

Moderate bottom with high leg opening.

Hipster bottom.

Microkini bottom.

B – by moving side seam down.

High-waist bottom is a swimsuit with waistline just below or above the belly button.

Moderate bottom is a swimsuit with average covering.

Hipster bottom is a swimsuit designed to sit low on the hips.

Microkini is a swimsuit bottom with extremely low coverage.

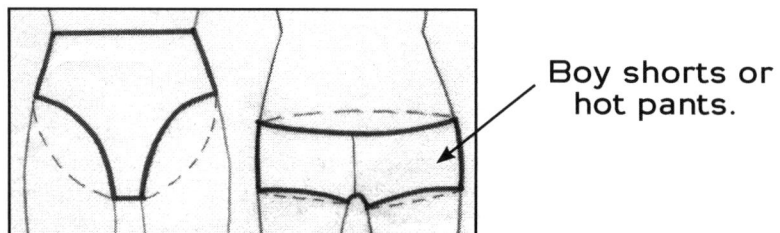

Boy shorts or hot pants.

C – by moving leg cut level (opening leg) and waistline down.

How to Draw Fashion Flats A practical guide to fashion technical drawing by Irina V. Ivanova

How to draw front view flat for swimwear
(simple pencil line)

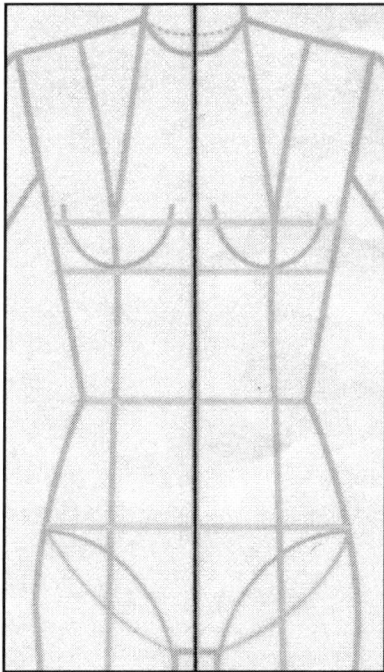

Step #1

Cover template with tracing paper and tape it to avoid shifting. Draw center line.

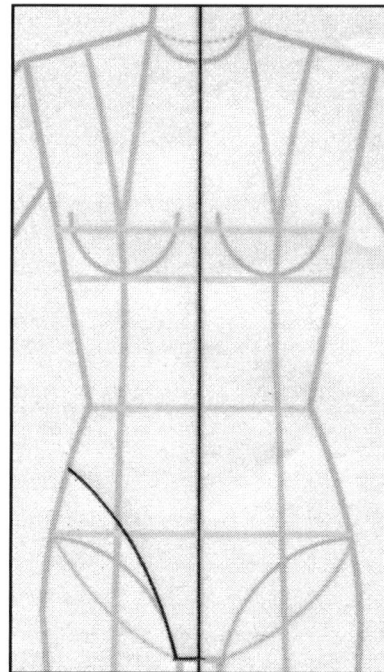

Step #2

Draw front leg opening and crotch seam.

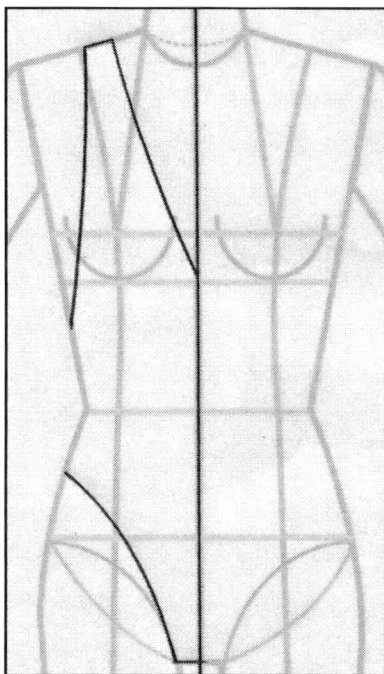

Step #3

Draw shoulder seam, neckline, and arm opening.

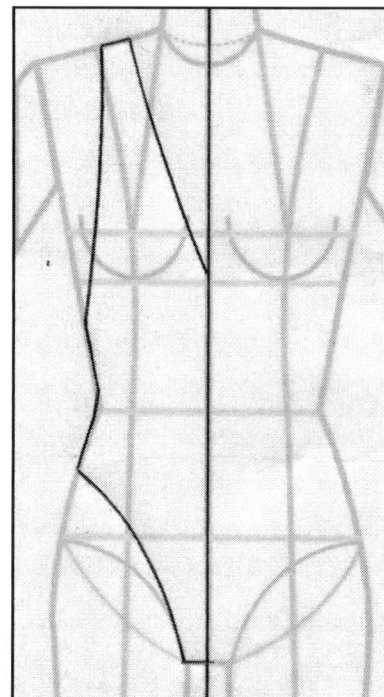

Step #4

Draw side line.

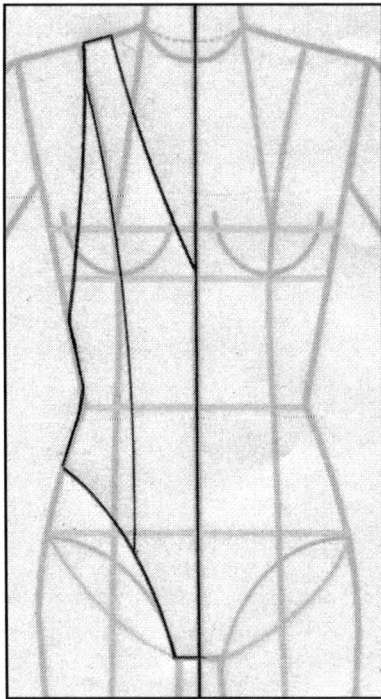

Step #5

Draw princess line.

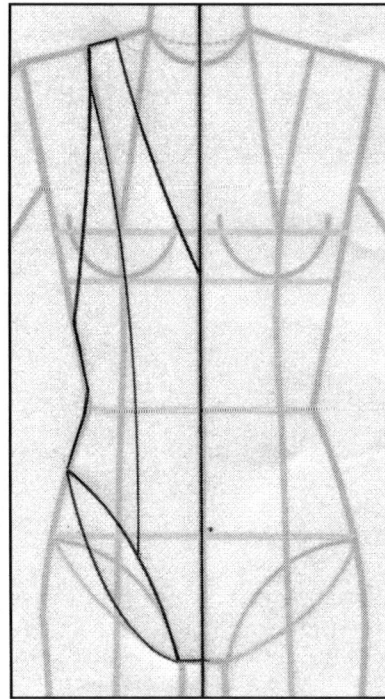

Step #6

Draw back leg opening.

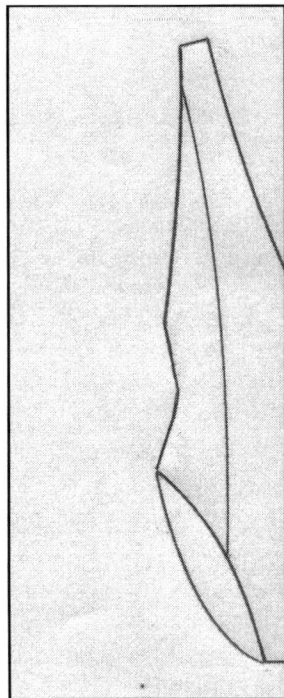

Step #7

Fold your flat along the center line and trace second half.

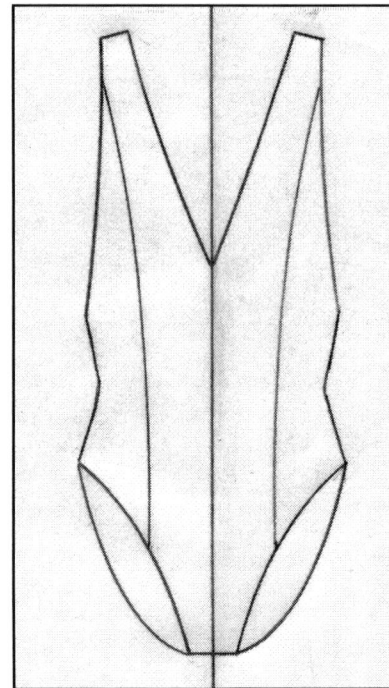

Step #8

So, front view of the flat is completed! It is time to do corrections if needed.

Now we are ready to do back view flat.

How to draw back view flat for swimwear
(simple pencil line)

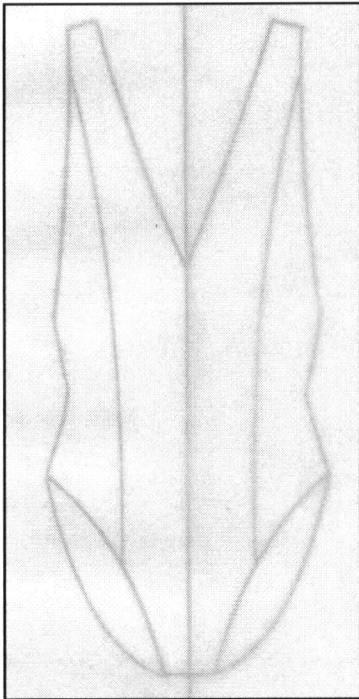

Tip

Never use the body template for drawing back view flat but for only a front view flat. A front view flat as underdrawing will help to keep the front and back views identical in general outlining.

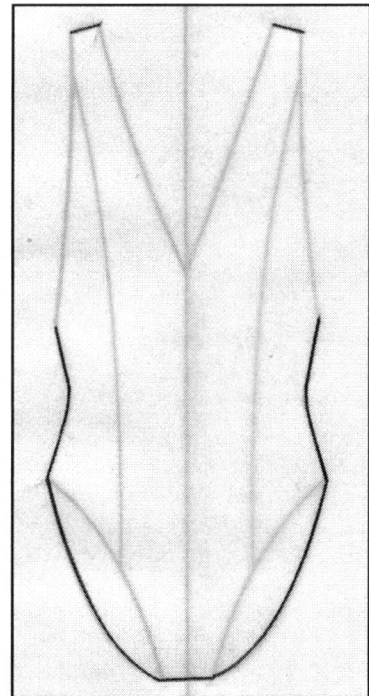

Step #9

Cover the front view flat with a new sheet of tracing paper.

Use tape to avoid shifting.

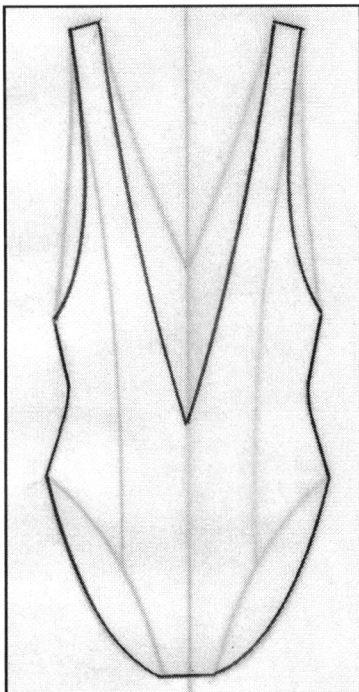

Step #10

Trace side seam, shoulder seam, crotch seam, and back leg opening.

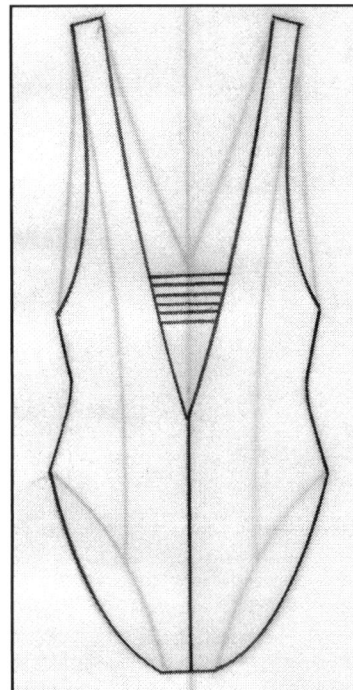

Step #11

Show back neckline.

Step #12

Draw all details for back view.

So, the back view of the flat in simple pencil line is completed!

How to draw final front view flat for swimwear (marker line)

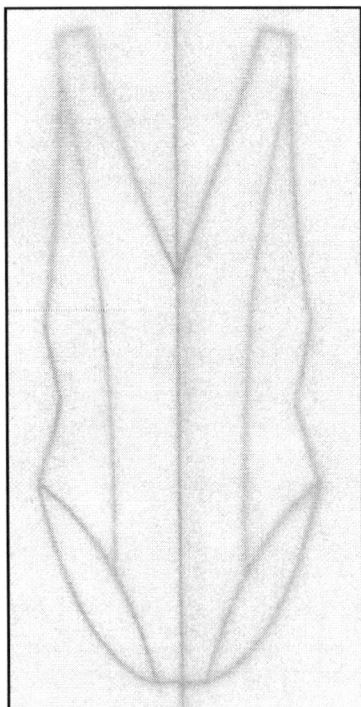

Step #13

To draw a front view flat with black marker line use a front view flat with simple pencil line.

Cover your simple pencil front view flat with a new sheet of marker paper.

Use tape to avoid shifting.

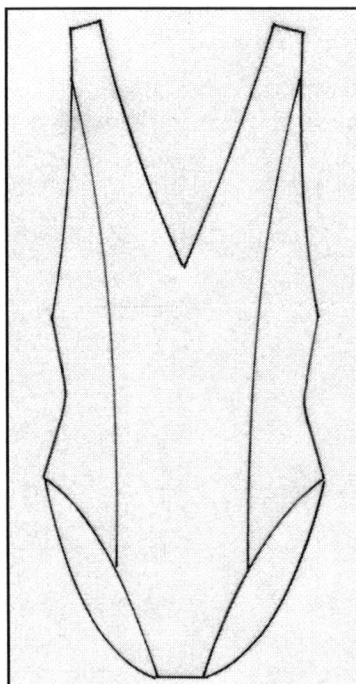

Step #14

Outline all line with marker.

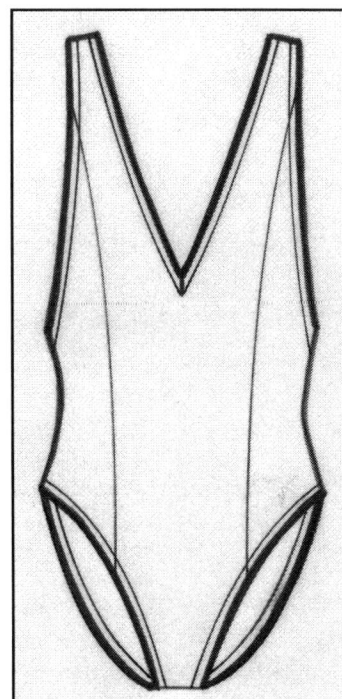

Step #15

Show binding around neckline, arm and leg opening.

For final outlining you can use a thicker line for the basic shape and skinnier lines for details and topstitching.

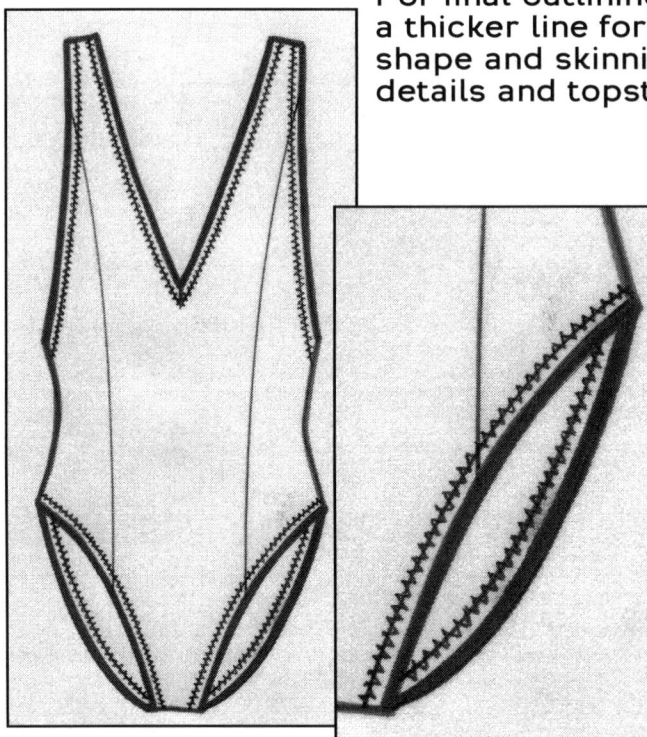

Step #16

Show zig-zag seam around binding if necessary.

How to draw final back view flat for swimwear (marker line)

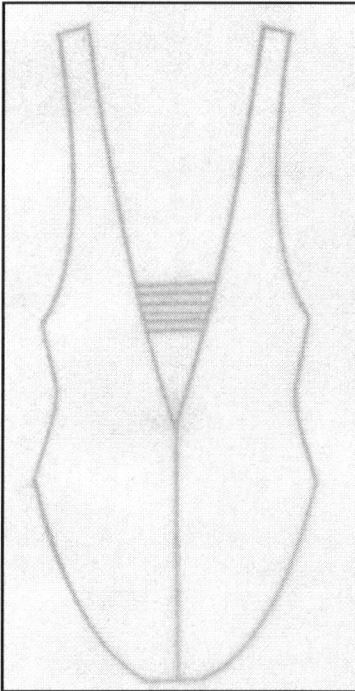

Step #17

To draw a back view flat with black marker line use a back view flat with simple pencil line.

Cover your simple pencil back view flat with a new sheet of marker paper.

Use tape to avoid shifting.

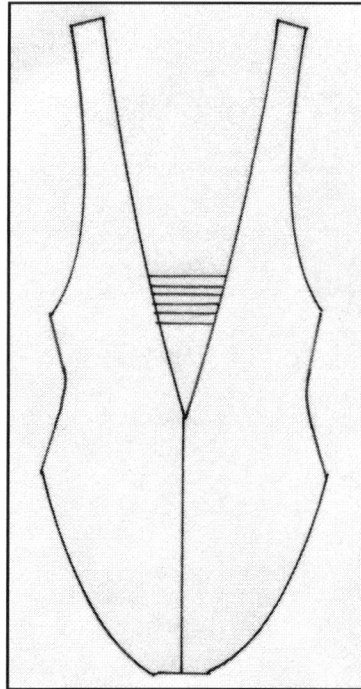

Step #18

Outline all line with marker.

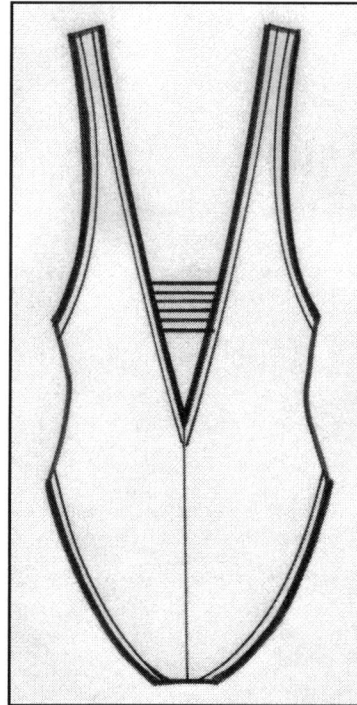

Step #19

Show binding around neckline, arm, and leg opening.

For final outlining you can use a thicker line for the basic shape and skinnier lines for details and topstitching.

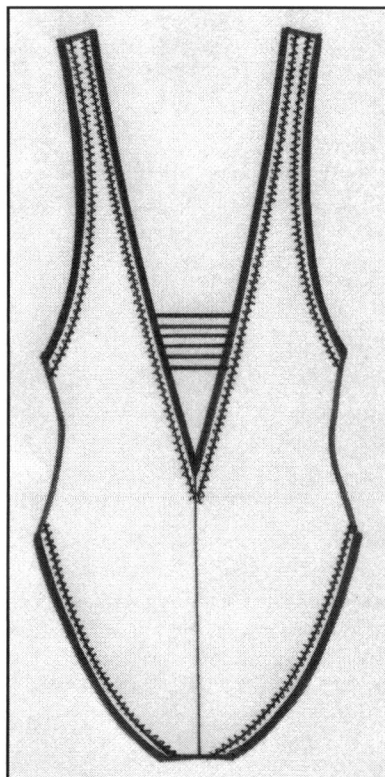

Step #20

Show zig-zag seam around binding if necessary.

Chapter 8

Figure templates for fashion technical drawing

Gallery of templates for flats
Women's wear croquis for flats

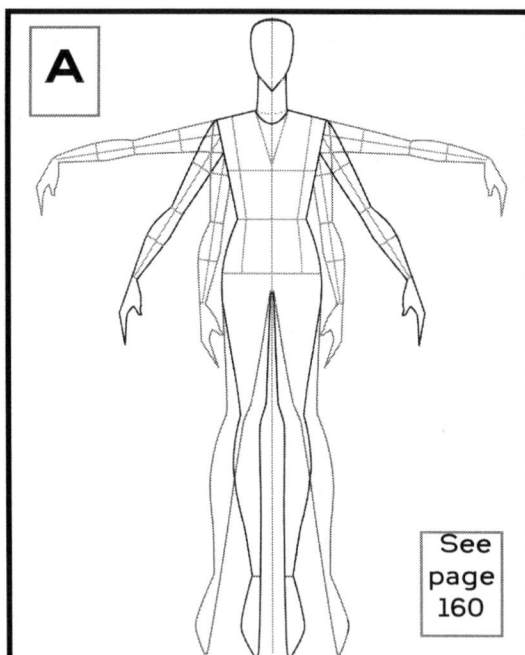

A

See page 160

Universal template (for a variety of women's garment) with
  · multiple positions for arms,
  · multiple positions for legs.

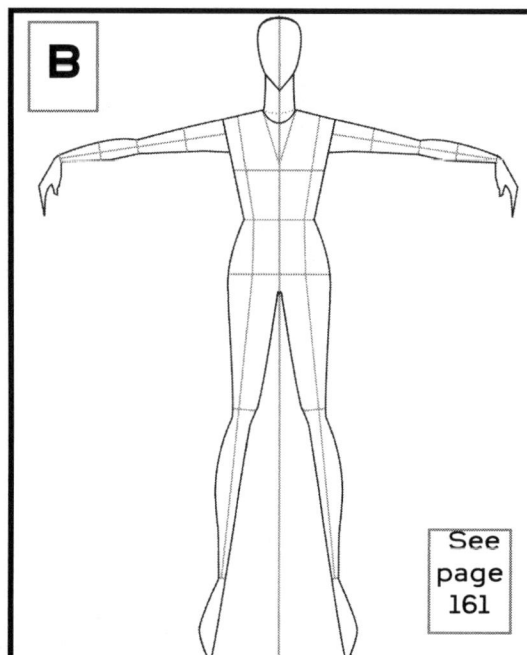

B

See page 161

Template for women's garment
(with one position of arms and legs).

This template is excellent for loose fitting kimono sleeves, flared dresses, skirts and pants.

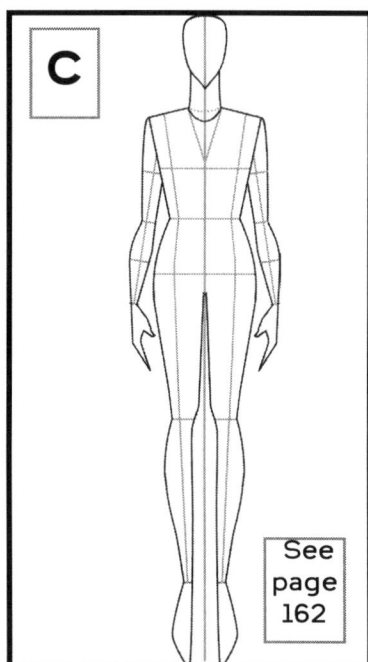

C

See page 162

Template for women's garment
(with one position of arms and legs).

The template is good for a fitted and a sleeveless garment.

Tip

Do not forget to leave a bigger technical ease (distance between body and garment) for upper garment and smaller technical ease for inner layers of a garment.

158

© 2016 Irina V. Ivanova

Tip

Pick a template which will help you to show your design in the best possible way with all necessary details.

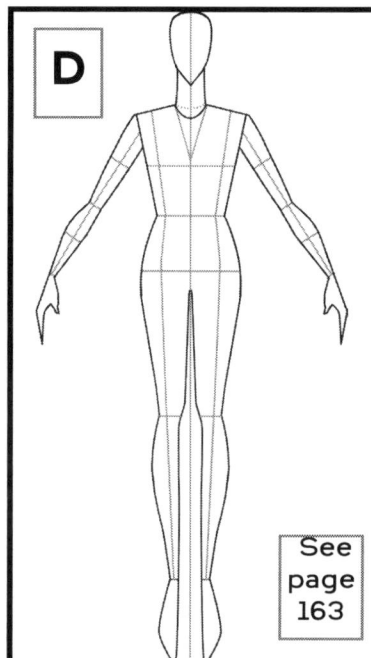

D

See page 163

Template for women's garment with one position of arms and legs.

Good to use for fitted garment.

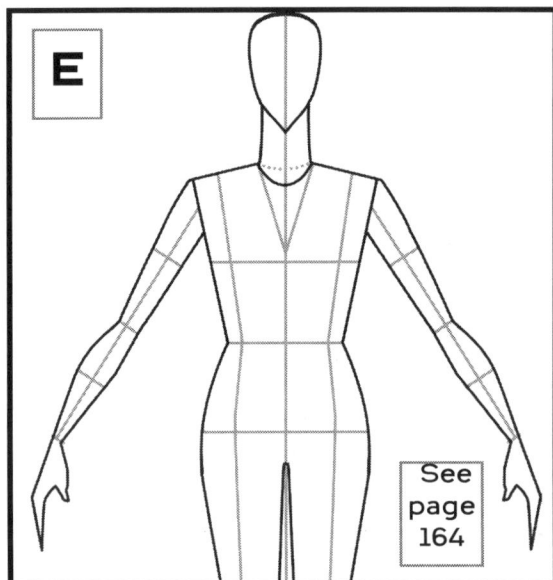

E

See page 164

Big scale template for women's garment (with one position of arms).

The template is easy to use for shoulder based clothing with a necessity to show small details with more preciseness.

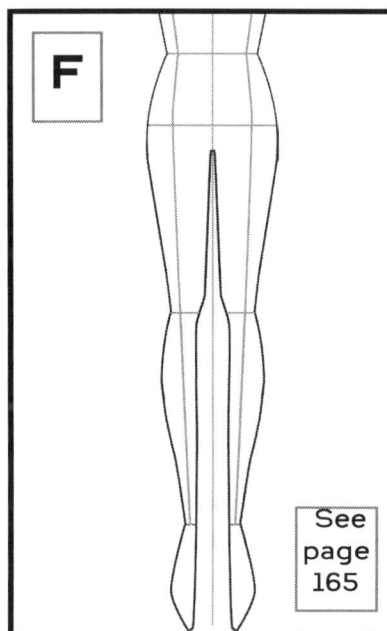

F

See page 165

Big scale template for women's garment (with one position of legs).

The template is easy to use for waist based clothing with a necessity to show small details with more preciseness.

159

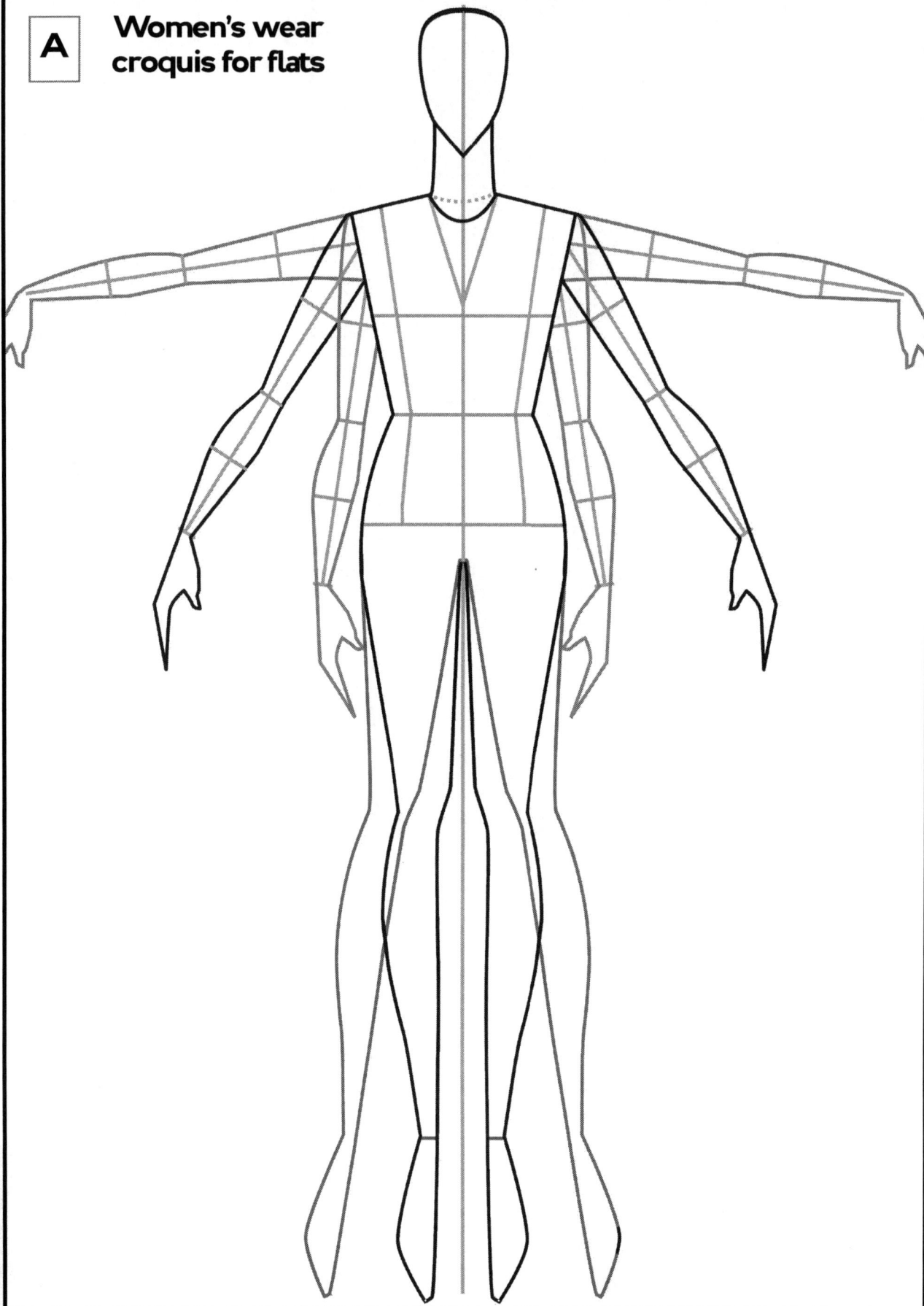

A — Women's wear croquis for flats

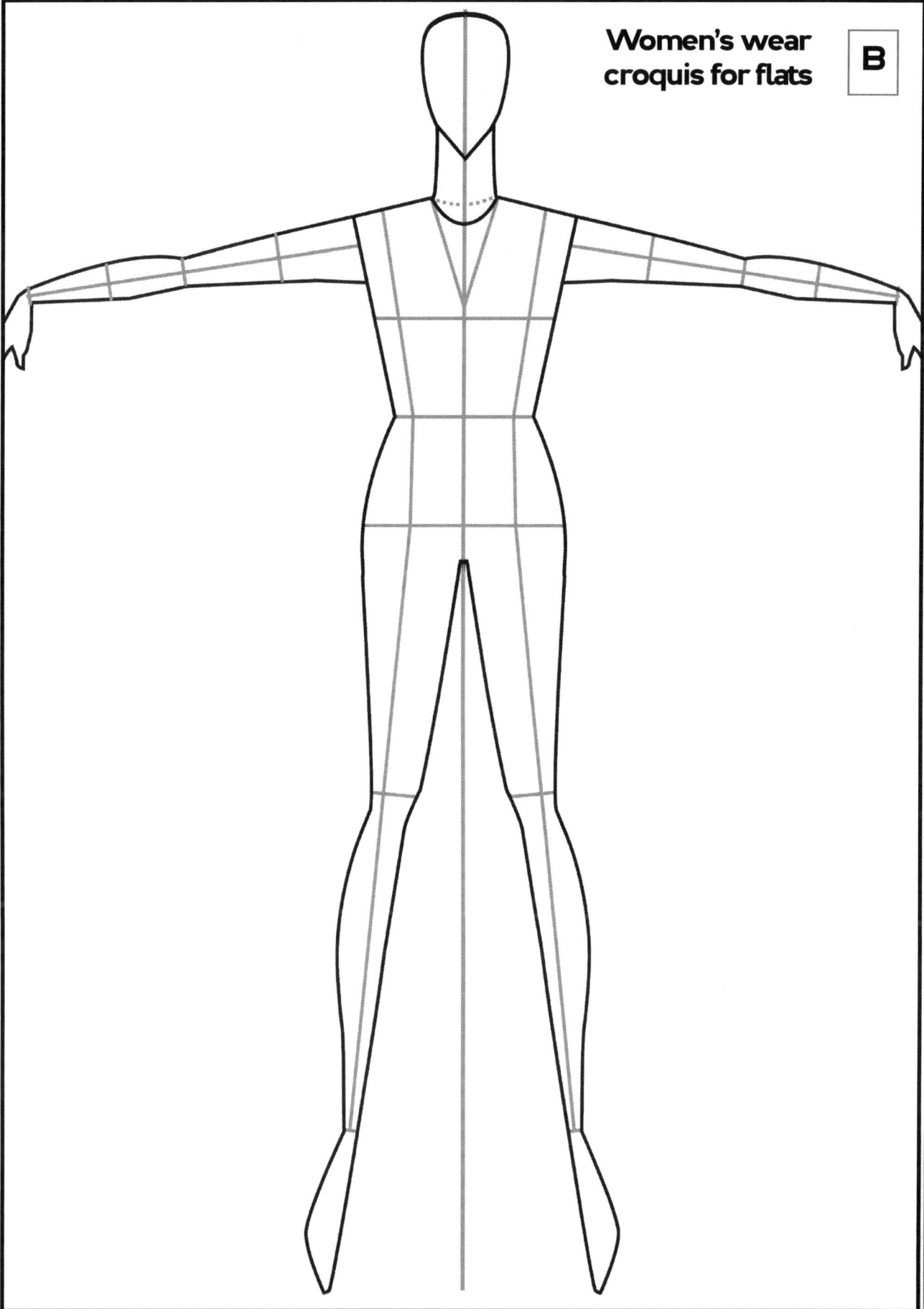

Women's wear croquis for flats

B

C Women's wear croquis for flats

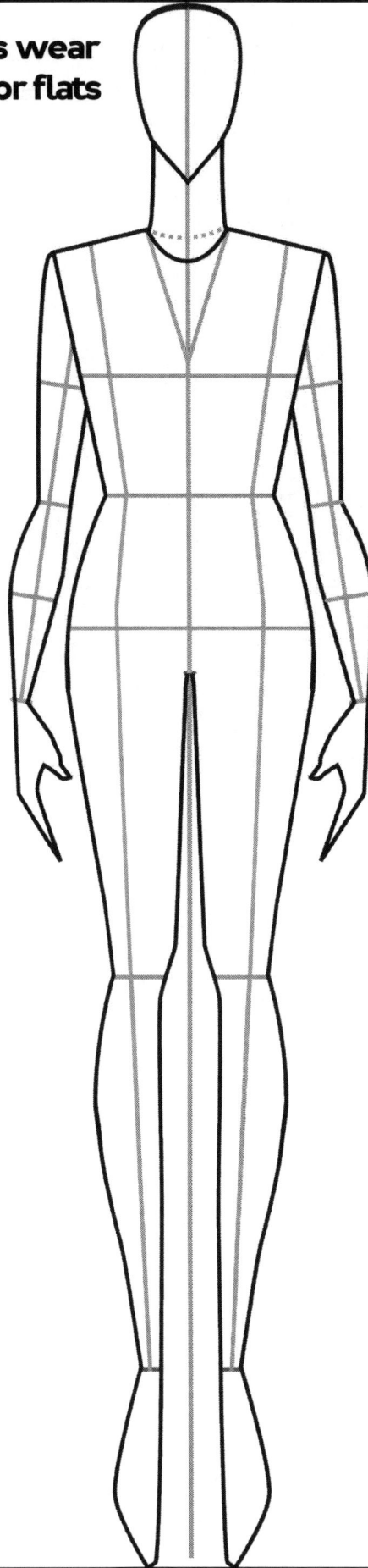

Women's wear croquis for flats

D

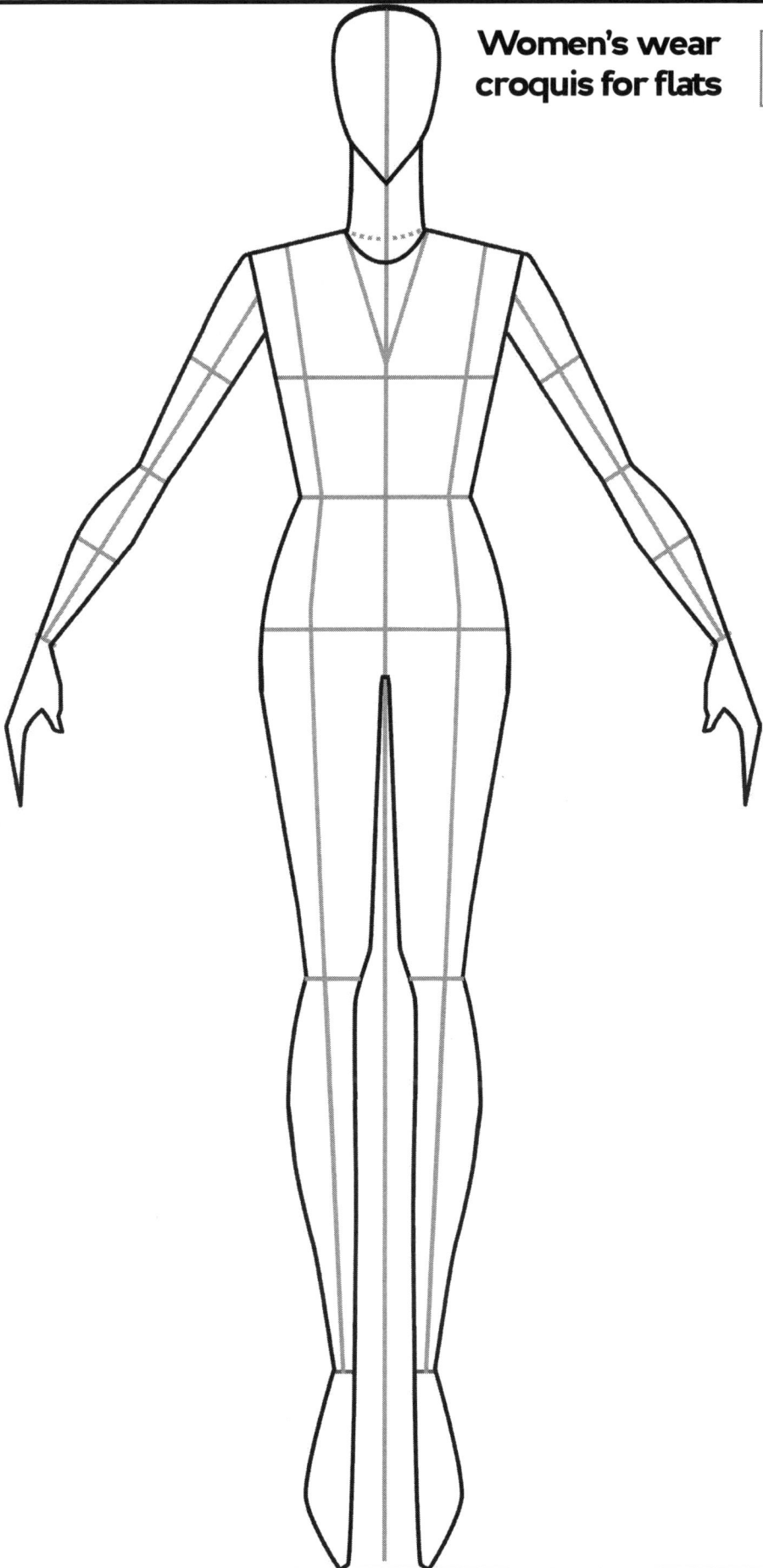

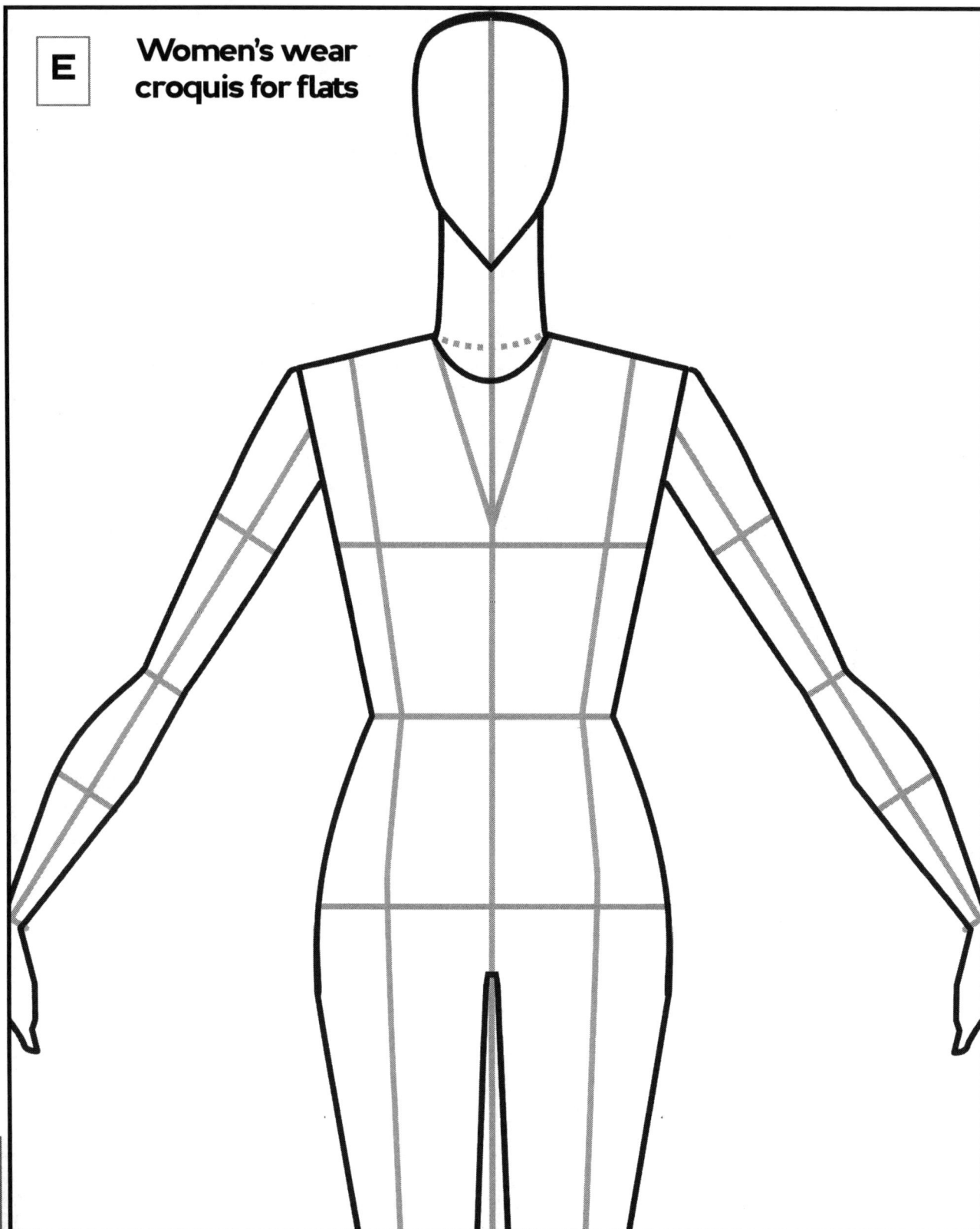

E Women's wear croquis for flats

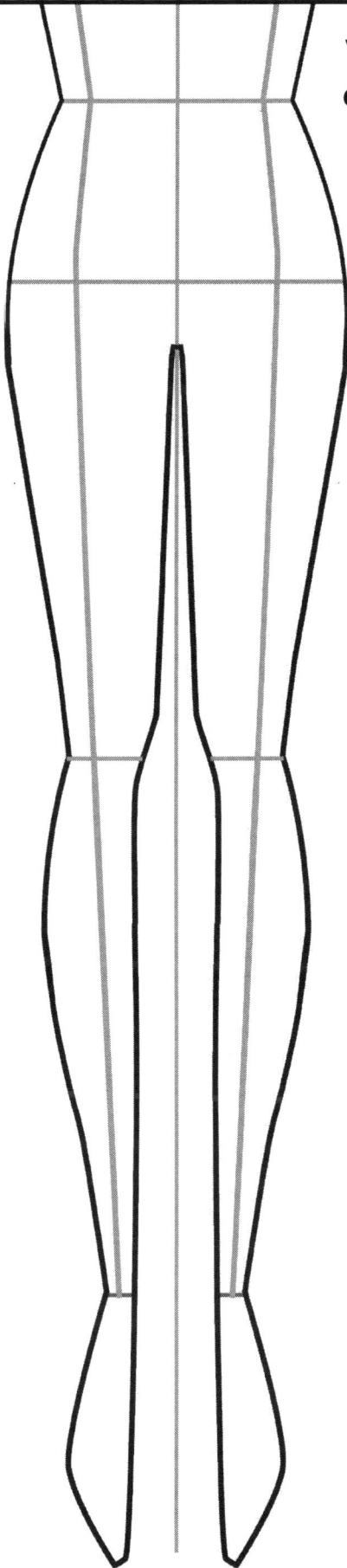

Women's wear croquis for flats F

A

See page 168

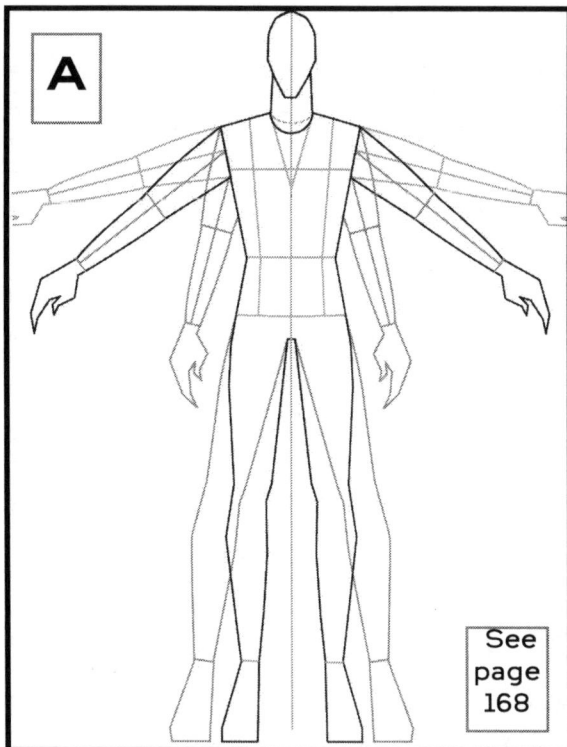

Universal template (for a variety of men's garment) with:
- multiple positions for arms,
- multiple positions for legs.

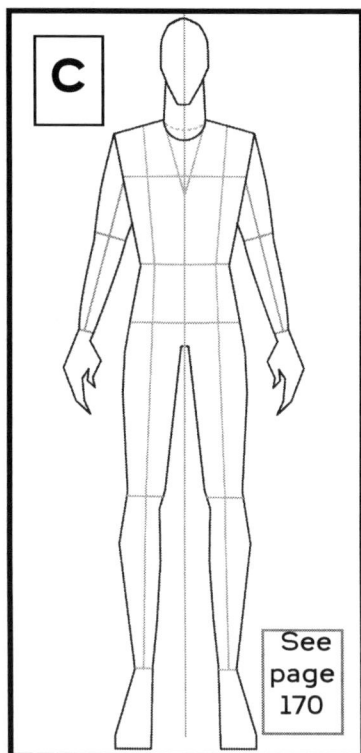

B

See page 169

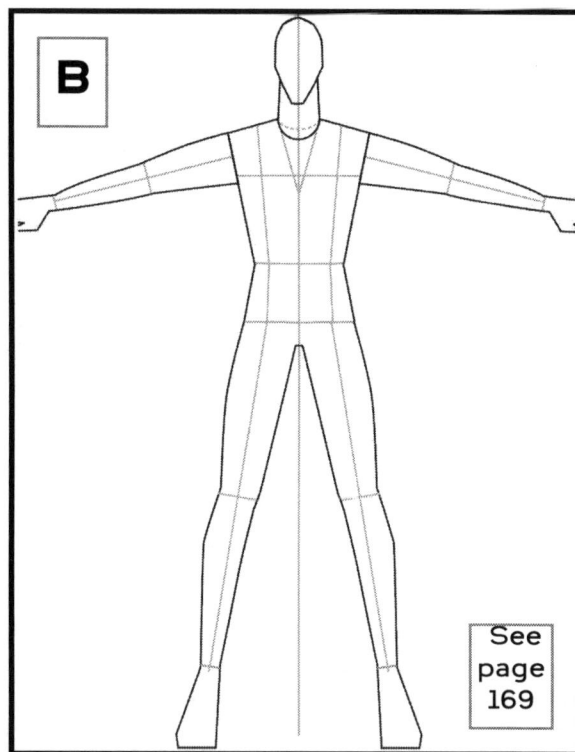

Template for men's garment (with one position of arms and legs).

This template is excellent for loose fitting sleeves with deep armholes and pants with a low rise.

C

See page 170

Template for men's garment (with one position of arms and legs).

The template is good for a fitted and a sleeveless garment.

CHAPTER 8

166

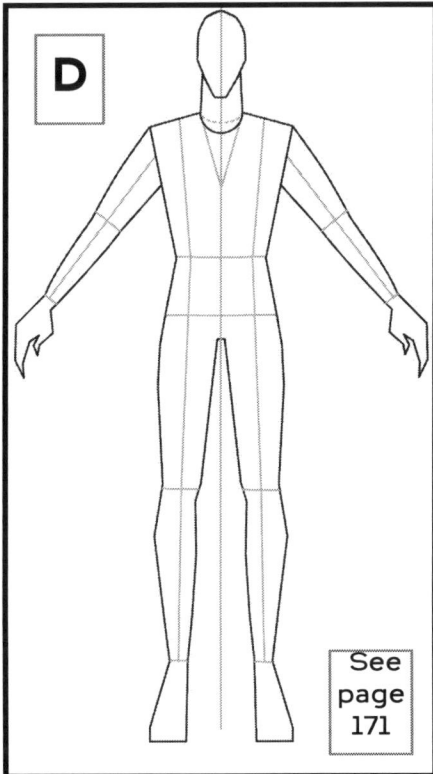

E See page 172

Big scale template for men's garment (with one position of arms).

The template is easy to use for shoulder based clothing with a necessity to show small details with more preciseness.

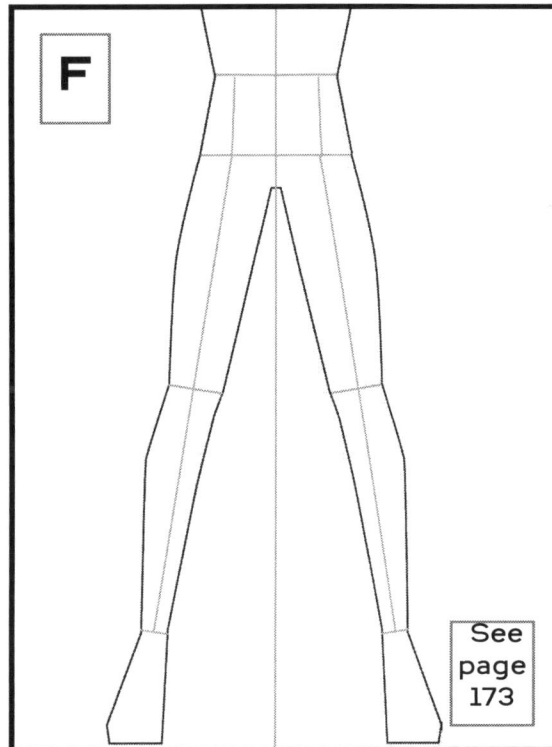

D See page 171

Template for men's garment with one position of arms and legs.

Good to use for fitted garment.

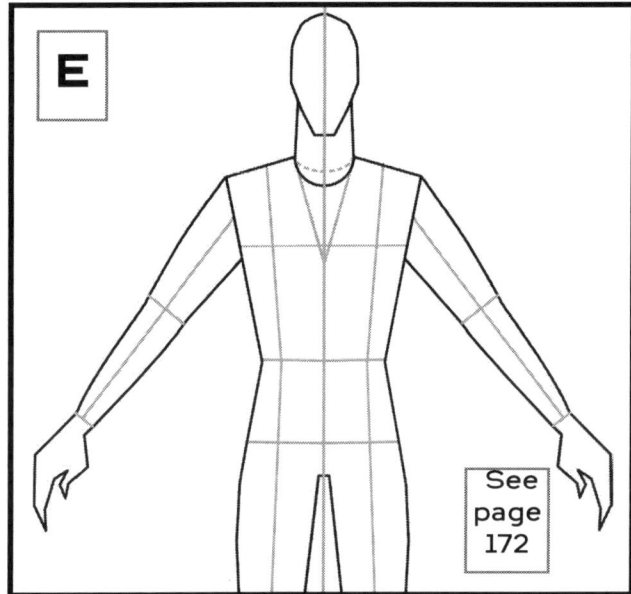

F See page 173

Big scale template for men's garment (with one position of legs).

The template is easy to use for waist based clothing with a necessity to show small details with more preciseness.

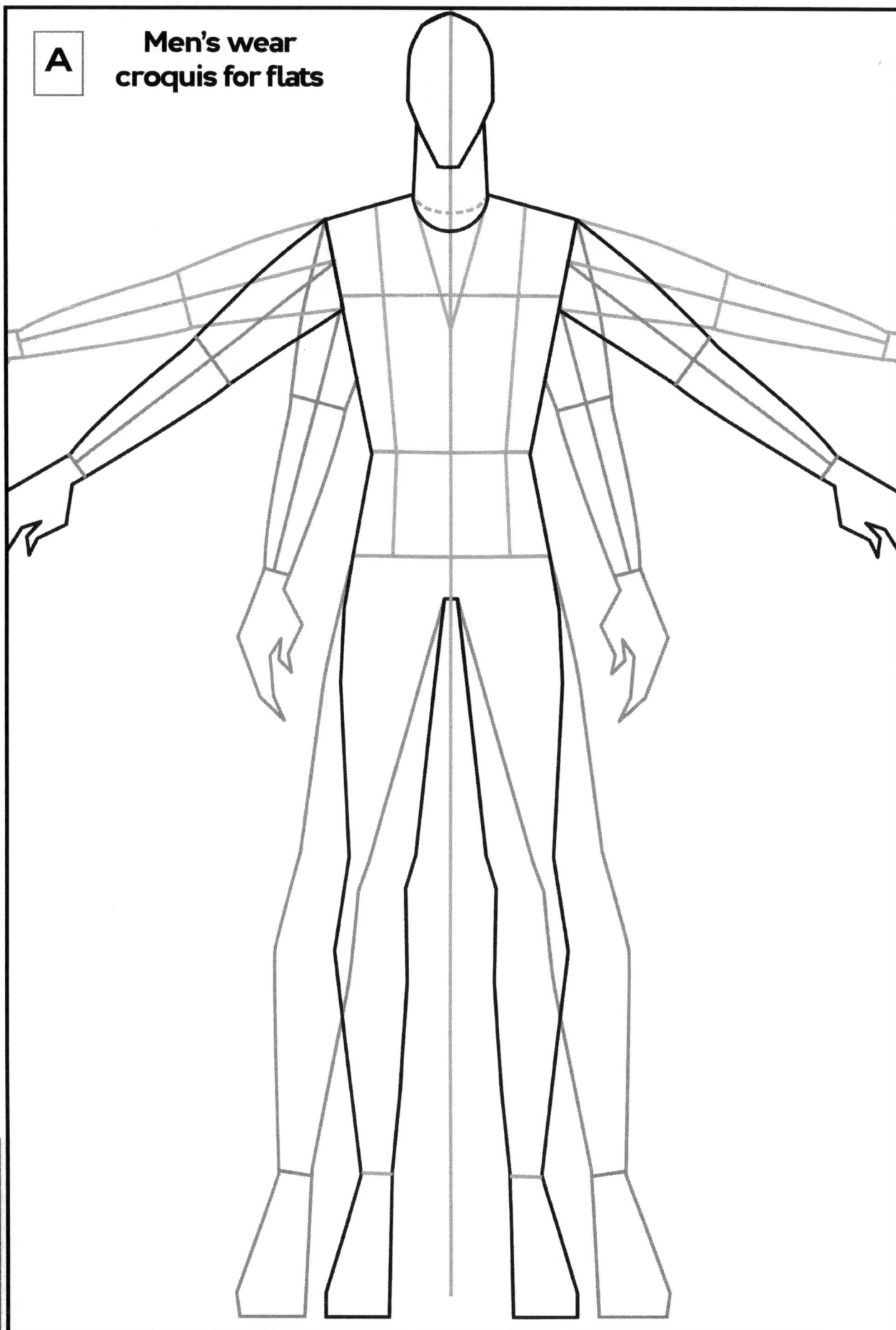

A — Men's wear croquis for flats

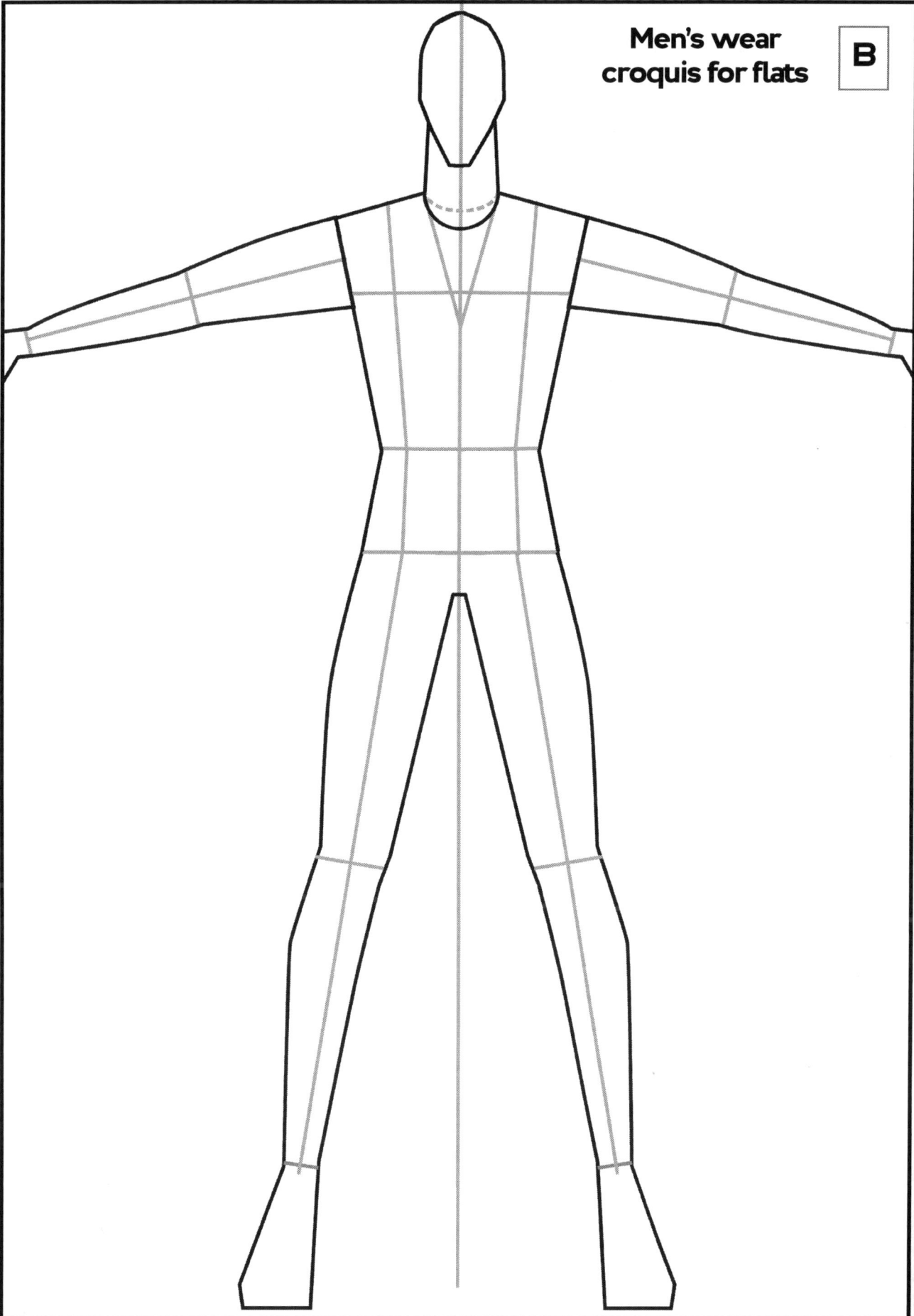

Men's wear croquis for flats B

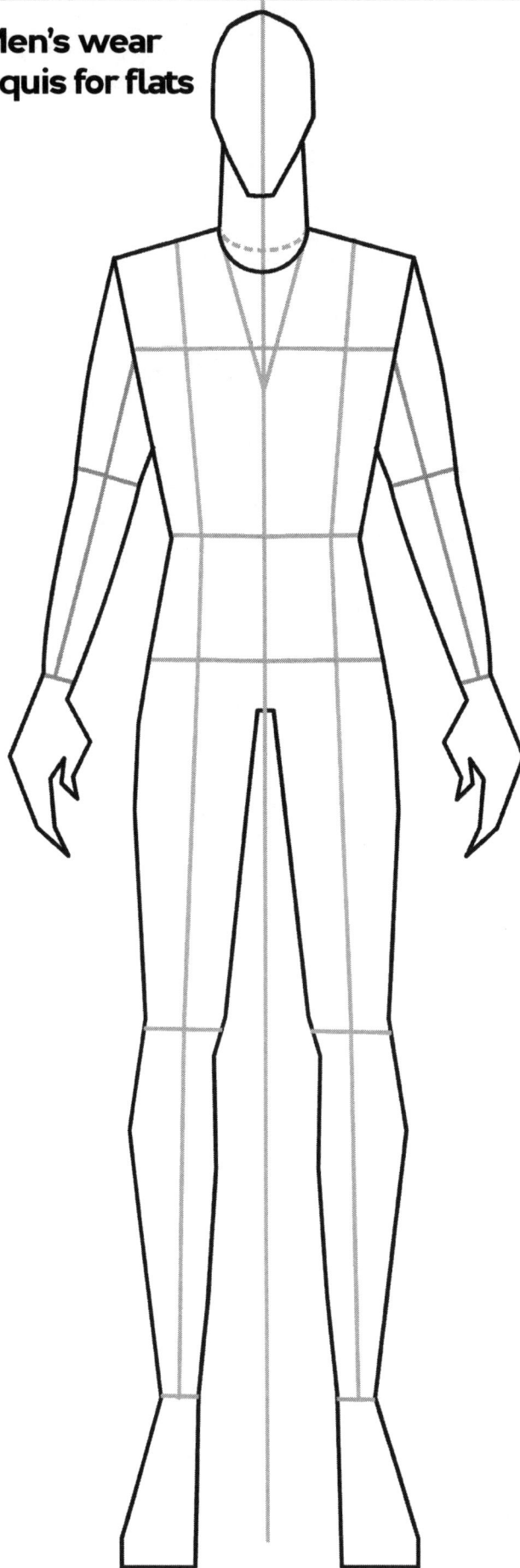

C

Men's wear croquis for flats

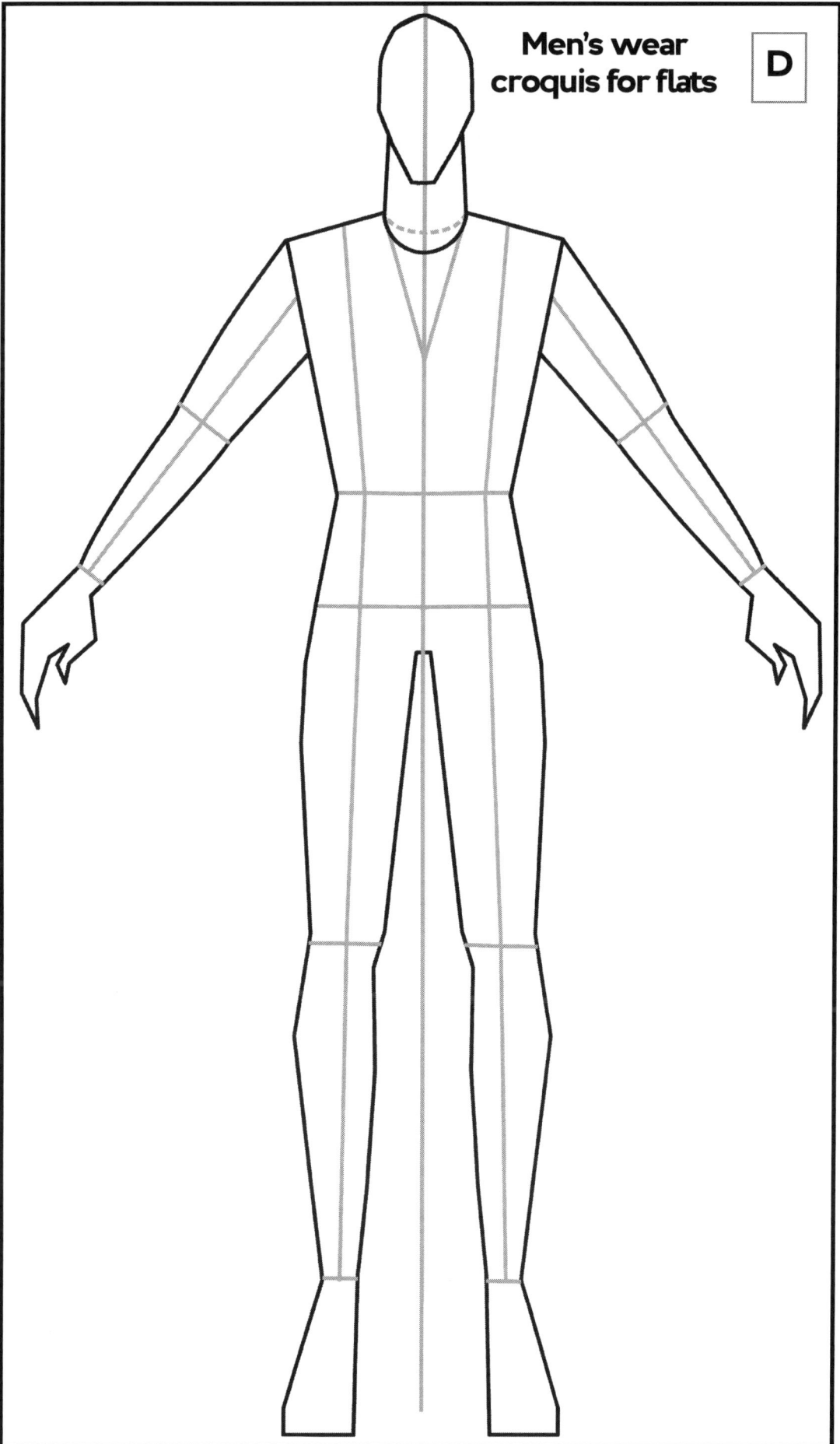

Men's wear croquis for flats

D

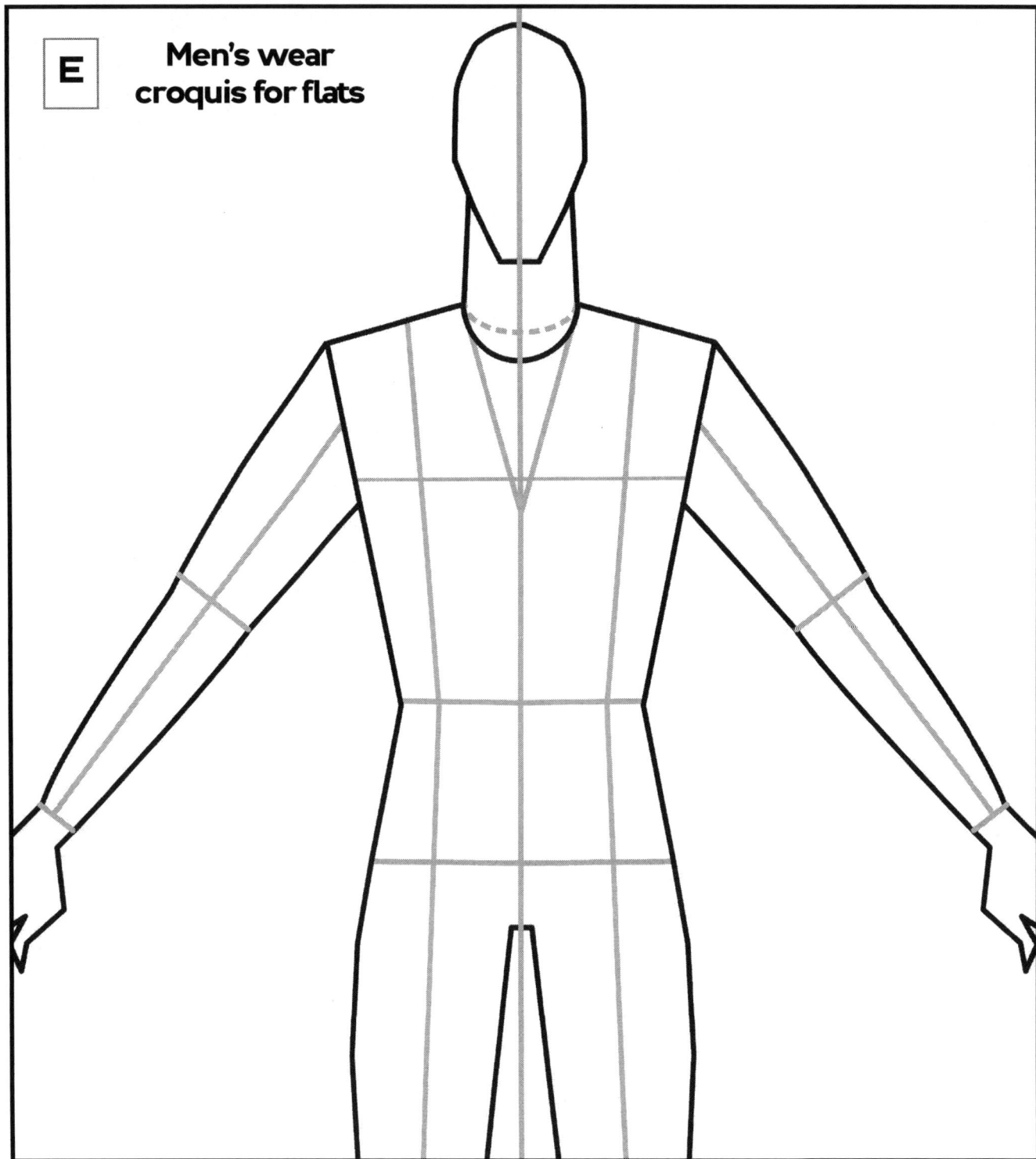

E Men's wear croquis for flats

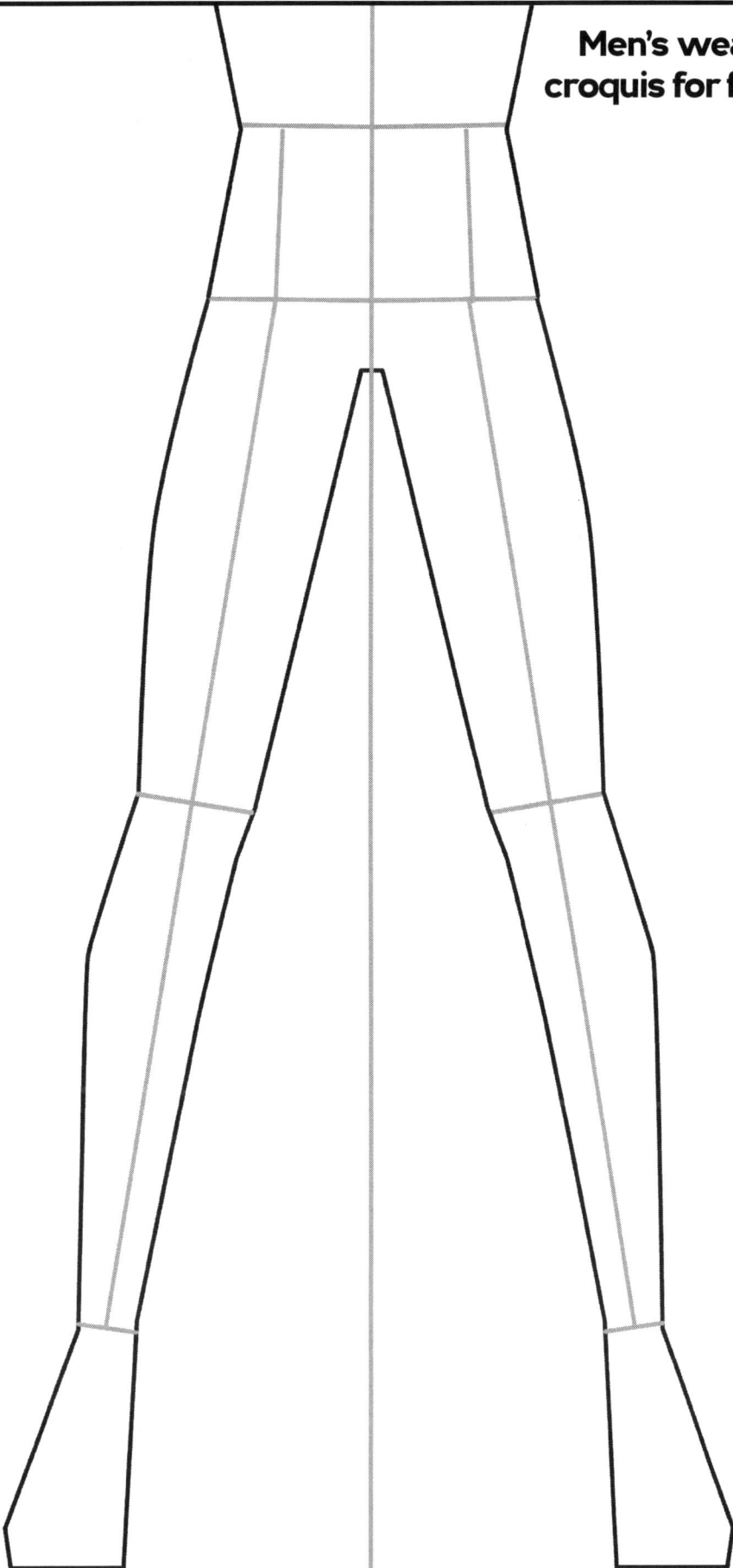

Men's wear croquis for flats

F

Children's wear croquis for flats

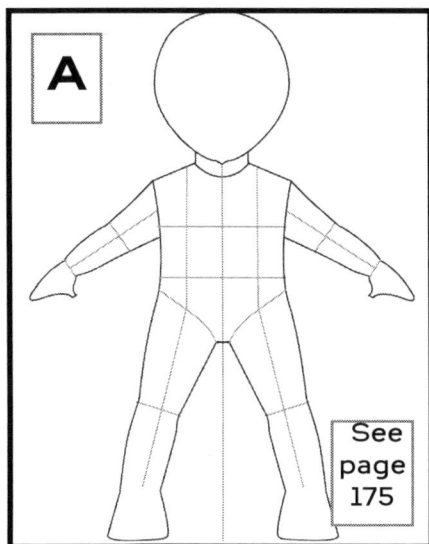

A

See page 175

Universal template for children.

Age group 0–1 years old.

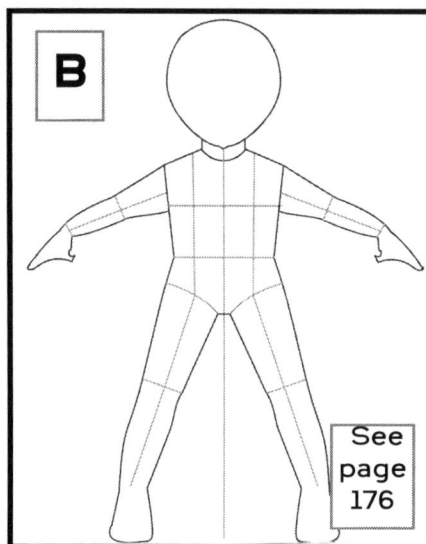

B

See page 176

Universal template for children.

Age group 1–3 years old.

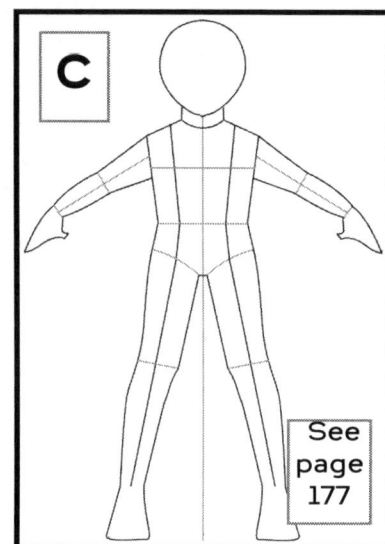

C

See page 177

Universal template for children.

Age group 4–6 years old.

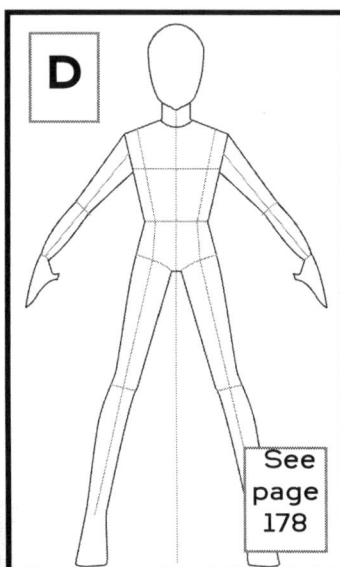

D

See page 178

Template for girls.

Age group 7–10 years old.

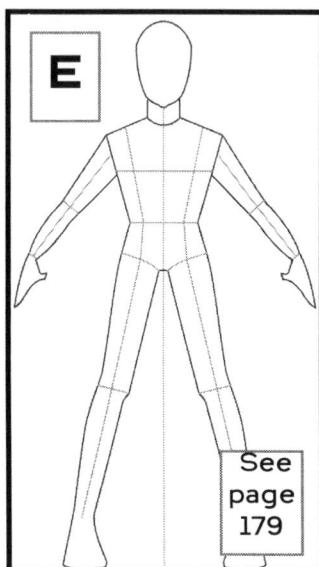

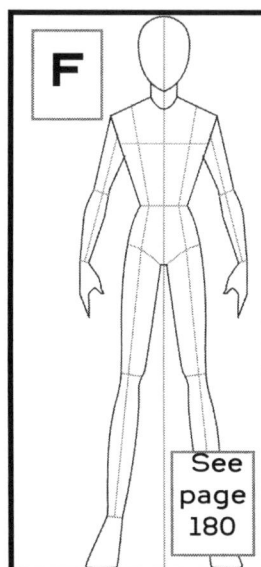

E

See page 179

Template for boys.

Age group 7–10 years old.

F

See page 180

Template for girls.

Age group 10–14 years old.

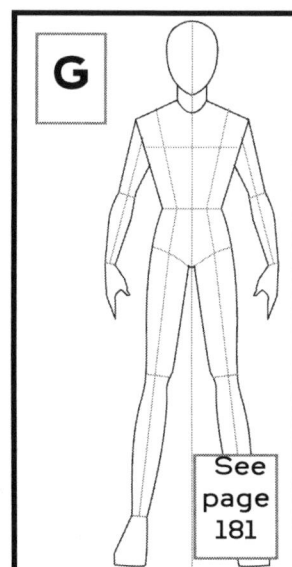

G

See page 181

Template for boys.

Age group 10–14 years old.

How to Draw Fashion Flats A practical guide to fashion technical drawing by Irina V. Ivanova

CHAPTER 8

174

© 2016 Irina V. Ivanova

Boys and girls 0–1 years old A

Children's wear croquis for flats

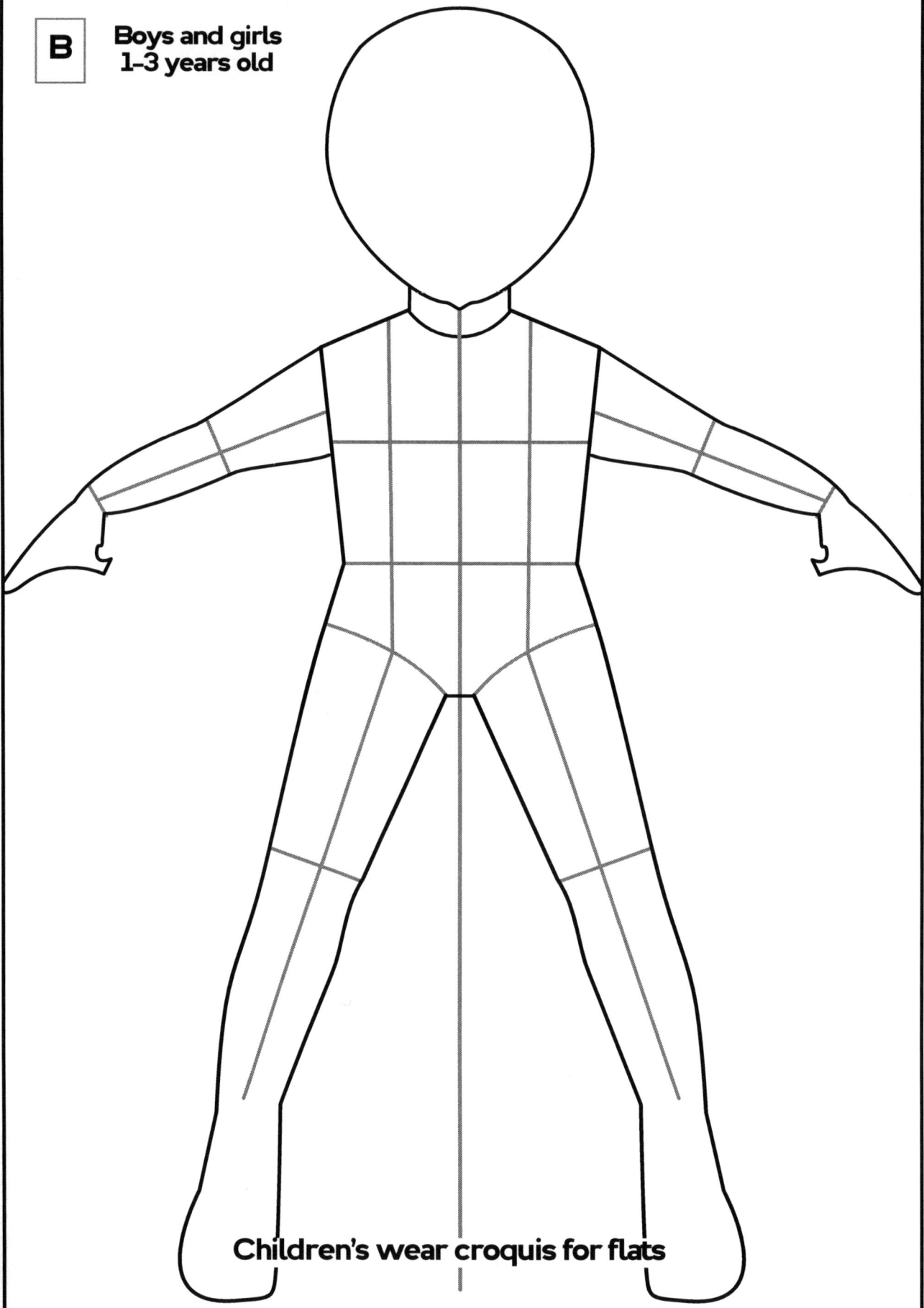

B **Boys and girls 1–3 years old**

Children's wear croquis for flats

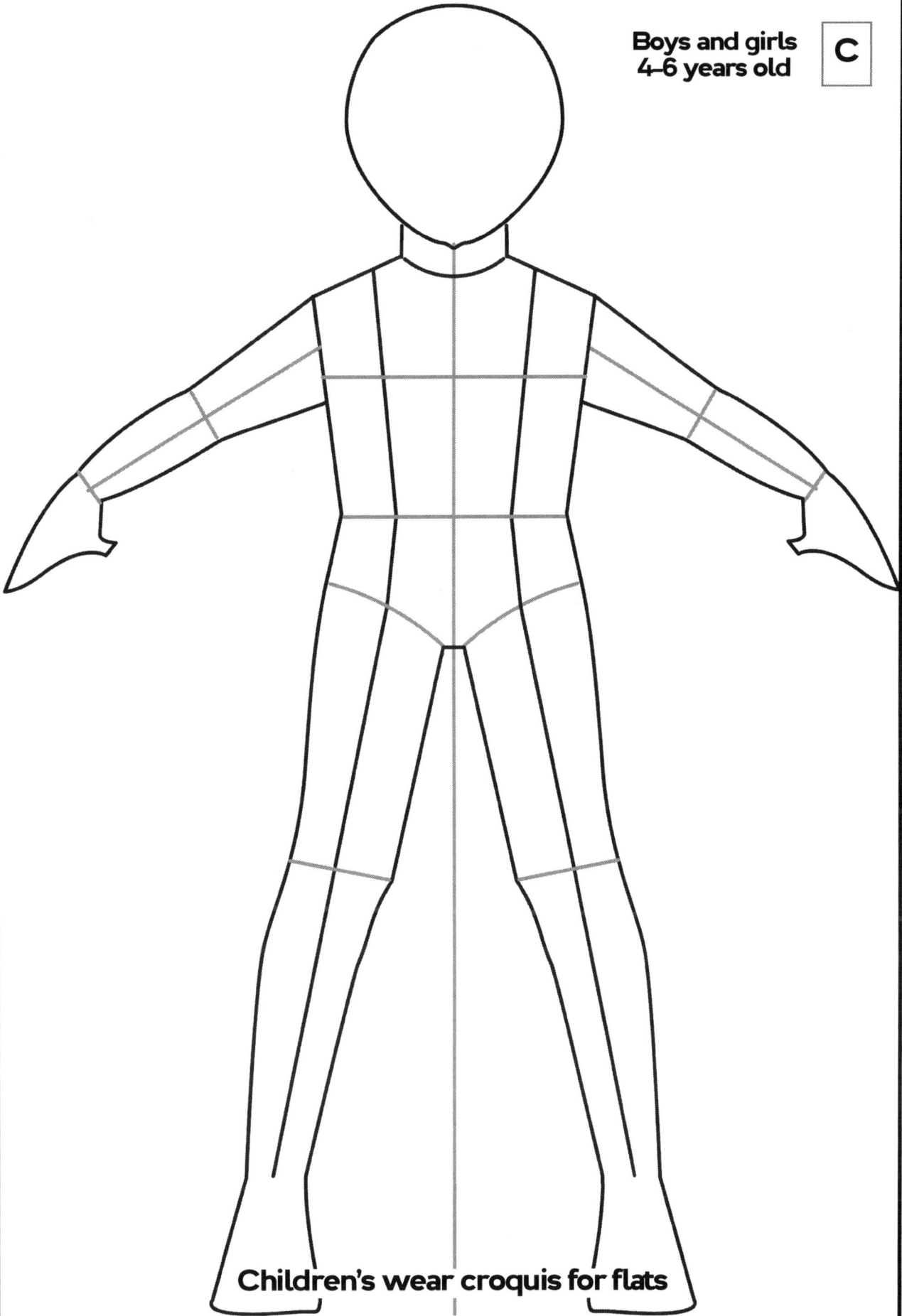

Boys and girls
4–6 years old

C

Children's wear croquis for flats

D

**Girls
7–10 years old**

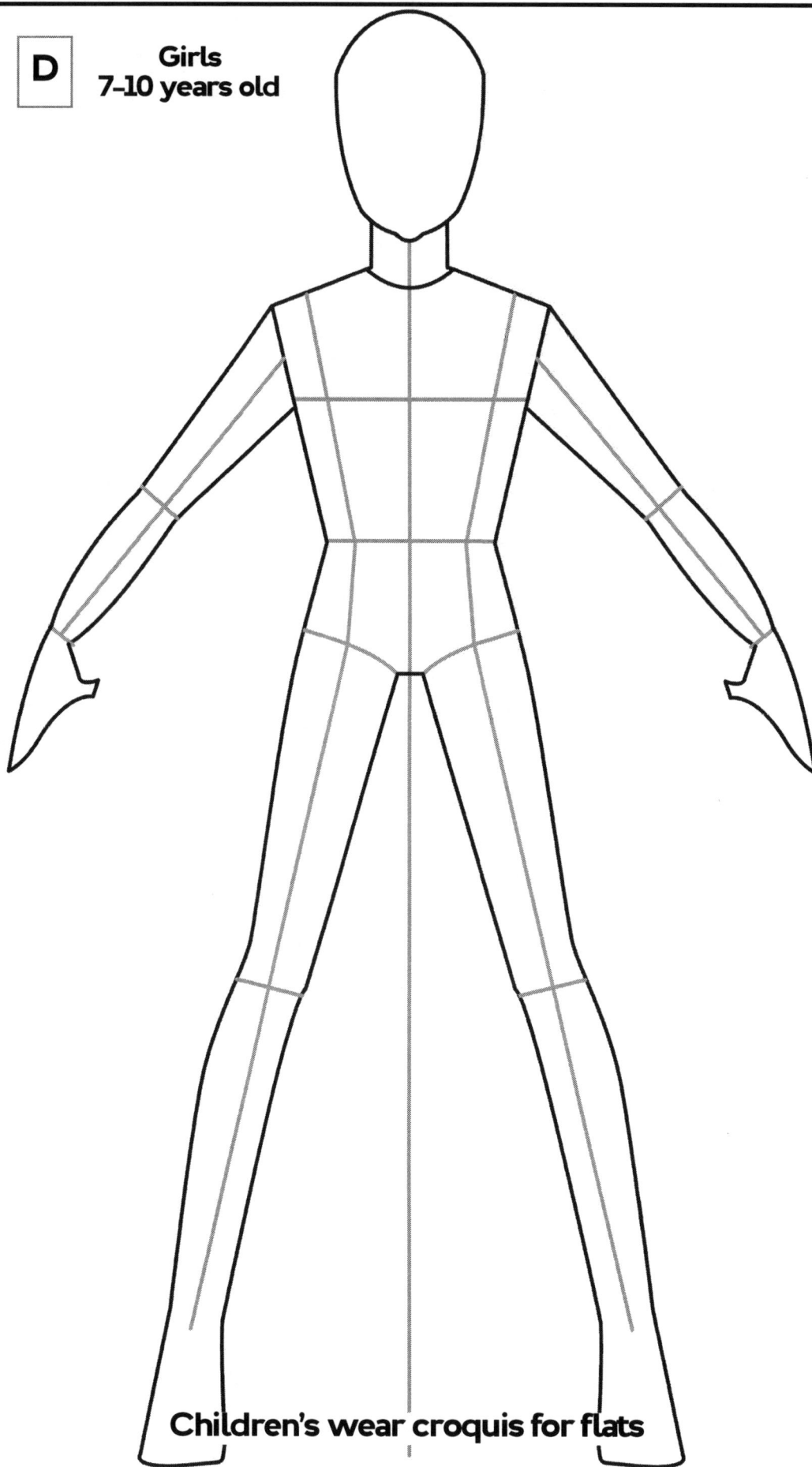

Children's wear croquis for flats

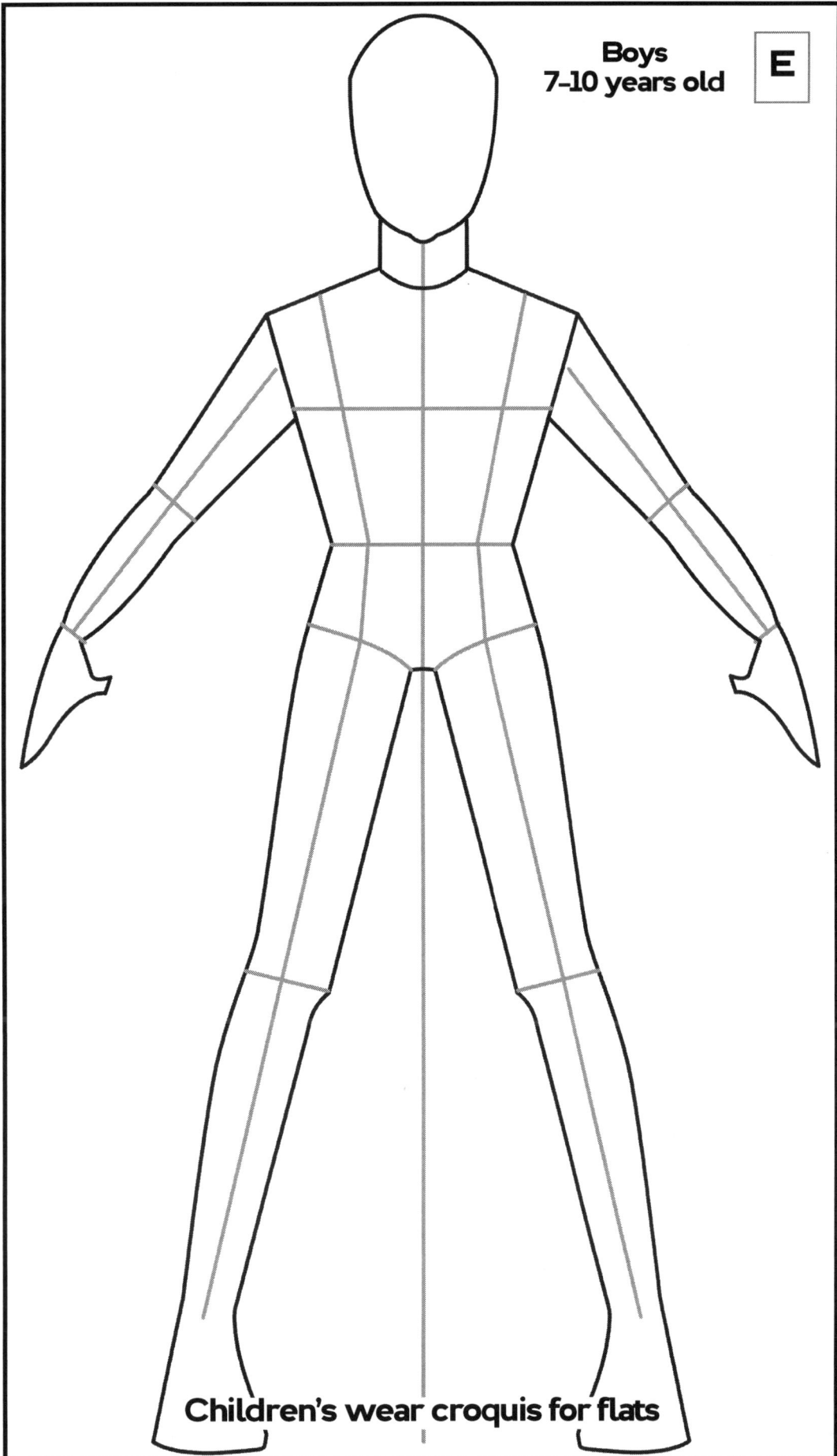

Boys
7–10 years old

E

Children's wear croquis for flats

F

Girls
10–14 years old

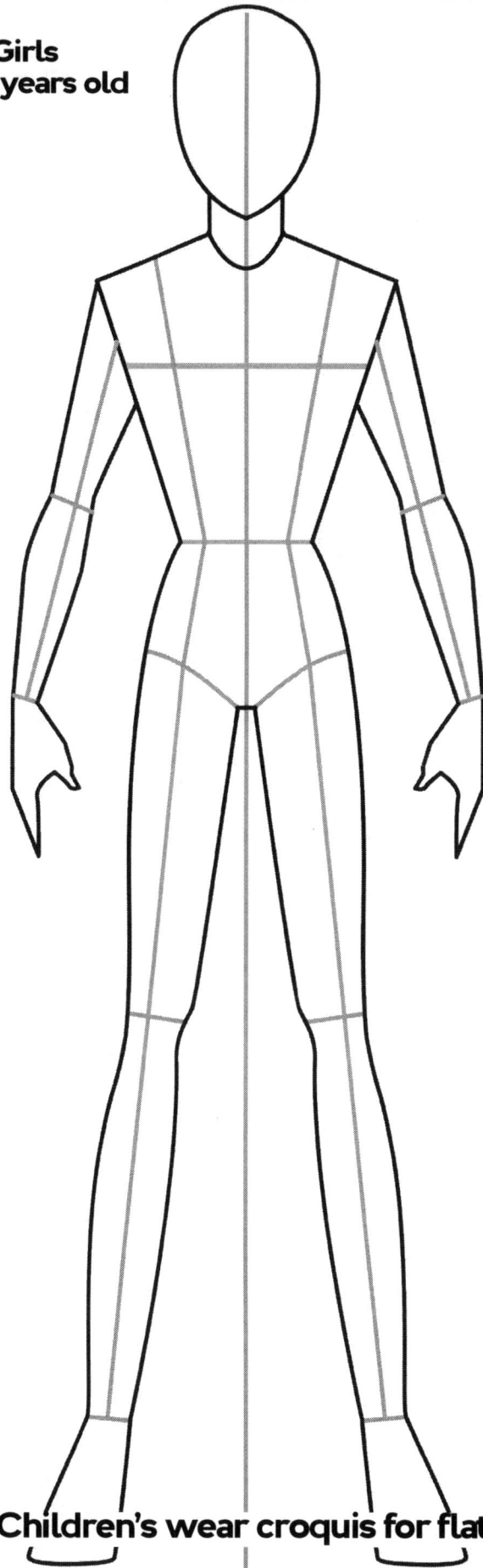

Children's wear croquis for flats

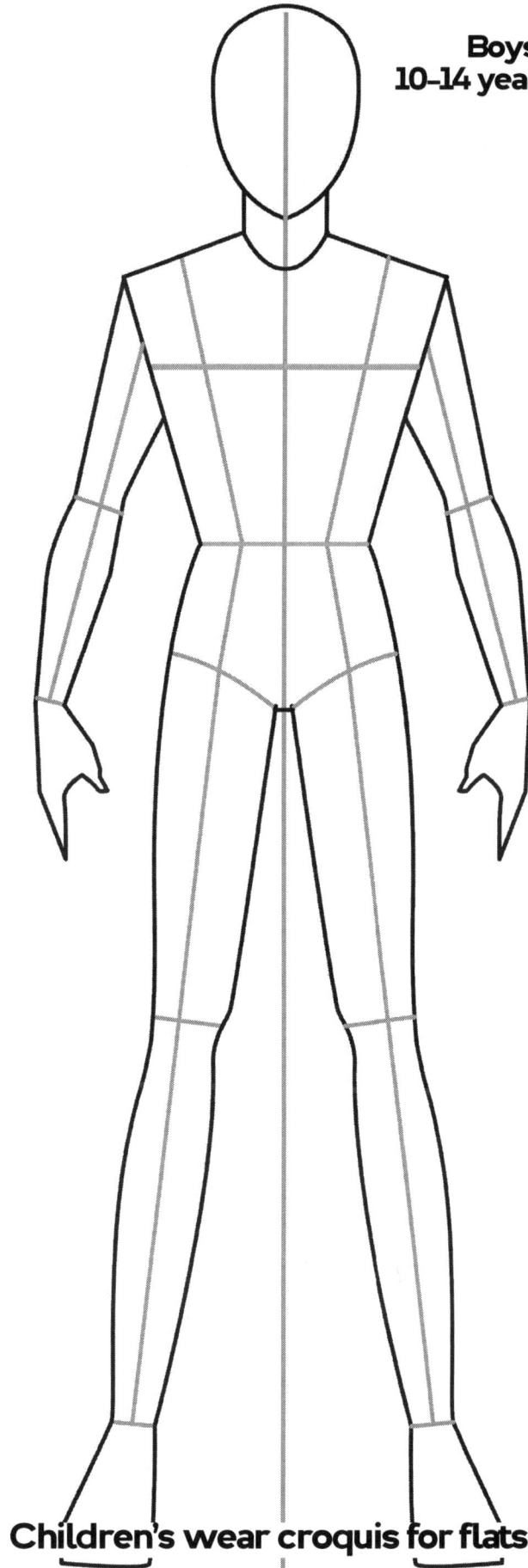

**Boys
10–14 years old**

G

Children's wear croquis for flats

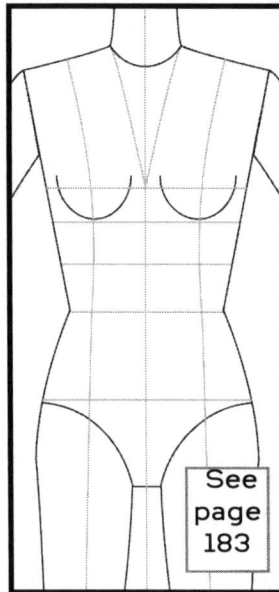

See
page
183

**Big and tall size wear
croquis for men and plus size wear
croquis for women**

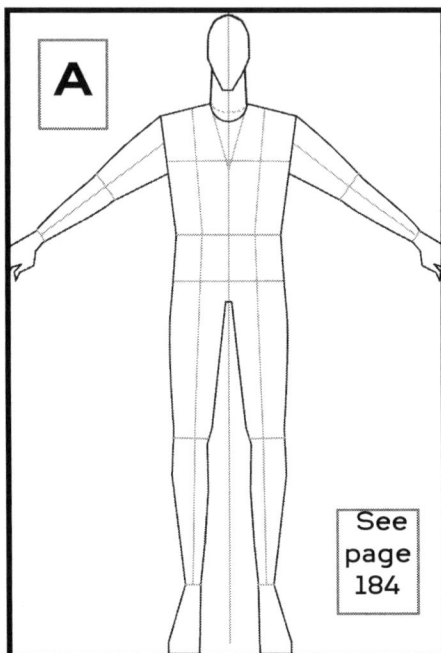

A

See
page
184

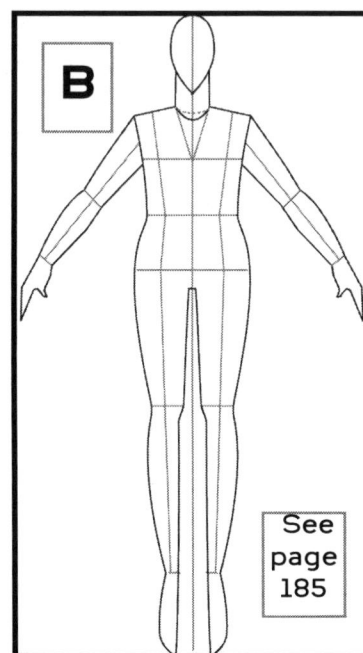

B

See
page
185

Women's swimwear
croquis for flats

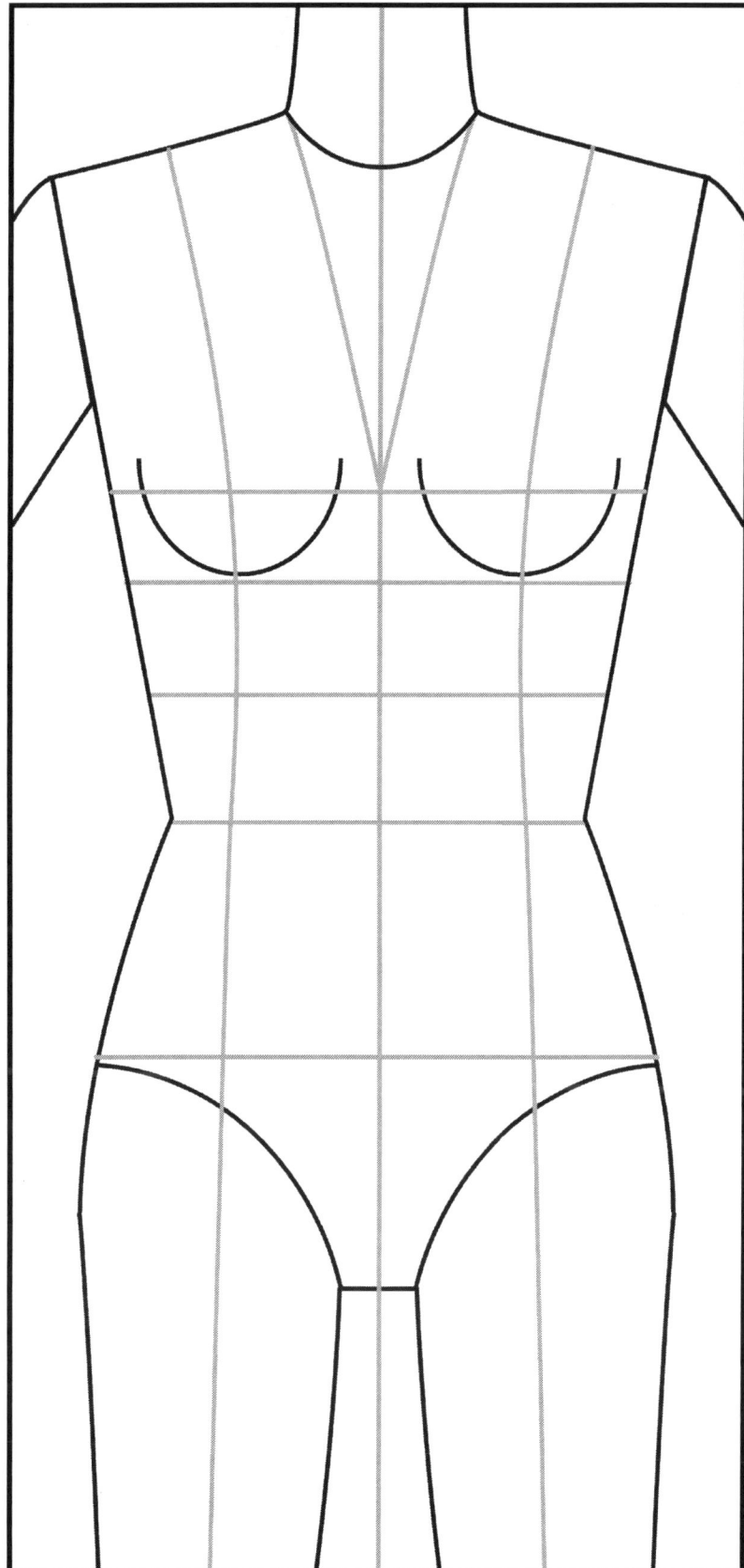

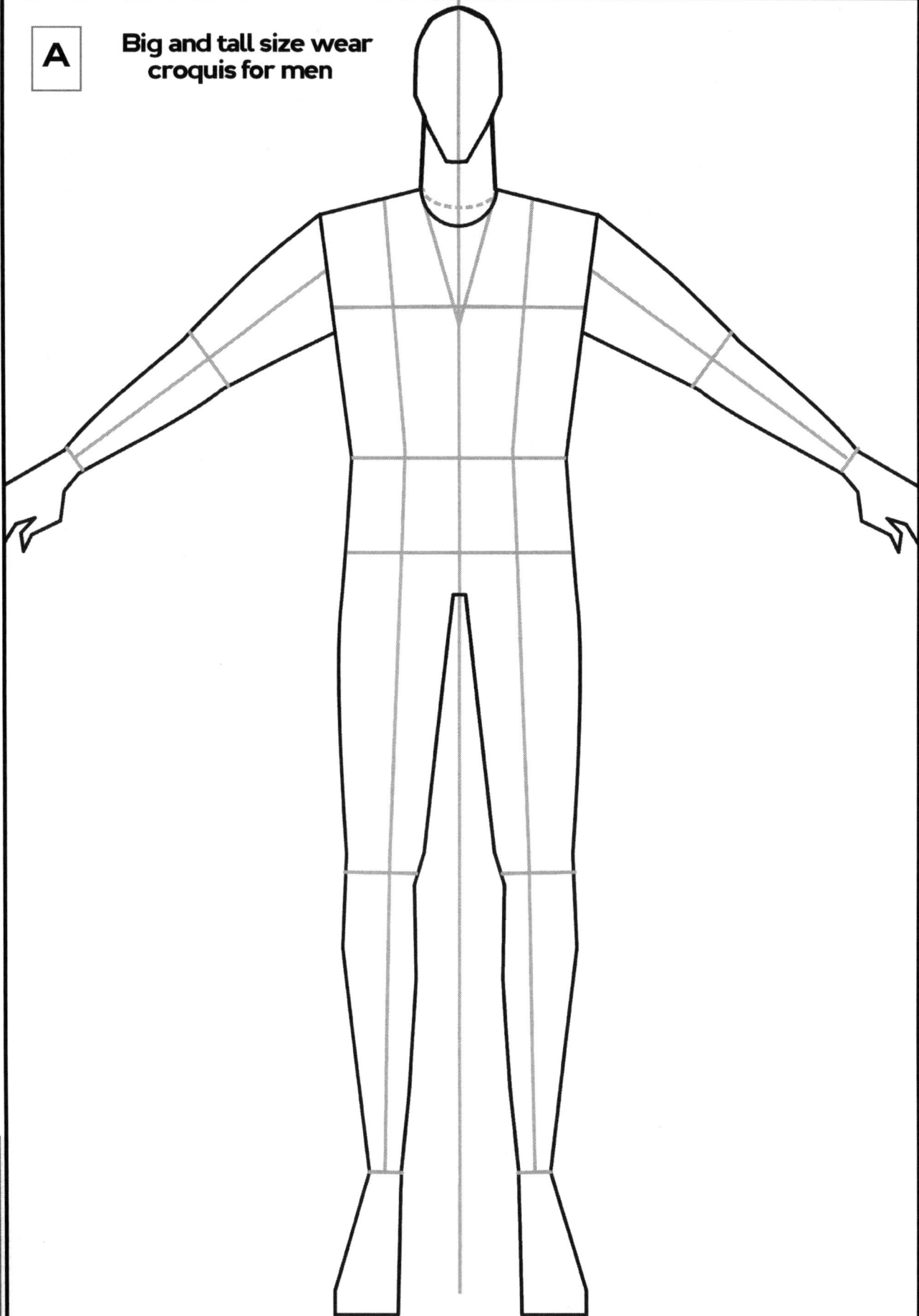

A Big and tall size wear croquis for men

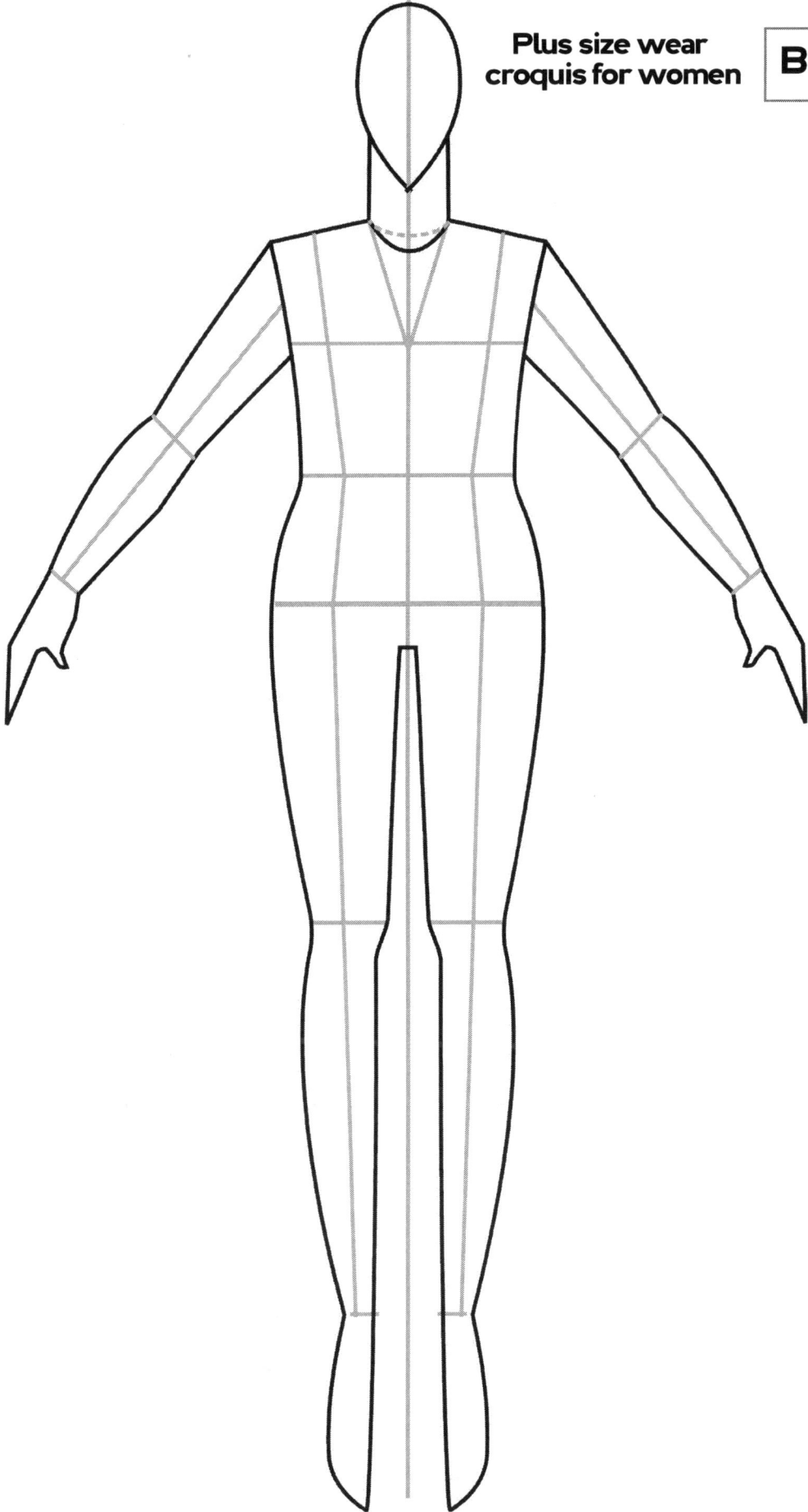

Plus size wear croquis for women

B

Chapter 9

Gallery of projects

Children's wear collection

A

Before you start your technical flats, you should sketch all your design ideas just to understand all elements and basic shape of garments which you possibly will consider as a part of your future collection.
Here are simple pencil sketches.

For all sketches, I used templates from "Children's Wear Fashion Illustration. Resource Book" by Irina Ivanova (ISBN: 9780692554074).

After visualizing all possible garment designs, I chose a few sketches for future development into flats.

B

C

188

D

E

F

G

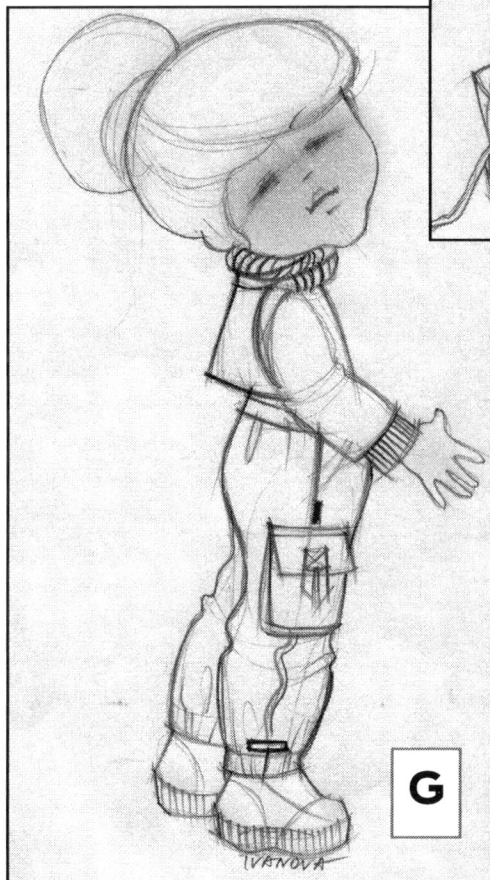

I have chosen sketches A, E, F and G for more specific development into flats.
See the whole process of flats development on pages 190–195.

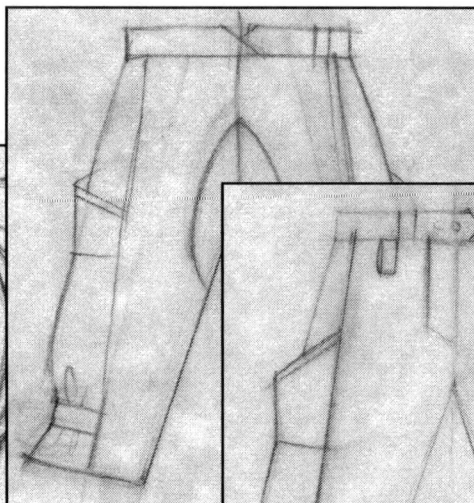

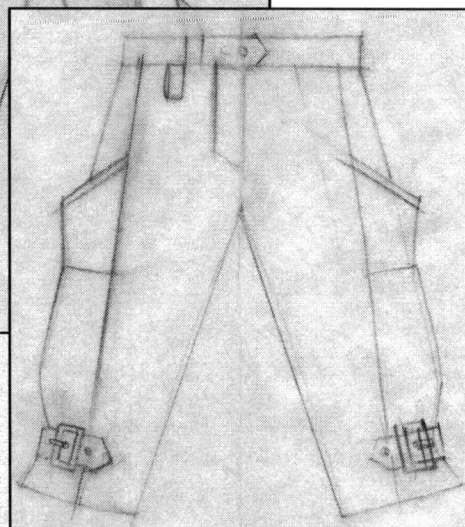

Preliminary simple
pencil flats for pants
(front and back views).

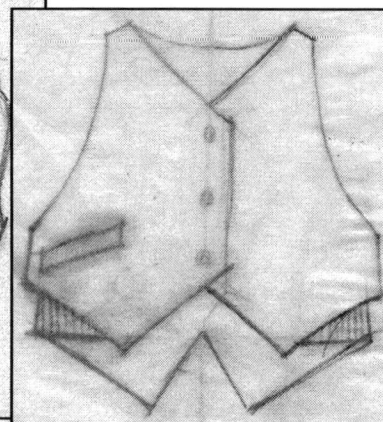

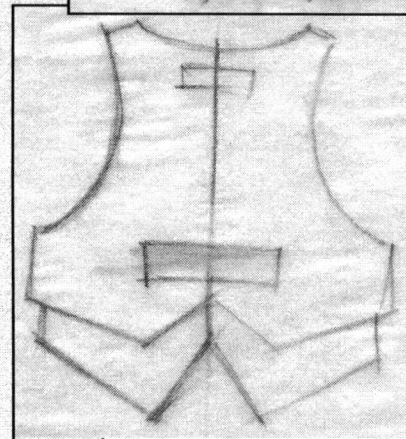

Preliminary simple
pencil flats for vest
(front and back views).

A

190

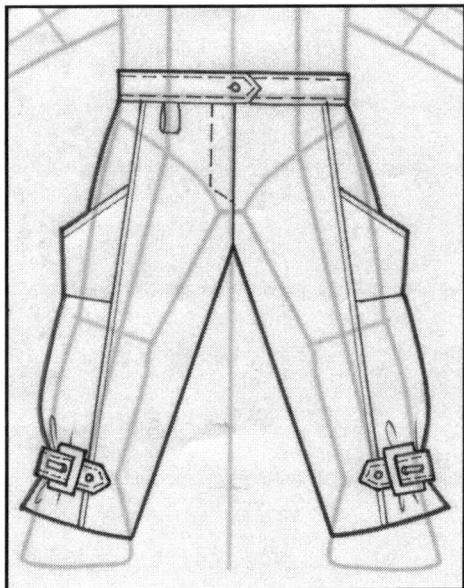

Final front view flats for vest and pants with template underneath to understand how garment is fitted to a body.

Final front and back views flats for vest.

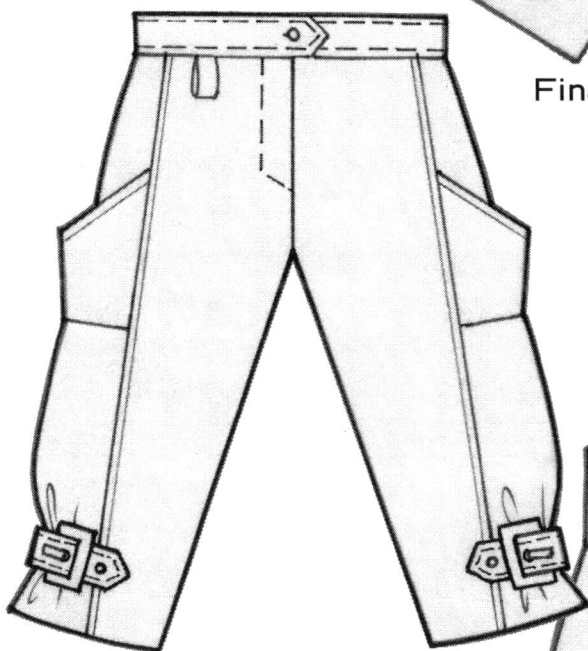

Final front and back views flats for pants.

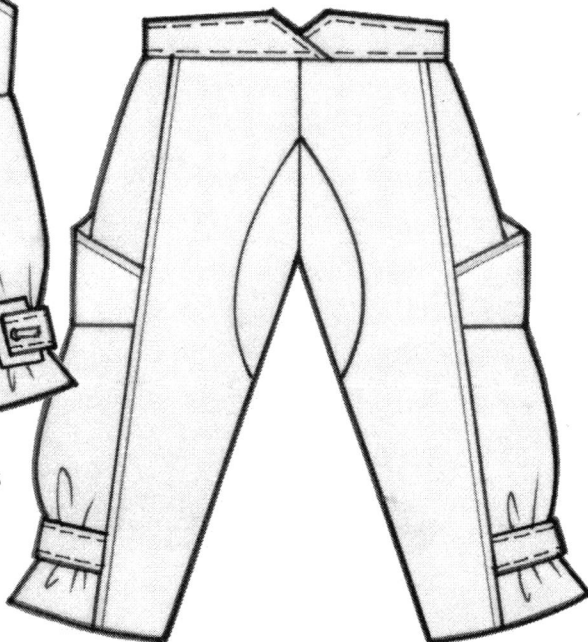

E

Final front view flat for shirt with template underneath to understand how the garment is fitted to a body.

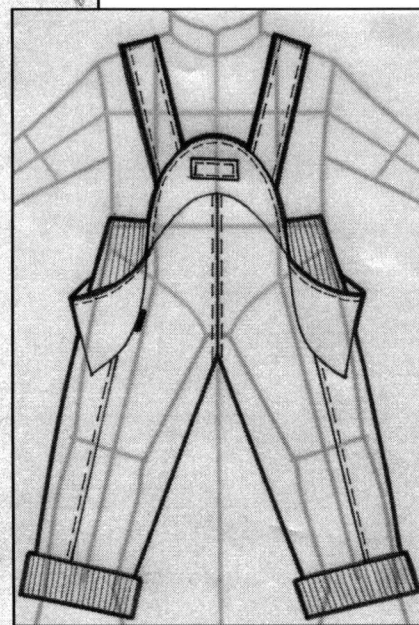

Final front view flat for bib overalls with template underneath to understand how the garment is fitted to a body.

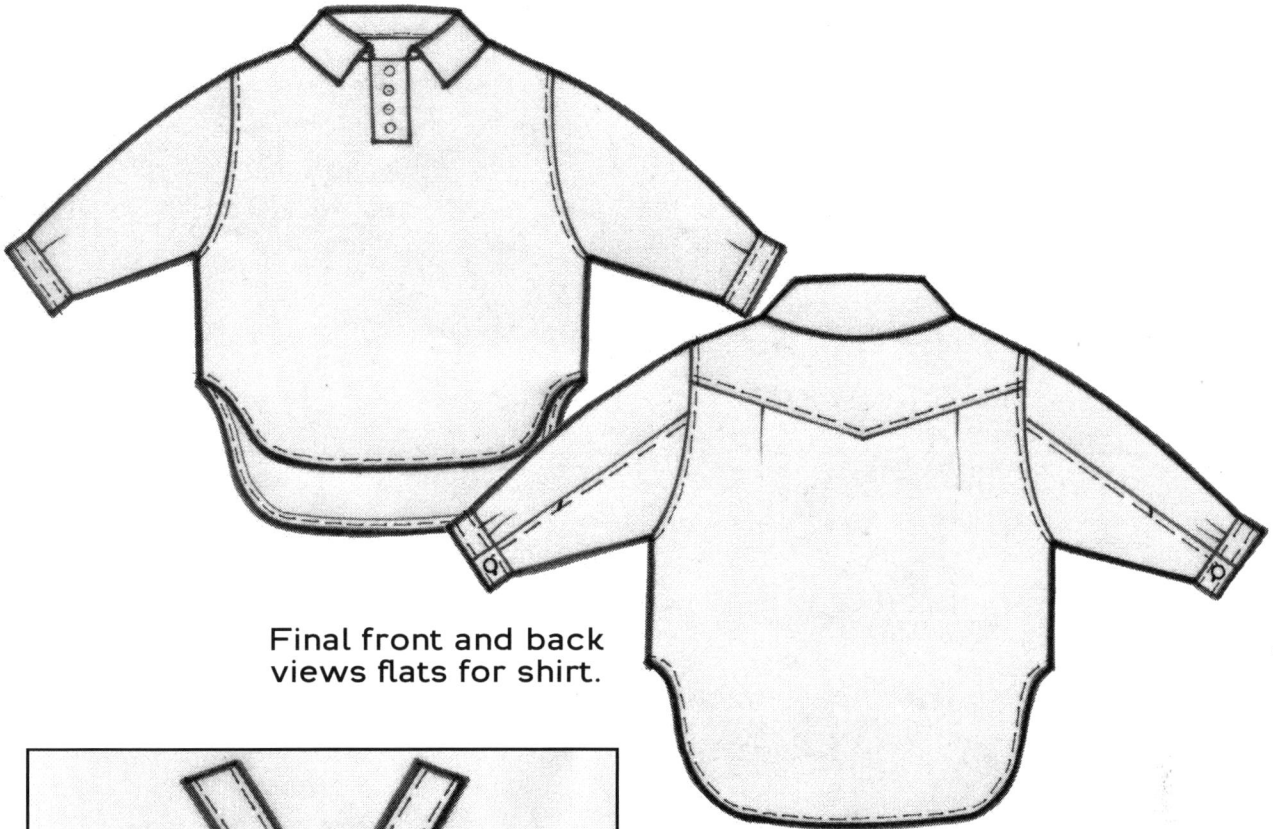

Final front and back views flats for shirt.

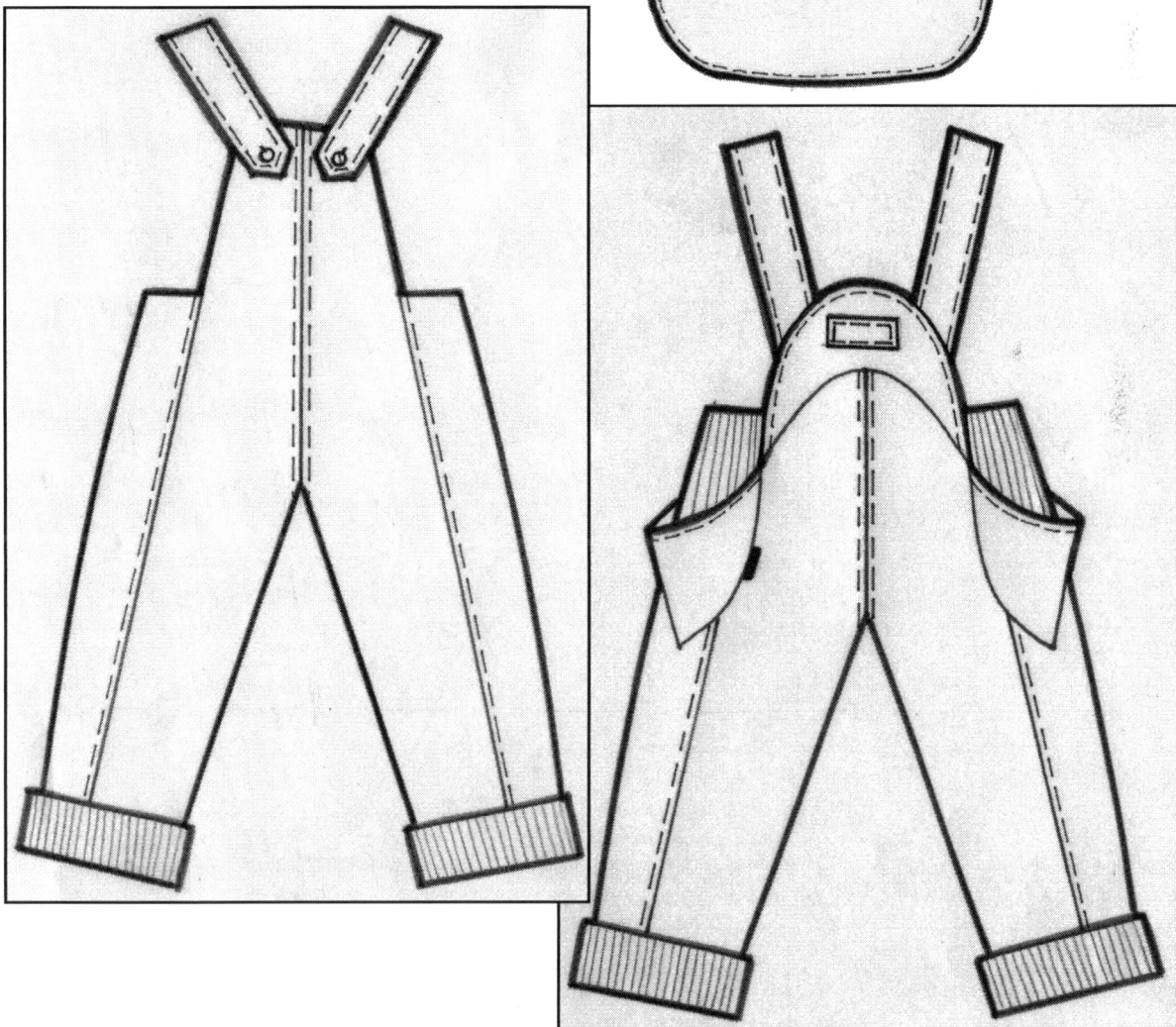

Final front and back views flats for overalls.

F

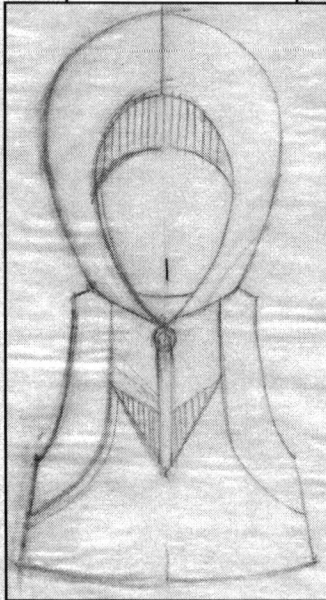

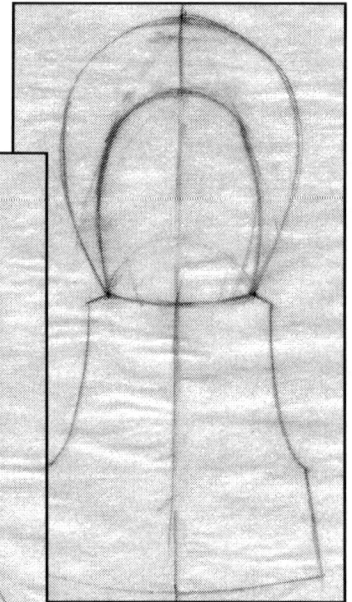

Preliminary simple pencil flats for vest with hood (front and back views).

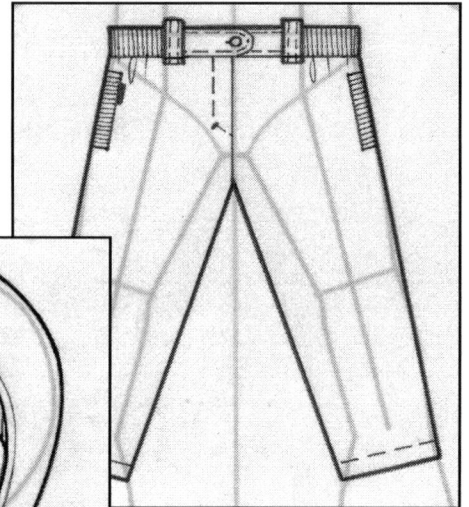

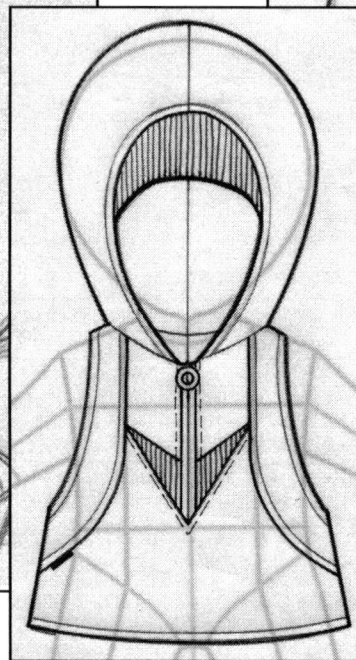

Final front view flats for vest and pants with template underneath to understand how the garments are fitted to a body.

194

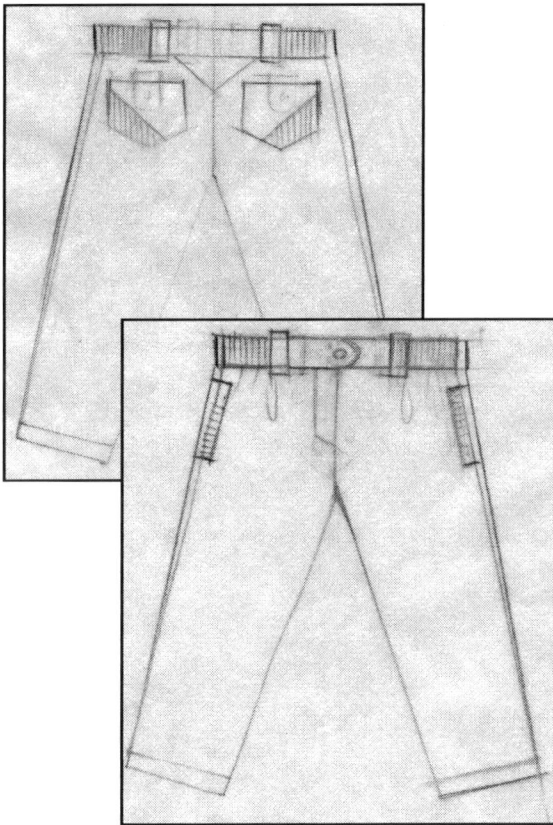

Preliminary simple pencil flats
for pants (front and back views).

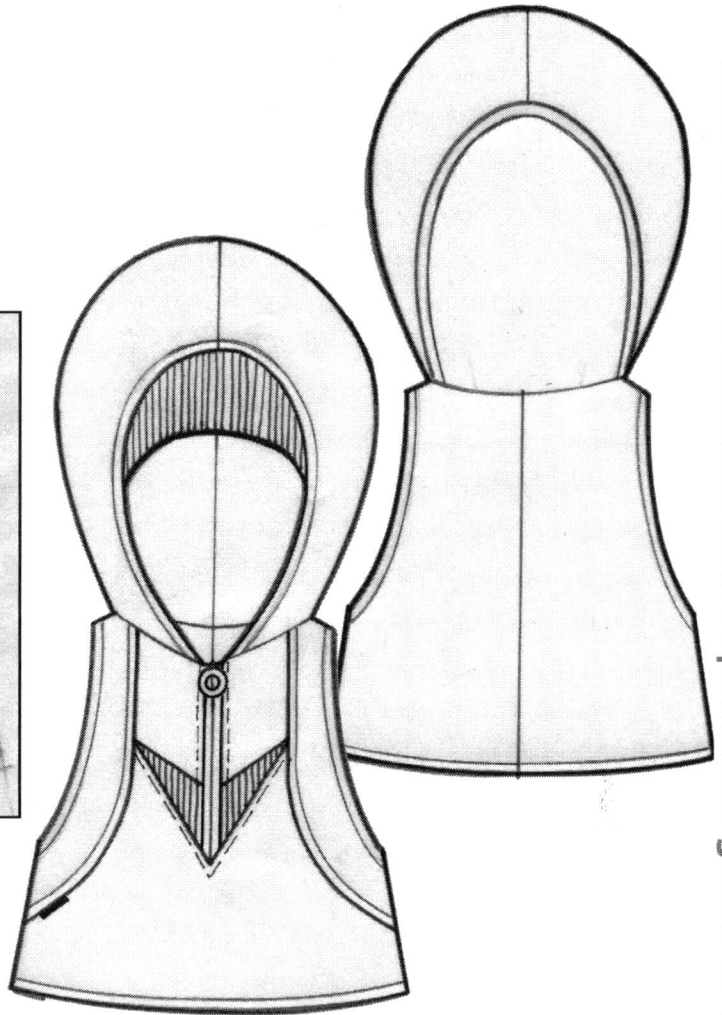

Final front and back views
flats for vest with hood.

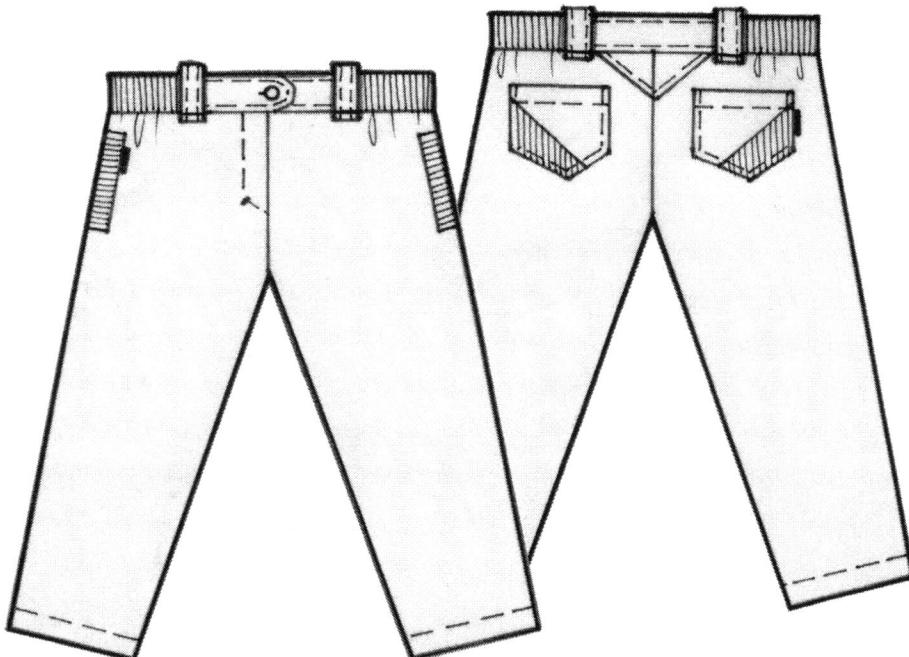

Final front and back views flats for pants.

Men's wear collection

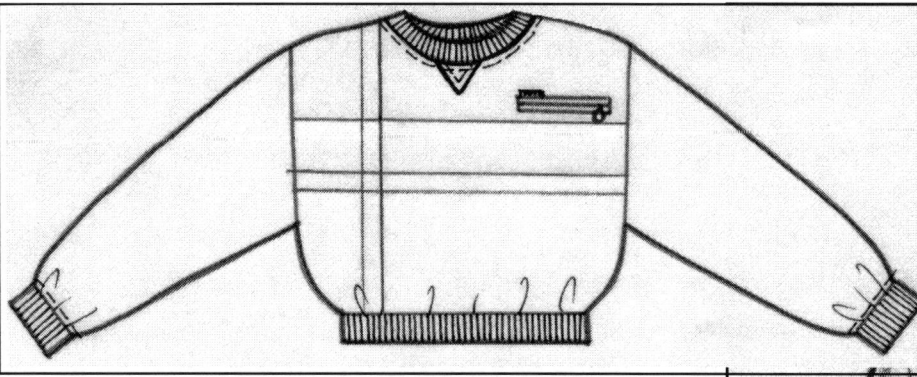

Final front view flat for knit pullover.

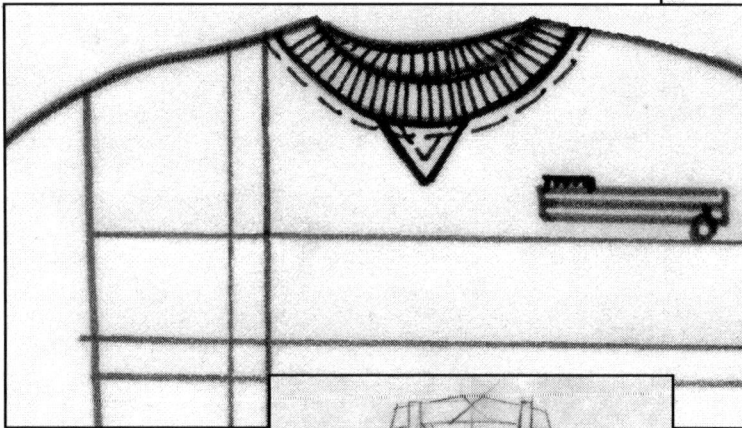

Details from final front view flat for knit pullover.

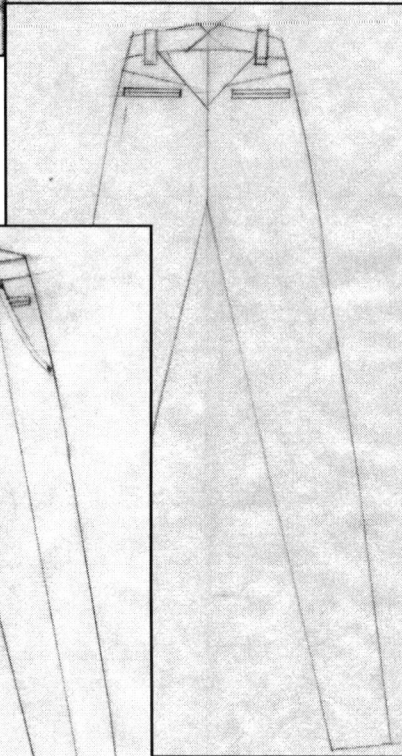

Preliminary simple pencil flats for pants (front and back views).

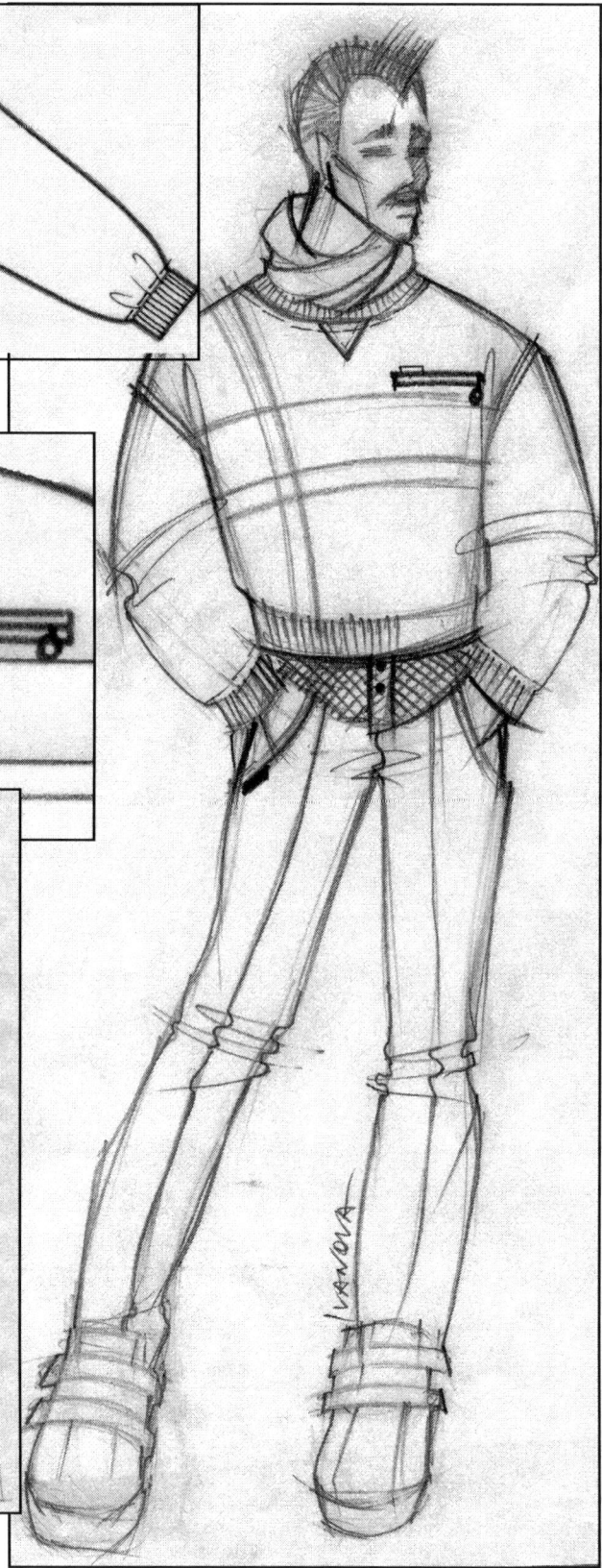

IVANOVA

196

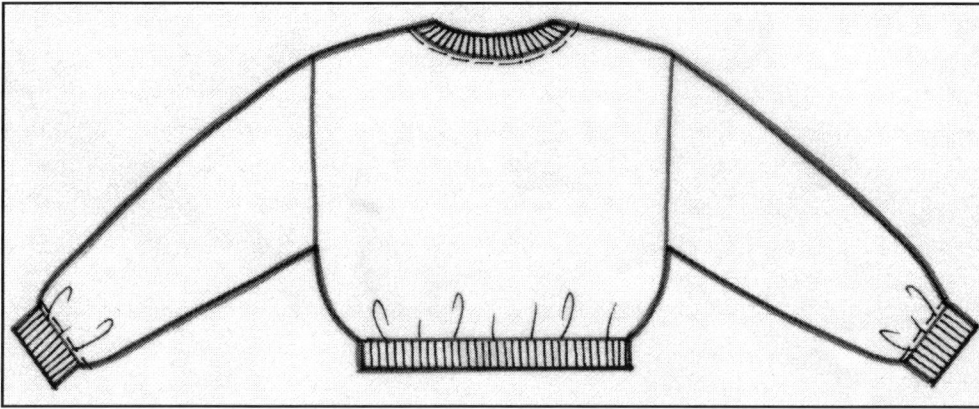

Final back view flat for knit pullover.

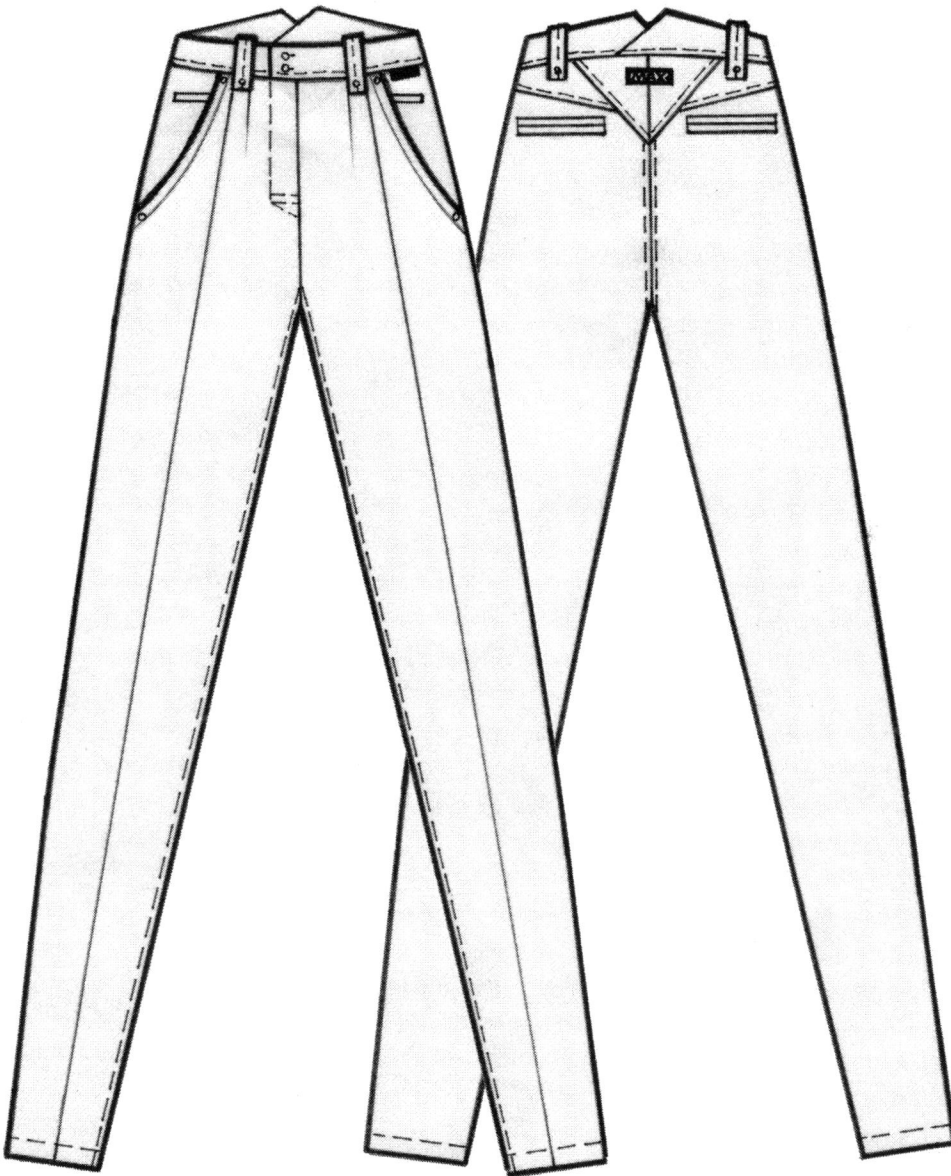

Final front and back view flats for pants.

Details from final front view flat for jacket.

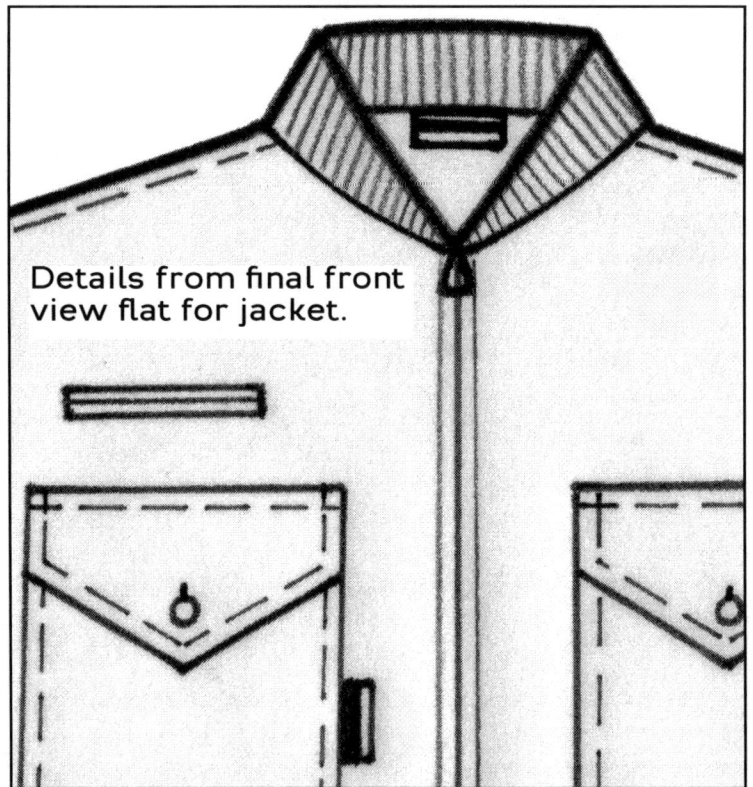

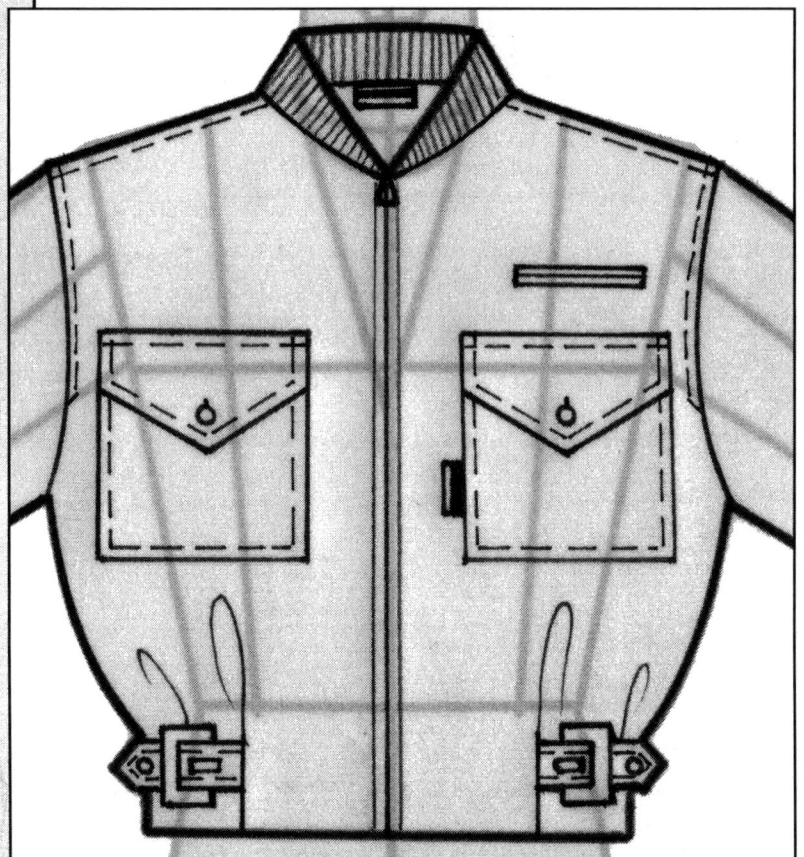

Final front view flat for jacket with template underneath to understand how the garment is fitted to a body.

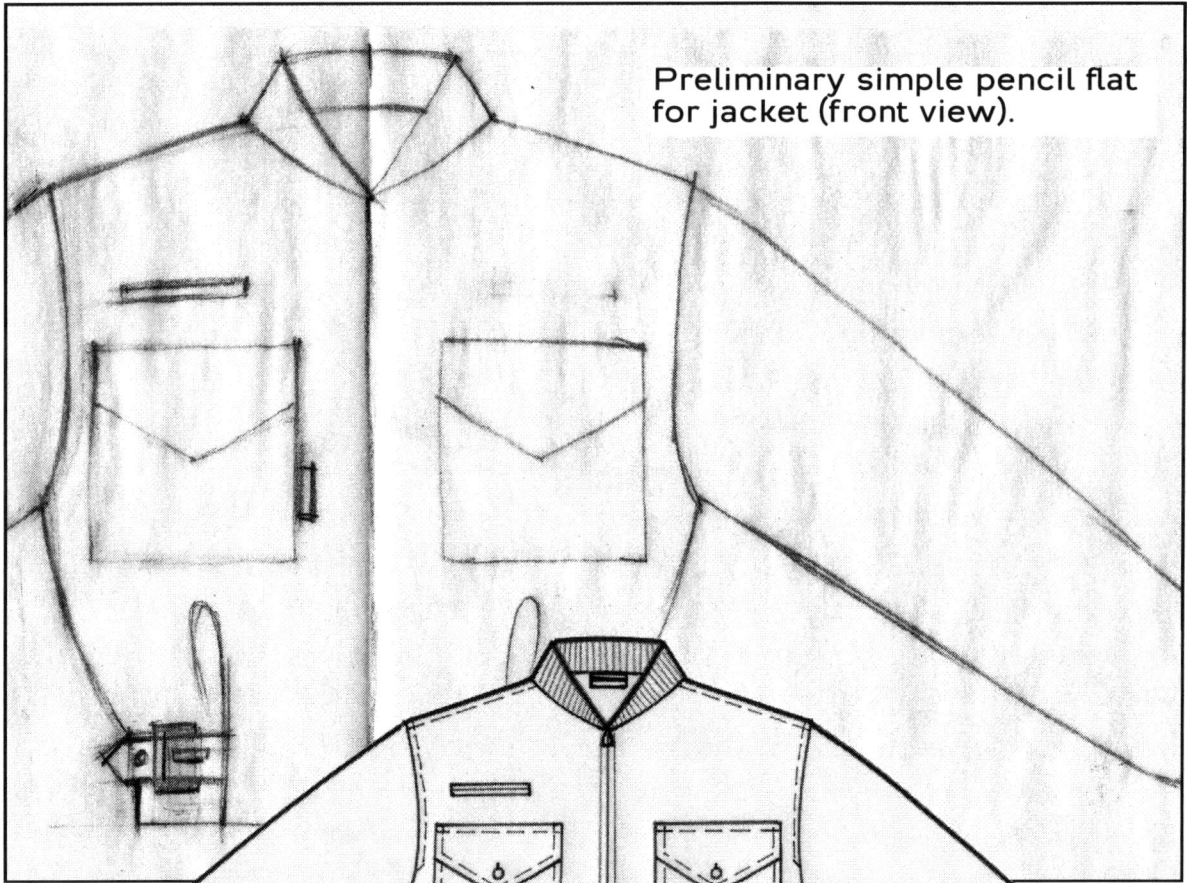

Preliminary simple pencil flat for jacket (front view).

Final front view flat for jacket.

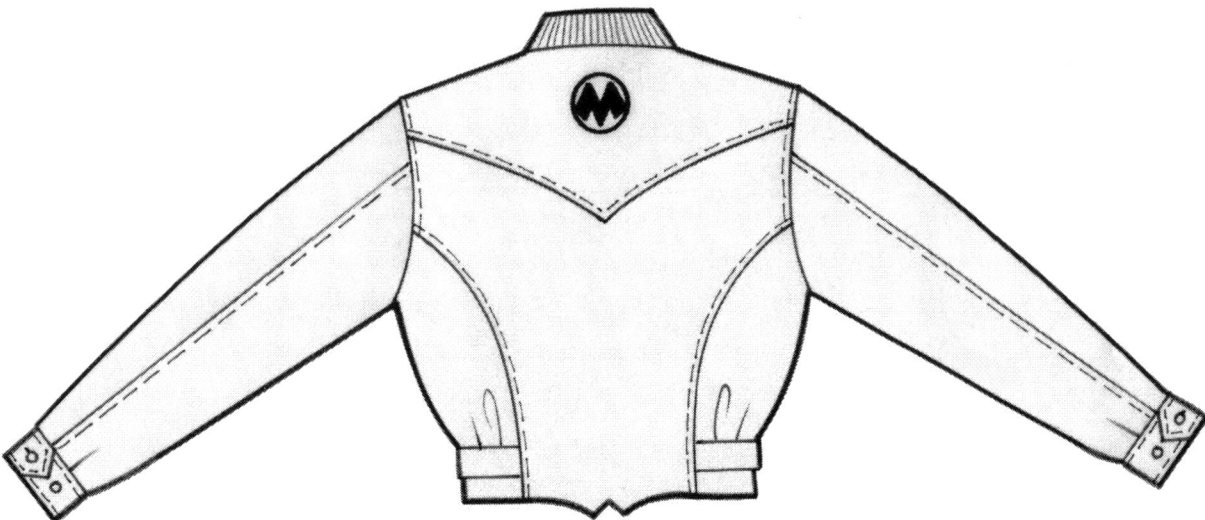

Final back view flat for jacket.

199

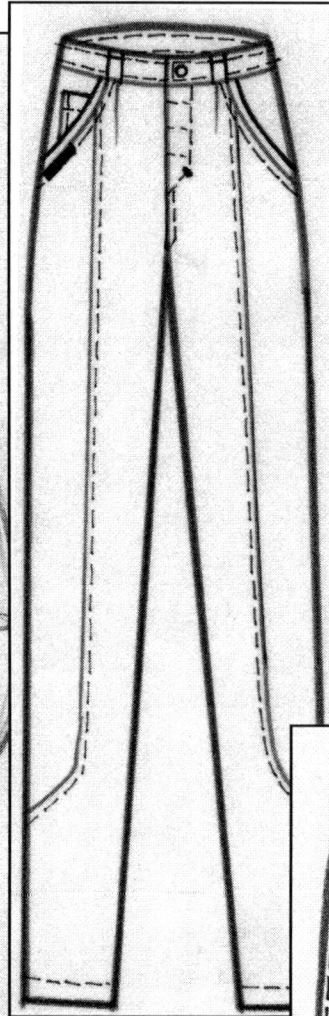

Final front view
flat for pants.

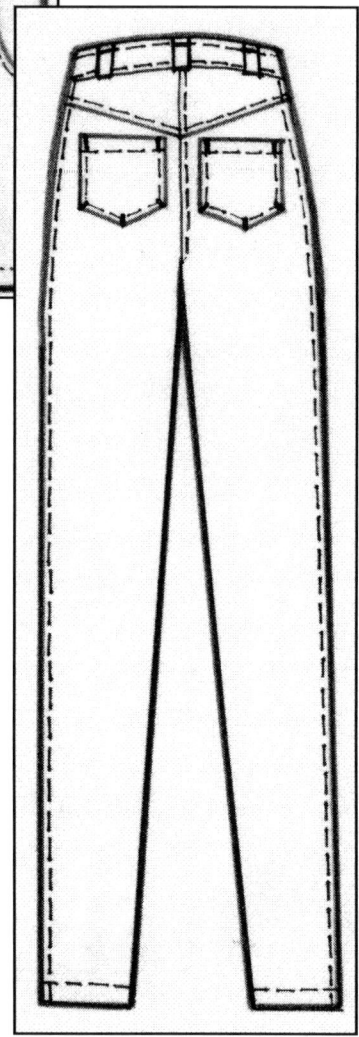

Final back view
flat for pants.

200

Final front view flat for jacket with template underneath to understand how the garment is fitted to a body.

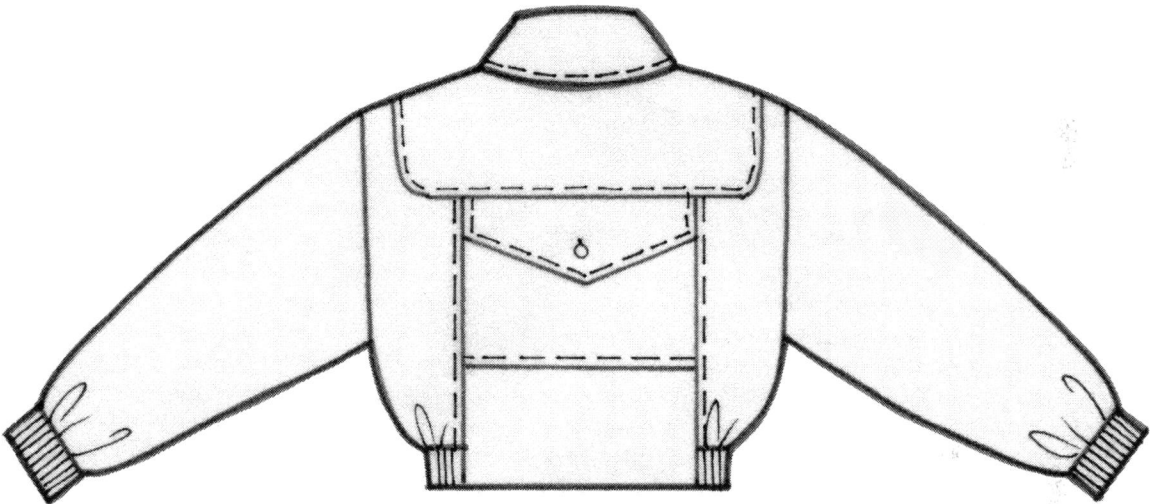

Final back view flat for jacket.

Final front view flat for jacket.

Women's wear collection: straight skirts

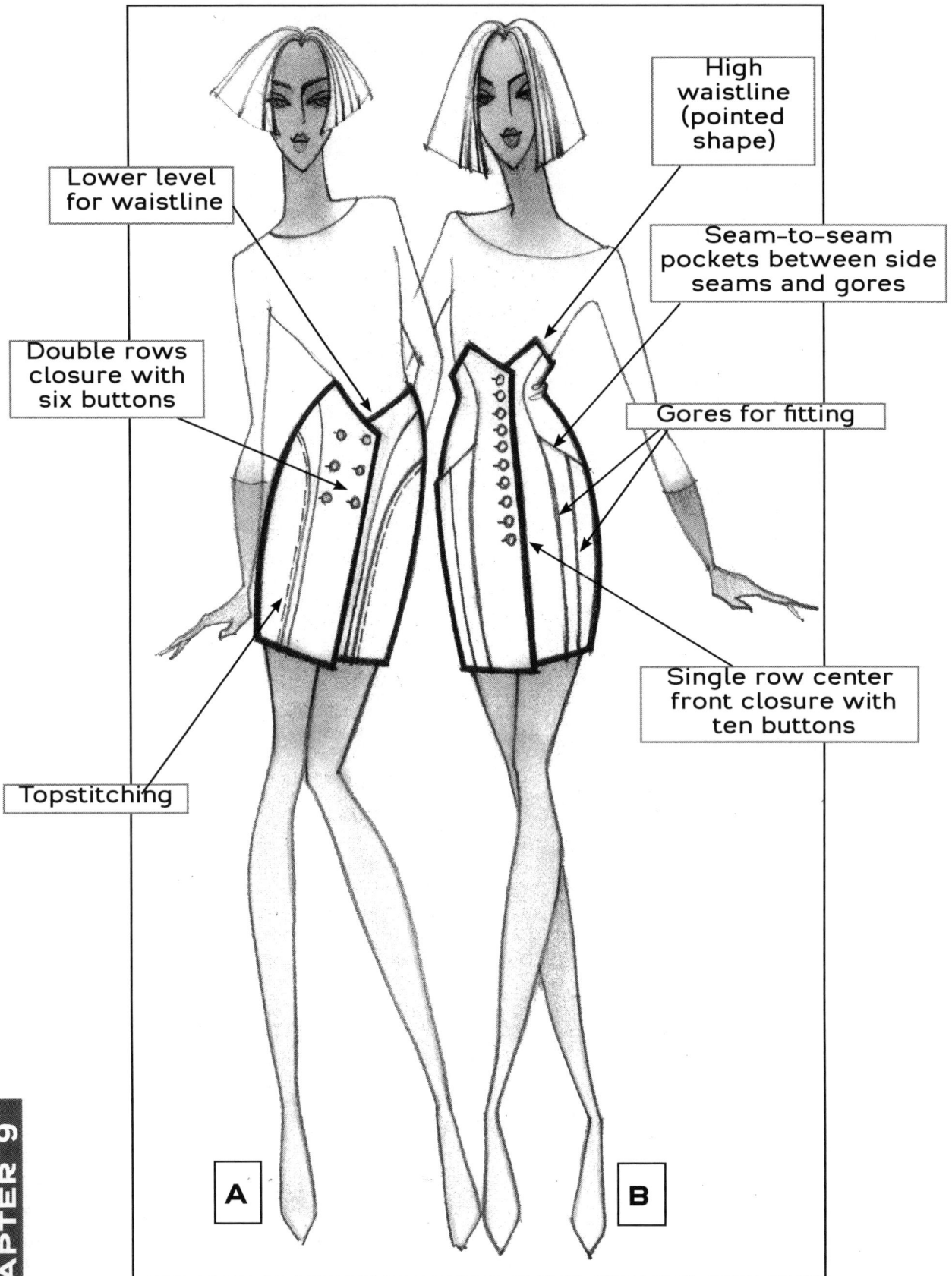

Lower level for waistline

Double rows closure with six buttons

Topstitching

High waistline (pointed shape)

Seam-to-seam pockets between side seams and gores

Gores for fitting

Single row center front closure with ten buttons

A

B

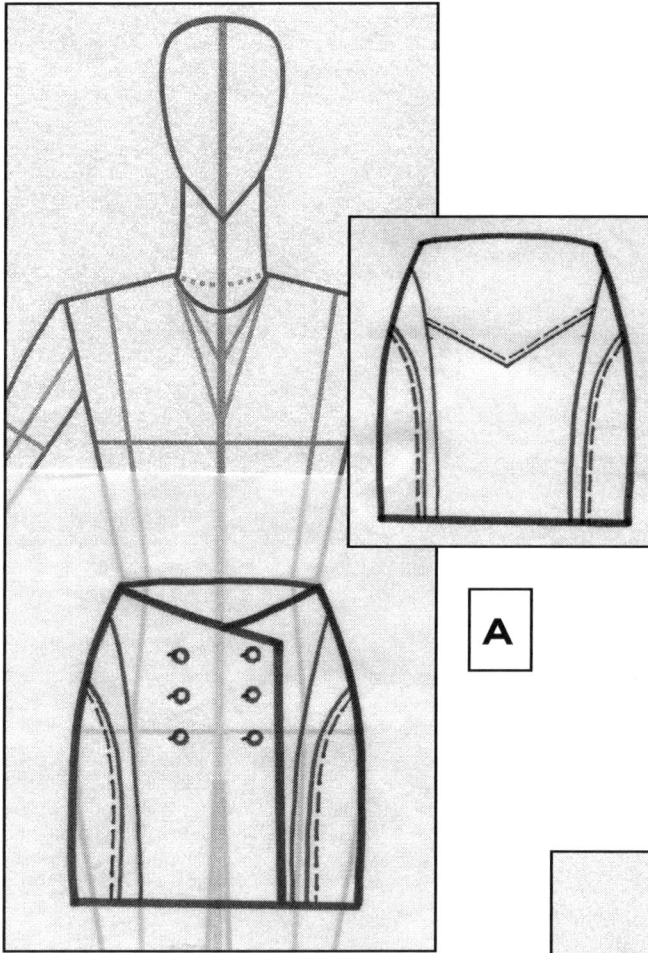

Flats (front and back
views) for Illustration A.

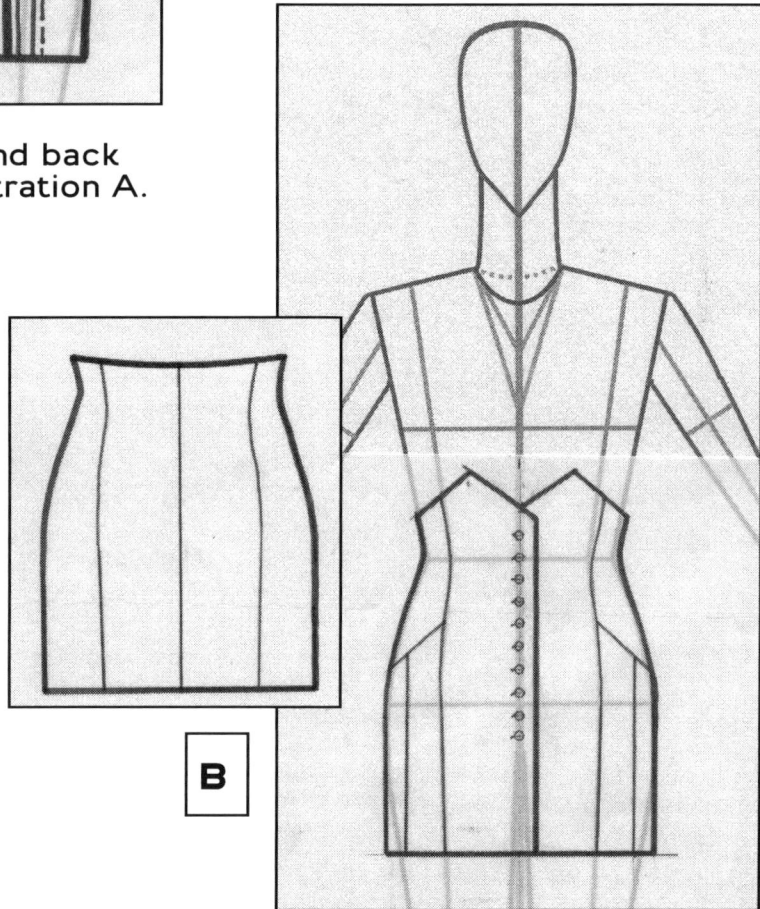

Flats (front and back
views) for Illustration B.

203

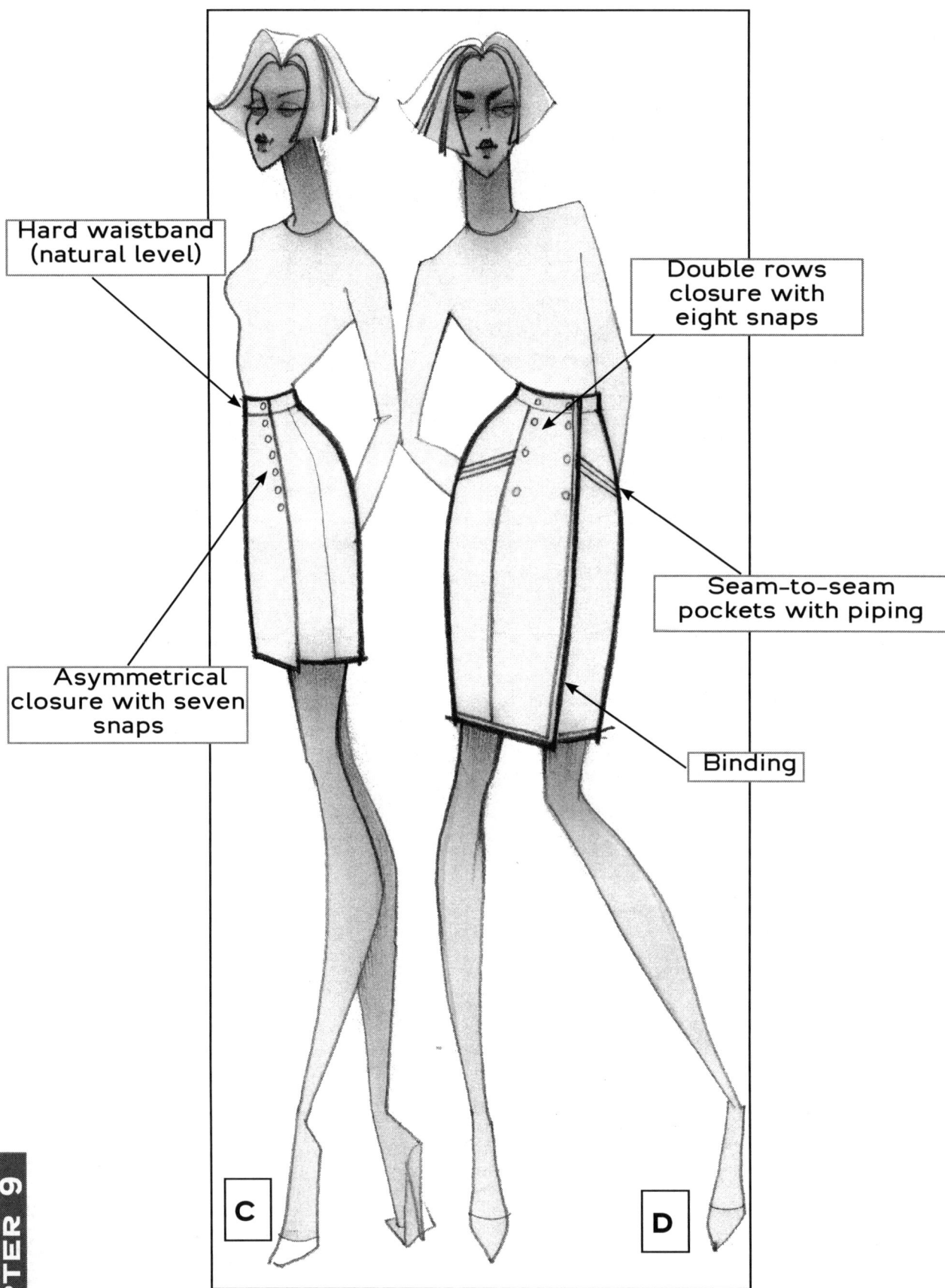

Hard waistband (natural level)

Double rows closure with eight snaps

Asymmetrical closure with seven snaps

Seam-to-seam pockets with piping

Binding

C

D

Index of terms

Index of terms

Index of terms

Index of terms

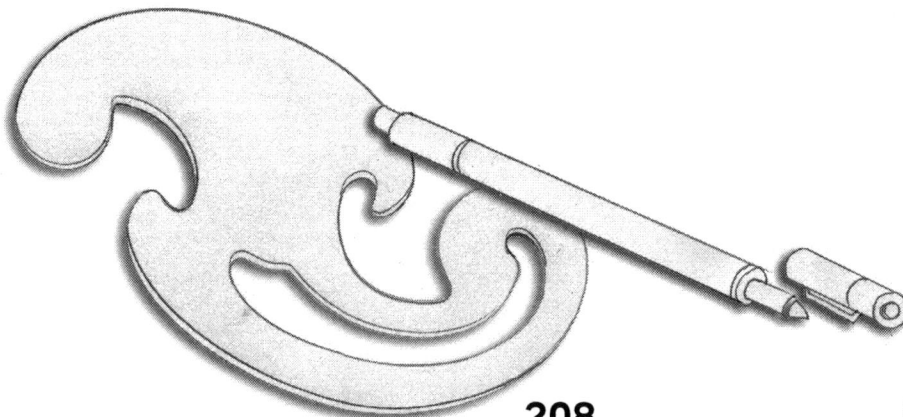

Index of terms (by topic)

Terminology:

Common mistakes:

Preview from new upcoming book from the Fashion Croquis series by Irina V. Ivanova: How to draw women's wear. Sign up for updates and special offers at www.fashioncroquis.com/signup.shtml

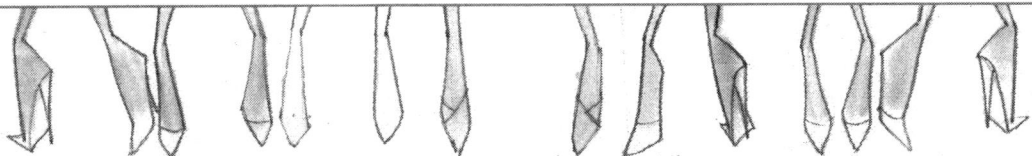

Book summary

Draw fashion flats with easiness, accuracy and confidence using this one of a kind book.

"How to draw fashion flats" is a comprehensive, practical guide to technical apparel drawing. The book focuses on pencil and marker techniques with rulers and French curves.

This expert, hands-on, guide make essential basic concepts of fashion flats easy to understand. Text in the book is concise and to-the-point. More than 700 hand drawn visuals are in the book to illustrate every step, every term, and every concept. It is a unique book, created by professionals for professionals. Book saves time and makes the complexity of technical drawing easy to comprehend.

Who should use this book?

- Independent designer or small business professional. Be more efficient by making the process of creating and correcting flats easier and more reliable.

- Professionals in the field of fashion design, apparel technical design and garment product development. Draw accurate flats with this book.

- Fashion merchandising professionals. Use the book as a reference for garment elements terms and a glossary of garment types.

- Students who study fashion design, patternmaking and fashion merchandising. With this book, a student's project can rich a level of professional competency.

With this book, you can draw accurate fashion flats, fast and with confidence.

Feedback

Please provide your feedback, suggestions and comments at
http://fashion-flats.com/feedback.html
and receive updates on books and fashion drawing resources created by Irina V. Ivanova.
Thank you!!!!

Visit www.fashioncroquis.com
for fashion drawing resources by Irina V. Ivanova

Fashion Croquis by IRINA V. IVANOVA
www.fashioncroquis.com

About the author

Irina V. Ivanova is a Florida-based educator, fashion designer, and visual artist. Irina delights in merging her versatile professional life experiences in a blend of fashion design, visual art, and teaching.

Trained in tailoring, Irina is experienced in all technical aspect of apparel design, apparel construction, and patternmaking. With an advanced degree in fashion design and extensive experience in fashion industry Irina understands every aspect of fashion design process.

As a fashion designer, she blends her technical knowledge of clothing design with artistry. Balancing creative and technical aspects of fashion process Irina creates her books in both a real world practical and artistically stylish way.

Apparel design is just one aspect of her multifaceted creative skills. In addition to expertise and experience in fashion design, Irina is professional illustrator and trained visual artist. Irina exhibited her paintings and illustrations on multiple art shows, illustrated for a major publishing house and is represented as a visual artist by a fine art licensing agency.

This fusion of insightful (even technical) aspects of apparel design with highly creative artwork makes Irina's books uniquely stylish and technically accurate at the same time.
Her books are a reflection of her versatility.

Art and fashion are merged in Irina's books helping each other for the benefit of a reader. Her books are not just "beautiful" books about fashion. Irina's books are practical guides on fashion subjects and collection of practical resources articulated with artistic talent and illustration skills.

Irina V. Ivanova is committed to creating informative, practical, visual and easy to comprehend fashion books for all levels of skills: from aspiring enthusiast to accomplished professionals in the field.

This book is a book in the series called "Fashion Croquis". The Fashion Croquis series is a collection of books with visual resources on various aspects of fashion drawing addressed to fashion professionals and students of fashion schools.

The series is a reflection of Irina's long term interest in merging all aspects of fashion design: from fashion technical drawing flats to fashion sketch and stylized fashion illustration into professionally accurate and easy to comprehend form.

Before starting the Fashion Croquis seriesIrina works from her art studio in Hallandale Beach, Florida, USA, creating visual art and producing fashion design publishing projects.

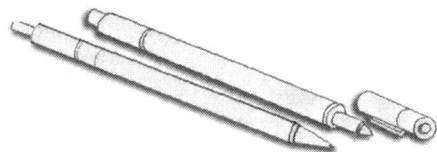

Fashion Croquis Sketchbooks

Choose a sketchbook for any project: children's, men's, women's wear.

Draw your sketches directly in the book. Draw right over the figures. Use gray figure as an underdrawing.

Who should use these sketchbooks?
- Fashion and clothing designers
- Students working on fashion design projects
- Anyone who have fashion ideas for clothing and need support in its picturing

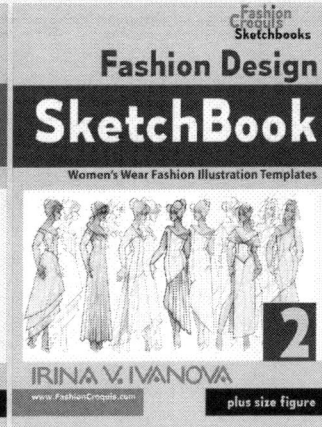

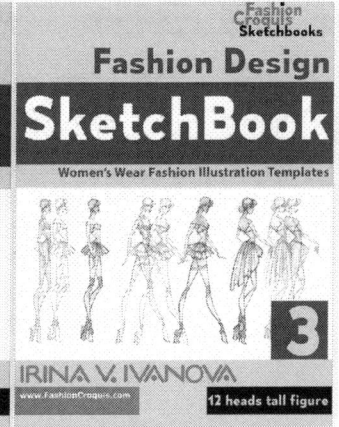

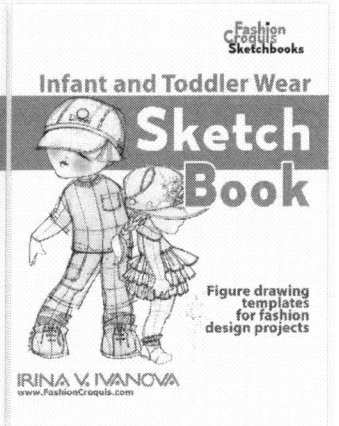

Fashion Croquis books: resource books for professional fashion drawing

Books for children's wear, couture and men's wear design drawing:

- Figure drawing templates

- Drawing step by step tutorials

- Main terms illustrated

...and much more in every book

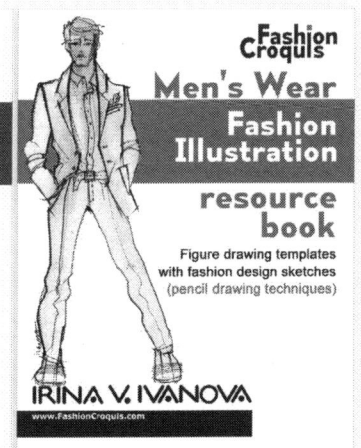

More books are coming: Sign for updates at www.fashioncroquis.com/signup.html

Printed in Great Britain
by Amazon

18131235R00122